Richard Norton is an independent theologian and former Director of Studies at the UK Centre for Monastic Studies and Culture. He has taught systematic theology and church history in a variety of contexts around the world. He is a Companion of Julian of Norwich (CJN) and an Oblate of the Order of Julian of Norwich (ObJN). He is a Fellow of the Royal Society of Arts and a member of the Royal Society for Literature and many other learned societies in the UK and America. Richard has given keynote addresses at academic conferences in Canada, Europe, the USA, and the UK, most recently at the International Medieval Congress in Leeds.

To Claire, Beckie, Edd, Seb, Freya, Jenny, Al, Jamie and Amelia, who, in their many different ways, know the strength and beauty of the inner space.

Richard Norton

LIVING ON THE EDGE

Monastic Spirituality and
the Development of Inner Space

AUSTIN MACAULEY PUBLISHERS®
LONDON * CAMBRIDGE * NEW YORK * SHARJAH

Copyright © Richard Norton 2025

The right of Richard Norton to be identified as author of this work has been asserted by the author in accordance with sections 77 and 78 of the Copyright, Designs and Patents Act 1988.

All rights reserved. No part of this publication may be reproduced, stored in a retrieval system, or transmitted in any form or by any means, electronic, mechanical, photocopying, recording, or otherwise, without the prior permission of the publishers.

Any person who commits any unauthorised act in relation to this publication may be liable to criminal prosecution and civil claims for damages.

A CIP catalogue record for this title is available from the British Library.

ISBN 9781035865659 (Paperback)
ISBN 9781035865666 (ePub e-book)

www.austinmacauley.com

First Published 2025
Austin Macauley Publishers Ltd®
1 Canada Square
Canary Wharf
London
E14 5AA

To my wife, Jacinta, who, for over a third of a century of our relationship, has proved to be a model of all that is good, thoughtful and loving in the world.

To my sister, Claire; my nieces, Beckie and Jenny; their husbands, Edd and Al; and their children, Seb, Freya, Jamie, and Amelia: I owe you an immeasurable debt of love and encouragement, even in my darkest hours. This book is dedicated to you with boundless gratitude.

To John Corkery, my oldest friend and often a rock in time of tribulation. It is an honour to have shared his life for nearly fifty years. Though we now work in very different specialisms, we have always supported each other, our families and our academic endeavours.

To all my fellow Oblates in the Order of Julian of Norwich, the Companions and Friends of Julian of Norwich, whose ability to create inner space, hospitality and the nourishment of the soul is unsurpassed.

To all my many friends, mentors and colleagues throughout the world who do not always understand what I do or why I want to do it but who continue to believe that it will come out all right in the end!

And finally, to everyone at Austin Macauley who have so generously and gently guided me through their processes so that what follows can see the light of day. The faults which remain are, of course, entirely mine.

Table of Contents

Preface	13
Part 1: Foundations	15
Part 2: Tradition and the Creation of the Inner Space	25
Part 3: Monasticism and Conflict	30
Part 4: St Benedict Then and Now	32
Part 5: Medieval Monasticism	43
Part 6: Contemplative Love and the Love of Contemplation	46
Part 1: Foundations	49
Chapter 1: The Four Pillars of Monasticism and the Example of Christ	*51*
Chapter 2: The Moral Features of Early Monasticism	*61*
Chapter 3: The Development and Structure of Early Monastic Communities	*72*
Part 2: Tradition and the Creation of the Inner Space	85
Chapter 4: What Is Traditional About the Orthodox Tradition?	*87*
Chapter 5: Stillness, Silence and the Art of Prayer in the Orthodox Tradition	*98*
Chapter 6: Orthodoxy and the Celtic Tradition: Unexplored Connections	*110*
Part 3: Monasticism and Conflict	125
Chapter 7: Monasticism in Britain Before the Conquest (1) Northumbria and the Synod of Whitby	*127*

Chapter 8: Monasticism in Britain Before the Conquest (2) Lives of the Saints — *137*

Chapter 9: St Augustine of Hippo: Monasticism and the Defeat of Heresy — *177*

Chapter 10: St Augustine of Hippo: Monastic Friendship in the Cloister and Beyond — *185*

Part 4: St Benedict Then and Now — **201**

Chapter 11: The Quest for the Historical Benedict: The Man, the Myth and the Rule — *203*

Chapter 12: Shared Virtue? The Possibility of Aristotelian Influences on the Rule of St Benedict — *222*

Chapter 13: Benedictine Spirituality Then and Now — *235*

Chapter 14: Benedict and Work in a Time of Recession — *247*

Part 5: Medieval Monasticism — **257**

Chapter 15: Revival and Reform (1): New Orders — *259*

Chapter 16: Revival and Reform (2): New Liturgies — *276*

Chapter 17: Revival and Reform (3): From Monastery to Marketplace — *287*

Part 6: Monasticism and the Heralding of God's Kingdom — **295**

Chapter 18: St Bernard of Clairvaux and the Sufficiency of Love — *297*

Chapter 19: Holy Poverty and Holy Preaching — *306*

Chapter 20: The Beguines — *323*

Part 7: Contemplative Love and the Love of Contemplation — **339**

Chapter 21: St Ignatius of Loyola: Spiritual Exercises for All — *341*

Chapter 22: "God's Bees": Carmelite Spirituality in the Inner Space — *349*

Chapter 23: St Francis De La Sales: Inner Space as a Loving Heart — *384*

Part 8: Widening Spirituality and the Inner Space in the Modern World — **399**

*Chapter 24: Parochial Monasticism: The Church of England and
the Book of Common Prayer* *401*

Chapter 25: Dietrich Bonheoffer: Life Together *410*

Chapter 26: Thomas Merton: The Relevance of Irrelevancy *419*

*Chapter 27: John Main Meditating on the Mysterious Shape of
God's Affection* *425*

Part 9 **439**

Chapter 28: Living in the Inner Space Today *441*

Chapter 29: Prayer, Reading and Hospitality *453*

Preface

Every Christian is called to holiness: "Be ye perfect, even as your heavenly Father is *perfect.*"[1] That is our unique calling and grace. Christ looks on a person, loves them and invites them to live in radical surrender to God and co-create with him the conditions under which the final Kingdom of God might come. It is a question of allowing ourselves to be guided by the Holy Spirit into the inner space of our souls and more deeply into the abiding love which God has for each one of us as the people we are, the people we might become. This development of the inner space comes about very gradually and always imperceptibly. But it gives us discernment, a desire to live differently, to repent of our sins, to love and be loved, to listen to the Word of God and enter more deeply into study, contemplation, meditation and prayer. In all of these ways we learn to love God more truly, to love ourselves and our neighbours and to persevere with those with whom we struggle too.

Everyone can achieve holiness for, having been called into being by God, we carry his indelible image even and especially in our fragility and brokenness. But some choose to do so by a path less travelled—the path of monasticism. They do so not because they are some sort of spiritual elite or because they have acquired an "extra" amount of grace—after all there is no such thing. They do so not as an "escape" form the world but as a separation from it. There is a great deal of difference between escape and separation. Monks and nuns do not escape from modernity either. However enclosed they may be, they are still "in" the world, just not of it. Even though their lifestyle and dress may appear to be archaic, it is not anachronistic, far less do they live in some sort of Christian historical theme park of interest only to "busloads" of curious tourists eager to shop for incense or honey.

---

[1] Mtt. 5:48. See also 2. Cor 7:1 Heb.12:4 and 1 Jn3:2–3.

Rather, the call of monasticism is to exercise a unique apostolate in the universal church. It is to be a visible witness to the *absolute priority* of God above everything else without anything else intervening and without the compromises which the rest of us beyond the cloister have to face and make day by day.

As we will see as this book unfolds, the path of monasticism has never been a straight one. If it is true that left wing political groups seem to have an in-built amoebic tendency to split and divide with alarming and almost monotonous regularity this is, in some ways, no less true of the history of monasticism. This has been made even more complex in our own day as increasing numbers of Christians seek to combine some of the insights of cloistered life, mission and ministry in their everyday lives, a "new monasticism".

The purpose of this book then is first to trace some of the twists and turns of the path of traditional monastic spirituality, second to explore how some insights that can be garnered along the way may be used to best effect by those deliberately seeking to establish a monastic spirit in society and thirdly to find ways in which the rest of us might develop the inner space of our souls as a result of both.

Part 1
Foundations

Foundations

Christianity has always produced people who do not quite fit and who, though loyal to the faith and to the church as institution, choose to do things differently. Not a few of these have been inspired to pursue rigorous aesthetic life styles. Indeed, even the most primitive expressions of Christianity, such as the writings of St Paul and the Gospels, contain a strong ascetic emphasis. These are people who live on the edge of the world, geographically, psychologically and emotionally as well as spiritually. But the emergence of monasticism as a distinct ascetic movement of the edge did not appear straight away. It emerged in many and varied forms only in the late third and fourth centuries.

The reasons for the appearance of monasticism at this time and not earlier have been explained in a great number of ways but there can be little doubt that monasticism sprang from a desire to recover and reinforce the understanding that from its beginning Christianity had always been a call to self-denial. Without such a willingness to part with one's old self, the new self could not arise. During the Roman persecutions, this call was often put before Christians in an unambiguous way: do you have the discipline to accept the pain of parting with the familiarity of your "fallen" life for the sake of your true life in Christ? Christians could not hide behind a nominal acceptance of the faith. During the persecutions, there were no secular advantages that might provide ulterior motives for becoming a Christian.

Persecution kept the line between being for Christ or against him. But after Constantine's toleration of Christianity, all that changed; the line was no longer as sharp. With peace between the City of God and the Kingdoms of this World, there was a real and present danger of forgetting Christ's injunction that "My

Kingdom is not of this world".[2] The call to self-denial for Christ's sake was no longer being put before Christians with such unmistakeable clarity. The invitation to take up one's cross (literally as well as metaphorically) now had to come from within. "The monks with their austerities were martyrs in an age when martyrdom of blood no longer existed; they formed the counter balance to an established Christendom."[3] Monasticism, a formal life of internally imposed self-renunciation for the purpose of developing the inner space of the soul, emerged for many reasons but especially in response to the diminishing presence of externally imposed self-renunciation.

It is for these reasons that the opening chapters of this study, **Foundations**, will examine whether and to what extent monasticism has its roots in the primitive expressions of the faith in general and in the life of Christ in particular. I will then trace some ethical and moral motivations for a movement which has always been an essential part of the Christian *kerygma, the* heralding of the Christian Gospel.

Throughout this study I will use the terms "monasticism" or "religious life" interchangeably to indicate that ascetic movement in Christianity that is characterised to greater or lesser degrees by an intentional withdrawal to the edges of Christianity and certainly to the edge of secular society. From the outset then it is necessary to bear in mind that while all Christian monasticism is ascetic, not all asceticism is monastic and that what distinguishes monasticism from the broader category of Christian asceticism—at least as I propose to use the terms— is monasticism's emphasis on withdrawal. Hence the title of this book "Living on the Edge".

But as so much in the study of monasticism, even this needs to be qualified. First, it is important to point out that the withdrawal which characterises monasticism does not either imply or entail a *total* disconnection either from the church as institution or the world at large, howbeit that there is a widespread and popular (though mistaken) idea that it does. The monk is, and must be, connected to the church and to society through his prayers. We might already think that that is at best a tenuous or negligible connection, but in characterising the motivations of the earliest monks we must be clear that they did not and do not share this view.

---

[2] Jn 18:36.
[3] Metropolitan Kallistos Ware (2015); *The Orthodox Church*. London. Penguin Books. Revised Edition. p 37.

Furthermore "progress" in the monastic life, measured by spiritual growth and an ever-growing unity to God in Christ, depends on how a monk or nun lives in community and on the communal consequences of pursuing that progress as individuals and as a religious community. So, for example, when St Athanasius described the many victories of St Anthony of Egypt over the demons that beset him, they are always portrayed as being a victory for *all* the people of God whoever and wherever they may be and in whatever style of life they might adopt.

Moreover, there were cases in which the monastic withdrawal was not at all permanent. After a time apart, some early monks returned to the rest of the religious community and/or the wider church. Again, St Anthony of Egypt is a good example of this. Fortified by the freedom and insight that his withdrawal helped him obtain, he was enabled to help countless others find their own freedom and vocation. What enabled him to be so helpful was precisely his withdrawal from society.

The second qualification that it is necessary to make is that (again contrary to mistaken common belief) monastic withdrawal *does not* imply or entail either a dualism between the body and the spirit, nor a hatred for the world. Early monasticism at least, was never about this but only about stilling the passions— the creation and development of the inner space of the soul. For them, the great battle was with demonic spirits, principalities and powers, not flesh and blood; and the battle line was drawn *not* between the physical and the immaterial, but between godliness and unbelief. In other words, they believed that the passions were as much spiritual as physical. As Peter Brown has observed:

"…attention to the body enjoyed almost oppressive prominence. Yet to describe ascetic thought as 'dualist' and as motivated by hatred of the body, is to miss its most novel and most profound aspects. Seldom, in ancient thought, had the body been seen a more deeply implicated in the transformation of the soul, and never was it made to bear so heavy a burden."[4] Indeed, the great burden the early monks placed upon the body was evidence of the great expectations they had for it. The body *together with* the soul was to be saved, and that is why not only the soul but also the body too, had to be brought under strict discipline Against all types of Dualism, pagan or pre-Christian, Anthony's perfection is

---

[4] Peter Brown (2008): *The Body and Society Men, Women and Sexual Renunciation in Early Christianity.* Columbia Classics in Religion. New York. Columbia University Press. Second Revised Edition. P 235.

shown reflected in his bodily condition, retained right up to his death fifty years later when he was still sound in all his senses and vigorous in his limbs, with even his teeth complete in number though down to his gums.[5] If the austere fasts, the minimal amounts of sleep and the frugal lifestyle of the earliest monks are not to be understood as a rejection of the body, what then is their meaning? They have a more positive aim: the acquisition of freedom, uniqueness and creativity. Slavery to the passions is an assault on all of these. After all, what is more boring and predictable than the behaviour of someone totally addicted to the affirmation of their own ego? This freedom from the tyranny of the passions, or *apatheia*, is a fundamental aim of all Christian asceticism in general and of monasticism in particular.

Freedom from a tyrant can be brought about in two ways. One can either alter the nature of the relationship with the tyrant, or simply get rid of him through "regime change". Similarly, ascetic and monastic spirituality tends to approach freedom from the passions in two ways. One can see the passions in Aristotelian terms, as neutral capacities capable of being put to either good or evil uses, in which case the aim of Christian monasticism would be to transform them so that they work for our benefit. Or one may see the passions as the Stoics did, as fundamentally diseased qualities, intrinsically evil, in which case the aim would be to get rid of them.

In the end, of course, both approaches share a common aim: the ascetic struggle is freedom from the passions, called *apatheia*, whether this "freedom" implies reform or complete revolution. We should note here that *apatheia* is not at all like our modern word apathy, or indifference. Still less is it a condition in which sinning is impossible. On the contrary, it is a state of *inner* freedom and integration in which a person is no longer under the domination of sinful impulses, and so becomes capable of genuine love. It is no mere mortification of the passions, but a state of the soul, the inner space, in which a burning love of God and for fellow human beings leaves no room for sensual and selfish impulses.

With these two qualifications in mind the hallmark of Christian monasticism is an ascetic struggle which succeeds, if at all, not by personal effort or labour but only in cooperation with God's grace. Monks throughout the ages have always been convinced that it is Christ who is at work in them and that without

---

[5] J. Derwas Chitty (1966): The Desert a City. Oxford. Basil Blackwell. p4.

Christ they can do nothing. Without Grace, their whole lives are meaningless. But with the grace of Christ, there is nothing that the monk cannot do that is worth doing.

These early chapters are also concerned with the developments of early monasticism in its eremitic and coenobitic forms, especially in Egypt and Asia Minor. They consider the unmitigated life of withdrawal and seclusion: the eremitic life—hermits. The great father of this form of monasticism is St Anthony of Egypt who, at the age of about twenty (circa 269 AD) heard Christ's words: "Go, sell all you have and give the proceeds to the poor. Then come and follow me"[6] read aloud in church. Taking this literally he did as the words bade him—although not without first securing a stable future for his sister, for whose care he was responsible at the time.[7] He followed Christ into the desert. His withdrawal was a gradual one: he moved further and further away from human society until (circa 285) he reached the deep desert, the outer mountain of Pispir, where he struggled day and night to free himself from the tyrannical delusions of the passions and the demons. By about 350 AD, having attracted a number of followers who were inspired by his discipline and holiness, he came out of seclusion to advise others in their own struggles.

In what sense is it characteristic of monasticism to follow Christ to flee into the desert? The answer to this may be found, I think, in Christ's own departure to the desert prior to his public ministry, as well as his departure to the desert following the execution of John the Baptist during it. Christ's decision to withdraw to the desert on the second occasion (with the mind of a hermit?) is certainly not a meaningless accident, an arbitrary selection of a place without significance.[8] St Anthony of Egypt was thus following Christ's model; indeed, he was following Christ himself. For, as Father Georges Florovsky has

---

[6] Mtt 19:21.

[7] He entrusted her to a Christian "Parthenon". It is not entirely clear to what such a group or institution might have been, how they lived, nor how they were regulated. But that there existed a group of women in which Anthony could have this sort of confidence might suggest that something which we might recognise as female monastic communities already existed.

[8] The Greek text of the Gospels suggests that on the first occasion, during which he resisted the temptations, the Spirit, pushed, shoved, cajoled, Christ into the desert. The implication is that it was against his will. Our more usual English translation of the same word "led" does not signify the use of force implied in the original.

explained, while Christ, as the second person of the Trinity is always and everywhere present, filling all things, there is something unique about the desert and the solitude which it symbolises and effects that makes Christ's presence more easily recognised. Florovsky goes on to say:

"By following Our Lord into the desert, St Anthony was entering a terrain already targeted and stamped out by our Lord as a specific place for spiritual warfare. There is both specificity and type in the desert. In those geographical regions where are no deserts, there are places which are similar to or approach that type of place symbolised by the desert. It is that type of place which allows the human heart solace, isolation. It is a type of place which puts the human heart in a state of aloneness, a state in which to meditate, to pray, to fast, to reflect upon one's inner existence and one's relation to ultimate reality—God…

[The desert] is the terrain of a battlefield…a spiritual one. And it is Our Lord, not St Anthony that has set the precedent. Our Lord says that 'as for what is sown among thorns, this is he who hears the word, but the cares of the world and the deceit of riches choke the world and it becomes unfruitful'. The desert, or a similar place, precisely cuts off the cares or anxieties of the world and the deception, the deceit of earthly riches. It cuts one off precisely from 'this worldliness' and precisely as such it contains within itself a powerful spiritual reason for existing within the paths of the Church. Not as the only path, not as the path for everyone, but as one, full authentic path of Christian life."[9] The eremitic life may have certain attractions and be regarded as the most potent of all forms of monasticism—but it is also the most risky. As Father Florovsky made clear at the end of the above quotation, it is by no means for everyone. For others, a more moderated form of withdrawal and seclusion is suitable. One such alternative form of monasticism, possessing great inherent safeguards against delusion, is the communal, coenobitic life.

Here a group of monks live together, under a common Rule and in one place, mutually supporting and encouraging one another. There are two great fathers of this form of monasticism, St Pachomius of Egypt and St Basil the Great. Pachomius's communities were established around Tabbenisi in the Thebaid, near the Nile. Pachomius personally attracted many followers so that at his death, he ruled over at least nine monasteries for men and two for women.

---

[9] The Collected Works of Georges Florovsky. Vol x. *"The Byzantine Ascetics and Spiritual Fathers."* At Florovsky Last Accessed March 2024.

In Asia Minor, Basil greatly encouraged coenobitic monasticism as being more suitable for most people than the life of a hermit. Basil feared that, among other pitfalls, the life of a hermit could lead a person to neglect the Christian duties of proclaiming by word and by deed, the need for social justice and for charity. This was readily summed up in his famous question: "Whose feet will you wash?" By asking this question, "Basil adds to the mystical and inner emphasis of monasticism, a strong emphasis on external acts of charity and philanthropy."[10] His monasteries were places from which such endeavours could occur. Basil also insisted on obedience as a check on the excess, the competitiveness, and the ostentation of histrionic individuals who were already bringing the monastic movement into disrepute:

"Basil was also careful to insist that monks remain mindful of the normal worshipping and liturgical life of the wider Cchurch, and made sure that they remained connected to the authority of the local bishop."[11] There was, in these early days of monastic history, a third form of monasticism which sought to combine elements of both the eremitic and coenobitic life. We may think of those who followed it as "semi-hermits". These semi-hermits did not withdraw into complete seclusion, but neither did they live a fully communal life either. Rather they lived in small groups coming together only to celebrate a common liturgy and a common meal on Sundays, so preserving a far greater degree of isolation and solitude than was common or indeed possible in a coenobium.

Nitria, for example, was near to Alexandria and formed a natural gateway to Scetis. It was a meeting place of the urbane "civilised" world and the desert where visitors, like John Cassian for example, could make first contact with the monastic traditions of the desert. Here we may suspect that the monasticism was more of a learned sort and that a more Greek-influenced type of monasticism evolved around a highly educated minority, of whom Evagrius of Pontus is the supreme example.

The "semi-hermetic" life was also found at Jerusalem and, much later and perhaps more surprisingly in Ukraine.[12] By the fifth century, the desert of Judea was home to many monastics especially in the region around Gaza and by the

---

[10] Henry Chadwick (1993): *The Early Church*. Penguin History of the Church Volume 1. Harmondsworth. London. Penguin Books. pp178–179.
[11] Loc cit.
[12] See below where I comment on my first visit to the Pescherk Lavra in Kiev Ukraine in May 2010.

sixth century there were still more monastics living in Palestine having moved there under the influence of St Euthymius the great (d473) and his disciple St Sabas (d 532). Judea became a Lavra.[13] Here a number of monks had their own cells in close proximity to a central leader and met weekly and on special occasions, just as in Nitria and Scetis. Another important difference between the semi-hermetic life and the coenobitic models is that the former often functioned as a preparatory phase for the full eremitic life which it tacitly deemed to be superior.

"This," says Henry Chadwick, "is a marked contrast with the ideal of Pachomius, or of Basil, for whom the coenobium is a lifelong vocation."[14] Taken together these chapters will show that before the emergence of monasticism in the fourth century, the practice of asceticism was widespread and that a number of Church Fathers, East and West, had already developed an ascetical theology. They will argue that Christian asceticism, if not yet monasticism, has its roots in the New Testament, and less dramatically perhaps to the Old Testament too. I will argue that there is a high degree of continuity between the pre-monastic and monastic ascetic theologies and that this continuity was quite deliberate so that, as Chadwick remarks: "In the writings of Clement of Alexandria and especially of Origen all the essential elements of an ascetical theology may already be found."[15] Clement, for example, emphasised that the aim of the Christian life is not to trouble ourselves with what lies outside, but to purify the eye of the soul and to sanctify the flesh and that Jesus heals the whole person in body, mind, spirit and emotion. Clearly for Clement salvation is not merely an extrinsic imputation of the righteous: salvation is always far more than merely a declaration of righteousness or a claim that somehow one is righteous because

---

[13] Op cit Chitty: The Desert a City. p15. 'The word Lavra does not appear in fourth century records and its *monastic use seems to originate in Palestine. Perhaps the sense of market comes instantly to mind when we connect it to the Arabic suq, which is not inappropriate. Here the ascetics brought together there produce on Saturday mornings, worshipped and fed together, and transacted all necessary business, taking back with them to their cells on Sunday evenings bread, water, and raw material for their handiwork for the coming week.'* I will argue below that by the eleventh century in Ukraine these features may well have been present too but that, by then, the word Lavra had a specific ecclesial meaning in the Orthodox tradition there.

[14] Op cit Chadwick p178–179.

[15] Loc cit p177.

one has been predestined to it. Rather salvation is ontological, the Christian has to be *made* righteous insofar and in the degree to which he or she is infused by and cooperates with the grace of God.

This idea is carried through into monastic theology:

"Anthony and the monks of the fourth century inherited a revolution; they did not initiate one. In the century that had elapsed from the youth of Origen to the conversion of Constantine, the horizons of the possible had already been determined…in a slow unfolding of the moral landscape of the Christian world. Total sexual renunciation had become a widely acclaimed feature of the Christian life."[16] And so, we already have a framework which can support Chitty's observation that:

"One thing can be certain. This making a City of the Wilderness was no mere flight, nor a rejection of matter as evil (else why did they show such ascetic sense in placing their retreats, and such love for all of God's animal creation?)."[17] In Origen too, there is a strong emphasis on the importance of martyrdom, a very highly developed understanding of the "senses of the soul" and the injunction to personal sanctification. Both Clement and Origen speak of mystical union with God and this emphasis would henceforth be a central feature of all monastic theology.

On the level of practice, many celibates or consecrated virgins could be found, be they widows choosing to remain in their bereaved state, young virgins choosing to dedicate their lives to God, clergy choosing to dedicate their ministry through celibacy (or living with their wives in a non-sexual relationship), married couples living among the laity also choosing to renounce the sexual element of their relationship, and even young men and women living together as "partners" but as brother and sister (howbeit that this last soon fell into disfavour!)

In understanding the many motivations of the early monks, I highlight two fundamental themes. First there is the ideal of martyrdom, the recognition that nothing—family, possessions, even one's own life—is more important that dedication to and final union with God. From this point of view, monasticism is indeed the renunciation of the present world, a sober recognition of its secondary status.

---

[16] Ibid.
[17] Op cit Chitty. p xvi.

Second, the monastic life is centred on another ideal, that of returning to (if not surpassing) the state of human beings before the so-called "fall". By pursuing an ideal type of what human beings may have been like before the "fall", the monk seeks not only his own salvation but also that of the whole created order round about him. Since it was through human beings that creation "fell", through human beings will it be restored. While, of course, full restoration will only come about at the end of time, the monks partially anticipate that restoration in their own selves and in the manner of their life. From this point of view, monasticism is indeed an affirmation of the created world; while the monks renounce the world, they renounce only the *"fallen state"* of the world. Their willingness to die to the created world reflects their conviction that all is not as it should be. It is a recognition with is surely shared by the world as it groans in anticipation of its final redemption. Thus, the created world rejoices in the monk's striving for divine union for it knows that, in some degree at least, its salvation is bound to the monk's "success".

In these ways, the monastic life can be seen as a supreme act of love for the world, striving to restore it to its true vocation and virtue. So, the monk's partial anticipation of the final redemption of all things is prophetic: it provides a glimpse of the world as it should and will be.

Part 2
Tradition and the Creation of the Inner Space

In these chapters, I distinguish between western and eastern monasticism for they took very different routes especially after the complexities of the Great Schism of 1054, which cannot simply be reduced, as so often, to a dispute about the primacy of Rome alone. The distinctive nature of the relationship between tradition and revelation in Orthodox theology and practice is considered in order to lay a secure foundation from which to consider the great gift of contemplative prayer that the Orthodox tradition has given to the church both in the east and increasingly in the west. This, in turn, leads to a discussion of how tradition, revelation and prayer combined in the Celtic tradition and tries to sketch out some of the ways in which both the desert dwellers and the practices of the Orthodox territories might have influenced Celtic monasticism. Once again, there might be much interesting research to be done to tease out just how widespread these influences might have been and how they arose in the first place.

I visited Kiev in May 2010 and again in 2012 and on both occasions had the opportunity to take an extensive and detailed look at the life and worship in the ancient cave monasteries known as the Pescherk Lavra. It was from these monasteries that the Rus, the original Russian tribes, continued to be converted and nurtured in the faith following the original mission and ministry of St Cyrill (of the Cyrillic alphabet) and Methodius in the late ninth and tenth centuries.

It is because these cave monasteries are of supreme importance in the history and faith of Eastern, that is Russian, Christianity that they have the title Lavra. It is here that I part company with Chitty who, as we saw above, equates "Lavra" with *"suq" or market*. The early Lavra in Jerusalem and Syria that concern Chitty may well have been that, but certainly by the eleventh century in Ukraine they were far more than that. The problem for western writers, like Chitty, is that there is no equivalent title in the western church, not even Basilica, and so misunderstandings may be bound to arise, however good one's research and knowledge.

In Ukraine, at least, Lavra indicates a place of enormous spiritual and theological importance without which the life lived by ordinary Christians would be diminished and indeed, especially at times of tribulation, may not exist at all. Perhaps we should think along the lines of the Hagia Sophia (howbeit that of course that also is in the East) or the Benedictine foundations at Subiaco or Monte Casino, Cluny or the later Cistercian foundation at Citeaux or even the importance of Assisi in the Franciscan movement in their heyday. At all events, the Peschersk Lavra of Kiev was, and is, regarded as a most holy site. To go there on pilgrimage, or indeed simply to be there is regarded as a privilege and a source of special grace—and so indeed it is.

These chapters further illustrate the mixture of historical fact and stories that make them live in the hearts and minds of ordinary people, a feature that can be encountered everywhere in monastic studies. It might be reasonably argued that nowhere is this more prominent than in the study of Orthodoxy. It is certainly at the heart of the "history" of the establishment of the Peschersk Lavra.

In 1051, a monk of Mount Athos called Anthony (later St Anthony of Peschersk) had a vision from God which directed him to go and live by the banks of the Dnipro River in the walled city of Kiev. Anthony, like so many in the west today, had only the vaguest idea about where Kiev was but knew that he didn't want to go there, fought over as it was by all sorts of pagan tribes roaming the steppes of Ukraine.

Even this is interesting, I think. For notice that as late as 1051 and despite the best efforts of Saints Cyril and Methodius, and their local disciples Vladimir and Princess Olga, the people of Ukraine are described as "pagan". This word is used not in the sense that they were agriculturalists (that is what the Greek word for "pagan" indicates), though they were. Nor are we being told that they are not Orthodox Christians, but rather that they are (still) actively worshipping idols.

Despite his fears and in obedience to God's call, Anthony summoned up his courage and off he went to Kiev. He settled in a small cave, about 14 feet long, in a forest just outside the city in Berestovo, and there, like the earlier western St Benedict he stayed for five or six years by which time (and again the parallels with Benedict at Subiaco are striking) he had been joined by twelve other men all of whom had committed themselves to the fully religious life. At least two of these were later proclaimed saints themselves, Nikon and Theodosius who are still venerated by the Ukrainian Orthodox today.

Quite obviously the small cave had to be enlarged and by 1056, it included an underground church as well as the living quarters for the community. Their religious life seems to have taken its toll too, because already a part of the cave had been reserved as a necropolis, or city of the dead. The underground Church of the Annunciation can still be visited though the iconostasis, the wall of icons, separating the sanctuary and apse from the body of the church is of a more recent date, perhaps only three hundred years old.

Soon the demands of the coenobitic life proved too much for Anthony who preferred to live as a solitary and in 1057 he announced to the community that while they could, and should, continue to live in community he at least would set himself apart as a hermit. He promised to find them a new abbot.

This again is interesting. Whatever "rule" governed the life of these monks (and I think that we can safely assume that it was related to a pattern with which Anthony would have been familiar on Athos) it seems not to have allowed the community to elect their own abbot but rather have one imposed upon them by appointment.

At first, Anthony retreated to his cell, but this proved to be entirely unsatisfactory. Whenever the monks had a problem, they would disturb him and did so with increasing regularity. (This echoes the disturbances that St Anthony of Egypt repeatedly suffered, perhaps). So, he had little alternative to move to another hill nearby and dig a new cave for himself there. It was, in fact, only two hundred yards away, but at least it was something! This cave became the centre of the "Near Caves" we know today. In the meantime, the little community of brothers had grown and they too had built a whole labyrinth of caves so that eventually the "far" and "near" caves joined up to form the present complex of the Lavra.

While all this building, or rather digging work was going on, Anthony still hadn't kept his promise about finding a new abbot and the brothers suspected that he had forgotten all about it—as indeed he had. So, they petitioned him to approve their choice of Theodosius as their new abbot. Here more questions arise: Where did final decision-making authority lie in this community, with Anthony, with the brethren or in some sort of informal convocation of both? To what extent, if at all, was Anthony still reliant upon and answerable to his original community on the Holy Mount? If he was, to whom, how and how regularly did he communicate? If he was not, why not? More locally, what were his dealings with the growing power of the Ukrainian Patriarchate which would soon become chief among the Slavic peoples?

There is much interesting research to be done in teasing out answers to these questions.

The community continued to grow and the far caves were expanded still further. These must have been exciting, if somewhat disturbing times to be an Orthodox monk at the Lavra including as they do the rise to prominence elsewhere of great thinkers and teachers like St Simeon the New Theologian and the controversies of the final great schism between the western and eastern churches. During the period, 1058–1062 a second underground church—the church of the Nativity—was fashioned. Eventually even the newly extended far caves and now two churches became far too crowded to accommodate all the members of the community, especially for common worship. The physical limitations of the caves could not keep pace with the rapid growth of the community. Like the most primitive community of the church described in the Acts of the Apostles, it seemed that many were added to their number every day.

So, they hit on a novel and indeed radical idea. They would build a church above ground! Theodosius consulted St Anthony who thought that this was a splendid idea even though, of course, it would bring about major changes to the ethos and way of life for the whole community. They had lived underground for a number of reasons, to directly imitate what they believed to be the way of life among the Desert Fathers, to be hidden as the leaven in the lump and salt adding savour to everything around, to be an exemplar of burial and resurrection. All that would now change. Only very careful spiritual leadership at the hands of Theodosius would ensure that it was not entirely lost. [18] So it was that Theodosius was commissioned to design and build yet another church along with

---

[18] It is interesting that this willingness to embrace change and innovation is so often a feature of formally constituted religious communities whereas those involved in "New" "Lay" or "Secular" Monastic groups often resist it. "New monastics" often struggle with change because they cannot, or will not, find that detachment which formal coenobites know so well which dissolves their own personalities into the community. For many "New Monastics", "the journey" "the life" or "the ethos" must be preserved in aspic even at the expense of expanding their mission and ministry to others. Too often this leads to a sense of moral and spiritual superiority over others.

enclosure walls (an innovation) and new cells for the community. The church, though not the rest of the structure was, at first, made of wood. It is this, I think, apart from the plentiful supply of birch timber in Ukraine and Moldova even now, that may account for the many wooden churches that still characterise the rural landscape of these countries. They are in direct imitation of Theodosius' efforts.

By 1062, this new church had become the main centre of worship for the community at the Lavra, although the underground complex continued to be used by those who wished to be solitary and live the life of a holy hermit. For the next eight centuries, the life of the hermit seemed to become increasingly attractive at the Lavra so that by the late seventeenth century, when the west was ravaged by civil wars and the traumas of the post-reformation and counter-reformation period, yet another church had to be built. During the Soviet occupation of Ukraine after the Second World War, the Stalinist regime closed the Lavra as being incompatible with collective atheism. But they did not succeed for long and soon the hermits returned to live underground once more, continuing the ancient tradition and doing so as a more or less overt form of non-violent, passive resistance to the regime.

The Lavra today is a major tourist attraction and a place of pilgrimage with all the glitz and kitsch that accompany all such places. But above all it is still a large and active community, which is one of the last examples (perhaps *the* last example) of a monastic community in a form which has largely past from history. For here, still, is a community which consists of those committed to the coenobitic life alongside those who are committed to the eremitic life as both pray for the reconversion of the Rus, after the physical and spiritual privations of Communism.

It is against this background that these chapters are set in order to give the context for an examination of Orthodox tradition, spirituality and prayer.

Part 3
Monasticism and Conflict

The chapters which immediately follow do not continue a strictly chronological pattern. They are placed here, rather than say between the Chapters on Augustine and those about Benedict because they concern monasticism in Britain before the Norman Conquest and so continue some of the themes explored in a previous chapter which tried to uncover some of the connections between the Orthodox and the Celts.

Here I will show how hagiographic writings were generally a means of venerating a saint's life. A monastic writer of the lives of the saints had two connected purposes in mind: to advance his own salvation and educate his audience in the proper practices of Christianity. I will argue that Anglo-Saxon hagiography, written after the Synod of Whitby in 664 also showed more support for Roman and not Celtic Christianity. In an era during which Christianity in England was culturally and religiously divided, unification under a single tradition regarded as the one "true" faith was increasingly regarded as being essential.

These chapters provide an analysis of four important hagiographical works from the late seventh and early eighth centuries, namely the "*Lives of the Abbots of Wearmouth and Jarrow*" by Bede the Venerable, the anonymous "*Life of Ceolfrith*", the "*Life of Wilfrid*" by Eddius Stephanus, and the "*Life of Cuthbert*", also by Bede.

These works are important for this study because they cover a period of immense change, crisis and continuity when most Celtic monks in and around the north of England, particularly in the Kingdom of Northumbria, resisted the transition to Roman monasticism and with it entirely new ways of thinking about the inner space of the soul. The lives written about Benedict Biscop, Ceolfrith,

Wilfrid and Cuthbert reveal how this transition began and steadily progressed after the Synod.

I next consider St Augustine of Hippo. Most people do not think of Augustine as having anything to do with those people who live by a "rule" (like monks and other "religious") and certainly his early life, as outlined in *"Confessions"* might be regarded as the worst possible preparation for the life of a monk! Or perhaps it was the best possible start for it gives comfort and hope, if only on the grounds that if such a renegade as he could, through grace, turn his life around and become not only one of the greatest systematic theologians of his or any age, a canonised saint and a doctor of the church—so can we! If we have a past, Augustine had one too.

We shall see that Augustine's "rules", one of which was especially intended for communities of women, shows an understanding and sensitivity to the needs and psyche of women which was unprecedented in his day when the patriarchy of the late Roman empire was at its height. Although it has been changed and adapted in ways which make it almost unrecognisable there is a sense in which the wisdom of St Augustine has enabled all religious communities to live by his *"Rule"* ever since. In order to fully understand why this might be so, we again need a historical context and so I set the Augustine's *"Rule"* firmly in the context of his many and varied attempts to defeat heresy and his emphasis on the importance of spiritual friendship both within the community of faith and beyond.

Part 4
St Benedict Then and Now

In this section, I review some of the many contributions made by St Benedict of Nursia to western monasticism and to so much that is fruitful for our spiritual lives today. So much has been said and written about St Benedict that it is almost impossible to find anything new or original to say about him or the monastic order he founded. I do even not attempt to do so in these chapters. Rather they revolve around two central themes: First, Benedictine ethics which, in my view, owe a great debt to the philosophy of Aristotle. Second, the distinctiveness of Benedictine spirituality and the ways in which it may be relevant to faithful Christian living during a time of austerity and financial recession. These chapters have another orientation too, which is to lay the foundations on which to build some of my arguments towards the end of this study where I will examine some of the themes of the so-called "new" monastic movements many of which, consciously or unconsciously borrow from Benedict and his "rule" for those enrolled in the "school of the Lord's service".

It is at this point that I should, perhaps, "declare an interest" as they say in parliament. Although I am not attached to the Benedictine tradition or a particular house in any formal sense, I am heavily influenced by "Benedictine-ism" in my own life of prayer and in my ministry as a Licensed Reader in the Church of England. Benedict, together with my most beloved Julian of Norwich are my spiritual counsellors and guides.

So, if the next few paragraphs, the chapters on Benedict are no longer value neutral or academic in a strict sense—that is the reason. While I acknowledge that this might be the case, I make few apologies for it.

The best way to declare the details of my interest in Benedict and his influence on me is to take a few passages from his *Rule* and show how I try to apply them to my life.

I begin with the *Prologue*. The opening word of the Prologue is "*Obsculata*", which is translated as "*Listen carefully*". I have never been very good at that! So here is the first reason why Benedictine spirituality attracts me; it holds me to a standard that I hold dear but so rarely accomplish. The Rule requires me *try* to listen to people as if they are the most important person in the world to me at that moment: listening to them as if they were Christ himself. Listening to people in the way I want to be listened to. I am not at all convinced that I ever entirely succeed. But that it the whole point of the rule, it draws me back to the principle and provides an encouragement to start all over again.

In Chapter 2 of the Rule, Benedict writes of the qualities required to be an abbot:

"An Abbott is worthy to be over a monastery and should always remember what he is called, and live up to the name of Superior."[19] All Christians are called to walk a life that is worthy of their calling, in other words to practice what they preach. But St Benedict says here that it is all the more important for those who, like me, have a position of leadership and responsibility in a local community of faith. This is especially true when I am called upon either in personal dealings or from the pulpit to provide some spiritual guidance, or at least, spiritual clarification. That is a central part of my ministry, so I am called to more actively follow what I teach. My actions must compliment, if not speak louder than, my words. This is exactly what the *Rule* asks me to do, just as the Bible does too. This then is another reason why Benedictine spirituality is important to me. Like listening, it is calling me to a higher perfection of something I already hold dear.

Yet listening and trying to make sure that actions and words are complimentary is extremely difficult and indeed have their specific dangers as Benedict himself makes clear a little later on in the same chapter:

"Let the Aabbot always bear in mind that at the dread judgement of God there will be an examination of these two matters: his teaching and the obedience of his disciples. And let the Aabbot be sure that any lack of profit that the master may find in the sheep will be laid to the blame of the shepherd. On the other hand, if the shepherd has bestowed all his pastoral diligence on a restless and unruly flock, and tried every remedy for their unhealthy behaviour, then he will be acquitted at the Lord's Judgement and may be able to say to the lord with the prophet. 'I have not concealed your justice within my heart, your truth and your

---

[19] Rule of St Benedict, Trans Abbot Parry OSB With an Introduction and Commentary by Esther de Waal. Leominster. Herefordshire.(2003) Chapter 2.

salvation I have declared' (Ps.39:11) 'But they have despised and rejected me' (Is. 1:2 and Ezek. 20:27).[20] So, if my congregations mess things up under the influence of my teaching I must take ultimate responsibility and this cannot just be shifted on to my incumbent tasked with the cure of the souls in our parish. The teaching is mine, the consequences are mine and the responsibility, therefore, is mine as well—unless, of course, I have tried everything, the incumbent has chastised me and tried to repair some of the damage—and they mess up anyway! This extract from the 'Rule' ensures that I take my vocation and ministry with absolute and ultimate seriousness."

"However, just as it is proper for the disciples to obey their master, so also it is his (the abbot's) function to dispose all things with prudence and justice.[21] Here Benedict deals with decision-making in the abbey. If the matter is especially serious the abbot must call the whole community together and seek the views of all the members. Each member is encouraged to make their points humbly and simply, without making a fuss about it. If the decision is of relatively minor importance, then the abbot need only consult with his senior advisors. The Abbott is expected to listen to everything everyone has to say. From his experience, Benedict says, that he often finds that the youngest members of the community have the beast ideas. Nevertheless, once the Abbott makes his decision, the decision is made and is no longer open to question."

There is a balance here. The abbot submits the problem to the community, and the community submits its ideas. The abbot is expected to receive these ideas in humility. After all, the voice of the newest member might just be the one with God's solution. The abbot is then expected to consider every point of view and then make his decision. The community is then bound by that decision.

All this has profound implications for my dealings at both a parochial and diocesan level, because the principle here is submission. It is not a question of power but of who has the authority to make the final decision. Yes, the abbot makes the final decision, but if that is only what is looked at then the members of the community are in danger of missing a key point of the Benedictine life: its mutuality and collegiality.

By changing the circumstances, so far, I have had had no problems submitting my ideas to my parish priest when she or I have identified a problem. This is certainly not always the case at diocesan level! Many years ago, I came

---

[20] Loc cit.
[21] Ibid Chapter 3.

to the view that a very serious mistake may have been made concerning the appointment to a key post of someone who, on his own admission, had no relevant experience in the role to which he was appointed, sought to evade the requirements of the job description—and yet who had an on-going influence over the future course of Licensed Reader Ministry. What was the Benedictine thing to do? Simply to submit my concerns, not as a complaint but merely as an observation of doubt in the right quarter and then to accept the decision that has been made—difficult as that may be.

For Benedict, that submission is necessary not only for the sake of recognising due authority, which is one thing, but because it makes an essential contribution to my spiritual growth and the development of my inner space—which is much more significant.

"In all things, therefore, let all follow the Rule as a guide, and let none be so rash as to deviate from it."[22] No lay person need ever adopt a monastic rule as a guide for spiritual living and development, and most do not. But if one does, what would be the point of deviating from it? Surely it would be better to lay it aside for a while or abandon it altogether. Here too is another reason why I am caught by the Benedictine Rule: it holds me to standards I *freely* choose to embrace.

"These, then, are the tools for the spiritual craft. If we employ them unceasingly day and night and return them on the day of judgement, our compensation from the Lord will be the wage he promised."[23] What Benedict calls the "tools of the spiritual craft" are 72 "Instruments of Good Works" each one of which can be found in Scripture and are to be exercised all the time. That is a very tall order, and one that I can only begin to even contemplate, let alone implement, by the grace of God—and that is precisely the point.

I like to think of redemption as a process of infusion. That is, in order to finally enter the kingdom of heaven I am required, in some sense, to *be* clean ontologically, not just be *declared* clean by some external agent however authoritative that agent might be. It is a slow case-by-case and day-by-day process. Like a recovering addict it always means being prepared to take one step forward only to find that I have taken two steps backwards. It is not a matter of trying to "earn my salvation" or prioritising "good works" over faith. Rather it is recognition that the tools to be found in the *Rule* originate in God and come from

---

[22] Loc cit.

[23] Ibid Chapter 4.

God through his Holy Spirit. Accordingly, there is no credit to me at all. And yet I am expected not only to use the tolls but to return the whole toolkit. My ability to use even one of these tools, let alone all 72, comes from the grace of God as well.

So, this part of the *Rule* reminds me that reliance on Grace is central to my calling for it is the calling of *all* Christians, "Benedictine-curious" or not. The Instruments of Good Works also give me a summary of a Biblical set of practices that can aid that process of redemptive infusion.

"The first degree of humility is obedience without delay. This is the virtue of those who hold nothing dearer to them than Christ; who, because of the holy service they have professed, and the fear of hell, and the glory of life everlasting, as soon as anything has been ordered by the superior, receives it as a divine command and cannot suffer any delay in executing it."[24] This quotation points to motivation. The point of entering any form of accredited ministry in the church is the love of God; it is for the seeking of God. This should, in my view, be the primary motivation for every aspect of the Christian life, but especially for those whose particular vocation, say that of a Reader, has been recognised by "the Superior". I would like to think that it is intuitively obvious—but I fear it is not!

"Having climbed all these steps of humility, therefore, the monk will presently come to that perfect love of God which casts out fear…all those precepts which formerly he had not observed without fear, he will now begin to keep by reason of that love, without any effort, as though naturally and by habit."[25] The seventh Chapter of Benedict's Rule is the longest because it gives a detailed account of the twelve-step ladder of humility: to keep the fear of God always before your eyes at all times, to not cling to your own will and desires, to submit to the superior, to practice patience, to be open and honest about failure, to be tractable, to stay close to the Rule, to find periods of silence, not to be a nincompoop, to speak and to be gentle, and to be so infused with humility that it is obvious to all without being showy. This chapter is, for me, the greatest challenge of all. I am not known for my humility! So, this excerpt shows me why I should try to do something about that: it is yet another way of seeking the perfect love of God. By not only standing at the foot of the ladder but putting my hand out to haul myself up to the first rung, then the perfect love of God might make humility not forced but more natural.

---

[24] Ibid Chapter 5.

[25] Ibid Chapter 7.

As I said, that for me is a high standard, but it is also a practical guide to achieving that standard, once again through the grace of God.

"When we wish to suggest our wants to persons of high station, we do not presume to do so except with humility and reverence. How much more, then, are complete humility and perfect devotion necessary in supplication of the Lord who is God of the universe! And let us be assured that it is in not saying a great deal that we shall be heard (Mtt. 6:7), but in purity of heart and in tears of compunction. Our prayer therefore ought to be short and pure, unless it happens to be prolonged by an inspiration of divine grace.[26] So often in our churches and elsewhere prayer is neither short nor pure. Quite often in my parish it is nothing but a long list of parish events, (with times and places) a reinforcement of 'the notices' or akin to the wailing of a toddler '*gimmie, gimmie, gimmie*'. At other times they are *not* so subtle attempt of someone to persuade the congregation to their point of view in everything from the nature of the church, through the great events of our day, and on to whether it is or is not theologically appropriate to pray the *lux aeterna* in remembrance of the dead. At other times too prayers read and sound like the executive summary of a set of financial report and accounts—so boring it is surprising that those who pray them might think that anyone, let alone the 'God of the universe', might be minded to listen to them in the first place!"

So, this quotation from Benedict reminds us that true prayer is about our legitimate needs and that through grace we can and must present them to God. There is a particularly beautiful image that might help us here. During the Last Supper, the disciple whom Jesus loved is said to have laid his head on Christ's chest. At that moment, he must have heard the very heartbeat of God. True prayer, whether public or private must surely be to listen for that heartbeat and adjust ours to his. The question then becomes: *how* do we present our prayers in a way that this is likely to occur?

There is much that I recall with a certain fondness from some of my forays into the more fundamentalist and charismatic approaches to the faith. But one thing that I never was fond of was the unspoken assumption that the degree of a person's devotion and holiness could be determined by how passionately one sang the bland, repetitive and uncreative lyrics to "worship songs" and how loudly one could pray in public using the sort of false voice usually associated

---

[26] Ibid Chapter 20.

with comic vicars on the stage. Moreover, if one could also "speak in tongues" no one could ever question your salvation or membership of "the elect".

As Willy Wonka said, probably quoting Belloc, "Let us never, ever doubt, those things we are not sure about!"[27] I have always thought that I probably missed the point somehow. True, God isn't nervous—but he isn't at a great distance either and, as Benedict points out we are unlikely to get very far with, say, a Councillor or an MP if we harangue them. Why should God be given less respect? One of the ways we can show that respect is, according to Benedict, through repentance and purity of heart. Decibel levels do not enter into it. So, this is another reason why I incline to Benedict. He understands my dislike, even distrust, of some uses of public intercessory prayer and the noise and nonsense that so often surrounds it.

"As cellarer of the monastery let there be chosen from the community one who is wise, of mature character, sober, not a great eater, not haughty, not excitable, not offensive, not slow, not wasteful, but a God-fearing man who may be like a father to the whole community."[28] Here Benedict speaks directly to my professional life and duties. A cellarer was the business manager of a monastery and I spend my days managing the fundraising and administration of a small international Christian charity. Look, however, at the qualifications that Benedict sets down for being a cellarer. It is easier in some senses to be an Abbot than Cellarer. Can such a person ever be found? Perhaps not, but in setting exacting standards the *Rule* provides me with aspirations to be sought in all my professional dealings.

"Above all things, let him have humility; and if he has nothing else to give let him give a good word in answer for it is written: 'A good word is above the best gift' (Eccles: 18:17)."[29] The repeated demand for humility here is important. Benedict is making sure that while his communities and its most prominent officials must struggle with humility, they do not confuse it with low self-esteem. It is form of self-honesty. Humility recognises that its good qualities are the result of God's grace whereas its failures and bad qualities are entirely its own. Low self-esteem, like high self-esteem, is grounded in self-deception. It views itself as something special, something unique: either too inferior or too superior to be

---

[27] Roal Dahl (2016). The Complete Adventures of Charlie and Mr Willy Wonka. Illustrated by Quentin Blake. London. Puffin Books.
[28] Op cit Benedict Chapter 31.
[29] Loc cit.

a "normal" human being. It is a hard reality and one which challenges many widely held understandings of Christianity and which I have long shared. That is, I am beginning to wonder whether God's greatest gift, apart from salvation, is *not* the "fruits of the spirit", or "signs and wonders" after all, but rather humility. Benedict's injunction of humility on those who would seek to be managers is a challenging concept but one which I choose to grapple with in the belief that if I continue to do so it will eventually re-orientate not only what I do, but why I do it, and some at least of its outcomes.

"Let him take the greatest care of the sick, of children, of guests and of the poor, knowing without doubt that he will have to account for all of this on the day of judgement. Let him regard all of the utensils of the monastery and its whole property as if they were the sacred vessels of the altar. Let him not think that he can neglect anything. He should be neither a miser nor a profligate squanderer of the monastery's substance, but should do all things with measure…"[30] This is another excerpt from Benedict's chapter on the role and responsibilities of the cellarer. It is concerned with how the physical plant and all the fixed and moveable property of the community are to be treated, namely, with the utmost care and respect. Every item is to be treated equally and carefully conserved. Even so, moderation and balance is also expected in the use of the possessions in his care.

But the greatest level of concern is to be given to the sick, to children, to guests, and to the poor. People before possessions and vulnerable people before others is the watchword here. I hope that this meets with my personal standards. I do try and take care of my possessions and most of the time I even succeed!

But I am not very good at caring for the sick, becoming anxious and irritated at my own helplessness in the face of their obvious difficulty. I do what I can but often I do not know what to do or, sometimes just as importantly, what to say. It is quite easy for me at such times to comfort myself with Chapter 36 of the Rule, where Benedict reminds us that the sick are to be taken care of before and above all things, but that does not give those who are ill the right to make unnecessary or unreasonable demands—and I do so knowing that I am using it as the greatest possible excuse!

If I could, though grace, free myself from that then according to Benedict, here is another indication of where I might reasonably expect to find Jesus: in

---

[30] Loc cit.

the sick. We serve Christ by serving each other. We find Christ in each other. This is part of the Benedictine challenge. It is, as I have indicated, a hard challenge for me to accept, as it also means that I have to find Christ in the face of those with whom I struggle and may even count as "lost" friends or enemies. But this is the banner under which I choose to fight for their restoration and mine.

The same is true of caring for the visibly poor. I have a near neighbour who has a bi-polar personality and other severe and complex mental health problems. He depends on Disabled Living Allowance and other benefits for his income. Even though it must be difficult to survive on such sums, he clearly has no idea of how to set a household budget or manage his money nor has he ever been shown how this might be achieved. So, when money comes in, he spends it all in one go leaving him with virtually nothing until the next payment date. As a consequence, he knocks on my door, sometimes three or four times each week and asks to "borrow" certain sums which, of course, are never repaid.

If something is returned on account, it is recycled to meet his next request. I say nothing more about this, certainly not as an advert for my philanthropy or as a complaint either. Rather I mention it only because it is completely symptomatic of the total lack of *real* care and transformative guidance that has always been at the heart of our benefit payment system in the UK. In contrast, as a neighbour and as a Christian, I am obligated to help him in any way I can, and in the ways of which Benedict writes—*taking the best possible care.*

Children and young people are a different matter, though I suspect that I would have been either too harsh or too soft to have been a parent. I respect what children have to say and I try always to treat them appropriately and with respect. I do not denigrate them or their contributions because their age is somewhat less than some arbitrarily decided figure.

Showing hospitality is easy! I am a reasonably good cook and I like to prepare meals for people. I flatter myself that I am able to create a relaxed and hospitable atmosphere for family, friends and strangers alike so I am pleased that Benedict has much to say about hospitality and that Chapters 61, 62, 63, 64 and parts of Chapter 65 of the Rule deal with little else. He begins from a set of general principles the first of which is that guests are to be treated as if they were Jesus—because, in fact, that is exactly what they are. There is something earthy, something "incarnational" about that. We meet and receive Jesus every day; in visitors to our homes and workplaces yes, but also in the poor, in the sick, the vulnerable and in each other.

Guests equally are expected to act responsibly, with discretion and humility, respecting the traditions of place in which they find themselves especially if those traditions are not their own or to their natural inclination. In this way, they honour their host who is as much Christ to them as they are Christ to him. Once more Benedict ensures mutuality and reciprocity in what he has to say. The host is expected to mull over any criticisms or concerns guests might raise. After all that might be, the very reason why they are "strangers within gates" in the first place. The host must do so lest he is "entertaining angels unawares". If, however, guests prove to be too exacting in their standards, prone to vice, or just generally a pain in the neck, they can be politely asked to leave, at least from the monastery[31] even if the rules of normal social etiquette might prevent one from ejecting them form one's own home. Hospitality is something which is offered, not something that can be demanded. St Benedict's attitude contrasts very strongly with that of a fellow undergraduate of mine in the late seventies. Andrew told me with a bemused smile that he wanted nothing whatever to do with Miss C who lived in another part of his hall. The implication was that I should have nothing to do with her either. She was, apparently, unfriendly, unhelpful and downright rude.

I discovered sometime later that he had asked Miss C to do his laundry on a certain day each week on the spurious grounds that he did not think that her degree demanded as much of her as his did of him, and unsurprisingly she had said, "No". The hubris of this request from a virtual stranger, to say nothing of his view of women and the value of courses of study in disciplines other than philosophy and theology is still quite mind-boggling!

Furthermore, Benedict insists that the offering of hospitality is a virtue, not a vice. I once visited numerous London conference centres preparatory to a holding a theological symposium. One centre owned and run by a Christian denomination *not* known for its stand on the matter of temperance, refused to take the negotiations any further because I had asked for wine to be available at the reception. I could not hire the room I had seen because I was *"obviously going to hold a party"*. That in itself would not have mattered, but then to be told that I *"couldn't possibly be a true Christian"*, because *"Christians neither go to nor hold parties because of the sins they encourage"* worried me a great deal, and still does. St Benedict would, I think, say the exact opposite and it is fairly safe

---

[31] Anecdotally, I know of one instance in which this occurred in a lay "new" monastic community in England some years ago.

to say that he would have been as amused by this rush to judgement on both counts as I was!

The long-term value of this encounter is to remind me, as does my daily encounter with Benedict's Rule, that I am far from perfect. I am still very sinful. Saying so is of course, politically incorrect even, perhaps especially, in the church. But I have a great redeemer and a calling. It is that which I try to honour as well. These passages from the *Rule* and my informal commitment to it are some of the things that help me to keep struggling onwards.

Part 5
Medieval Monasticism

Part of the ebb and flow of the developments in monasticism and the creation of the inner space of the soul is a cycle of great zeal and fervour at the outset of any new form of communal living followed by periods of decline, and sometimes failure and extinction. When caught in the downward turn of the cycle, monastic communities are faced with a choice: reform or die. I suspect, however, to think of the reforms of the eleventh and twelfth centuries as being the child of decline in monasticism is all too easy and an example of sloppy thinking, howbeit that it has been the main-stay of the arguments of a wide variety of scholars ever since. No reform movement ever admits of a single explanation and it is a good philosophical principle to be deeply suspicious of anything or anyone which suggest that one thing is "nothing but another". To say that it is, is simply reductionist. Rather, the reforms of the eleventh and twelfth centuries were attempts to redefine and recreate the development of the inner space, both for individuals and for whole monastic communities.

It could be argued that western monasticism has reached such a point at present and this may account for the rise of the so-called "new" monastic movements. Whether this is so or not, the cycle of rise and fall goes to prove that all religious communities, as human institutions are prone to human weakness. This was something that Robert of Mosleme, Stephen Harding, St Bernard and other early Cistercians knew well and influenced St Bruno as he encouraged the first Carthusians to collectively recreate the conditions of desert hermits in the Charterhouse.

The centuries that followed saw further developments and reforms in at the hands of Saints Francis of Assisi and Dominic. These were very different characters indeed, but one thing that unites them is their understanding that the monasticism, while not of the world, is very much in the world and that the religious life both influences and is influenced by, the prevailing political, social and economic circumstances which surrounds it. At the time of Francis and Dominic, trade and manufacture were becoming much more commercial and the thirst for profit increasingly dominant. The foundations of the capitalist mode of production were being laid. The merchant classes were beginning to emerge as a distinct stratum in civil society and some members of it were enjoying unprecedented riches, honour and prominence. There was a need in the church for someone to witness to poverty and, in very different ways, Francis and Dominic did just that.

Strictly speaking those who gathered around Francis and Dominic were *not* monastic at all. They were, and are, not to be thought of as following a cenobitic life and they are certainly not hermits. Rather they are mendicant friars. "*Mendicant*" comes from the Latin verb "*mendicare*"—to beg. Hence mendicant friars were to live by begging. This posed a series of difficult and challenging questions both to the existing monastic orders and to the church at large, and still does.

To what extent should churches and individual Christians seek to make financial security a major priority in their lives? Have we such fixed revenues, so much land and property that one of the central Gospel values, namely trust in divine providence, has become a rhetorical question instead of a lived reality? The mendicant friars remind us that begging in some form, especially for grace before God in our prayers is a basic and essential part of the Christian life.

I mentioned a moment or two ago that Francis and Dominic were very different characters indeed. Francis was not a learned man and was deeply suspicious of those who were. It was only with some difficulty, and then reluctantly, that the Franciscans entered the fields of formal education and other sophisticated ministries. Dominic, on the other hand, wanted his men to be learned from the outset. He wanted them all to be learned priests, eloquent preachers ready able and equipped to defend the faith by the truths of reason.

For Dominic, faith and reason are not in conflict but rather complement each other as sisters dwelling in the same house. Both are equally the gift of God. Dominic held this view so strongly that, while there were universities throughout Europe before his arrival on the scene, there is no doubt that it is to him that we owe the idea and form of the university as we know it today. It was Dominic who saw that Christians should not only know what they believe but why it makes sense to believe it and in a way that is at least as articulate as other forms of rational discourse.

Part 6
Contemplative Love and the Love of Contemplation

In the meantime, there was another crisis: a Protestant reformation. Most people think that this occurred in the sixteenth and seventeenth centuries, and so it did. But this was merely the flowering of the stem the roots of which go much further back in time. Indeed, it could be reasonably argued that the dispute between Thomas Becket and King Henry II concerned the extent and limits to which the church in England might, (or might not) become semi-autonomous from the central authorities in Rome.

Shortly afterwards the demand for a vernacular version of the scriptures and the liturgy grew more intense, and with it an increasingly intense clerical resistance to it. The build-up of this pressure ensured that the later great crisis of the sixteenth and seventeenth centuries would sweep across northern Europe like a hurricane. St Ignatius believed that it was his task to meet that crisis and calm the storm. The only way to do that, he thought, was (like Dominic) to educate priests to the highest possible level and in as many aspects of human endeavour as possible—and then ensure their total loyalty to the Pope with all the rigour of a military campaign.

Yet there is always a huge price to be paid in trying to reform other people's lives, as the examples of St Ignatius Loyola, St Teresa of Avila and St John of the Cross make plain in their very different ways. In the case of Teresa and John, it is not at all clear from their writings who gave spiritual direction and comfort to whom as they set about reforming the Carmelite tradition. Perhaps the relationship was mutual; for there is no doubt that they respected and loved each other deeply. In any case, there was a grave need for the reform of the contemplative life and the development of the inner space.

Teresa made sure that even the most active communities were reformed along with those who were most contemplative. This is a clear instance of something we noted earlier, the choice to reform or die. Teresa and John knew that the reform would need to be as wide ranging as possible or death would inevitably ensue as much of the Carmelite tradition had grown moribund. If that was true in their day, and it was, the need in our day is greater still and that is why this work will spend a very great deal of time looking in some detail at their spiritual doctrine and teaching.

There was, inevitably, a personal cost to be paid for seeking reform. John spent a great deal of time in prison, held captive by his fellow Carmelites. Teresa, in travelling from one community to another suffered great hardship and difficulties. More than once, she believed that members of the community she was about to reform were intent upon killing her. There were convents in which she ate only moderately avoiding everything that might have been poisoned. Both she and John quickly learnt that if we want a quiet and serene life, it is better not to try to reform anybody!

The Carmelite vision comes to a climax in the life and thought of St Theresa of Lisieux. Superficially at least she makes the religious life and the attainment of sanctity look easy. Like St Augustine, the idea is that if she can make it, so can we. But like St Augustine and like St Benedict too her life of prayer and sacrifice were remarkably apostolic. She was canonized, the church tells us, mainly in order to teach us that God is pleased with the creation and development of our inner space.

Part of that creation and development is to struggle in prayer and in living a life devoted to love of God and of people. In any study of the development of the inner space, including this one, Theresa reminds us that what we do and how we live can often determine the strength of faith, or lack of it, not only in ourselves but in others too. So, we will consider her *not* because she is a central character in modern popular piety, but because she is a salutary lesson to us all.

We will then turn our attention to St Francis de Sales. St Francis de Sales gave to the world what is one of the most influential and certainly most popular spiritual classics: *"The Introduction to the Devout Life"* which is a theology of the dynamics of Love. With this book, we enter a totally new vision of how the inner space develops and nourishes the soul. With it and for the first time in Christian history, it became possible for Roman Catholic women to take simple vows, be members of orders recognised and approved by the Pope, yet living in communities and encouraged to fulfil their apostolate *outside* the walls of the convent.

It may be that it is in this book we have the foundations of a "new" monasticism, rather than the much quoted passage in the works of Dietrich Bonheoffer. At all events, it is this book which encouraged thousands of people to see their so-called secular lives as an active apostolate.

For the Beguines, the idea of the active apostolate in the "secular" world had many advantages, not least of which was that it provided a way of communicating the faith to the laity and equipping them to communicate the faith to others. Though there are not I think any formal links between the Beguines and St Francis de Sales it is clear that he thought that this had two interconnected features.

The first was the apostolate of sanctification. That is, the main purpose of communicating the faith to others is to show how every person is a unique child of God, always firmly held in God's loving embrace no matter who or what or where they are.

The second aspect is to perform what used to be called the corporal acts of mercy so that everything a Christian touches, thinks or is engaged in is a sign and token of the constant loving presence of God in us and around us.

Part 1
Foundations

Chapter 1
The Four Pillars of Monasticism and the Example of Christ

There are many reasons for beginning this study of monastic spirituality and the development of inner space by paying some attention to the New Testament in general and the example of the life of Jesus Christ in particular. The first is that whatever else might constitute the content of monasticism it must always and everywhere be grounded in Scripture. The New Testament is, as it were, *the* foundation document of monasticism, its articles of association and much more besides. It is nothing less than the Word of *The Word*. [32] As such it speaks of the way in which our whole life in all its joys sorrows and passions is, or may be, devoted to God. Yet, this sort of commitment is impossible without a strong motivation and a willingness to make sacrifices along the way. The strongest motivation a Christian can find for that sort of devotion is the belief that the foundations of such a life lie in divine revelation—the life of Christ himself as pattern and guide. In order to dedicate our lives to God, we need to be sure that it is *Deus Volt* (= because God wills it) and the reading of Scripture will also tell us why he wants it.

The second reason for starting with the New Testament is that there are many voices both in the church and outside it at present that raise doubts as to whether monastic spirituality and certainly the quest to develop an inner space is really *Christian* at all. Perhaps this is to overstate their case but there are certainly those who doubt that either of these things is anything more than a redundant addition or even a distortion of the Christian message. If they are right, spirituality would not properly belong to Christian revelation. It would be the creation of the

---

[32] Jn1:1.

church, no doubt under divine guidance, but what the church can create it can also destroy. It would no longer be *Deus Volt* at all.

So, to begin with the New Testament is to try to discover whether, and if so how, there is anything in the life of Christ that laid the foundation from which monastic spirituality might legitimately follow. In order to do that, I will group Christ's life and example into four groups: Christ's Love, Christ's Service, Christ's Sacrifice and Christ's Grace. I have chosen Love, Service, Sacrifice and Grace because I believe these to be the four pillars of his own life and of the Christian life in general. They provide us not only with the motive but the means of imitating him. They are the prime tools by which the inner space is fashioned.

Love

If Christ is the exemplar of monasticism, we need to make sure that that he followed this mode of life because he wanted to. We need to make sure that he did so out of the purest sense of freedom and not because of any internal or external pressure or coercion to do so. Human beings choose freely, with no compulsion, no coercion *only* when we love. Pure freedom is pure love. Was this true of Christ? The short answer, if we take the Chalcedonian formula seriously, is "yes". God became man out of love of humankind. God in Christ did all that he did, lived in the way that he did not in order to please himself, or us, but that through pure love we might be saved and be free. But here we must be careful in case we fall into false thinking and, eventually, erroneous theology. Did God *have* to become a person in order to save the world and everything in it? No. As a human being was it *necessary* for him to suffer and die in order to win our freedom? No, but it was sufficient? Did he have to die on a cross? No.

All of this was free choice and if there is one thing that stands as the keystone in the arch of the faith it is the loving freedom with which people follow Christ. They do so because they love. When we are in love, we don't have to give reasons for it or explain it because love is a state of being. Love is the highest reason. In the end, it is the *only* reason. Everything else is argument.

Service

In order to be itself, Love must result in some action or deed between the lover and the beloved. Traditional Christian doctrine tells us that the parts of the Holy Trinity, Father, Son and Spirit, love each other with bonds of mutual dependence. It is a fertile, fruitful love. Without dividing the parts of the Trinity, we can conceptually say that the Son manifested his love for the Father when he undertook to serve the needs of that which they and the Spirit had created and specifically, human beings. He did so because he loved the people he had created albeit that they had also freely chosen to offend against love. They badly needed a saviour, and what is that unless it is love in action to the ultimate extent? Christ loved by serving and saving.

This pillar of service in Christ's life is of central importance as an example of our service and this is nowhere seen more plainly than in the accounts of his temptations in the wilderness. They show that we, like him, are faced with a choice. We can serve reluctantly, even rebelliously, or we can serve joyfully and with eagerness. Or we can be shrewd and look around. There are many ways of serving and many of them are cheap. Christ's example shows that true service is not only and expression of love—it is always costly. Another name for costly service is sacrifice.

Sacrifice

Sacrifice is the third pillar on which the argument that Christ might be the first monastic rests. His life and work and ministry were acts of total self-surrender as we see from the fact that, despite their many narrative and contextual differences, all four Gospels end with the shedding of blood. Blood belongs to the essence off the religious life, not just sacramentally but physically. I did not know that when I first became a Christian and it was still a somewhat abstract concept when I took my vows as Reader in the Church of England. Even yet I am not sure whether a bleeding of the spirit is not greater and more painful than bleeding from the body. But it is real all the same. If you are afraid of blood, the Christian life is not for you and a life lived under some form of religious vow, monastic or secular, quite impossible.

Grace

Why is so much effort and exertion involved in this active love? Why even, perhaps especially, crucifixion at Calvary? After all, the Son didn't need any of this. All he got for becoming a human being was rejection, abandonment, blasphemy and death. It is worth reminding ourselves that the Son, in his divine nature, foresaw all that and *still* chose it. He chose with a purpose and that purpose was to win Grace. It was to merit salvation and sanctification for everyone who because of his suffering and death would benefit.

We, like Christ are to have finality to all of this as we develop the inner space and grow in—sanctity, becoming more united to God. But that does not mean that we pursue holiness for our own sake. It is not a way of boosting our spiritual egos in a way that might say, "Look at me, covered with medals because of my battles with temptation and my victories in overcoming vices with virtue. Look at me bulging all over with sanctity so that I'm fit to pop." No—and while we are on this point, let us also never forget that people can, and do, pursue the religious life for twenty, thirty, fifty years and never know the reason why. The reason why is Christ's reason why: it is to obtain for souls. The souls of others as well as our own, and our own, last of all.

Love, Service, Sacrifice and Grace, these are the marks of the truly devoted religious life. They make us co-redemptive disciples with Jesus. There is, of course, a big and fundamental difference between him and us. Unlike Christ, we are prone to sin no less than the people we are called to love and to serve. So even as we labour, in the imitation of Christ to obtain grace for other people, we all need a bit more grace ourselves.

These four pillars are linked by a fifth which is closely associated with the monastic life but which is by no means exclusive to it.

Total Dedication

There are several kinds of totality which identify the religious life as lived by Jesus Christ and his immediate followers. Each of them has been regarded as the key features of the monasticism since the earliest days of Christianity.

The first is a totality of sacrifice. What does this mean in practice? It means a special Grace to give up the exercise of any right to property or possession. This is often called the monastical to poverty, but it is only one aspect of it.

The second totality is the giving up of the natural desire to marry and have sexual relationships. This is often called the monastic call to celibacy and so it is but, again the sexual aspect is only one aspect of what it means to be celibate.

The third, and in our own day the most unbelievable, is refusal to exercise the right to autonomy and self-determination. This is often called monastic humility. There are few more important or popular words than "autonomy" in our contemporary vocabulary. Autonomy is so often confused with a radical individualism which allows the individual to do whatever she wants, wherever she wants, with whomsoever she chooses and under equally chosen circumstances. Autonomy is understood to be and to confer unrestrained freedom so that there are no limits to the choices we make from when to get up in the morning to whether or not to have an abortion. But all this is far from what "autonomy" actually means.

Our English word is derived from two in ancient Greek. The first meant "self" and the second "under the law". So, whereas we commonly think of "autonomy" as meaning a law created by ourselves to suit our desires, actually the ancient Greek concept speaks of the individual internalising the bond of law which gives cohesion to the whole community and freely deciding to be bound by that sense of communal good. Autonomy then is about subjecting oneself to a higher authority, the community. This has always been a key feature of the monastic way of life and is the first kind of totality that Jesus practised.

According to Luke, Jesus' teenage years were spent in subjection to Mary and Joseph, not because they were "superior" to him but in order to preserve the common bond of family and community and in order to develop a true sense of his own individuality and purpose within the limits these things impose.

This has direct links with another form of totality, the totality of service. Christ came into the world to serve and not be served (Lk. 22:24–27). His disciples followed him in order to serve too. But they did not do so randomly or according to their own inclination but only according to his teaching and direction. In the same way, those who seek or are part of the religious life fulfil their vocation and serve others only by subjecting themselves to the aegis of the *magisterium* (teaching tradition) of the hierarchical church.

The next totality is the totality of duration, or stability. One of the most telling statements of Jesus was on the cross, "*It is finished*". His service of others pertained until death. This means that everyone who has a genuine calling to the religious life intends to make a lifelong and not just a temporary or part-time commitment of sacrifice to God and commitment to the church. There are not, or should not be, any associate members of the religious life. It is not like a job where we "put in" thirty-five or forty hours a week. That is why it is another slippage of language and thought of when priests or readers, monks or nuns or anyone else with a vocation that has been officially recognised by the church claim to be "retired". Retired from what? Following Christ's own example, our commitment is to be twenty-four hours each day, seven days each week, three hundred and sixty-five days each year—until death.

Against this background of some of the distinguishing marks of the religious and monastic life, it makes it easier to move on to a particularly vexed question we must now try to resolve. At this point, I want to be as clear and as cogent as I can be because the answers we give, may be of central importance to what follows in the arguments in the rest of this study.

The question is this: Did Jesus make a distinction between his close followers and those who were not "close" and yet heard and believed? An immediate and tentative answer, based on what appears to be the general thrust and trend in the New Testament as a whole, is "yes he did". The New Testament seems to make the distinction obvious. There were always people who listened to Jesus, who heard his teachings, sermons and parables, sometimes in their thousands. And when the day of Pentecost had come, thousands more presented for baptism—but there were always also those which Jesus called his "friends".

Let us now look at this in closer detail. *"If anyone wants to be a follower of mine..."* This is one of the most crucial passages in the whole of the Gospels. It forces us to consider exactly what it means to be a follower, a friend, or lover of Jesus. Are we prepared to give what it takes in all the *totality* we have been considering? We read of Jesus asking the disciples, *"Who do you say that I am?"* (Mtt.16:13–20)

Peter replied, *"You are the Christ, the Son of the living God,"* with the title "Christ" being loaded with all sorts of understandings and expectations of a people that had been nourished by the prophetic Word of God and who had a keen sense that the messiah would appear among them.

Jesus then told his friends that the Son of Man was destined to suffer and even to die. Not for one moment did Peter think that Jesus was speaking figuratively. He started to rebuke Jesus. Far from telling Peter to calm down and not be so literal, Jesus almost loses his temper, *"Get behind me, Satan! You are thinking not as God thinks, but as human beings do."*

Well, yes of course, Peter was after all a human being! Or is Jesus facing a temptation to depart from his totality of love and service in doing the will of the Father even to the point of death, and is that why he uses the same language as he previously used to defeat the temptations in the wilderness? Is Jesus losing his temper with himself? The answer may indeed be "both", for this incident clearly shows that Jesus only wanted followers who would accept him as the rejected one and then later as the one who surmounted this rejection by rising to new life. And what is more such a follower would have to be prepared to be rejected as Jesus would be. Jesus warned them that in loyalty to him there would be renunciations for them to make and crosses for them to carry. They would need to have the courage of his convictions, and in doing so they would transcend all the hostility that might be thrown at them.

As Jesus laid down the ground rules for his friends what must he have been thinking? Knowing that he was the Christ, the Suffering Servant, he had to come to terms with what it would mean for him. In Gethsemane he would pray *"My soul is sorrowful to the point of death...Abba Father! For you everything is possible. Take this cup away from me...but not as I will, but as you will."*[33] This is Jesus in an intensely loving relationship with the Father and yet it is a tortured relationship too. The torture is not one of resentment but one of deep apprehension at the pain that loving obedience would impose.

Many of us might be living out our faith to the full while others may do so in fear of their lives. Yet others, in an increasingly secular society, may be beleaguered by legislation that deeply offends their consciences. There may be a heavy price to pay domestically and in terms of career development if our convictions prevent us from following cultural and political leaders. Other people may be subjected to victimisation and vilification for no other reason than that they dare to speak of the love that dare not speak its name. No longer, as Lord Alfred Douglas wrote,[34] the love between homosexuals—but the love of Christ for women and men. What identifies a true friend of Jesus is that we can identify and espouse his convictions and insist on living by them, in the full knowledge that this will involve much personal sacrifice. More than this, since our idealism is drawn from Jesus these convictions are, for us, *the way* to be followed, *the truth* to be told *and the life* to be lived. As his followers we too live in a loving relationship with Christ. It is a relationship that is, contrary to popular opinion, far from comfortable, far from cosy. In fact, it is in many ways a tortured relationship, grounded in our resolve to remain his disciples, no matter what the cost to ourselves.

Part of this is also to be aware that the Evangelists and St Paul speak of different levels of intimacy between the followers and Jesus himself. In English, the word is "friends", but the Greek word in the earliest manuscripts is closer to the concept of "lover". If we reread key passages of the New Testament substituting the word "lover" wherever "friend" occurs we will be shocked to

---

[33] Mk 14:36 and Mtt.26:38.
[34] Lord Alfred Douglas (1892) 'Two Loves' A poem. *The Chameleon*. Oxford. December 1894.

discover just how often and how subtle the degrees of intimacy between Jesus, his friends and the other followers could be.

This becomes especially apparent in the days following his triumphant entry into Jerusalem and leading up to the trials and the crucifixion and again after his resurrection. With whom and for whom did Jesus give his most intense teaching and consecrate the bread and wine as his body and blood? His close friends, his lovers. After the resurrection, of the tens of thousands who probably witnessed his slow and painful journey from the place of scourging to the place of the skull, he appeared to only a few. Jesus chose. He picked. He selected. Whereas many are called few are chosen to be lovers. Whereas many could be disciples only some could be apostles but these were the most unexpected people imaginable. There were not even reliable. There was Judas—a traitor. There was Peter—a denier. There was Thomas—a sceptic and an empiricist. That is quite a high percentage of a small group of twelve.

It is not, and let us be clear here, that Jesus did not want others outside the inner group of friends to be holy. He did. But he also called those who needed to be frequently and *intimately* in his company more often than others and gain an additional insight into his message, ministry and purpose. Only thus could these things endure and the work of salvation be extended to all generations.

Having said all this, what does it imply or entail? I think that it shows that the New Testament foundations of the monastic life are to be sought among those people who are chosen selected and inspired with a particular calling to sanctify others through their love and their service. Since Christ instituted the church there are to be, as St Paul later adds, not all evangelists, not all prophets…and so forth and so on. There are to be in the church, as there was in the beginning, those who are called to a specialist form of spirituality and holiness in order that they might become the channels, through which the whole people of God might be, in turn, infused with a special sanctifying grace.

At this point, there is a temptation to argue that since all the faithful are called to holiness, all degrees of holiness are the same and that no one can enjoy a greater degree of intimacy as a "friend" of Jesus than anyone else. That might appeal to our current quest for fairness in all things (even at the expense of doing justice), it may be democratic, but is it true? Are some people called to a greater degree of holiness than others? If the answer is "yes" then we have also to decide by what criteria this might be judged and how people grow in holiness. Behind this lies another question. How, as far as we can ever tell, does God want the church to be sanctified and to be a sanctifier? The answer is through building relationships with other people. In other words, it seems that God wants some people to be providential instruments or channels to promote holiness in other people.

We may then conclude that already in the first century and even among Christ's closest friends, this is precisely what occurred. Some were called and chosen—by name—to "follow me". Not all received this invitation. Some were called to a higher order of sanctity. Beginning with Mary, the Mother of Jesus and John the Baptist and going on through all the great figures of the Gospels and through the apostolic age; they were called to be God's channels, his means to other people so that being holy themselves, they might also sanctify the lives of all with whom they came into contact.

From the argument made in this chapter, the following points (in no particular order) can be drawn out.

1. The essentials of the religious life are divinely revealed. This is to say rather more than that they are based on the Bible. There is more to revelation than the Bible. Revelation concerns the whole work and ministry of Christ in his own person and in the Tradition of the Church ever since. So, for example, we can put a statue by its base. But the statue is not the base. In the same way, revelation is not merely the base of the religious life; it is the religious life revealed.
2. Everyone is called to holiness. But not necessarily the same kind of holiness.
3. Superiors are necessary in any community. It is impossible to have community, especially a religious community, without them.
4. Effective renewal of the religious life is mainly the interior renewal of the spirit. But this renewal must be demonstrated in loving acts toward other people. The religious life is not a call to personal holiness or personal sanctification but to be a channel of grace by which others are sanctified.
5. The religious life demands a totality and constancy of commitment and that commitment must be made freely and without coercion.
6. Contemplation and the exercise of the apostolate are both essential elements in the religious life but they are by no means the same. To exercise an apostolate is to put contemplation into action. People who

do so contemplate even as, or while, they do whatever their work is. Thus, for St Benedict, "laborare est orarare" (work is prayer) and vice versa.
7. The unqualified centre of the religious life is Christ himself—especially as made known in the events of his passion and resurrection and present with us now in the bread and wine as his body and blood.
8. The spirit in which the sacrifices of love, service and grace are made should be generous.
9. The pursuit of the holiness of others in the religious life is both primary and necessary.
10. That which distinguishes the religious life from secular society is the sense of community and obedience.

In short, the monastic life is a witness to the world just as Christ's was. This witness is more than what monastic do; it concerns what they are, indeed what we all are—the most beloved sons and daughters of God—and to rejoice in that through a lifestyle that is based on a totality of commitments which are not comparable to any other, and cannot be. The monastic life, whether in its cloistered or secular forms is not so much a matter of speaking or doing as of being. Hence St Francis of Assisi is reputed to have said, "Preach by all means possible—and use words if you need to."

Chapter 2
The Moral Features of Early Monasticism

What did the early Christians believe about the dedicated religious life beyond the minimum essentials of keeping the moral law and achieving the intimate friendship with Jesus that I outlined in Chapter One? There we noted that from the very beginning Jesus seems to have distinguished between the majority of those who listened to him, broadly the disciples, and his inner circle who were called to be apostles. This chapter try to determine whether, and if so, where and how, this distinction was maintained in the early Christian community from, say, 100 to 325AD, and in such a way that a distinctive class of persons emerged which might be recognised as the earliest monks and nuns.

The best way of doing so is to consider some of the main features of the monastic life in this period. These features may not appear in any logical sequence but, as we will see, each collides with each much like billiard balls upon a table. Each feature, as we will also see, has a definite relation to the times I am describing. So, the purpose of this chapter is very specific: to identify what might be called the spiritual patrimony of the early church as the foundation on which all future religious communities were built.

The first feature is Christianity as separation. That does not necessarily mean physical separation, but it does mean a moral distinctiveness that must characterise the true lover of Christ. Christians, we recall, must be "in the world but not of the world". When Christ himself distinguished between those who believe in him and "the world" and when St Paul later wrote to the early Christian churches about being pilgrims in a strange land, we get some idea of the sort of separation this is.

This is nowhere brought out more plainly than in the *"Didache"*, also known as "The Teaching of the Twelve Apostles".[35] This important text was probably written somewhere before 100 AD. The first sixteen chapters have been called *"The Book of Two Ways"*, because it poses Christians with a choice, the way of life, or the way of death. Like Moses who posed the same choice to the people of the Exodus it is a choice seeking its own answer; to choose life. The way of life is made up of four duties, to love God, to love people, to love enemies and to practice liberality. So, the mark of the Christian is not only what Christ said it would be but what the first Christians actually did after the ascension based on their understanding, frail and fragmented as that might have been. It is, after all, one thing to have a recipe and quite another to have a cake. It is as if the teaching of Jesus was the recipe and the practical life of the early church the cake. The proof of the pudding, as they say, is in the eating and our participation in the feast proves not only that the recipe was faultless but that the first cakes set the standard by which all the others which follow might be judged. In other words, that the teaching of Jesus could be encapsulated and emerge as a distinctive form of life, proves that what Jesus taught was no idle dream. What he taught he taught well. He taught so well because he conferred Grace on his followers, equipping them live up to what he told them to do.

The second feature is the personal duties of those who follow *"The Way of Life"*. This consists in the practice of virtue and the overcoming of vice in its widest sense. More specifically, especially for those called to the monastic life in an ordered community, it is about the avoidance of sensuality and the physical pleasure of sexual acts. This is commonly thought to be *the* key feature of the monastic life. It is not. Many writers and recent paedophilic scandals have shown how difficult the strict observance of this personal element in the religious life can be. Father Hardon SJ has highlighted its unintended social and negative evangelistic consequences too.

He argues that it is the avoidance of sexuality that non-Christians find as repulsive as to confirm their unbelief.[36] Hardon's position is not that the avoidance of sexuality should therefore be abandoned by monks and nuns and parish clergy, but rather that so often it is ripped out of context and made so important that it becomes more than it actually is. He, rightly, believes that the

---

[35] Didache.

[36] Father J.A. Hardon.SJ. *History of the Religious Life up to Vatican II*. The Real Presence Association. LaCrosse WI. USA. See also Last Accessed March 2024.

church in general and members of religious orders in particular have an intellectual and moral duty to place it firmly where it properly belongs; as part of the totalities of commitment we considered in Chapter 1. Only by explaining the importance of the total commitment required by the religious life can the avoidance of sensuality make sense to the modern mind which is, often, sexually obsessed. If this could be done cogently and clearly, and without communicating either a sense of superiority or a devaluation of sex, this would, I think, help to underscore the importance of chastity and faithfulness in marriage and so promote its importance to society and family life. Whether and to what extent there is a willingness to do so in ways which are not prissy, sentimental and pious is, of course, an open question.

But sensuality is not just sexuality; it includes other passions, such as cruelty and anger too. The old saying that "sticks and stones may break my bones but words can never hurt me" is simply untrue. As we know only too well, cruelty can be practised by the tongue as painfully as the cut of any knife and its wounds sometimes never heal. Indeed, in the worst case, words may even damage the soul itself.

The third feature concerns the social duties of those who follow *"The Way of Life"* both within and outside the church. The social duties are based on giving and receiving respect whenever and wherever it is due, and especially to those in positions of authority. To give and receive respect maintains the bonds of communal living, and those in positions of authority have a particular responsibility to maintain it.

No aspect of human life or endeavour is off-limits to the practical expression of the social duties and this may take various forms. But there are three areas which Christians in general, and monastics in particular, have made their own and so have become most closely associated with the church.

The first is the maintenance of peace. So often our public prayers are for peace at the macro-political level. We pray for peace as if it were an absence of war or conflict. We pray for the sort of peace which we can influence only indirectly through the ballot box and by lobbying. Rarely, if ever, do we publicly pray for peace in those things of which we are part and over which we can, and must, bring our immediate and personal influence to bear; peace in broken, discriminatory and hurting relationships.

Since we fail to do that, we similarly fail to pray for the peace which passes understanding and penetrates into our own souls and for the sake of our life with

God. We fail to pray for the sort of peace which is, according to De Caussade and Brother Lawrence,[37] available to us when we abandon ourselves into the providential will of God and become keenly aware of his presence with us, around us and within us. One way of remedying this tragic situation is the practice of contemplative meditation as recommended by John Main and Richard Rohr and which we will explore in greater detail towards the end of this study. The second aspect of social duties is faithfulness. Faithfulness to one another, the immediate community of which we are part, faithfulness to ensuring that all creatures have the ability to be and become what God intends them to be, and faithfulness to the teaching of the church, to name but four. Too often faithfulness becomes moribund and unless we are very careful decays into a Christian antiquarianism. We believe that faithfulness is about preserving the status quo at all costs, or worse, we think that it means preserving our notion of some previous "golden age" of the past which probably never existed in reality. Some Christian views of marriage do just that. But faithfulness is, rather, the recognition that we are but one link in a long chain. We are linked to the past, yes, but we are not that link. The forging of our own link must be sufficiently distinctive, lively and life-giving so that it receives from the past, appropriate to the present and ensures that there will be something for our successors to bind into in their turn.

The third area in which the social duties are most commonly exercised is in education. Those who are most effective in education in any of its many forms have a generosity of spirit which is derived from peace and from a true sense of what it is to be faithful. The problem is that all too often we think that education is nothing but formal education or conducted by those who have a special skill officially recognised at degree level. Alternatively, we think that education is nothing but the acquisition of some skill or talent such as being good at sport or being "computer literate". Both are profoundly mistaken. Education begins and ends in experiencing, maintaining and extending good relationships; good relationships with the material to be studied, but also good relationships with the people who compose it and present it to us.

This is illustrated by a quiet corner of the Under Croft of York Minster. Beyond the tomb of St William, there is a small and rather beautiful medieval

---

[37] Fr Jean Pierre De Caussade (2008) Abandonment to Divine Providence. Mineola New York Brother Lawrence of the Resurrection (2000) Practice of the Presence of God. New York. Bantam Doubleday Dell A Division of Penguin Random House New Edition viii.

statue of St Ann teaching the young Virgin Mary to read. At the entrance to the Quire, there is a wall tablet of somewhat later date in which St Ann and Our Lady sing together the "Song of Hannah". (No wonder then that St Ann is the patron of teachers and lecturers!) Both of these ancient artefacts not only illustrate the point I have just made but remind us that the church has been involved in building healthy educative relationships since before apostolic times.

The fourth feature which characterises those who have chosen "The Way of Life" is the *confession of sins*. It is interesting to note the ways in which the church has approached this subject over the centuries and especially in, say, the last forty years or so.

When I was a young man, the teaching on sin had many similarities to the myth of Sisyphus. Everyone had their own heavy load to haul up the hill of Calvary with the intent and purpose of leaving it there at the foot of the cross and to see it roll away as Pilgrims did in Bunyan's *"Pilgrims' Progress"*.[38] It was a time when popular Christian literature spoke about how members of New York gangs had, through Grace and the tireless work of pastors and evangelists, managed to do just that and become honourable and hard—working members of the establishment. We even used to sing songs about how "burdens are lifted at Calvary"[39]—though fortunately we were spared the imagery of massacre imposed on our parents' generation which sang of "fountains filled with blood drawn from Immanuel's veins"[40] and of white robes being "washed in the blood of the lamb".[41] But somehow, however hard I tried, whatever efforts I made and however fervently I sang the songs, I still found myself back at the bottom of the hill with my rock intact.Having been encouraged from an early age to develop an enquiring mind, I sought an explanation and to my horror discovered that it was *my fault*. I was the guilty one—and at least doubly so! First, I had my own burden of sin in having tried, but failed to "hit the mark" of God's love (even though I was conversely told that salvation was by faith and not by works). So

---

[38] John Bunyan (1678) *Pilgrim's Progress from this World to That which is to Come.* 1815.

[39] A more recent version is that of Ladye Love Smith on the album *"In the Easter Garden: Easter favourites from Bill and Gloria Gaither and Friends."* (Live) 2015.

[40] William Cowper: There is a Fountain Filled with Blood. A hymn at www.hymnal.net/en/hymn/h/1006 Last accessed March 2024.

[41] Elish Albright Hoffman: *Have You Been to Jesus for the Cleansing Pow'r?* A hymn. Www.hymnal.net/en/hymn/h/1007 Last Accessed March 2024.

clearly, I did not have enough faith. It was lack of faith that prevented my having sufficient strength to build up enough force to move my rock. If the mark of a Christian was to have faith and I only had a very small amount, perhaps none at all, then I could not be a "good Christian".

Perhaps I wasn't a Christian at all. Yet I believed I was, and others believed it too. This produced feelings of great doubt and uncertainty. Was I a fraud? Was I living a lie? Was I Jonah in the ship of faith, a hireling or even a wolf set among the flock? Was I really me at all? How, when it came right down to it, could I be certain that there was anything "real" about my life at all? This was, of course, long before I discovered that thanks to St Anselm's ontological argument and its rebuttals, existence (reality) is not a predicate!

I could hardly turn to God to sort all this out because even though, allegedly, he saw me through the filter of the sacrifice of Christ for me and for all things seen and unseen; surely the weight of my personal "manifold sins and wickedness" was too great for him to do other than condemn me to nether hell.

If all that were not bad enough, I was also guilty of being complicit in the original sin of Adam and his fall from Grace. Why Adam could not be as responsible for his sin as I, apparently, was for mine was never fully clear to me. But there it was. I was guilty *because* Adam was guilty of allowing himself to be *seduced* by his wife into disobedience. Stop there! This was already beginning to be too much.

How was I complicit if, assuming that Christianity does not admit of a doctrine of reincarnation, I could not possibly have been an accomplice before, during or after the seduction? Well, it turned out I was *seminally* present in Adam. Seminally present…eh. Now this was far too much information for a young person coming to terms with and exploring his sexuality and forging relationships in London in the mid-nineteen seventies.

Then in the eighties and nineties more burdens of sin were added to my already heavy load in the form of "structural sins". In some ways, these "structural sins" were far more deadly than the ordinary type. In structural sin, I not only sinned against God but against those who were not born into free, democratic, western capitalist societies and did not have the benefits of a good education or the other benefits I enjoyed.

In so far as I did (or did not), purchase fairly traded Bolivian chocolate powder (or some such), did (or did not) join the appropriate action committee on everything from race relations to the atom bomb, and in so far as I did (or did not) make a religious "option for the poor" I was more or less in sin. In fact, everything I did, or did not do, was an occasion for sin. I came to believe that my entire existence was one enormous sin and that therefore it was extremely unlikely that I would encounter the God who in Christ was reconciling the world to himself. Far less was it likely that he should encounter me!

The legacy of this is with us to this day. It is why the general confession at the Anglican Eucharist speaks of sins *"against our neighbour"* and the Roman Catholic equivalent speaks of sins against *"you my brothers and sisters"*. There is surely some interesting research to be done in the connection, if any, between guilt inducing theology, the decline in church attendance and the increasing secularisation of society.

No one, I think would wish to return to the theology which asked people to emotionally and spiritually beat themselves up as I did, over the slightest misdemeanour rather than experience the joy of being a sinner saved by Grace. But I am equally certain that the current state of ecclesiastical affairs, in which we hardly ever mention sin, never mind feel guilty about it, is *not* an improvement. Nowadays we can go for whole seasons in the liturgical year without ever hearing about sin at all. Sadly, the so-called penitential seasons of Advent and Lent are not exempt from this generalisation either.

We hear much about the unconditional love of God for everyone, and this is surely right. But the difficulty with this is at least twofold: First, it presses dangerously close to crossing the barrier between creatures and their creator. While it brings God near as *"truly a person"* and refuses the notion that God is out to punish us at every opportunity, it also diminishes his divine nature. It tends towards an anthropomorphism in which we see God as a more perfect and larger version of ourselves. This leaves Christians and Christianity exposed to all the critiques of Feuerbach, Marx and Freud (to name but three) in ways which could only have been dreamed of by them when they originally wrote. We have created God in our own image. In short, we struggle to see Jesus as *"truly God"*.

Second, it weakens the prophetic voice of the church to society. Rather than confronting society it confirms it, especially the tendency to speak of rights and recognition rather than duties and responsibilities. It presses close the belief that Christians don't have to *do* anything or live in a particularly distinctive way. No matter what they do, or how they live and whatever their morality, God will love them anyway. Fine. But will he, can he, forgive? While God's love is always and everywhere unconditional this may not be true of forgiveness. Love and forgiveness are not synonyms. Can there be forgiveness if there is no acknowledgement of fault and the responsibilities that attach to it? Perhaps not.

For if forgiveness is to mean anything at all, it is surely a mutual exchange and meeting between the perpetrator and the one who is aggrieved. Apology, repentance, is met with forgiveness and a new basis on which the loving relationship can continue. Merciful forgiveness is primary, love follows.

That is, in order to cooperate with Christ's saving work, we need to confess the ways in which we have contributed to the suffering of the world and in the lives of individuals closer to us. In order to do that, we must not only also experience suffering but also allow ourselves to be hurt by the world and by those same individuals who are closet to us. That demands patience and a practical love of our neighbour and enemies alike. Perhaps it is time for us to recover the obligation to confess sins which given our contemporary state of affairs could be of two kinds. Individual confession to a group in which the individual would admit to what they had done wrong to whatever group has joined together.

We might also develop a more "official" confession which might be of a more sacramental nature than the general confession at the start of the celebration of the weekly Eucharist. In order to underpin this, we need to examine why the notion of "structural sin" is often so vacuous: it is devoid both of personal experience and of suffering.

Time and time again the early Christians were reminded of how important personal experience and suffering help to create and develop the inner space. They understood that personal experience and suffering the quintessence of the Gospel and they, like us, quickly discovered that selfless "love of neighbour" can mean a great many things even within the community of faith. For example: when a person does not believe what we believe, or in quite the same way, she can become our enemy. When she dislikes what we hold dear, we may smile and be "nice" to her, but she is still our enemy.

When she scorns what we cherish and would make any sacrifice in order to obtain, she is still our enemy. When she despises us, opposes us, puts every conceivable obstacle in our way surely, she remains an enemy. When she persecutes us, reviles us and, when all else fail imprisons and tortures and attempts to kill us, surely, she is our most deadly enemy.

Providentially for all future Christian generations, however, the early Christians were called upon to practice heroic charity in loving people they were absolutely sure were their enemies. They loved so successfully that, though many died as martyrs in the process, they converted much of the pagan world by their witness to suffering love. Nothing converts like the power of suffering love especially at the hands of the one who causes the pain.

It is precisely this sort of love that brought about our redemption. But so often we read the passion, study with horror all that Christ endured and then forget all that his death teaches about the love that suffers. That is the third feature of pre-Nicean spirituality.

The fourth feature of this early period which formed the basis of the life of future monks and nuns is the practice of ascetics. There was a strange logic in the spirituality of the early church which being historically speaking so close to Christ in time, remains a pattern for us to imitate. What is strange about that early spirituality is that it was not content with the practice of heroic patient and suffering love towards those who utterly opposed the followers of Christ. If the early church was a persecuted church, it was also an ascetical church. To place this in context we have to remember that we are talking about a people living over seventeen hundred years ago when the access to good and services and the comfort we enjoy could not even be dreamed of.

Yet there was comfort in the late Roman Empire and with an indulgence of the passions which, as the letters of St Paul make clear, could be extreme. The asceticism of the post-apostolic age was especially centred on the virtues that were the direct opposites of the vices of those days.

In this regard, the writings of Tertullian are especially instructive. Tertullian was a great man whose writings are often overlooked in favour of those of his near contemporary Justin Martyr because of his personal spiritual journey. Tertullian moved from being a staunch Christian to a semi-Montanist and then a fully convinced Montanist so that he (heretically) broke with the church that he had formerly defended so well. One reason why Tertullian finally broke from the church was precisely over this question of asceticism.

In his, at first, laudable zeal to preserve the purity of Christian morals he urged the faithful to avoid contamination with the lecherous paganism that surrounded them. His message was that Christianity is not just distinctive in the manner of its thought and spirituality, but especially in its mode of life. He was caustically witty and satirical in delivering this message and reserved his ire especially for those who saw no such distinction. Here he is on the matter of Christian women using hair dye and cosmetics to appear younger than they actually are:

"God says, 'Who of you can make a white hair black? Or a black white?" And so, women proved the Lord wrong. 'Behold,' they say, 'instead of black or white we can make it yellow and more pleasing with a more graceful colour. The age we fervently pray to attain blushes for itself.' And so, a theft is committed. Youth, the period of sin, is sighed after; the opportunity for grave seriousness is wasted. The more old age tries to conceal itself the more it will be detected. This then is your idea of true eternity is it: hair that is ever young? This is your idea of incorruptibility—that we have to put on for the new house of the Lord one guaranteed by cosmetics? When do you hasten to greet the Lord? When do you speed to depart from this iniquitous age? You to whom the near approach of your own end seems unsightly!"[42] That was one of his more tolerant and mild rebukes! Tertullian, in common with many of the early masters of Christian asceticism, insisted on self-denial of the body, restraint of the senses and control of the appetite if a Christian wishes to be and remain a true disciple of the suffering servant. But great as he was, Tertullian went too far. He so stressed external mortification that he neglected what is the essence, the bed-rock of all Christian asceticism. Other writers in the generations that followed him, such as Evagrius of Pontus and John Cassian, did not make the same mistake. They too were oppressed by the lewdness and looseness of non-Christian life styles in the late Roman Empire, but they took a more nuanced and balanced approach to mortification.

They taught the faithful to practice asceticism but mainly an asceticism of the mind by internal humility. From this, flowed an asceticism of the will in childlike obedience and an asceticism of the imagination through emotional self-control. Above all, they taught an asceticism of the spirit through constant prayer, such that Evagrius famously remarked that there can be no theology without prayer and that all who pray are theologians.

Already then, control of sensuality, mortification, humility, self-control and constant prayer—the familiar hallmarks of monasticism—are beginning to emerge. But what of poverty?

In general, the Christians of this period developed two understandings of poverty both of which they believed could be derived from the New Testament. The first was a liberality, a sharing of goods, skills, money and possessions with those who lacked them or whose resources in this regard were meagre. We might

---

[42] Tertullian: *On The Apparrel of Women* At Last Accessed March 2024.

call this a relative poverty. This was enjoined on every Christian. In practice, it meant then—and means now—a belief that nothing, could be kept as a personal possession or attribute. Christianity is a community faith and all things must be put at the disposal of the community. It was and is easy to see this simply in terms of financial resources, but it goes much deeper. Economic resources increase from skill and the practical workings of the human intellect.

So, the early Christians also understood that God had given them intellect not in order to be big-headed but in order to share. For them, acquisition even of intellectual prowess made no sense whatever unless and until it was shared. One received in order to share and that, they correctly thought, is the very heart of our faith.

The second was a poverty of dispossession, an absolute poverty. Not every Christian was, or is, physically, psychologically or emotionally capable of this. It demands a special Grace that, like chastity, is by no means given to all. But when it is given, it provides the religious, monastic life with a distinctive element and a unique structure to communal living. It is to the development of those structured communities that we now turn, in the next chapter.

Chapter 3
The Development and Structure of Early Monastic Communities

This Chapter concerns the development and structures of the earliest monastic communities. It will concern itself, mostly, with the Christian West, but will note the towering importance of the work of St Basil in developing monasticism in the East. It will include something of the people whose life and practices set the pattern of later monasticism before going on to look at the distinctive features of those practices in more detail and how they in turn became organised into established "Rules".

Academics and others dispute when the first structured religious communities began to emerge in the immediate post-apostolic era. There is almost a competition between them to find as early a date as possible. Here I shall join the competition by reminding them that as early as the late first century we have records of gathered groups of Christian Holy Virgins (female *and* male) who appear to have built a common life together based on consecrated chastity. Their chastity seems always to have been associated with, and perhaps a consequence of, the poverty of dispossession.

The possibility of sensuality and sexuality was regarded as a great personal good, otherwise to be celebrated and enjoyed, but also to be renounced as part of receiving the special Grace of dispossession. From a modern point of view, we might think that the life of Holy Virgins would be a short-lived phenomenon, but even in the late second century the Fathers of the church praise their mode of living.

Shortly after the Holy Virgins there appeared those whom the Fathers called *asketi,* or ascetics. This Greek word is confusing to the modern mind since it now carries with it an implication of cultural sensitivity or high-mindedness. This is a mistaken view and we might more appropriately think of them as Confessors.

They too adopted chastity and the poverty of dispossession as their prime mode of life. A number of these *asketi* whom we do not usually think of as adopting a lifestyle which could be understood as monastic, probably did. For example, Eusebius, in his fourth century "*History of the Church*",[43] claims that St Cyprian, St Ignatius of Antioch, St Clement of Rome and St Polycarp were all at various times numbered among the Confessors and what he has to say about the modes of life of each of them shows marked similarities to that of later monks. As we noted in the introduction, there is almost universal agreement that by the fourth century, we find clear traces of what we might now think of as the life of monks and nuns. These early monastics were chaste and voluntarily poor but to this they added a third dimension: seclusion from the world. Until then Holy Virgins and Confessors had edified the world by being in it but not of it, keeping themselves pure in the midst of corruption and focussed in the midst of dissipation. But as the Letters of St Ambrose make clear[44] the earliest communities of monks and nuns saw their seclusion from the world as a protest against all that the world holds dear. Thus, the life of the solitary and the monk (they are *not* the same thing) was one of withdrawal and austerity. Part of the austerity was withdrawal because most people like to talk, but the withdrawal was often for the purposes of silence. Their Christian contemporaries were astonished by this, and so are many today. Chastity, Poverty, Austerity and Withdrawal constituted a war against what they believed to be fallen human nature. The strategy and goal of this war was to achieve and then witness to a victory of divine grace over human nature—and what wild natures some of these early monks seem to have had! But then a series of persecutions occurred, the most severe of which was during the reign of Emperor Decius in the mid-third century. It was at about this time that the settled communities of the desert mothers and fathers began to form.

Indeed, many of them may have fled to the desert as a direct result of the persecution. This flight was justified not on the grounds of escape, but in order to more closely imitate Christ. Their reading of the New Testament showed them that Christ escaped from his would-be assassins on more than one occasion, not because he was afraid of them but because his divine vocation and mission was not yet fulfilled. The desert mothers and fathers wanted longer to witness to their vocation and calling too, not only by words but especially in deeds.

---

[43] Eusebius; *History of the Church.* At Last Accessed March 2024.
[44] Ambrose: *Letters* At Last Accessed March 2024.

One of the greatest commentators on the desert communities was St Anthony (251–356). That is not a misprint—the austere life obviously suited him! At the age of twenty he retired to the desert for a different reason. Reading and meditating on the Gospel concerning the Rich Young Man, Anthony decided to do what that would-be disciple did not, or could not, do. Anthony wanted to expiate and so he went to the desert where a number of disciples decided to join him and live in monastic villages. There they lived in clusters of like-minded people, mostly if not exclusively men, who were all seeking the perfection that Christ promised and in which they could find encouragement from one another.

One of St Anthony's contemporaries was Pachomius. He did not enjoy a long life and died at the age of 54. But he made a major contribution to the future development of monasticism in the whole of Christendom, East and West. Unlike Anthony, Pachomius insisted that all his monks should live under one roof and under a common Rule. With Pachomius, we see the development of a concept of the monastery and a written Rule that has set the pattern for all the others that have followed down to our own day. This cenobitic life seems to have been very attractive to large numbers of people for it is said that when he died Pachomius was superior to seven thousand monks, of whom thirteen hundred were in one place, Tabenniesi. The others were in monasteries of various sizes elsewhere.

The structure of the religious communities which Pachomius founded was very simple: First, there was the Superior or Abbot (Abba/Father) over *all* the monasteries. Second, the abbot had a subordinate or superintendent (from the Latin *praepositus*) in each monastery whose task it was to ensure that the abbot's directives were carried out and to maintain good order and godly discipline. Third there was a role which is best described as "the weekly leader", (from the Latin *hebdomadarius*). The holder of this office changed, as its name suggests, at the start of every week in order to ensure that the brother fulfilling its functions would not be prey to the sin of pride or abuse his privileges.

The job of the "weekly leader" was to call the community to prayer, lead the liturgy at the appropriate hours, relate the directives of the Superior and the Superintendent to the communities and relay any complaints from the community to the other two tiers of the hierarchy. His was an unenviable position and the "weekly leader" may well have been glad to serve for so short a period of time until his time came to serve again.

It is important to note that the members of Pachomius' communities, like those of Anthony, were *not* priests. Monastic priesthood is a much later development which was fiercely resisted for some time. One of the problems was a conflict of role. It was thought that once a monastic became a priest, with all the education that implies, they would want to engage in pastoral ministry in the world in the same way as the non-monastic clergy. What then would happen to their specific calling to monasticism, drawn apart from the world to pray in silence? So, at this early period all those professed to the life of monasticism were laymen. Priests were called in on Saturdays and Sundays to hear confession and celebrate Mass.

The simplicity of the non-clerical communities which Pachomius founded was eminently successful for four main reasons. First, his "Rule" was cogent clear and well set out. Everyone could understand it whatever their level of education and experience. This meant that it was attractive to large numbers of people many of whom, at first, believed they were called to be hermits but who came to understand that since Christianity is a shared, communal religion (*Our* Father, *We* believe…) it was far better to practice it in organised communities of like-minded brothers and sisters.

Second, Pachomius appealed to both men *and* women. Whereas Christian men had a number of options open to them through which they might exercise their vocation, women did not. They were either Holy Virgins, or wives of Christian men—and nothing else. Pachomius had the insight to see that women could take the austerity and hardship of the monastic way of life—even in the desert—too! At the time of his death, Pachomius ruled nine foundations for men and two for women. Unequal numbers, certainly, but this constituted a huge advance recognising the spirituality and religious capacity of women on their own account and not as a mere adjunct to that of their father before marriage and their husband afterwards.

Third, Pachomius was successful because he inspired other leaders to follow his example and to organise communities like his because, fourthly, Pachomius was always practical. The way of life he set down was detailed and yet remarkably adjustable depending always on the interpretation of the abbot according to local conditions and the specific needs of a particular community over time and in this way Pachomius' Rule became a prototype for all monastic Rules in both the west and in the east.

If Pachomius was pre-eminent in the development of Christian monasticism in the west, it was St Basil who enjoys the same towering position in the east. It can be said without exaggeration that Basil made the greatest contribution to monasticism in the east, than anyone else before or since. His contribution was many and varied but largely rests on a clear distinction between the solitary and the communal monastic life. Basil stressed the advantages of living in a gathered Christian community, not least of which is that it provides an opportunity to practice Christian love.

For him, it is quite impossible to survive communal Christian living without the daily practice of love. Moreover, while Basil always criticised the desire of some monks to practice excessive mortification of the flesh and the suppression of desire, he encouraged the Superior to regulate the religious life by reason. He was determined to find a right and reasonable balance between chastisement and cheerfulness.

Perhaps the greatest development brought about by St Basil was to encourage his monks to engage in the education of children, not just by way of catechesis important as that is, but through formal general education too. Basil may be credited as being the originator of what was once known as Aspirancy.

Aspirancy is no longer a feature of Christianity but it was once the main source of vocation both to the monastic life and to the priesthood. It was a system through which children were sent to a monastery, as it were, on permanent loan, to be educated and to become familiar with the rule and rhythm of the religious life in much the same way that Hannah "lent" the young Samuel to Eli.

Basil foresaw that one of the dangers of Aspirancy would be that vulnerable parents living in extreme poverty might use it as a means of abandoning their children. To avoid this, he put a series of checks and balances in place to ensure that the child was not compelled to enter the religious life but did so, as far as possible, freely and willingly. This immediately excluded very young children, those who could not make their own decision and those who had not yet reached the so-called "age of discretion". While this system was by no means entirely close to abuse it did last for over a thousand years and only began to wither with the rise of the merchants, like Sir Thomas Chipsey in Northampton and his foundation of the grammar school there.

As the system of Aspirancy disappeared, the church went out in search of vocations by other means. That search was successful insofar as it went but the problem was that it divorced the calling to the religious life (either monastic or priestly) from the "ordinary" experience of life and education that had been delivered through Aspirancy. It made the calling "special" and so elevated it to a higher plain suggesting, sometimes unintentionally, that only people with a direct revelation from God could aspire to such a life. So, unsurprisingly, most did not and do not.

In recent years, the church has joined forces with the marketers and advertised for vocations. I recall two series of advertisements in the back pages of the Roman Catholic newspaper "*The Universe*". One sought to be amusing and to emphasise that the religious life is freely chosen. The caption read "I was not born an Augustinian Recollect" (or whatever), "I chose to be one".

This had unfortunate unintended consequences at a time when socially, politically and medically there was a great debate as to whether and to what extent homosexuality is derived from nature or nurture. There was even a somewhat pointed joke doing the rounds which was supposed to originate from graffiti on a toilet door. The first line read, "My mother made me a homosexual." To which some wag had added, "If I gave her the wool would she knit me one too?" No doubt this joke would now be regarded as an example of extreme "homophobia", to say nothing about its view of women, but the point is that the Augustinians (or whichever order it was) failed to notice the echoes of this debate in using such a slogan.

This, quite obviously, had the effect of separating the religious life from lived experience even further.

The second campaign spoke of a "Special Bargain Offer" for men falling within a specified age range. Here the religious life was reduced to some commercial exchange, a contract for goods and services, rather than a dedicated rule of life through a lifelong commitment. Whether large numbers of men and women answered the advertisements and whether those who did subsequently became fully absorbed into the monastic way of life were of the highest quality are both, I think, to be doubted.

It may be time then for the present church to reassess and re-establish some aspects of Aspirancy. My case in support of this comes from my experience of having taught at St Kitzio Minor Seminary in El Obeid, Sudan during the great famines of the early nineteen eighties. The parallels are not, of course, exact but there is no doubt that the mixture of formal education, communal living and an introduction to the religious life had a great influence not only on those who experienced it but also on the wider community too. It helped many young people and their families survive the ravages of famine where they would not otherwise have done so.

It gave an education and a place of safety that was free from the disturbances and bias of the civil war that was being fought all around them. But far more importantly it was as a result of his early experience at St Kitzio that a local Dinka found his vocation and was later the first member of that ethnicity to be ordained priest. The Minor Seminary drew many of the hitherto animist Ashanti people into the life of the cathedral and thereby enhanced the music of the liturgies and our cultural life too.

Similar claims might be made by the great African Christian boarding schools of Michaelhouse and Peterhouse in South Africa and Zimbabwe respectively. But their orientation has always been somewhat different, leaning towards an understanding of the obligations of an effective and Christian lay leadership in the secular world of administration, politics and business rather than instilling and developing a vocation to the monastic life.

Yet, if all this is true of a Minor Seminary and perhaps of major public schools too, how much more might be achieved if we were to recreate a system of Aspirancy suitable to our own time and situation both within the church and beyond?

As we leave this brief overview of St Basil's contribution to the development of monasticism, we should note that it is as a direct result of his teaching and influence that the religious life in the east has remained non-clerical even to this day. Most monks in the east are *not* priests. Monasticism was integrated into the social and apostolic life of the church, but not in its priestly state. That is why, for example, St Ignatius of Loyola could never have founded his Society of Jesus in the east. The combination of the monastic with the priestly is largely western invention. The roots of this process are found in the early life of the west other major contributor to monastic history to whom we must now turn.

Eusebius, Bishop of Vercelli, organised the clerics of his cathedral into a community living under a common Rule in about 360AD. It may be that this is the earliest example of an exclusively clerical monastery. It is clear that these priests were already conducting their secular pastoral and sacramental ministry, but Eusebius decided that it would be good for them and beneficial to the whole diocese if they formed a religious order. A similar arrangement was made by St Paulinus in Nola and by St Ambrose in Milan—all three in Italy. Of these, the most significant was that of St Ambrose in Milan for it was from there that the great theologian and doctor of the church, St Augustine of Hippo emerged.

In Gaul, John Cassian had already distilled the essence of eastern and desert monasticism for a western readership and adapted so that it could be lived in the very different conditions prevailing in Western Europe. Cassian influenced both St Martin de Tour and St Caesarius of Arles. Of these St Martin is the most famous because of having divided his cloak with a peasant stranger—an example of seeing the divine image in another person, the sharing of goods and the renunciation of personal property.

But it was St Caesarius who had the more profound and lasting effect on the development of monasticism, for it was he who reinforced the notion of stability in the monastic community. St Benedict thought that stability was so important that he elevated it to be included as one of the Benedictine vows. It has been a feature of much monasticism ever since.

Having given a brief historical note of some of the developments in early monasticism and of those responsible for them, we turn now to a consideration of some of its salient features.

The first of these features is the purpose of the religious life. The life of monks and nuns was now much more systematised than those of their predecessors, the Holy Virgins, Ascetics, or dwellers in the desert. Whereas they sought perfection in a more or less structured way the reason and goal of systematisation was to bring it about more quickly through communal prayer, Bible study, communal living and victory over individual desires by living together in one place. Four p's typify this purpose; prayer, praise and penance (lead to) perfection.

The monks and nuns did not aspire to the fifth p, priesthood. Indeed, for the most part they desired to not to be priests, despite Augustine's formation of clerical communities. It was, in this early period, priests who became religious and not religious who became priests. This dialectic between the monastic way of life and that of the priesthood would remain throughout the centuries and remains with us still with all the tensions and potential conflicts we noted earlier. The primary purpose of monasticism at this time was perfection; the means of obtaining it were prayer, praise and penitence.

The second feature is the emergence of obedience. As Christians, of course, they owed obedience primarily to God, but for all practical purposes this meant obedience to the bishop or abbot. Obedience and monastic community life were now inseparable and mutually dependent. Increasingly, monastic communities could not function efficiently and effectively without obedience.

The third feature is Poverty which can be summed up as a prohibition on all private and separate property. At this time, there were few simple vows of poverty. It was not an ideal to which to aspire, but a practical reality. The choice was clear; either you give up everything or you cannot be a monk or as nun. They had to receive everything they needed to use from their Superior and return it when used.

I recall from my childhood and youth in the nineteen sixties how shocking the practice of absolute dispossession then was, and perhaps may still be. My family had befriended an aged Anglican nun, Sister Gabriel, who had spent many years in silence as a member of a community near the site of Tyburn Tree where so many English Catholics and Protestants were butchered because of the version of the faith to which they adhered. She had become ill and now spent her days with the community of St Catherine of Egypt at Parmore House, the former home of the Cripps family in the Thames valley.

One Christmas, my grandparents offered her a fountain pen as a present but she refused to receive it unless or until her Mother Superior gave her permission to do so and assuming too that it should not become a communal pen or given away. As someone who longed to own such a pen this was strange beyond belief! Perhaps I secretly hoped that it could be given away to me!

Sister Gabriel also had something of a sweet tooth and a special fondness for Polo Mints which my grandparents would give her at the end of each visit to them. Again, at first, she was reluctant to accept them and for the same reason, but then decided that the best thing to do was to eat them on her long walk back to the convent through the woods and fields. After all, she reasoned, by the time the decision concerning the "ownership" of the mints was made they would probably have lost their sweetness. She was, as Jake Thackeray might have sung, "a very naughty nun indeed"[45] and all the more endearing for it. Perhaps absolute dispossession was observed in the breach after all! But for all that she was one of the most prayerful and holy people it has ever been my privilege to meet and she continues to have a profound influence, some half a century or more later, on my spirituality and approach to the faith.The fourth feature was chastity. Despite their subtle but important differences, chastity and celibacy had now

---

[45] Jake Thackeray: "Sister Josephine".

become synonyms and were used interchangeably as they are today. Celibacy was a presumed prerequisite for the monastic life. Yet, as the supreme case of St Augustine makes clear, this did not mean that those who had not lived chaste lives before entering the monastery were excluded from the religious life. Moreover, provision was made for widows and widowers, and also to married persons and children whose spouse or parent gave themselves to the live of a monk or nun.

From now on, the inclusion of marriage or sexual relationships of any kind in the life of a monk or nun was simply unthinkable and especially after the pronouncement of Pope Siricius in 385 AD. He branded as infamy any sexual act by a monk or nun. St Cyprian was more direct and called it adultery since through their vows monks and nuns were "married" to Christ.

The fifth feature is the greater emphasis on the vows themselves. The earliest complete formulation of vows in the religious life comes from Egypt in about 400 AD. Vows were taken for life and the penalties for breaking them were severe. So, having once entered the life of a Holy Virgin or Ascetic a Monk or a Nun, the person felt a clear obligation to persevere. The scriptural grounds for this, coupled with a divine warning, was found in the words of Christ himself; "No man putting his hand to the plough and looking back is fit for the Kingdom of God."[46] The sixth and most remarkable feature of this early period is the emergence of Canon Law. Almost as soon as the church became one of the officially recognised religions in the late Roman Empire the church authorities set about creating a legal system to govern its life and produce good order and discipline. This might be the point at which the church became institution but it was important that a legal system which was both complimentary to and independent of the civil powers was created if the church was going to survive the collapse of empire which many could see could not be long delayed.

The first Canon Law regulating gathered communal religious life was passed at the Council of Gangra in Asia Minor, in 315 AD. It was addressed to three different groups of people. First, Holy Virgins. Second those who were chaste but not virgins, namely married people. Third, those people who had mainly or wholly withdrawn from the world in order to practice their faith more fervently *and at the same time* care for their parents, children, husband or wife who needed special care and attention.

---

[46] Luke 9:62.

This third group was clearly a widespread feature of religious life in this early period. If this were not so, the council would hardly have thought it necessary to legislate for it. This group show how care for the vulnerable was regarded is a distinct form of religious life, to be honoured as a unique vocation ministry and service to be ranked alongside those of priests and monks and nuns. It is this group too that provided the historical precedent for the notion of the Lay Apostolate which was so much in contention at Vatican II and strengthens it. Might it also be that modern oblates, members of "Third Orders" and the "new" monastic movements can trace their spiritual lineage to this group?

Until detailed research is conducted into this often-overlooked group I think we can say the following: there was from an early period a class of Christians for whom, for a wide variety of reasons, there was little or no prospect of entering a structured monastic community. These people had obligations and those obligations were regarded as given to them by God, sacred and unbreakable. Those they cared for formed their religious community and it was with them and for them that they exercised their faith and the virtue of patient, charitable love.

Indeed, the people they cared for bore the very image of Christ himself. In serving those for whom they had a special care, they served a Christ visibly and actually present in the flesh of another. They had his real presence among them just as much as any monk or nun perceived it in the bread and the wine of the Holy Mass—though clearly, they did that as well.

In comparison, the other canonical legal decisions we should note seem almost paltry. The first was a little noticed decision at the Council of Chalcedon, 451AD, which is of course better known for its momentous decision about the divine and human natures of Christ. But it also concluded that no monastery could be erected anywhere except by the express permission of the local bishop. This ruling is still in force so that no community exists without the approval of the hierarchy, but the passage of time has thrown up a few anomalies.

From their foundation the Jesuits, for example, were free from Episcopal control, owing their allegiance directly to the Pope; nevertheless because of the Chalcedonian decision, they may not enter a diocese unless they are invited to do so by a bishop. The other legislative decisions regulating the religious life arose from a series of councils held mainly in fifth century France which concerned perseverance.

Thus, fifteen centuries ago the church felt that she should make general laws for monastic living alongside and in addition to those that regulated Christian doctrine and practice. So, we have two levels of legislation. The first is legislation imposed on all the faithful and enforced by the hierarchy; while the second level applies to monks and nuns in particular and in a way which was quite separate from any monastic Rule that might govern their daily lives.

By the end of this early period, the daily life of most monks and nuns were governed by two great Rules, those of St Basil in the east and St Augustine of Hippo in the West. As we will see in later chapters two other great Rules were to follow not least of which were those of St Benedict and of St Francis of Assisi, but for the moment, we will consider the centrality of stillness and silence leading to prayer in the Eastern Orthodox tradition before moving on to the doctrinal and community structure of those communities in the west that lived according to the Rule of Augustine.

Part 2
Tradition and the Creation of the Inner Space

Chapter 4
What Is Traditional About the Orthodox Tradition?

It is becoming something of a truism to say that our contemporary world is marked by tragedy. We appear to be pursuing a course of action that can only end in tears (if it has not done so already) for countless millions of people, a path that leads to nihilism and despair. Ours is a world so caught up in its own futility that, according to Orthodox Christians, the church comes to show another path and to offer another mode of existence based on a clear vision for the present and a hope for the future. After all, was it not Christ himself who said, "*I am the Way…?*" Thus, it is that the church comes to pit itself against the tragedy of human history.[47] Within the uncertainty of the contemporary world, the church emerges as the only possibility of a genuine and existentially authentic life. The Church enters the world as a "*new cosmos*" as the "*creation of another world*".[48] Of course, it is evident that when Orthodox Christians speak of "Church" in this way they do not mean the institutional organisation or even those parts of the social construct concerned with the moral betterment or welfare of human life. By "Church" they mean the life-giving Body of the God-man: Christ himself transmitted and extended throughout the ages. Like St Paul, by "Church" they mean nothing less than the transmission and transformation of life itself.[49] How this might be so is the subject of this essay which will consider it through seven interconnected themes.

---

[47] See 1 Jn 1:2.
[48] St Gregory of Nyssa in *Canticum Canticorum* (Song of Songs) Ed H. Langerback. Pp384–386 (PG 44.1049BC 1052A).
[49] Col 2:6–8.

Theme 1: The Church as Tradition, and the Traditional Church

In Orthodox thought, tradition and church are not parallel concepts. They are realities which are essentially interrelated and are bound into each other. While they cannot be confused either in thought or in fact, they exist together so that the church *is* Tradition and Tradition *is* the conscience of the church.[50] Hence it is quite impossible to speak of church without speaking of Tradition and *vice versa*. The teaching of Tradition *is* ecclesiology; indeed, the very heart of ecclesiology as we shall see, and since that heart is nothing other than Christ incarnate, crucified, risen, ascended and glorified, the church *is* the visible embodiment of Christ himself. When we say that Tradition is the church and the church is Christ, we mean that the church always and everywhere refers back to Christ and through Christ to the sovereign principle of God the Father understood as the source of Trinitarian and ecclesiastical unity.[51] Thus, we arrive at the source of the church's unity, at the source of tradition, at the cause of every good gift and spiritual blessing.[52] In the internal life of the Trinity, God the Father "gives himself over" to the other two divine Persons, generating the Son and causing the Spirit to proceed.[53] Here, again, we should understand that this "giving over" (*paradosis*) as a communicating of all the divine essence of the Father to the Son and to the Holy Spirit as a complete *kenosis* of the Father at the utter limits of love; the *paradosis* of the Father for the benefit of the other two persons. The Son and the Spirit respond to this pouring out of the Father's love. They neither usurp the Father's love nor do they seize it[54] but in their turn offer their existence and life—similarly in love—to the Father. This loving exchange (*antidosis*) is expressed as absolute obedience to the Father's will.[55]/[56] Similarly, in the church, which is the image and reflection of the Trinitarian God, the Son gives himself up for the life of the world[57] and here too there is an abundance of

---

[50] Where "*is*" is understood as the "is" of identity and not or mere predication.
[51] Eph.4:4–6.
[52] 'For every good gift is from above and comes down from you, the Father of Lights…' The Divine Liturgy of St John Chrysostom.
[53] M Farantos (1977) "Orthodoxy and Contemporary Reality" *Koinonia* (a journal). p32.
[54] Phil 2:6.
[55] ibid.
[56] Loc cit Farantos.
[57] Jn 6:51.

love and offering. Here we have a giving over of in love.[58] The Son's absolute obedience to the father leads him to *kenosis*, an outpouring, of humility for the sake of the world's salvation. In the same way, the Holy Spirit lives in the world to be a constant witness to the truth.[59] Proceeding, (according to Orthodox theology which greatly differs from that in the west on this crucial point) from the Father and being sent *through* the Son, the Holy Spirit continues the work of Christ as the comforter of all people. The presence of the Holy Spirit in the Church ensures the preservation of truth and its new life. The Holy Spirit is given over to the church; it does not repeatedly descend on the church but abides and dwells in it. Pentecost, then, is not the celebration of a past event and is certainly not regarded as so often in some more Protestant western churches as "the birthday of the church" (whatever that may mean); rather it is a continuous present in the life of the church. Pentecost is the recognition of a universal reality which embraces the whole church in love and makes Christian living an image of eternity firmly embedded within the history of the world.

So it is that both in the relationships between the Persons of the Trinity as well as in the church itself, God's love is manifested *as paradosis*, as a constant outpouring of divine love. God the Father gives himself over for the sake of the other two divine Persons. The Son, out of love becomes one of us and gives himself over in order to save us. Finally, the Holy Spirit dwells in the church until the consummation of the ages and, in the meantime, continues the work of the Son in the world.

Theme 2: Tradition, Revelation and Changelessness

The continuous presence of the Holy Spirit in the Church ensures the preservation of truth and revelation in the same way as the body can be said to preserve the life of the soul. Revelation—the culmination of which comes about at Pentecost—constitutes the primal factor in the life of the church. The Church is alive because she possesses and preserves the revelation that has been given to her. She possesses it precisely so that she can exist. In the final analysis, however, when we say that the church possesses and preserves revelation, we mean that the church does this because revelation *is* Tradition (*paradosis*) and becomes Tradition within the church.

---

[58] Jn 3:16.
[59] Jn 15:26.

Revelation *is* Tradition precisely because it was transmitted in Christ and in the Holy Spirit, and it becomes Trinitarian because the church preserves it throughout the course of history, as the power of her life. Tradition, the, is the unceasing existence of Revelation in the Church and is the inner creative and cohesive power which holds the church together. Through Tradition, the church is preserved alive and *changeless* simply because *only* in Tradition can the authentic message of revelation be found, and *only* in Tradition does the life of the church arrive at a particular moment in time.

From the very beginning of her existence up to the present time, the Orthodox Church is aware—with the same intensity now as then—of the abiding presence of Christ and the Holy Spirit. Thus, the church has always experienced a *lived* revelation and will continue to do so until the end of time for nothing can prevail against it.[60] This lived Revelation in the Church, this continuous "now" of revelation which is realised in Tradition, constitutes the very life of the church and its Gospel.[61] Consequently, Tradition is the certainty that what the church possesses today is not something suspended in mid-air, not attached to some vague and often undefined notion of apostolic succession or a supposed event in past history, but rather is continuously and organically connected with the life of Christ and his illumination of the first Apostles. In other words, Tradition in the Orthodox Church gives an assurance of eternity, an assurance that human time is embraced by God, an assurance of the universality and applicability of the Gospel through the ages which is lived in the church at every particular historical moment and which, through the church, is proclaimed to the world as its salvation.

Theme 3: Tradition and the Contemporary Church

At this point, it is probably worth noting that Tradition in the Orthodox Churches is not, as is sometimes mistakenly supposed, a voice from the past. It is, rather, the voice of eternity. Tradition is not some kind of sacred archaeology, or even a reference back to an experience in the past. Tradition's value and significance is not to be found in that it is based on an historical authenticity, but in that, it is based on the unchanging and ever living voice of revelation. This fidelity in Tradition does not simply mean recognition of the historic past, but

---

[60] Mtt.16:18.

[61] 1 Cor. 15:1-2.

also an acceptance, in humility, of the Word of God. Tradition is not only the testimony of history, the "yes" to the life of the past; rather, it is chiefly a reference to the truth which was revealed in Christ and is preserved in the church through the Holy Spirit. Fr Georges Florovsky wrote this about it:

"Tradition is not a principle striving to restore the past, using the past as the criterion for the present. Such a conception of tradition is rejected by history and by the consciousness of the church. Tradition is the <u>authority to teach, posestas magisteri, authority to bear witness to the truth</u> not by reminiscence or from the words of others, but from its own living, unceasing experience, from its Catholic fullness[...]."

"Therein consists that 'tradition of the truth', <u>traditio veritatis</u>, about which St Iranaeus spoke. For him, it is connected with the 'veritable unction of truth', <u>charisma veritatis certum</u>, and the 'teaching of the Apostles' was for him not so much an unchangeable example to be repeated or imitated, as an eternally living and inexhaustible source of life and inspiration. Tradition is the constant abiding of the Spirit and not only in the memory of words. Tradition is a charismatic, not a historical principle.'[62] 'Tradition is a charismatic, not a historic principle' and so it is an unceasing revelation of the Word of God in the Holy Spirit at each specific historical moment. It is not something distant, something springing from a time and a culture dimly remembered or altogether lost to us, rather it is a reality which is extremely contemporary, just as the fruits of the Spirit[63] are extremely contemporary for people living now. It is always open, always ready to embrace the present and accept the future. Just as the church at every given historical moment accepts new members, so too is tradition tangible and believable in every age and culture—simply because the church *is* the living bearer of Tradition. The idea of a contemporary Tradition is based on the unbroken presence of Christ in the church, and on the certainty that the teacher of the church is the Holy Spirit. In his *Confession* of 1672, Patriarch Dositheos of Jerusalem wrote:

"We believe the Catholic church to be taught by the Holy Spirit. For he is the true Paraclete, whom Christ sends from the Father in order to teach the truth and dispel the darkness from the minds of the faithful. The teaching [didache] of

---

[62] Fr G Florovsky (1934) "Sobornost; The Catholicity of the Church", *The Church of God, An Anglo-Russian Symposium* ed. E.L. Mascal London. p64–65. Emphasis in the original.
[63] Gal.5:22–23.

the Holy Spirit, however, does not directly make the church brilliant and splendid, but indirectly, through the fathers and leaders of the Catholic church."[64] To deny the importance of Tradition in the contemporary life of the church is to deny the work of the Holy Spirit in history and to doubt its *charismata* now. In the final analysis, to reject Tradition means to reject the church as the Body of Christ and as the vessel of the Holy Spirit. By calling into question the fact that Tradition possesses tremendous importance for the here and now of the church, if we deny that Tradition is the image of the Catholic and inter-temporal nature of the church, we reduce and alter the church from its "God-Manness" to a simple society of human beings, based exclusively on human standards. Rejecting Tradition is a little like accepting that Christ has forsaken the church, that his words of assurance that he will not[65] are a cruel deception. By accepting the promise that *today* we are able to understand and to interpret the Gospel by basing ourselves solely on our own brilliance and experience, without Tradition, we strip the church naked of Christ. More than this, we sever the body from the head and take away its life-giving Spirit, thus leaving the interpretation of the Gospel open to individual judgement and to the arbitrary whims of subjectivity.

The Orthodox Patriarchs of the East had much to say about this in an *Encyclical* of 1848. It described in simple but nevertheless systematic terms something of the fullness of this living continuity of Tradition:

"For our faith, brethren, is neither from men nor by man, but by the revelation of Jesus Christ, which the holy Apostles preached, the sacred ecumenical councils upheld, the most great and wise doctors of the oikoumene transmitted through their teaching, and the holy martyrs confirmed with their blood. We hold pure the confession we have received."[66] We cannot deny the life of the church, "that unbroken chain", which defines the "sacred enclosure" of the church, "the door" of which is Christ and in which the entire Orthodox fold is shepherded.[67]

J.N. Karmiris (1968) *The Dogmatic and Symbolic Moments of the Orthodox Church*. Ii. Graz. P835.
[65] Mtt.28:20 and Jn.14:16.
[66] Op cit Karmiris; p1002.
[67] Ibid p1003.

Theme 4: Tradition and the People of God

We turn now to two key questions: who can test that Tradition is genuine? And how might his be achieved? In the *Encyclical* quoted above the Patriarchs of the East gave this answer:

"The defender of the faith is the body of the church, that is, the people [laos]."[68] The people of God, taken as a whole, possess a spiritual sense with which it can test whether or not, and to what extent, actions and core teachings (*kerygmata*) are in accordance with the life of the church. Thus, Tradition is protected within the entire community of faith. The hierarchy of the church teaches, that is interprets Tradition, and the people in their entirety make declarations concerning its faithfulness to Tradition. Here we have an inner reciprocity. The teachers of the church interpret Tradition; they transmit the Gospel to the people, and the people judges whether or not the interpretation that has been transmitted to them is authentic. This means that all who interpret the Gospel can never disregard the people, because the people are the ultimate arbitrators and bearers of Tradition.

Thus, it is that both those who teach and those who learn, both hierarchy and the people, constitute a whole which labours for the preservation of the truth, for the protection and understanding of Tradition.

Each contributes to this same task even though their viewpoints might be very different. The hierarchy passes judgement on Tradition and the people judges the judgements of the hierarchy. Thus, the people endorse (or reject?) the teaching they have received and with it, the decisions of the hierarchy. When St Paul told the Thessalonians to "hold the traditions"[69] he was acknowledging precisely this: the right which the people have to maintain the tradition and to reject every alien element which might affect the purity of the life of the church. So it is that in the Orthodox Churches the people are entrusted with the tremendous task of testing and preserving the genuineness of Tradition. The Orthodox Churches are regarded, certainly in the west and among the more Protestant denominations, as being anti-democratic. But here we see that the reverse is true. The people have ultimate power. Their power flows from the living *experience* of Tradition itself which provides a discernment as to whether

---

[68] Ibid p1000.
[69] 2 Thess 2:15.

what they have received lies within the *"consensus partum et apostolorum"* (the teaching of the fathers and the apostles) or remains outside it.

This special spirit of discernment which the people of God possess and which, in the end, makes the people the sole guardian of the faith, is nothing less than the fruit of the very same experience lived by the Apostles and received and lived by the fathers and the saints of the church and preserved alive in every historic moment of the life of the church in the world. Once again, it is the identity of the *experience* which ensures the faithfulness of the Tradition.

The Church preaches, interprets and lives the same Gospel throughout the ages and the same truth. Of course, this truth is not an idea, a concept, but a specific person, the theandric (=God/Man) person of Christ.[70] Christ then is *"the same yesterday, today and forever"*[71] and the Holy Spirit who vivifies the faithful and ensures the unity of their life. Thus, the experience of the people of god today is not of another order than the original experience of the apostles, saints and martyrs, and it is this one and same experience of the people of God that ensures fidelity to Tradition. To speak about Tradition in this way is not an attempt to deprive the church of her right, indeed obligation, to proclaim the Gospel message in a new way which is relevant to each and every generation. On the contrary, fidelity to Tradition often compels us to abandon the schemes and methods of the past because they are no longer relevant and a hindrance to proclamation. Fidelity to tradition never hindered the fathers from doing this, or expressing in new terminology and in a new fashion all that the church had already lived and experienced from the very beginning of her existence. Hence, in Orthodox thought, whatever the Fathers or ecumenical councils sated in later times is of equal value and authenticity with whatever was said from the very beginning, precisely because of its congruence with the fullness of the Gospel.

Theme 5: Tradition and Traditions

At this point, it is necessary to mark the difference between (the) Tradition and traditions, and what has been written so far has attempted to keep this distinction in mind. The tradition of human beings should not be confused with the Tradition of the Church in her fidelity to the fullness of the Gospel. In contrast to the Tradition which endures through the ages, the traditions which human

---

[70] Jn 14:6.
[71] Heb 13:8.

beings create come and go, they change and are supplemented, they are rejected or sustained depending on the prevailing spiritual climate and the context in which they appear. The traditions that we create for ourselves can be positive and useful, but they can also be quite meaningless. They may possibly help in the understanding of Tradition, but then again, they may also be insurmountable obstacles to proclaiming and approaching the authentic Gospel message.

So, when Orthodoxy speaks of Tradition it does not mean all those human elements which are encountered in the historic church. It speaks only of the deposit of faith which is "the pillar and ground of truth".[72] The Joint Declaration of the Commission appointed by the Ecumenical Patriarch and the Archbishop of Canterbury which was set up in 1930 to consider points of theological and doctrinal similarity and difference between Orthodoxy and the Anglican communion had this to say on the matter: "We agree that by Holy Tradition we mean the truths that come down from our Lord and the Apostles, through the fathers, which are confessed unanimously and continuously in the Undivided Church, and are taught by the church under the guidance of the Holy Spirit.

Everything necessary for salvation can be founded on Holy Scripture as completed, explained, interpreted and understood in the Holy Tradition, by the guidance of the Holy Spirit residing in the church.

We agree that nothing contained in Tradition is contrary to the Scriptures. Though these two may be logically defined and distinguished, yet they cannot be separated from one another nor from the church."[73]

Theme 6: Holy Tradition and Holy Scripture

As the above quotation makes clear, generally speaking Scripture and Tradition cannot be separated or confused: "…though these two may be logically defined and distinguished yet they cannot be separated from each other nor from the church." Scripture and Tradition *together* constitute one unbroken whole. Tradition is contained, though not limited, by Scripture and *vice versa* as St Paul himself made clear.[74] Tradition is channelled into the church through word and through Scripture and in this relationship, there is neither superiority nor subordination. Both the spoken word and the word of Scripture possess mutuality

---

[72] 1 Tim.3:15.
[73] *Lambeth Occasional Reports* 1931–1938. London 1948. Pp 52–53.
[74] 2Thess.2:15.

and an agreement, a mutual fulfilment and confirmation. As St Basil put it "both have equal force for piety"[75] to which St John Chrysostom added: "...they did not transmit all things through the epistles; much was handed over not in writing. In like manner, both these and those are worthy of belief. Hence, we consider the Tradition of the Church also worthy of belief. Is it Tradition? Then enquire no more?"[76] In the western church, of course, the distinction between Scripture and Tradition was, and is, stressed more firmly. Either they are considered to be two sources of revelation (Roman Catholic and some Anglicans) or Tradition is rejected completely so as to create the concept of *sola scriptura* (scripture alone) in Protestantism. From an Orthodox viewpoint, there is little to choose between Roman Catholicism and Protestantism on this point. In both instances, the distinction between Scripture on the one hand and Tradition on the other is emphasised. Rome views Scripture and Tradition as *two* sources of revelation, while the Protestants opt for Scripture *alone*.

In both cases, the belief that Scripture and Tradition are distinguishable because separate—two quite different things—is presupposed. Against these viewpoints which, according to Orthodox thought, reduces the spiritual relationship between Scripture and Tradition to a legalistic one (of equality *or* superiority) the eastern churches posit their own understanding of the matter, which is based on the principle that Scripture and Tradition *co-exist* within the Orthodox Church. The Orthodox Church, guided by the Holy Spirit, understands Scripture (composed with the inspiration of the Holy Spirit) in the light of Tradition, which is also the work of the Holy Spirit.

Theme 7: The Earthly Trinity—Church, Scripture and Tradition

In other words, Tradition *is* Scripture interpreted by the church. Just as the Orthodox Church understands Scripture in the light of Tradition so, in the same way, it understands Tradition in the light of Scripture. Tradition is full of Scripture; that is why theology, especially that of the Fathers and the Ecumenical Councils is nothing other than Biblical theology.

Scripture and Tradition are to be mutually understood together because they exist together. Both are united unshakeably within the church. Scripture is born

---

[75] St Basil. *De Spirito Sancto* PG.32. 188A ff.
[76] St John Chrysostom: Homily 4.2 in 2 Thess. Ed B de Montfaucon.11. 532B.

in the church and for the church, and Tradition bears the seal of the church from the very beginning. It is in the church that both Scripture and Tradition appear and are contained. So Church, Scripture and Tradition are all linked together existing as one entity in which the relationship of the parts to the whole are harmonious and form a community of love—reflecting the relationship in the Holy and Undivided Trinity which is God.

So, for the Orthodox, any community of faith that separates Church, Scripture and Tradition cannot properly reflect the life of God on earth. Such a community must come to false conclusions that either Scripture is superior to the church and Tradition, as in Protestantism, or that the church is superior to Scripture and Tradition, as in Roman Catholicism. The hyperbole of both approaches must lead, again according to Orthodox thought, to damage to the whole concept of what we mean by "Church" because the essential balance in the relationship of the parts to the whole has been disrupted.

In conclusion then, the answer to our original question "What is Traditional about the Orthodox tradition?" amounts to this; only if we accept that the church, Tradition and Scripture are neither separated nor confused, being united without confusion, will we be able to understand that the church is the only organ that can find the true meaning of Scripture, just as the Son is the only person of the Trinity who hears and understands the words of the Father.[77]

---

[77] C Scouteris (1975) 'Holy Scripture and the Councils', *Sobornost. A journal.* 7:2 pp112–113. See also D Staniloae (1970) 'Holy Scripture in relation to the Church and Tradition', *The Living Logos: A Spiritual Symposium on Holy Scripture,* Athens. P83.

Chapter 5
Stillness, Silence and the Art of Prayer in the Orthodox Tradition

"…When you pray, go into your room and shut the door and pray to your father who is in secret, and your father who sees in secret will reward you. And in praying do not heap up empty phrases as the Gentiles do; for they think they will be heard for their many words. Do not be like them, for your father knows what you need before you ask him."[78] These words of Christ have often provoked the following question: what is the sense of praying if God already knows what we need?

In answering this question by reference to some key aspects in the history and theology of Orthodoxy, we should remember that prayer is not just petition, it does not just ask for something. Indeed, in the Orthodox tradition prayer it is hardly that at all. Prayer is, in the Orthodox tradition, first and foremost an encounter—a dialogue with the living God. According to Evagrius Ponticus, "Prayer is the communion of the intellect with God."[79] In prayer, we encounter the God who is a person—the personal God, who hears us, responds to us and is always ready to come to our aid. In prayer, we communicate with the divine reality which is the only true life. Compared to it every other reality is only partial and imperfect. As we will see, for the Orthodox Christian life without prayer is but a pathway to spiritual death, a gradual dying. We live in so far and to the degree in which we participate in God, and we participate in God through prayer.

Why does Christ forbid verbosity in prayer? Precisely because it is not in words that true prayer is born. Prayer is not the sum of our requests addressed to

---

[78] Mtt 6:6–8.
[79] Evagrius.(1992) 'On Prayer', Writings from the *Philokalia* 1 On Prayer of the Heart. London. Faber and Faber Limited p57.

God. Before they are formed into words (if at all) prayers must be "heard" in the heart. All true masterpieces of music and poetry are not simply composed out of disconnected sounds or words; they were first formed in their author's heart and only then became incarnate, as it were, in words or musical tones. Prayer is like that. Prayer is also a creative work, born not of verbosity, but out of deep stillness, out of concentrated and devoted silence. Before embarking on the path of prayer, we must inwardly fall silent and renounce all human thoughts and words.

It is in the stillness that prepares us for prayer that a person's heart, mind, mouth and senses fall silent. Words, sounds, and worldly impressions disappear from the heart; our face is bowed to the ground and then we begin to glimpse the stillness of God himself. "Intelligent silence is the mother of prayer…The friend of silence draws near to God and, by softly conversing with him, is enlightened by God." [80] according to St John Climacus, and Metropolitan Kallistos of Diokleia has more recently written: "To achieve silence: this is of all things the hardest and the most decisive in the art of prayer. Silence is not merely negative—a pause between words, a temporary cessation of speech—but, properly understood, it is highly positive: and attitude of attentive alertness, of vigilance, and above all of listening. The heychast, the person who has attained hesychia inner stillness or silence is, par excellence, the one who listens. He listens to the voice of prayer in his own heart, and he understands that this voice is not his own but that of another speaking within him."[81] Like every other conversation, then, prayer is a dialogue and its aim is not only to express oneself but to hear that of *another speaking within him*.

"Silence is a mystery of the age to come, but words are instruments of this world," wrote St Isaac the Syrian.[82] In order to attain stillness and silence monks deprived themselves of encounters and conversations with others, departing for the deep desert, or hiding themselves in forests and mountains. But in the Orthodox tradition this stillness and silence was not and is not the preserve only

---

[80] St John Climacus (1982) *Ladder of Divine Ascent* 11. Trans. Colm Luibheld and Norman Russell with an Introduction by Kallistos Ware. Classics of Western Spirituality Series. Mahwah NJ USA. See also Fr. John Mack (1999) *Ascending the Heights – A Laymans' Guide to The Ladder of Divine Ascent.* Ben Lomond Clifornia. Conciliar Press.
[81] Metropolitan Kallistos (1991) *The Power of the Name: The Jesus Prayer in Orthodox Spirituality.* Oxford. SLG Press. p1.
[82] St Isaac the Syrian: *Homiliy number 65. (The Ascetical Homilies)* p 321.

of monks or clerics, rather it is essential for everyone who would learn the "*art of prayer*". To achieve this experience, we do not have to withdraw into the physical desert, but we do need to spend some time every day quiet alone, shutting the door as it were on the outside world and praying to the God who is in secret. Our usual temptation, or deception, is that we are always too busy, we have no time for this stillness and silence, and we must keep busy. Anything else is wasted time. We believe, wrongly, that if we spend time in prayer, we will not have the opportunity to do all these important things. But on the contrary, the experience of many people shows that time spent in prayer seldom, if ever, affects our business negatively, in spite (or perhaps even strangely because of) our initial concerns. Prayer teaches us to concentrate far more on the matters that will be in hand. It makes our minds more disciplined. The net effect of this is that time spent in prayer is time won, rather than time lost.

Contemporary society does not like stillness and silence very much. It distrusts it and fills it with all sorts of images and sounds. Many people are even scared of remaining in silence, being alone or having free time. They feel far more comfortable being constantly occupied or distracted away from themselves. They need words and impressions; they always hasten in order to create an illusion (for it is exactly that) of an abundant and saturated life. But life in God begins when words and thoughts and images fall silent, when the cares of the world are forgotten, and when the inner space is opened and freed to be filled by him.[83] The great saints of the Orthodox tradition, following Jesus Christ himself, emphasise that prayer should be simple and unsophisticated. St John Climacus compared one who prays with a young child speaking to its parents:

"Let your prayer be completely simple…Do not be over sophisticated in the words you use when praying, because the simple and unadorned lisping of children has often won the heart of their heavenly Father. Do not try to be verbose when you pray, lest your mind be distracted in searching for words. One word from the publican propitiated God, and one cry of faith saved the thief."[84]

---

[83] Something of this was ably illustrated by an experiment conducted television's favourite Abbot, Fr Christopher Jamison, (formerly of the Benedictine community at Worth) who took a group of ordinary women and men into an 8-day silent (Ignatian) retreat. The course of the experiment and its "results" were broadcast on BBC2 as "*The Big Silence*" in the autumn of 2010.

[84] Op cit Climacus 28. P213.

Childlike faith must be combined with a deep humility of heart, as St Isaac the Syrian emphasises:

"Walk before God in simplicity and not with knowledge…When you fall down before God in prayer, become in your thoughts like the ant, like a creeping thing of the earth, like a leech, and like a tiny lisping child. Do not say anything before him with knowledge, but with a child's manner of thought draw near to God and walk before him that you may be counted worthy of that paternal providence that fathers have for their small children."[85] Prayer, stillness, silence and humility are deeply embedded in repentance: "A man, who loves conversation with Christ, loves to be alone. But he who loves to linger with many is the friend of this world…if you love repentance, love stillness also."[86] But, of course, being left alone in a room with the door shut does not yet constitute stillness. Neither does the avoidance of speech constitute silence. Both are inward states which presuppose peace of mind and tranquillity of thoughts. Very often people who are alone and about to pray, find turmoil and chaos in their mind. Although they say prayers with their mouth their mind wanders far away.

The early Orthodox fathers called this distraction of mind during prayer *meteorismos,* light mindedness. The reason for this distraction, they maintained, is that the human person is quite unable to control thoughts, or the different images or fantasies that appear in the mind. To control our thoughts, we must learn the art of *nepsis* (=watchfulness, alertness, vigilance, sobriety). *Nepsis* is based on the understanding that every thought captures the mind gradually and by degrees. Thought in the mind passes through several stages of development.

The first stage is called *"assault"*, which is simple conception, or a sudden apparition of something in the mind, an image or an idea that comes from outside. At this stage, there is nothing in the mind not first through the senses. The second stage is *"converse"* or conversation in the mind when it ponders or enters into dialogue with the assault. The dialogue may soon become a struggle, when the mind opposes the attacking thought and either accepts or rejects it. The acceptance of the thought by the mind is called *"captivity"*: it is a *"forcible and involuntary rape of the heart, or a permanent association with what has been encountered"*.

The last stage of the development of thought is *"passion"*; it is "that which for a long time nestles with persistence in the soul, forming therein a habit, as it

---

[85] Op cit St Isaac the Syrian *Homily 72* p351.
[86] ibid *Homily 64* p316.

were, by the soul's long-standing association with it since the soul of its own free and proper choice clings to it."[87] Every passion begins with a sinful thought: "*No cloud is formed without a breath of wind, and no passion is born without a thought.*"[88] The so-called "Fall" of Adam and Eve is interpreted by St Philaret of Moscow in terms of acceptance of a thought and its gradual development into a passion: "When the woman saw that the tree was good for food, and that it was a delight to the eyes, and that the tree was to be desired to make one wise, she took of its fruit and ate."[89] "Saw" is an assault of thought. "Was good" and "was a delight" are a conversation and struggle with the thought. "Was to be desired" is an acceptance of the thought, Eve being captivated by it. "Took and ate" is the passion where it is actualised and put into practice. "A sinful disposition of the soul," says St Philaret, "begins with the powers of the intellect being orientated in the wrong direction…The multiplicity of one's own desires, which are not centred around the will of God, is connected with one's own deviation from the oneness of divine truth into a multiplicity of one's own thoughts."[90] In other words, distraction is deviation from primordial simplicity and the state of unification into multiplicity and complexity. Distraction is a consequence of the "fall", and the mind's acceptance of the sinful thoughts is a sort of illness and a sin of the mind. It is a "*mental adultery*" of the intellect.[91] The art of *nepsis* is the ability of a person to refuse the sinful thought at the very moment of its first appearance in the mind and before it develops into a passion. "The beginning of prayer", says St John Climacus "consists of banishing by a single thought"[92] the thoughts that assault us at the very moment they appear.[93] According to St Hesychios the Priest:

---

[87] Op cit Climacus 15 p 115–116. On the technical terms used by the Orthodox Fathers to describe the development of thought and its impact on stillness, silence and prayer see *Philokalia* 1 pp365–367.
[88] St Mark the Ascetic, *On the Spiritual Law* in *Philokalia* 1 p122.
[89] Gen 3:6.
[90] St Philaret of Moscow (2009) *Zapiski na knigu Bytiya* [Notes on the Book of Genesis] pp57–58 at Last Accessed March 2024.
[91] Evagrius 'Texts on Discrimination in Respect of Passions and Thoughts', *Philokalia* 1 p39.
[92] Or "by a single word of prayer" [Gk m*onologistos*].
[93] Op cit Climacus 28 p214.

"The science of sciences and the art of arts is the mastery of evil thoughts. The best way to master them is to see with spiritual vision the fantasy in which the demonic provocation is concealed and to protect the mind from it. It is just the same as the way we protect our bodily eyes. Looking sharply about us and doing all we can to prevent anything, however small, from striking them."[94] Evil thoughts must be "opposed", they must be "struggled with". Thus, on this view, prayer is not only a peaceful dialogue with God but also a heavy labour. It is nothing less than a fight for the purity of the mind. The one who prays must always keep watch on the intellect, memory and fantasy:

"Try to make your intellect deaf and dumb during prayer; you will then be able to pray…When you pray, keep close watch on your memory, so that it does not distract you…For by nature, the intellect is apt to be carried away by memories during prayer. While you are praying, the memory brings before you either fantasies of past things, or more recent concerns, or of the face of someone who has irritated you. The demon is very envious of us when we pray, and uses every kind of trick to thwart our purposes…he is always using our memory to stir up thoughts of various things and our flesh to arouse the passion, in order to obstruct our way of ascent to God…Stand on guard and protect your intellect from thoughts while you pray."[95] Orthodoxy has developed a special form of inward meditative prayer called *krypte melete*, or "secret occupation". This type of prayer was certainly already known and discussed in the fifth century and is still widespread in the Orthodox world. It consists of a short prayer formula, such as the "*Jesus Prayer*" which takes various forms: "Lord Jesus Christ have mercy on me a sinner" or "Jesus, Son of God have mercy on me" or even "Lord have mercy, Christ have mercy". The entire theory of *krypte melete* is expressed in the following, if somewhat lengthy monastic story which comes from the sixth or seventh century:

"A brother came from the coast to ask Father Philmon, 'What shall I do to be saved? For my intellect vacillates to and fro and strays after all the wrong things.' After a pause, the father replied: 'This is one of the outer passions and it stays with you because you still have not acquired a perfect longing for God. The warmth of this longing and of the knowledge of God has not yet come upon you."

---

[94] St Hesychios the Priest *On Watchfulness and Holiness* in Philokalia 1 p183.
[95] Op cit Evagrius *On Prayer* 11, 45–47, 70 in *Philokalia* 1 pp58–63.

The brother said to him: "What then shall I do father?" Abba Philimon replied, "Meditate inwardly for a while; for this can only cleanse your intellect from these things."

The brother, not understanding what was said went to an Elder and said: "What is inward meditation father?"

The Elder replied, "Keep watch in your heart; and with watchfulness say in your mind with awe and trembling, Lord Jesus Christ have mercy upon me."

The brother departed; and with the help of God and the Elder's prayers, he found stillness and for a while was filled with sweetness by this meditation. But then it suddenly left him and he could not practice or pray watchfully. So, he went again to the Elder and told him what had happened. And the Elder said to him, "You have had only a brief taste of stillness and inner work, and have experienced the sweetness that comes from them. This is what you should always be doing in your heart; whether eating or drinking, in company or outside your cell, or on a journey, repeat your prayer with a watchful mind and undeflected intellect…Even when carrying out needful tasks, do not let your intellect be idle but keep it meditating inwardly and praying."

For, in this way you can…give unceasing work to the intellect, thus fulfilling the apostolic command: "Pray without ceasing" [1 Thess 5:17]. Pay strict attention to your heart and watch over it, so that it does not give admittance to thoughts that are evil or in any way vain and useless. Without interruption, whether asleep or awake, eating, drinking, or in company let your heart inwardly and mentally at all times be meditating on the psalms, and at other times repeating the prayer: "Lord Jesus Christ, Son of God, have mercy on me."[96] The "Jesus Prayer": "Lord Jesus Christ, Son of God, have mercy on me"—or one of its many variants has a special power because the holy name of Jesus is contained in it. It was Jesus himself who commanded his disciples to pray in his name[97] and spoke of the wonder working power that such prayers have[98] "…for there is no other name under heaven given to men through which we must be saved."[99] There are, of course, many references to the power of the name of Jesus in early Christian literature, the most important of which are to be found in the second century text, "The Shepherd of Hermas": "The name of the Son of God is great

---

[96] *A Discourse of Abba Philimon* in *Philokalia* 2 pp 347–348.
[97] See Jn 16:23–24.
[98] See Mk 16:17–18.
[99] See Acts 4; 7–12.

and boundless, and upholds the entire universe...He supports those who wholeheartedly bear his name. He himself is their foundation and he carries them with love because they are not ashamed to bear his name."[100] The practice of prayer in the name of Jesus has lived within the Orthodox tradition ever since. St John Climacus (7th century), St Gregory of Sinai (13th century), St Gregory Palamas and other Byzantine Hesychasts in the 14th century, St Noicodemos of the holy mountain in the 18th century and St Seraphim of Sarov, St Thophan the recluse, St John of Kronstadt in the 19th century and St Silouan of the Mount Athos in the 20th century—all these authors, to name but a few, taught extensively on the "Jesus Prayer".[101] According to this centuries old tradition, the power and energy of God is present in the holy name of Jesus. In the beginning of the twentieth century, Monk Hilarion, a Caucasian hermit, wrote in his remarkable book "*On the Mountains of the Caucasus*":

"The Son of God...in the fullness of his divine nature is present both in the Holy Eucharist and in the Christian churches. He is also fully and entirely present in his name, with all the perfection and with the entirety of his divinity."[102] He then quoted the following words of St John of Kronstadt:

"Let the name of the Lord...be for you instead of the Lord himself...The name of the Lord is the Lord himself."[103] A heated dispute arose on Mount Athos in the 1910s around these words and around the teaching of those who were known as "the adorers of the Name". They were accused of dogmatic inaccuracy (heresy?), in confusing the name of God with his essence. As far as Monk Hilarion's book was concerned, however, it was very much part of the Hesychast tradition of the veneration of the name of Jesus. Regrettably, with the outbreak of the arguments around the meaning and power and use of the name of Jesus, this book was regarded as a manifesto for the "adorers of the name" and suppressed. It remained virtually unknown, especially in Russia and the territories of what we now think of as the former Soviet Union, until very recently.

---

[100] *The Shepherd of Hermas* Similitudes 9, 14.
[101] For an outline of their teachings on the Jesus prayer, see A Monk of the Eastern Church [Archimandrite Lev Gillet] *The Jesus Prayer*. New York. 1995.
[102] Monk Hilarion (1910) 'Na gorah Kavkaza' [*On the Mountains of the Caucasus.*] *Balalpahnik*. p16.
[103] Loc cit.

Of considerably more fame is a Russian book on the Jesus Prayer, which was written in the second half of the nineteenth century and is known in English as *"The Way of the Pilgrim"*[104] the hero and supposed author of this book was a simple Russian peasant, who heard in church the words of St Paul *"Pray without ceasing"* [1 Thess 5:17] and was caught by a desire to learn this unceasing prayer. For a long time, rather like the young monk in the long story quoted earlier, he could find no one who would teach him what this meant or give him spiritual direction. Eventually, again as in the earlier story, an Elder a *"starets"* told him of the practice of the Jesus Prayer and commanded him to repeat it three thousand times each day The quantity soon increased from three thousand to six thousand—and then doubled—after which, he tells us, he certainly knew how to pray without ceasing! "And that is how I go about it now, and ceaselessly repeat the prayer of Jesus, which is more precious and sweet to me than anything in the world. At times, I do as much as 43 or 44 miles walking each day and I do not feel that I am walking at all. I am aware only of the fact that I am saying my prayer…I thank God that I now understand those words I heard from the father: pray without ceasing."[105] The basic rule which applies to the Jesus Prayer, as well as to other prayers in the Orthodox tradition was set by St John Climacus and it is that one should "enclose one's thoughts within the words of the prayer".[106] But there is a difficulty here that many people only become fully aware of when they pass through times of great spiritual crisis and, once again, it concerns the mind. When the mind is located in the head, in the brain or intellect, it is very much subject to distraction and it cannot concentrate. In order to overcome this and so achieve concentration it is necessary to remove, as it were, the mind from the brain to its proper place in the heart, in the core of our being. It is the "proper place" because the spiritual journey is not one marked by spiritual experiences—or even great prayer—but by an ever-deepening practice of faith, hope and love. Only these three bring us to and ever closer and final union with God. The ancient method of removing the mind to the heart, which was developed in early monasticism, was summed up in the Orthodox tradition by St Theophan the recluse in one of his *Letters*: "You should descend to your heart from your head… As far as I remember you wrote to me that you had a headache from attentive prayer. This happens when one acts only with one's

---

[104] Anonymous (1954) *The Way of the Pilgrim*. Trans R M French London.
[105] Ibid p17–18.
[106] Op cit Climacus 28 p214.

head. But when prayer descends to the heart, there will be no difficulty in prayer, for the head will become empty from the thoughts. Al the thoughts are in the head, they follow one another, and it is impossible to control them. [But] if you discover your heart and are able to stand within it, then, as soon as thoughts appear, you can descend therein, and the *thoughts* will disappear…The life is in the heart, so you should live there. Do not think that this is only for the perfect. No, it applies to everyone who begins to seek out the Lord."[107] It may well have applied to everyone, but nevertheless the monastic tradition developed a special physical technique for exercising the Jesus Prayer.[108] An unknown author of the famous "*Method of Sacred Prayer and Attentiveness*"[109] says that in order to acquire attention during prayer a person must sit in a dark corner on a low chair, close his eyes, bow his head and hold his breathing; his mind should find the heart's higher part and being enclosed there pray with the prayer of Jesus. This method, however, is only a secondary means of attaining attentive prayer, which might also be achieved without any special exercises. The Orthodox spiritual writers of the nineteenth century were very reserved about this method. For example, St Theophan the Recluse, when translating the "*Method*" into Russian, deliberately omitted everything connected to physical techniques. "These external means," he wrote, "may scandalise some, divert others from prayer, and may distort the very practice of prayer…The essence of them is to get accustomed to holding one's mind within the heart…How to reach this? Seek and you will find.[110] The easiest way to find this is to walk before God and labour in prayer."[111] "Walking with God" or "walking before God" are, of course, expressions found in the Old Testament[112] where it is applied to the righteous people who are faithful and observed God's commandments.[113] In the later

---

[107] Quoted in "*On the Jesus Prayer*" Sotavala. 1936 P109.

[108] For a more detailed discussion of this see Metropolitan Kallistos Ware "*The Power of the Name*" pp 20–25.

[109] This treatise is usually ascribed to St Symeon the New Theologian, but more recent scholars incline to the view that it was composed during the thirteenth century—the debate continues!

[110] Mtt 7:7.

[111] This quotation from St Theophan appears as a footnote in the translation of the Writings of St Symeon New Theologian vol 2. Moscow. 1990 p188.

[112] Most famously perhaps at Micah.6:8.

[113] Cf.Gen.5:24, 6:9 17:1 et al.

Christian context, tines expression also points to the agreement of the life of a person and the teaching of Christ. To walk before god then, means to measure every thought, every action, by the standards of the Gospel, to remember God always, and to feel his presence. Prayer is helpful only when it its combined with faithful living according to the Gospel. The Christian ideal is that the whole life of a person should be transformed by unceasing prayer so that our very words and every deed by penetrated by prayer. "If you are a theologian," wrote Evagrius Ponticus, "you will truly pray. And if you pray truly, you are a theologian."[114] These words stress the interrelationship between prayer and theology; one cannot truly exist without the other. For the Early Church Fathers, theology was not an abstract theory about an "unknown God", but rather a search for a personal encounter with Him. Genuine theology then, is not "about" God, but is "in" God. It does not consider God as an object, but converses with him as Being itself. On this view, Christian theology is an eminently practical, political, matter because it is derived from prayer and mystical experience. It is not simply a matter of objective scholarship detached from God, but rather brings an experience of God into the smallest and seemingly unimportant actions of the everyday. So it is that stillness, silence and prayer are necessary for the proper conduct of theology: "Discussion of theology is not for everyone…It is not for all men, but only for those who…have undergone, or at the very least are undergoing, purification of the body and soul. For one who is not pure to lay hold on pure tings is dangerous, just as it is for weak eyes to look on the sun's brightness. What is the right time (for theology?) Whenever we are free from the mire and noise without, and our commanding faculty[115] is not confused by illusory, wandering images…we need to be still in order to know God…"[116] Prayer, in turn, derives from theology and is based on it. There can be no true prayer outside true dogma; this is an essential belief of the Orthodox Churches. Distortion of dogma leads to a distortion of the practice of prayer and *vice versa*. Wrong forms of prayer give birth to erroneous dogmatic teachings. A true prayer is one practised within the context of the church community, even if the question is about private prayer. "Nobody is a Christian *by* himself, but only as a member of the body," wrote Father Georges Florovsky. "Even in solitude, 'in the chamber', a Christian prays as a member of the redeemed community…the

---

[114] Op cit Evagrius Ponticus: *On prayer* 61. in *Philokalia* 1. P62.
[115] i.e. the intellect.
[116] St Gregory the Theologian: Fr *Oration* 27.3 . At last Accessed March 2024.

church."[117] The personal prayer of every Christian is always connected to the prayer of the whole church; it is nothing less than a continuation of divine worship. The entire life of a Christian is the liturgy which a person celebrates in their heart and addresses to God as a Trinitarian community, Father, Son and Holy Spirit.

The practice of prayer might be strikingly similar in different religious traditions, but its content is altogether dissimilar depending on the dogmatic and theological basis of prayer in every tradition. There are, for example, some similarities between the physical techniques associated with the Jesus Prayer of the Orthodox Churches and those employed in Sufic Islam. But in Sufism we do not find dogmas of the Trinity or of Jesus Christ as God and saviour which, quite obviously lie at the very heart of Christian prayer. As Metropolitan Kallistos has written:

"The essential point of the Jesus Prayer is not the act of repetition itself, not how we sit or breathe, but to <u>whom</u> we speak…The prayer is not just a device to help us concentrate or relax. It is not simply a piece of 'Christian Yoga', a type of 'Transcendental meditation', or a 'Christian Mantra'…it is, on the contrary, an invocation <u>specifically addressed to another person</u>—to God made man, Jesus Christ as Son of God and saviour…Secondly, the context of the Jesus Prayer is always one <u>of community</u>. We do not invoke the name as separate individuals…but as members of the community of the church."[118] St Paul wrote about the Holy Spirit entering the heart in order to pray with and alongside the Christian.[119] Thus for the Orthodox Christian prayer is a listening to the voice of God in our innermost being, "the heart". In a sense, it is not the human person who prays; it is God himself who prays deep within the human person—*Cor ad cor loquiter,* (heart speaks to, or with, heart). "Why say more?" asks St Gregory of Sinai "Prayer is God, who accomplishes everything in everyone."[120] If prayer is God as Trinity acting through Christ, there is not much in common between this prayer and that outside the Christian tradition. *But if the one who prays truly is a theologian, then there is no prayer outside the ultimate truth—the incarnate Christ. Why indeed say more?*

---

[117] Cited in Metropolitan Kallistos of Dioklieia *The Orthodox Church*. P310.
[118] Op cit Metropolitan Kallistos: *The Power of the Name* pp23-24 (my emphasis added).
[119] Gal 4:6.
[120] St Gregory of Sinai: *On Commandments and Doctrines*. In Philokalia 4 p238.

Chapter 6
Orthodoxy and the Celtic Tradition: Unexplored Connections

"Kindle in our hearts, O God, the flame of that love which never ceases, that it may burn in us, giving light to others. May we shine forever in thy Holy Temple and set us on fire with thy etern*al light, even thy son, Jesus Christ, our saviour and redeemer.*"[121] With the imagery of fire and light contained in this prayer we move directly to an incident in the life of the Celt St Columba which shows how he experienced the celestial light, which the Orthodox recognise as a vision of the One Uncreated Light spoken of in Scripture and by the Fathers as the image of God himself (God from God, light from light, true God from true God…):

"One winter's night a monk named Virgnous, burning with the love of God, entered the church alone to pray. The others were asleep. He prayed fervently in a little chapel attached to the side of the oratory. After about an hour, the venerable Columba entered the same sacred space. Along with him, at the same time, a golden light came down from the highest heavens and filled that part of the church. Even the separate alcove, where Virgnous was now trying to hide himself as best he could, was also filled with this light, to his great alarm."

Just as no one can look directly at or gaze with a steady eye on the summer sun in its midday splendour, so Virgnous could not at all bear the heavenly brightness he saw because the brilliant and unspeakable radiance overpowered his sight. This brother, in fact, was so terrified by the splendour…that no strength remained in him. Finally, after a short prayer, Columba left the church.

The next day Columba sent for Virgnous, who was still very much alarmed, and spoke to him these consoling words: "You are crying for good purpose my son. Last night you were very pleasing to God by keeping your eyes firmly fixed

---

[121] Prayer ascribed to St Columba.

on the ground. If you had not done that the brightness would have permanently blinded you. You must never, however, disclose this great manifestation of God's brightness as long as I live…"

Here, in the Celtic tradition we see something which we remarked of the desert dwellers, namely that they radiated a celestial light, a notion which has its roots in the experience of Moses after having spoken with God. Celestial light is always linked to grace as we see in this story from the life of St Adomann:

"At another time when the holy man was living on the island of Hibna, the grace of the Holy Spirit was poured out on him in abundance and in an incomparable manner. It continued marvellously for three days and as many nights. Remaining with the house barred, and filled with heavenly light, he allowed no one to go to him, and he neither ate nor drank. From that house, streams of immeasurable brightness were visible in the night, escaping through holes in the door and through the key hole. Spiritual songs, unheard of before were heard being sung by him."

"Moreover, as he afterwards admitted in the presence of a very few men, he saw, openly revealed, many of the secret things that have been hidden since the world began. Also, everything that in sacred scriptures is dark and difficult became plain and was shown more clearly than the days to the eyes of his purest heart. And he lamented that his foster son, Baithene was not there, who if he had had a chance to be present during these three days, would have written down from the mouth of the blessed man very many mysteries both of past ages and of the ages still to come. Mysteries unknown to other men…"[122] In the introduction to his translation of the *Vita Patrum; the Life of the Fathers*[123] Fr Seraphim Rose of Platina wrote appreciatively about the Orthodox saints of the pre-schismatic west in Gaul, but of course he could have been writing about the Celtic saints of the British Isles from exactly the same period of time. "A touchstone of Orthodoxy," Fr Seraphim wrote, "is the love of Christ's saints. From the earliest Christian centuries, the church has celebrated her saints—first the apostles and martyrs who died for Christ, then the desert dwellers who crucified themselves

---

[122] Both the story of St Columba and this from the life of St Adomann are quoted by Fr Gozrad Vorpatny in his "*Celts and Orthodoxy*" at www.orthodoxireland.com/history/celtsandorthodoxy/view

[123] St Gregory of Tours. *Vita Patrum – Life of the Fathers*. With an Introduction by Fr Seraphim Rose of Platina. Place unknown. St Herman Press USA.

for the love of Christ, and the hierarchs and shepherds who gave their lives for the salvation of their flocks.

From the beginning, the church has treasured the written lives of her saints and has celebrated their memory in the Divine Services. These two sources—the lives and services—are extremely important to us today for the preservation of the authentic Orthodox tradition of faith and piety. The false "enlightenment" of our modern times is so all pervasive that it draws many Orthodox Christians into it puffed up "wisdom" and without their even knowing it they are taken away from the true spirit of Orthodoxy and are left only with the shell of Orthodox rites, formulas and customs…To have a seminary education, even to have the right views about Orthodox history and theology—is not enough.

A typical modern Orthodox education produces, more often than not, merely Orthodox rationalists…lacking the true spirit and feeling of Orthodoxy. The spirit and feeling of Orthodoxy are communicated most effectively in the Lives of the saints and in similar sources which speak less of an outward side of correct dogma and rite, than of an essential inward side of proper Orthodox attitude, spirit and piety.

With Seraphim's principle in mind—that the lives of the saints are of crucial importance if we are to understand and pass on every element of Christianity to the next generation—it is important at this point to say what I mean by "Celtic" and "Celtic spirituality". It often comes as a surprise to people to learn that the "Celts" never described themselves in this way. It was a derogatory term applied to them by others having its roots in the Greek word *"keltos"*, meaning "the others" or "the strangers". It was a word which distinguished "people like us" from "people who are not like us at all". So, the word "Celts" was used by those who came in contact with them and saw them as being radically different from other tribes and people in the ancient world. And so indeed they were.

While the Celts did not lose their love of war, they no longer expressed it so lustily but channelled their energies into the faith with a single-mindedness rarely seen elsewhere except, perhaps, in the Orthodox tradition:

"Monasticism appeared attractive to a warrior people who were drawn to an ascetic lifestyle…it appealed to a marginalised people who saw the monk as one who lived on the edge of things, on the very margins of life."[124] We see this in the lives of monks like St Cuthbert and St Guthlic who *"were uncompromising*

---

[124] Timothy Joyce: *Celtic Christianity: A Sacred Tradition, a vision of Hope – A Spiritual Tradition for Today.* New York. Orbis Books 1998.

solitaries and their ascetic practices aroused wonder…"[125] and in the life of St Columba who we are told heroically *"leapt over his mother's grieving body, which was draped across her threshold, in order to head for a monastery"*[126] following the death of his father.[127] In that moment, he chose to live at the limits and his life thereafter has close similarities with the life of St Anthony in the deserts of Egypt. But this is not surprising, because their Christianity—that is their monasticism—was formed and influenced by the desert, and only incidentally by the continent of Europe. This means that Celtic monasticism was more like Byzantine or Salvic Orthodox monasticism than Latin or Northern European Christianity.

We see this in the physical arrangement of Celtic "monasteries". They were not an elaborate complex of buildings but a relatively modest "village" of separate cells gathered around a small church or chapel for communal worship. The monastic village usually had a stone wall around it to keep animals in and thieves or the merely curios out. Within the walls the many cells, small huts shaped like rounded bee hives, were usually wooden, or wattle and daub, thus emphasising the temporary nature of human existence and physical structures alike. Later, especially in the west of Ireland, stone buildings were erected. Remains of many of these stone "clochans" can still be seen scattered across the countryside, but there is no evidence that even these was intended to be permanent features of the landscape.[128] "Other monks and nuns lived out their days alone…in small wood-and-mud huts; they kept a cow or two, and accepted gladly the gifts of an occasional loaf or a basket of vegetables from local farmers.

---

[125] Benedicta Ward: High King of Heaven – Aspects of Early English Spirituality. London and New York. Continuum International Publishing Group 1999.

[126] Lisa M Bitel: *Ascetic Superstars* at www.chrisitanitytoday.com/ch/60h/60h022html Last Accessed March 2024.

[127] It is perhaps not surprising then to learn that the brave and heroic stories of King Arthur (believed by the Celts to have been a real person) originated among them and only much later were picked up by the medieval troubadours and scribes and expanded to suit their own purposes. These included the familiar tales of the Round Table and the Noble Quest for the Holy Grail, as well as the accounts of Arthur's "spiritual director", Merlin. "Merlin" may well be a contraction of Ambrosius Merlinus, after St Ambrose of Milan, teacher and confessor of St Augustine of Hippo. If this is so then Merlin is not the wise old Druid of popular culture but rather a key figure in Church history and doctrine.

[128] Op cit Joyce.

The desire for a solitary life and time to spend simply yearning for God…must have drifted through even the busiest abbot in the most bustling monastery."[129] Monastic life was seen as an absolutely essential part of Christian life—the norm for all Christian life, not the exception—and monks and nuns and hermits were the great heroes of the common people, who saw them, as St Cuthlac put it, as "tried warriors who serve a king who never withholds the reward from those who persist in loving him."[130] Indeed, it is this quality of persistent, even stubborn heroism that particularly stamps the character of Celtic Christianity and especially its monastic life. For Christian Celts, the heroes were monks and nuns, not political leaders, nor bards, nor any other cultural figures. The writings of John Cassian (still carefully read and studied by Eastern Orthodox monks today, and recommended reading in the closing chapters of the Rule of Benedict) were known to the Celtic monks. Cassian had spent years as a monk in Bethlehem and in Egypt and wrote his reflections on his conversations with the desert dwellers, later establishing a monastery in Marseilles. The life of the Egyptian father St Anthony, by Athanasius, was translated into Latin around the year 380AD, and we know that this was studied by the Celtic monks who depicted both St Anthony and St Paul of Thebes on some of the great Irish "High Crosses".

The literacy rate among the Celtic monks must have been very high and it was from their study of both Cassian and Athanasius that they learnt the daily practice of "Confession of Thoughts". It was from them too that they adopted a habit made of animal skins so that to all outward appearance they would appear to be like John the Baptist in the wilderness and so a complete contrast to the coenobitic practice elsewhere in Europe and a preference for woven cloth.

But there are also records of Celtic monks travelling through the Orthodox territories on their way to the Desert fathers, before about 680AD. An ancient Celtic litany mentions seven Egyptian monks who came to Ireland and were buried there and there is an inscription on a stone near a church in County Cork which reads: "Pray for Olan, the Egyptian." It is also interesting that even though there are no deserts in the British Isles, the Celts called their monastic communities "diserts" or "deserts" which shows not only their links to Egyptian but their understanding that the desert experience is a fundamental part of authentic Christian living. This was especially true of island monasteries or

---

[129] Op cit Bitel.
[130] Ibid.

hermitages—those spiritual fortresses—where *the* sea itself was like a desert. As an ancient anonymous poet said of St Columba's island home:

"Delightful, I think it be, to be in the bosom of an isle on the peak of a rock, that I might often see there the calm of the sea…That I might see its heavy waves over the glittering ocean as they chant a melody to their father on their eternal course."

We have an interesting description of a visit to the monks of Egypt near the close of the fourth century, written by Rufinus of Aquileia. He wrote: "When we came near, they realised that foreign monks were approaching, and at once they swarmed out of their cells like bees. They joyfully hurried to meet us." Rufinus was particularly struck by the solitude stillness and prayer among these monks. "This is the utter desert", he observed, "where each monk lives alone in his cell…There is a huge silence and a great peace there…"[131] More interesting still, I think, is the fact that St David of Wales, who lived in the sixth century, came from a monastery which had been founded by a direct disciple of John Cassian. St David had the gift of tears, spoke alone with angels, subdued the flesh by plunging into ice cold water, knew all the psalms by heart, and spent the day praying with many prostrations. All these are key features of desert monasticism and indeed can be found in the Orthodox tradition too. "He also fed a multitude of orphans, widows, sick needy and feeble pilgrims".[132] According to the Roman Catholic scholar Edward C Sellner: "Thus he began, thus he continued, thus he ended his day. He imitated the monks of Egypt and lived a life like theirs."[133] Sellener assures us that "…because of its [the Celtic church] love of the Desert fathers and mothers, it has a great affinity with the spirituality of the Eastern Orthodox [today"[134] and Fr Gregory Telepneff claims that the interlocking knots and complex designs on the famous standing "High Crosses" are of Orthodox influence.[135] Culturally then, Celtic monasticism and spirituality was a unique and intriguing blend of Egyptian, Orthodox and Middle Eastern influences with

---

[131] Quoted by Elizabeth Reess: *Celtic Saints—Passionate Wanderer* London. Tames and Huson 2000.

[132] Edward C Sellner: *Wisdom of the Celtic Saints*. Place Unknown. Bog Walk Books. 2006.

[133] ibid

[134] Ibid.

[135] Fr G Telepneff: The Egyptian Desert in the Irish Bogs: The Byzantine Character of Early Celtic Monasticism. Etna California. The Centre for Traditional Orthodoxy. 2003.

native and indigenous cultural elements. Before going further, it is important to say what I mean by "spirituality" in this context, especially since "Celtic spirituality" has recently become a Humpty Dumpty word so that it means anything we want it to mean. In the last decade interest in the attitudes and beliefs of Christians of the Celtic lands in the first millennium has swollen from being a specialist pursuit among medievalists and historians of theology into what is virtually a popular movement. In the process, more than a few books have appeared claiming to uncover the soul of Celtic Christianity in all its beauty. All too often, their authors operate by offering their own definitions of "Christianity" past and present, and then setting these against their definition of "Celt" or "Celtic". In this way, they can reach the conclusion they want.

This is typical of our modern intellectual arrogance and our spiritual poverty which feels the need to project our own feeble ideas back on to a supposed golden age of "spirituality". As a result, we are free to treat the rich heritage of Celtic Christianity as a smorgasbord, where we take those things we already "like" and put them together to form our own very distorted, and hence quite false, "version" of the Celts. To give just one example: while it is true that in the early Christian centuries Ireland, Scotland and many parts of Wales were never subject to Roman hegemony, this does *not* mean that "Celtic Christians" were anti-Roman, *nor does it mean* that they automatically opposed the idea of an organised patriarchal church.

The reality is, I contend, much more subtle than that. Although in fact, the Celtic Christians *did* have a quite different way of organising local faith communities than did Christians on the continent, this was *not* out of rebellion but because their models were drawn from Egypt and the Orthodox territories, not from Western Europe. The simple fact is that the Irish church has always theologically and geographically been living at the edges of Roman Christianity and in some sense considered a barbarian church of limited interest to the Popes. Although the climate and situation of Britain were very different from the hot deserts of Egypt, there were principles such as simplicity, prayer, fasting, spiritual warfare, wisdom and evangelism that were easy to translate to the communities of these islands. Thus, any attempt to enter into the spiritual, mental, emotional and physical world of a Celtic Christian is extremely difficult—not impossible, but extremely difficult and if we are to do so at all we need to take the following factors firmly into account:

First, our Celtic ancestors had no concept of privacy or of individuality such as we have today. Families did not live in separate rooms, or even separate houses, but all together; no one thought about compartmentalising physical space and claiming ownership of it, "My space". Only hermits and anchorites felt a calling to be alone in spiritual solitude with God and while monks lived in separate cells none of these would have thought of their hermitage or cells as belonging to them. They were seen only as a shelter from the elements and a place to search God, and this notion came directly from the monasticism of the Egyptian Thebaid.

The idea that people are separate individuals from the group with rights of personal ownership was not only unheard of, but would have been considered spiritually dangerous to the point of being heretical because the focus of their primary concern would shift from God to themselves. All tendencies towards self-absorption, "moods" and being temperamental were regarded are part of spiritual warfare because they can be "demonic" as the writings of Evagrius and Cassian, known to the Celts and providing a manual of monastic organisation and life, make abundantly clear.

Indeed, I do not think that it is too unreasonable to argue that our ideas of individuality and certainly of private property only came about with the Plantagenet King Henry II of England and the establishment of a structured legal system. It was at about this time that people began to keep detailed records and inventories, write journals and diaries and so increasingly singled themselves off from family, group or community. Until this time, there were no "real life" portraits of individuals which were painted in response to the medieval idea of romance. The portrait was a means of making a person present in their absence away on the crusades; in much the same way as an icon makes present the presence of a saint or Biblical character.

Second, "…the dominant institution of Celtic Christianity was neither the parish church nor the cathedral, but the monastery, which sometimes began as a hermit's cell and often grew to become a combination of commune, retreat house, mission station…school…a source not just of spiritual energy but also of hospitality, learning and cultural enlightenment."[136] Part of this is to note that the early Celts were not gathered into parishes and that it was only much later that they adopted the idea of a diocese based on geographical borders with a bishop

---

[136] Ibid.

as its head. For the most part, a bishop was simply a pastor, a shepherd of a given tribe or group, not a ruler over a specific piece of land. Our notion of a bishop "ruling a diocese" would have been quite foreign to them.[137] Now, if we begin to think about what this means in terms of how we currently understand ourselves, the world we create for ourselves and the values we hold, we can begin to see, I think, just how difficult it is for us to enter the world of the Celts. Today we are quite obsessive about such things as privacy and individuality, of "being our own selves" and "getting in touch with our inner person" and other ideas that lead to the self-absorption that the Celts explicitly rejected as potentially heretical nonsense. But Celtic Christians understood, just as Orthodox Christians still do, that human beings are saved in community. If we go to hell, we go alone.

So, the orientation of those Christian Celts to God and the "other world" was very different from the orientation of our modern world, no matter how devout or pious we may be, and this makes the distance between us and the world of Celtic monasticism far greater than merely the passage of many centuries. While this might be said of much of early Christian history, the distance is greater for the reasons I have given and as Sir Samuel Dill also made plain when writing more generally about Christians in the west at a similar period of time:

"The dim religious life of the early Middle Ages is severed from the modern mind by so wide a gulf, by such a revolution of beliefs that the most cultivated sympathy can only hope to revive in faint imagination…a world of…fervent belief which no modern mind can ever fully enter into…It is intensely interesting, even fascinating…[but] between us and the early Middle Ages there is a gulf which the most subtle and agile imagination can hardly hope to pass. He who has pondered most deeply over the popular faith of the time will feel most deeply how impossible it is to pierce its secret."[138] To enter the world of Celtic monasticism then we must try and find a way of seeing things as they did, not as we do today, to hear, taste, touch, pray, and think as they did. And that is what I mean by "spirituality" in this context, their whole world view. We must examine them in the full context of that whole world view, which was a world of faith, not just any faith but the faith of Christians in *both* the Western and the *Eastern* halves of Christendom in the first thousand years after Christ for whom spirituality was (and is) a living, dogmatic theology. This is the only way that we can begin to understand Celtic monasticism and the ways, if at all, it can be the

---

[137] Ibid.
[138] Quoted in Fr Serpahim Rose op cit.

model for contemporary sanctity that so many wish it to be. But even this may raise problems for what exactly do we mean by "model"?

Presumably we mean a standard that can be imitated, but how can this be when their world ceased to be over a thousand years ago? This being so it is, I think impossible to use Celtic monasticism as a model for external things such as, say, architecture, style of chant, style of prayer, monastic habits etc, since these are all cultural "accidents". This is, of course, quite contrary to the swollen "popular movement" which suggests that it is precisely these things that provide the model. I contend that it is *not* these things that provide the model at all but rather something inward, an inward spirit and awareness of God in all things. This inward spirit and awareness might indeed be captured in so-called "Celtic" Christian music, prayers and even liturgies, but let us be aware that these things are nothing more than a modern expression of that spirit and are not "authentic". Disappointing as this may be for some; this is neither surprising nor unique. It is true of all our attempts to translate the essential elements of monasticism to our secular lives. It is only in this inner sense that Celtic monasticism can be, for those who wish it, a model of sanctity in today's world.

Similarly, we must be clear about what we mean by "sanctity in today's world". We must be careful not to slip into some vague, New Age fuzziness which is more Gnostic that Christian and has more to do with being a "nice person" than encountering the true and living God in (Celtic?) simplicity. The Celts were masters of spiritual simplicity. Nowadays there is often a movement in our culture to recover some simple basics, but the model tends to be of the Quakers, Shakers or the Amish rather than the Celts. Perhaps that is because they are easier to imitate, after all adherents of some of these sects are still with us. For the Celts, however, simplicity was not so much a matter of externals—like furniture, architecture and so on—but something internal, founded on the Lord's Prayer and especially the phrase, "Thy will be done…"

That this was the basis of Celtic Christianity is repeated again and again in the later commentaries of the Venerable Bede of Jarrow and in the writings of Alcuin when he was at the court of Charlemagne. They tell us that the phrase, "Thy will be done…" was central to living a simple Christian life, it meant pursuing God's will and not the will of the group. It meant absolute trust in providence, trusting God for everything, health finance and community living. It also meant not judging others, seeking forgiveness and having the grace to forgive. This is where Celtic simplicity began and from there it easily expressed itself in outward forms, such as not owning five tunics where two were quite sufficient.

Celtic simplicity did not mean plainness. Celtic Christians were not "plain people" like, say the Amish, and their Christian culture (being derived from Egypt and the Eastern Orthodox) was not "plain" either, as the "High Crosses" show. They may not have been "plain people" but they were "simple people" in that they were single-minded and intensely focussed on God and the journey through this life to God and since their concepts of individuality was as yet unformed in any modern sense, they would not have understood our practise of "private prayer".[139] This practice too belongs to a later period in religious history, when privacy and individualism had become more important than traditional ways of seeking God through prayer. This did not mean, however, that Celtic Christians only prayed when gathered for communal worship any more than an Orthodox Christian prays only during the divine liturgies. But for the Celts, as for the Orthodox, prayer at times other than communal worship was the repetition of the psalms. Occasionally, a particularly gifted monk might compose a prayer such as the one written by St Columba with which this chapter began. But in moments of joy or need or despair it was remembered phrases from the psalms that quickly sprung to mind.

Central to Celtic Christianity was the cross another feature, as I mentioned above, which may well have been a direct influence from the Orthodox east where wayside crosses were, and are, prominent features of the landscape. It is interesting to note, however, that some Celtic Christians in the seventh and eighth centuries did not feel comfortable with the cross and chose to ignore it, just as some Christians do today. But generally, the Celts had a very clear understanding of the Cross. As Benedicta Ward has pointed out:

"The cross was not something that made them feel better, nicer, more comfortable, more victorious, more reconciled to tragedy, better able to cope with life and death: it was, rather, the centre of the fire in which they were to be changed."[140] It reminded them that they were to pick up the cross and carry it if they were to follow Christ faithfully and according to the Gospel imperative. Thus, the Celtic monks saw themselves as warriors of the spirit in a similar way and for similar reasons as the monks of the White Monastery at Atripe when

---

[139] By "private prayer" here I mean the ability to spontaneously create words and phrases to address to God in contexts other than communal worship.
[140] Op cit.

Shenoute was abbot. Even though the Celtic monks were not physically violent (which was the case at the White Monastery), both the Celts and the monks at Atripe believed that there was no greater act of heroism than to defend the faith of the tribe. Celtic monks and nuns, like those at the White Monastery, were fiercely dedicated women and men in whom the old warrior spirit, if not the practice, was alive but now put to the service of Christ, their High King of Heaven:

"The way of the cross for [Celtic Christians] was the way of heroic loyalty, obedience and suffering. It involved study and thought, doctrine and Orthodoxy[141] art and imagination. It was a complete, unified way of life, lived intimately with God…[Our] fragmented modern world…has a lot to learn from it."[142] No wonder then that the cross was loved and cherished in the monasteries where "High Crosses", sometimes 15 feet high, were erected. They were not the suffering bloody crucifixions with which we might be familiar in, say, modern Spain and Italy but shared the peace and serenity of the Orthodox crosses encountered in, say, Moldova and Ukraine. Like the Orthodox crosses, Celtic crosses rarely, if ever, depicted the slumped, crucified and dying Christ. Where he was shown, however, he was always erect, eyes wide open, his body fully vested like a priest about to celebrate the Holy Mysteries. In this form, as the "great High Priest" of Hebrews, Christ was a symbol of victory over sin and death; he radiated invincibility. This, in turn, influenced early English poetry such as the Anglo-Saxon *"The Dream of the Rood"*[143] In this poem Jesus is understood as a young, confident hero who prepares for battle. He strips and climbs up onto the gallows intent on saving his people from the massed forces of sin and death. He is in control, revealing himself as the second person of the Trinity and fulfilling the will of the Father. The cross, now personified and able to speak, trembles at Christ's self-determination and under the weight of his embrace:

"Unclothed Himself God Almighty when he would
Mount the cross, courageous in the sight of men.
I bore the powerful king, the Lord of heaven; I durst not bend.
Men mocked us both together. I was bedewed with blood.

---

[141] In the sense of right practice and belief.
[142] Op cit Cavil.
[143] A "rood" was the ancient word for "rod" or "pole" or, as in this case, the "gallows" on which our Saviour died.

Christ was on the Cross.

Then I leaned down to the hands of men and they took God Almighty..."[144] The interlacing, knot work, plaiting, weaving patterns and spiral designs, with animals, plants and saints, which decorate almost every surface of a Celtic High Cross proclaim Christ's victory in which all created things now participate. Many of these patterns may have their origins in Egypt, but they also show Orthodox influences. For example, there are no loose ends in these patterns; this symbolises the continuity of the Holy Spirit throughout existence—for God has no beginning and no end. Only Christ is the Alpha and Omega.

The same is true of the knot work patterns, which are endless and cannot be untied. The Holy Spirit proceeds from the Father, rests on the Son and embraces all things in a never-ending stream of divine love. The spiral patterns speak of God the Father, the "motionless mover" of (Christianised) Greek philosophy around whom all things revolve and to whom they tend. The many other complex geometric patterns refer to the complexity of the doctrine of *kenosis*, the self-emptying of Christ.

One of the main contributing factors to the eventual decline of Celtic monasticism was that the cross began to lose its central importance. According to Dom David Knowles:

"If monastic life...did not have at its centre the reality of the cross, it became a source of corruption...[for] once a religious house or order cease[d] to direct its sons to the abandonment of all that is not God and cease[d] to show them the narrow way...it sank to the level of a purely human institution and whatever its works maybe they are the works of time and not eternity."[145] But even in decline the Celts never really lost their native enthusiasm, exuberance and sheer joy at being alive as a most beloved child of God. Nowhere do we see this joy more plainly expressed than in a prayer by Abbess Brigit who lived in the fourth century and with whom I bring this chapter to and end:

"I should like a great lake of ale for the King of Kings, I should like the angels in heaven to be drinking from it through time eternal!"[146] So much for Christian temperance and those puritanical attitudes that seek to condemn all celebration, feasting and dance as evil and likely to lead us into mortal sin! How can we fail to be charmed by Brigit who, though a woman was a great leader of

---

[144] Op cit Ward.

[145] Dom David Knowles quoted in Ward. Ibid.

[146] Ibid.

Celtic monasticism? How can we fail to be intrigued by her claim to have been baptised by angels, and later fled a violent and arranged marriage by plucking out one of her eyes and finally, how can we not feel an empathy with a woman who was so bored by a sermon of St Patrick that she fell asleep.

Part 3
Monasticism and Conflict

Chapter 7
Monasticism in Britain Before the Conquest (1) Northumbria and the Synod of Whitby

Monasticism, East and West, had been gradually evolving and developing since the time of the Desert fathers, but, in the seventh century, monasticism in England confronted a crisis that asked the question as to whether the Celtic or Roman Church represented the one true faith of Christianity. Eventually, and perhaps inevitably, these two great factions met and clashed in the north-eastern region of Britain, more specifically the Kingdom of Northumbria. Once a decision was made in favour of one tradition over another the face of monasticism changed not only in Britain but throughout Western Europe—and changed forever.

Britain ceased to be province of the former Roman Empire in the fifth century when Emperor Honorius recalled his troops from the northwest frontier. The withdrawal of troops not only created a military power vacuum into which the Saxon invaders soon sped, but it also diminished the influence of many features of cultural and religious life—including Christianity. It is important to emphasise that Roam culture and Christianity did not disappear altogether to usher in the so-called "Dark Ages" as is so often commonly believed. In fact, the stories of St Patrick are only one instance which shows how Christianity in Britain survived after the Romans departed and before Pope Gregory the Great attempted to re-establish the authority of the Roman Church through the missionary programme of the sixth century.

They show too how Christianity had to resist being overpowered by the religious practices of the Saxons which were largely "pagan". The missionaries sent by Pope Gregory were to establish not just Roman Christianity, but Christianity itself. This was by no means an easy task. But with the additional influence of Irish and Frankish missionaries, Christianity once again spread throughout the country in less than a century.[147] With the exception of a few pagan practices linked to the cult of the Anglo-Saxon warrior, Christianity once again became the dominant religion in Britain. Celtic monasticism developed in Ireland in the sixth century and especially in those eastern regions which bordered the Irish Sea from whence it spread to south-west Scotland, Wales and, perhaps, parts of what is now Devon and Cornwall too.[148] It was in these areas that a form of Christianity very different from that of its Latin, Roman, counterpart emerged. The Latin culture of these regions was strictly based on Latin texts that were available to the Irish at the time,[149] namely, "the Bible and a selection of vivid texts of Latin Christian literature of the late fourth and early fifth centuries—the cultural debris of a ravaged Roman province that had been preserved in western Britain and Wales after the collapse of Roman society in large areas of the island."[150] Out of these limited resources a different kind of "Latin" emerged and with it a type of Christianity that had developed from the texts alone; a "Christianity of the mind"[151] the differences that developed were largely due to the Irish dependence on these texts, some of which were at least two hundred years old. The problem was that most of continental Europe in the sixth century was using a different form of Latin than that which had been used in the fourth. The Irish and Welsh, isolated in their own far-flung corner of the world, began to teach themselves "Latin" in order to communicate their Christian beliefs to one another.[152] Moreover, since Ireland had never been part of the Roman Empire or otherwise been influenced by it, it "owed little or nothing to Rome".[153] It was largely from this muddle that the debate as to whether Celtic or Roman Christianity more nearly represented the one true faith of Christ began. Both sides claimed this honour, but it was one that could not be shared. There could only be one true representation of the one true faith. The Synod of Whitby

---

[147] D.H. Farmer, J.F. Webb (1965) *The Age of Bede* London. Penguin Books Group, p14.
[148] Some legends about local saints still prevalent in Cornwall, such as that of St Ives who is said to have floated from Ireland to Cornwall on a leaf, show similarities to those of the Irish saints—in this case the voyage of St Brendan.
[149] Peter Brown (2003) *The Rise of Western Christendom*, Oxford and Malden Blackwell Publishing. p239.
[150] Ibid. p240.
[151] Ibid. p241.
[152] Ibid p239.
[153] Ibid p240.

in 664 concluded (perhaps somewhat reluctantly) in favour of the Roman tradition, but that did not mean that Celtic Christianity ceased nor it did not bring to an end its long monastic history. Some Celtic monasteries, such as Iona and Lindisfarne, remained loyal to their Celtic heritage and maintained its "…austerity, learning, calligraphy, [and a] pioneering missionary endeavour"[154] and even Bede the venerable approved of Celtic saints like Aidan.[155] As we will see, especially in the next chapter, the concern of monastic writers after 664, was to root the superiority of Roman Christianity in Britain while at the same time recognising that Celtic forms could not be totally eradicated even the monastic life. The monastic writers with which we will concern ourselves here produced works of hagiography. Hagiography is, by definition "writings about the saints".[156] The title "saint" in this period was given to a holy man or woman "who had lived a life of heroic virtue and then been posthumously judged by God to be worthy of entrance into the kingdom of heaven. In theory, all who resided in the divine court were saints, but in practice Christian churches accorded a relatively small number of people the title of saints and, with it, public veneration."[157] The veneration of saints at this time was a fundamental part of religious practice because "…saints were both during their lives and after their deaths, key members of the Christian community."[158] By the seventh century, hagiography had become a popular means of recording and disseminating the message of the "true faith". For the Roman Church, it was a matter of convincing their faithful to cling to the practices they had adopted, whereas for any Celtic readers, the stories gave comfort that while the traditions which no longer found favour on earth they were still blessed in heaven. Hagiography is often held in low esteem because it does not purport to be accurate history and because of its tendency towards gushing and pious sentimentality. While both criticisms are true hagiography does, I think, offer a glimpse into the ideal Christian life. This was particularly important for the early Middle Ages and for a number of reasons. One of the more obvious is that it was in this way that Christian saints and heroes could be immortalised. Their stories could be kept alive and their

---

[154] Op cit Farmer & Webb p16.

[155] Loc cit.

[156] Thomas Head (2001) *Medieval Hagiography; An Anthology* New York & London. Routledge p.xiv.

[157] Loc cit.

[158] Loc cit.

memory preserved for future generations. Another reason is that by writing about the saints and heroes, authors could convey to their readers the proper and ideal way of conducting their own ascetic, religious (and monastic) life.

The stories of the saints were intended as exemplars. These reasons correlate with what Thomas Head has to say about hagiographic writings in this period in his book *Medieval Hagiography: An Anthology*. He says that a writer of hagiography on this period intended "both to advance his own salvation and to educate his audience in the proper practice of Christianity."[159] Head, however, also says that "…hagiography can also tell us at least as much about the author and about those who used the text—their ideals and practices, their concerns and aspirations—as it does about the saints who are their subjects. Hagiography provides some of the most valuable records for the reconstruction and study of the practice of pre-modern Christianity."[160] For what it is worth, I agree. The hagiography written in England the late seventh and early eighth centuries is important not only as records of the saint's lives, but also as a record of how transition, continuity and change in Northumbria affected monastic life. It tells us not only how the saints dealt with that transition, but also how the monks who were undergoing similar crises dealt with them. As such these works are highly demonstrative of their author's ideals and opinions in regard to monastic life. Each of the hagiographical works that will be analysed in here[161] were written after the Synod of Whitby and come from that area of Anglo-Saxon England which was most sorely affected by the struggle between Celtic and Roman Christianity. By looking at these *Lives,* I will show how this transition progressed in some of the Northumbrian monasteries, and I will also show how the hagiography written during this crisis placed a special emphasis on Roman Christianity and helped further erode the Celtic traditions.

In extracting these hagiographic materials from a deep and rich mine of extent literature, a main factor to be taken into account was the author himself. The authors were all monks who had either known the saint in question personally, or who had a lively relationship with those who had known the saint. At worse then, the knowledge they have of the saint is only at one remove—

---

[159] Ibid p.xiii.
[160] Loc cit.
[161] *"The lives of the Abbots of Wearmouth and Jarrow"*, by Bede. The anonymous *"Life of Ceolfrith"*, the Life of *Wilfrid*, by Eddius Stephanus, and the *Life of Cuthbert* also by Bede are examples.

whatever they make of that knowledge thereafter. Bede, for example, was placed in the monastery at Wearmouth by his relatives, when he was only seven years old. He immediately came under the care and influence of Benedict Biscop.

Sometime later he removed to Jarrow under the supervision of Ceolfrith.[162] The anonymous author of the *Life of Ceolfrith* is also believed to have been a monk at Wearmouth.[163] Eddius was a monk at Ripon while Wilfrid was still alive, and his firsthand knowledge of some of the events recorded in the *Life of Wilfrid* might lead us to believe that he not only knew Wilfrid but twice accompanied him into exile.[164] As for the *Life of Cuthbert,* Bede did not know Cuthbert personally, but he conducted a "…thorough investigation of the whole of the saint's glorious life, with the help of those who had actually known him."[165] I suspect that this might be a literary conceit, but even if we allow for that it is clear that Bede used existing lives of Cuthbert as a resource and added material of his own to fill in the gaps left by anonymous authors.[166] These four works were also chosen because they offer much clearer evidence as to how monasticism in England developed after the decisions taken at Whitby than others which might have been in contention. They were selected because of their common objective, which was to persuade northern Christians to embrace the Roman Church in preference to the Celtic traditions, since it was affecting critical matters in the church not least of which was how to calculate the date of Easter, acceptable tonsures and the apostolate of bishops.

It is well known that at Whitby the Roman system for dating Easter prevailed over the Celtic system, but that did not bring about a total transition. The Celts put a lot of emphasis on the skill of "*computas*" which was the "compiling of ecclesiastical calendars"[167] the most significant aspect of which was the ability

---

[162] Bede (1994) *The Ecclesiastical History of the English Peoples*" ed Judith McClure and Roger Collins. Oxford. OUP. p293.
[163] Clinton Albertson ed. (1967) *Anglo-Saxon saints and Heroes*. Fordham. Fordham University press. USA. p245.
[164] Ibid p87.
[165] Bede. *Life of Cuthbert* in Farmer and Webb. Op cit.
[166] For more on the resources available to Bede about Cuthbert see Bertram Colgrave (1940) *Two lives of Saint Cuthbert: A Life by an Anonymous Monk of Lindisfarne and Bede's Prose Life,* London. CUP. P3.
[167] Marilyn Dunn. *Emergence of Monasticism – From the Desert Fathers to the Early Middle Ages.* Oxford. Blackwell Publishing. 2003. p153.

to calculate Easter.[168] The between the *computas* of the Celts and the Roman calculation was often a difference of more than one month.[169] In a region like Northumbria, where the two traditions met and clashed, doubt in regard to the "correct" date of Easter led to other uncertainties about monastic and secular life. For example, according to Peter Brown, the date of Easter "…affected the timings of mass baptisms of the newly converted and upset the rhythms of the royal court, where a warrior-king was expected to show his most exuberantly Christian face at the Easter feast."[170] The Celtic monks may have begrudgingly accepted the Roman system, but they were not as easily persuaded to give up their distinctive monastic practices. In the end, certain aspects of the Celtic world managed to prevail throughout Britain and what eventually emerged in the Celtic monasteries was a sort of fusion between the two traditions.[171] An example of this is seen in some of the Celtic art that survives from this period.[172] The hagiography which will concern us here does not, in my view, offer examples to illustrate how much of the Celtic tradition still existed in Anglo-Saxon England, since the hagiographers were far more concerned with writing to put a greater emphasis on the triumph of the church of Rome and the authority of the papacy, while still writing to ensure their own salvation and that of their audience and this, I think, reflects one of the most interesting aspects of monasticism in Britain at the time, namely that it developed on two fronts. In the southern kingdoms, missionaries from Rome (such as Augustine of Canterbury) sent by Pope Gregory the Great, began their efforts in Kent and from there the Roman tradition spread into the nearby regions. In the northern regions, such as Northumbria, it was still the Celtic missionaries from Iona that were most influential.[173] This meant, of course, that two different missionary groups were spreading two distinctly different monastic traditions around Britain. The main differences between the Celtic and Roman traditions stem from the fact that the Roman Empire never managed to reach Ireland which, in turn, makes it almost impossible to determine how, when, or by whom developed monasticism

---

[168] Ibid p154.

[169] Op cit Brown. P361.

[170] Loc cit.

[171] Op cit Farmer & Webb.p15.

[172] Op cit Brown. p 372.

[173] C.H. Lawrence. *Medieval Monasticism* (more bibliographical refs needed) p50.

reached the island.[174] A number of possibilities have been debated. They have been ably reviewed by CH Lawrence in his book *Medieval Monasticism* but as he there makes clear it is not known whether monasticism spread westwards from Britain, northwards from Gaul, or indeed from Eastern Europe.[175] Lawrence argues, however that there is some evidence to show that all three had a greater or lesser influence in Ireland, and it is known that missionaries from Britain and Gaul worked hard to try to evangelise Ireland.[176] Bede tells us about "*English nobles [who] travelled to Ireland to pursue religious studies to lead a life of stricter discipline*"[177] and in the *Anonymous* Life of Ceolfrith, there is a story of Ceolfrith's brother, Cynefrith who went to Ireland precisely because it was the most important centre for Biblical exegesis.[178] Situated in the theological centre of this "spiritual empire which stretched from Ireland along the North-West coast of Scotland as far as the Hebrides, Loch Ness and to the north of the Great Glen of Scotland"[179] was Iona, an island located in the seaways between the northern regions of Ireland and Scotland. In 565, Columba arrived on Iona as a self-imposed exile.[180] Within fifty years of his death, the influence of the monastery had grown beyond anything he might have believed possible, or indeed intended. Iona then had an "unusually extensive spiritual empire" which "stretched from western Scotland deep to the southwest into the heart of Ireland, and to the southeast, it ran throughout northern Britain, through the influence of its sister monastery, Lindisfarne."[181] It was in 635 that a group of monks from Iona, one of which was Aidan, travelled to Northumbria at the request of King Oswald. Oswald granted them land a parcel of land on Lindisfarne on which to build a monastery. The community was governed by the "*regula*" (rule/code/cannon) which Columba had set some seventy years earlier on Iona but, as Dr Jonathan Wooding has pointed out, it is most unlikely that this was the

---

[174] The Romans were almost compulsively obsessed with record keeping, whereas the Celts hardly regarded this as a priority at all.
[175] Op cit Lawrence. p38.
[176] Ibid p38–39.
[177] Op cit. Dunn p152.
[178] Anonymous "Life of Ceolfrith" op cit Albertson.
[179] Op cit Brown. P328.
[180] Ibid p 327.
[181] Ibid p328.

only "rule" by which the Celtic monks lived.[182] Aidan and his fellow monks managed to convert the principal Saxon warlords in the northern kingdoms.[183] This created a favourable environment in which other monasteries were established at Melrose, Gateshead, Hartlepool, Ripon and Lastingham[184] each of which adopted a similar strategy: "…they addressed themselves initially to the court aristocracy, and monastic foundation went forward with the active collaboration of the Northumbrian kings, who provided the landed endowment."[185] Another interesting feature of Celtic monasticism in Britain at this time was the "double monastery". According to CH Lawrence these were the result of "links between the English courts and the women's abbeys in Gaul"[186] and modelled on a similar pattern, a nunnery attached to a monastic community of men and both under the authority of an abbess[187] and almost certainly living according to a mixture of rules,[188] Celtic (such as the so-called *Columban Rule*), pre-Benedictine (such as those of Lerins, perhaps) and the Rule of Benedict itself. The "*Columban Rule*" was developed by a Celtic monk called Columbanus. Columbanus, like Columba, left Ireland to become a self-imposed exile.[189] He settled in northern Gaul and proposed his own "*Monastic Instructions*".[190] As we have already noted the most important of these "double monasteries" in England in the generation before that of Bede was at Whitby, governed by Abbess Hilda. Hilda was also Abbess of Hartlepool, and had been a pupil of Aidan. Whitby was, therefore, a double monastery of the Celtic tradition. Whitby's importance to Christianity in Anglo-Saxon England is apparent in the fact that King Oswy chose it as the place of the Synod of 664.[191]

---

[182] Dr J Wodding: "*Celtic monasticism: a pre-Benedictine way?* An unpublished paper given at the Fourth Annual MONOS conference. Douai Abbey. July 2010.

[183] While this is sometimes portrayed as evidence of the persuasive power of the Gospel and of Aidan's preaching it is surely also evidence of Oswald's astute use of a combination of religion and politics to extend his sway over the warlords and subdue any thoughts of possible rebellion against him.

[184] Op cit Lawrence p 51.

[185] Loc cit.

[186] Ibid p 52.

[187] Hilda of Whitby was an abbess of the "double monastery" there.

[188] Op cit Wooding.

[189] Op cit Brown. P247.

[190] Ibid p 249.

[191] Op cit Lawrence p52–53.

He clearly understood it to be a place where external gestures and matters were just as important as spoken loyalties for both monks and lay folk alike. In addition to the correct dating of Easter, the other main point at issue revolved around the difference between the Celtic and Roman tonsure. At this time, the way a person's hair was cut indicated his social status, class and identity. At a glance, it was possible to distinguish a lay person from a monk or a cleric, or a warrior from a farmer, a civilised "Roman" from a barbarian.[192] The Roman tonsure was cut to resemble Christ's crown of thorns at the passion, whereas the Celtic tonsure merely indicated that the monk had renounced his membership of the warrior class.[193] So instead of cutting the hair on the top of the head Celtic monks shaved "the front half [of their head] for ear to ear."[194] The reason that this became such an important issue at Whitby was that "…the precise nature of visible gestures and the precise timing of festivals spoke volumes. Conflicts over fully visible practices counted for far more than any conflict of ideas."[195] In conclusion then, we can say that the Synod of Whitby was far more than a declaration over which tradition, Celtic or Roman, represented the "true faith" and although the dating of Easter was important the Synod deserves to be remembered as being far more important than that, crucial though that issue was too. The Synod was the result of an enduring dispute concerning customs in an area divided by two dominating loyalties, the saints of Ireland on the one hand and St Peter and the martyrs of Rome on the other. The decisions made here changed the face of monasticism not in Anglo-Saxon England, but the whole course and direction it would take in Britain in future.

When the Roman tradition became the "one true faith", the one true monasticism, measures were taken to cement the influence of Rome in the hearts and minds of people in northern Britain after 664 and to eradicate as far as possible any trace of Celtic approaches. The larger presence and influence of Rome in northern Britain after 664 is, I think, undeniable, but the extent of that power is another subject of debate altogether, especially since the transition, challenge and change was gradual and was often met with opposition by those

---

[192] Op cit Brown p361.

[193] Ibid p360. This raises an interesting question to which, I think, Brown does not give an extended answer, namely was admission to Celtic monasticism only open to the warrior class, and if so, why?

[194] Op cit Albertson p42.

[195] Op cit Brown p 360–361.

who remained loyal to the non-Roman practice and customs. As Dunn has persuasively argued, it was the Irish in Northumbria who, for the most part, strove to conform to Rome after Whitby—but it was not until very much later that Iona would agree to conform as well.[196] The hagiography written in the late seventh and early eighth centuries offers a glimpse into these struggles and decisions which all monastic communities in Britain had to face head on. Two of the leading monastic figures during this transition and change were Benedict Biscop and Wilfrid of York. Both had their own agendas and methods for obtaining the goal of a universal conformity to Roman authority, but whereas Benedict Biscop was willing to find ways of making the Roman tradition more acceptable to those who had followed the Celtic ways Wilfrid took a more aggressive stance against Celtic monastic ideals. Two different approaches for the same objective, but both, along with the other *Lives,* reveal some of the progress made during this period of transition in the monastic life of Britain and it is to this we now turn in the next chapter.

---

[196] Op cit Dunn p154.

Chapter 8
Monasticism in Britain Before the Conquest
(2) Lives of the Saints

Much of the Anglo-Saxon hagiography that survives came predominately from the ancient Kingdom of Northumbria, and these *Lives* recount those who were influenced by as well as those who helped influence monasticism in Britain after the Roman traditions were recognised as the "one true faith". At this time, northern Britain was experiencing a change that held both religious and cultural significance, and each of the Lives selected for this chapter deal with people who helped establish Roman authority. With the possible exception of Wilfrid of York, there seems to have been a conscious effort to make Roman tradition more acceptable to those who maintained the Celtic ways and Celtic monasticism. An interesting aspect of Anglo-Saxon hagiography is that it outlines the discord and fusion of these two traditions.[197] In addition to the hagiographies that will be considered here, there is another important source of information on the transitions and changes to monastic life at this time, namely the works of the Venerable Bede which are by no means confined to his well-known *Ecclesiastical History of the English Peoples*. Bede entered the monastery at Jarrow at a very young age and it is there that he was taught and inspired by some of the most important monastic thinkers of his day, especially Ceolfrith.[198] Benedict Biscop was another influence on Bede but he was often travelling back and forth to Rome and other places on the continent, while Ceolfrith tended for the most part to remain in Jarrow. The influence of both Biscop and Ceolfrith is less pronounced in the *Ecclesiastic History* than it is in some of his other writings

---

[197] D.H. Farmer, J.F. Webb (1965) *The Age of Bede*. London. Penguin Group p14.
[198] Bede: *Lives of the Abbots of Wearmoth-Jarrow* in *Anglo-Saxon Saints and Heroes*. Ed. Clinton Albertson SJ. Fordham. Fordham University Press. p223.

which will concern us here such as his *Lives of Abbots of Wearmoth-Jarrow*. The *Lives of the Abbots of Wearmouth-Jarrow* is a most important work because it was written by a monk who was an eye-witness to some of the events that happened in the lives of Biscop and Ceolfrith and so is a commentary on the debates which lay at the heart of the transitions and changes which beset monastic life in Britain at this time. A recurring theme in Anglo-Saxon hagiography which helped to establish Roman domination is its emphasis on a devotion to the Apostles to the saints and martyrs of Rome, and the primacy of St Peter as the first Pope.[199] This emphasis reduced the importance of other central figures in Christianity such as the Blessed Virgin Mary. Mary, though important in her role as the Mother of God, seems to have been otherwise somewhat sidelined in Anglo-Saxon monasticism. If this is an exaggeration, then it is certainly clear that Mary was no more and no less important than the Apostles. This is most apparent, for example in the *Life of Wilfrid* in which the Archangel Michael appears to Wilfrid in a dream to comfort him in his illness: "I am Michael, the herald of the most high God, who has sent me to tell you that years have been added to your life because of holy Mary, God's mother virgin, who has interceded for you, and the tearful prayers of your people have reached the ears of the Lord. This will be a sign for you that from this hour your health will grow better day by day until you reach your homeland. And all those things that are most dear to you shall be yours again, and you shall furnish your life in peace. But you must also be ready, four, after the space of four years, I will visit you again. And now call to mind how you have erected churches in honour of St Peter and St Andrew, but for holy Virgin Mary who is interceding for you, you have built nothing at all. You must put this right and dedicate a church in her honour."[200] Benedict Biscop built a church inside the monastery at Wearmouth which he dedicated to the Blessed Virgin Mary[201] and from one of his visits to Rome brought back an icon of the of the Mother of God which he placed in a church dedicated to St Peter.[202] These are, however, the only references to his dedicating anything to Mary. Thomas Head has claimed that "literary expression of the legend about the Virgin's life and her miraculous powers tended to be

---

[199] A concept derived from a particular reading and interpretation of Mtt: 16:18-19.
[200] Op cit Albertson SJ. p15–152.
[201] Op cit Bede p 235.
[202] Ibid p231.

restricted, in the west at least, to the liturgy until the twelfth century."[203] This assessment seems to be true of seventh-century Anglo-Saxon hagiography, despite the facts that the cult of the Virgin Mary "was the oldest in Christendom" and that the "*Ave Maria* was one of the best-known Latin prayers among the laity." Feast days to Mary were, of course, an important part of the calendar but it was usually to the Roman saints that the monks turned for guidance.[204] All of this is of a piece with the emphasis on the Roman aspects of Christianity after the decisions of the Synod of Whitby in 664. Monastic leaders who displayed a personal commitment towards a particular Roman saint were doing far more than showing love and devotion. It was a political statement too. Whether they were consciously aware of it (but how could they not be?) This sort of private devotion stressed the importance of the ultimate authority of the See of Rome over any other possible influence or power, particularly Celtic.

Bede: Lives of the Abbots of Wearmouth-Jarrow

Bede's *Lives of the Abbots of Wearmouth—Jarrow* follows the lives of Benedict Biscop and Ceolfrith, the founding fathers of these two monasteries, who were two of the most influential abbots in the whole of Britain at the time. The majority of *Lives of the Abbots* deals with the life of Biscop since he was the principal founding father. It is only in the last few chapters that Bede turns his attention to Ceolfrith, so for the purposes of this chapter we too will concentrate mainly on Biscop. The next section will deal more explicitly with Ceolfrith's life and work for it is there that the Anonymous Life of Ceolfrith will be analysed. Thus, the last few chapters of Bede's *Lives of the Abbots* will be disregarded in favour of this other life of Ceolfrith.

Bede says that Biscop was a "devout servant of God"[205] who at the age of twenty-five left England to travel to Rome in order to fulfil his long-held desire to "see with his bodily eye the shrines of the bodies of the Blessed Apostles and pray in their presence. Then from the moment he returned home he never avoided an occasion for speaking enthusiastically, to all who would listen, about the various forms of religious life which he had seen and which he so loved and

---

[203] Thomas Head (2001) *Medieval Hagiography: an anthology*. New York and London Routledge. p xxi.
[204] Loc cit.
[205] Op cit Bede p 225.

reverenced."[206] In 665, after returning from Rome for a second time, Biscop went to monastery at Lerins in Gaul. By this time, the monastery at Lerins had become a leader in monastic education and its "Rule" was widely used. At Lerins, Biscop "joined the community of monks, received the tonsure, took the distinguished vow of a monk, and followed the regular discipline with all due earnestness. After two years of instruction in the proper principles of the monastic life, he was overcome again by his love for Peter, prince of the Apostles."[207] These words clearly emphasise a Roman bias: Biscop receives the tonsure;[208] he took vows,[209] followed the discipline of the Rules of Lerin and developed his devotion to Peter, the prince of the Apostles.[210] By 668, Biscop had been consecrated bishop. Shortly thereafter, the Pope asked him to return to Northumbria. The Pope "bade him in the interests of a greater good to give up the pilgrimage for Christ that he had undertaken and return to his country so that he could bring with him the master of truth whom he had been seeking so diligently, and for whom he could serve as an interpreter and guide not only on the journey to Britain but after he had settled down there to teach."[211] According to Bede, the Pope demanded this of Biscop because he saw in him a "man of wisdom, industry, *piety* and nobility of soul"[212] and because he had spent many years studying Roman values. Biscop's mission then was to enrich England both ecclesiastically *and* culturally[213] something which the Pope though possible to accomplish in view of Biscop's status as a Northumbria nobleman. Biscop did as the Pope had asked but within two years he was on his travels to Rome once more. On his return, he met and befriended Ecgfrith, king of Northumbria. The king became intrigued by Biscop's travelogues because Biscop "could not conceal the religious zeal which consumed him; he disclosed all that he had learnt about ecclesiastical and monastic Useage in Rome and elsewhere; he displayed how many sacred volumes, how many relics of the Blessed Apostles

---

Ibid p226.

[207] Ibid p 228.

[208] For the differences between the Celtic and Roman tonsure see the last chapter.

[209] Those required of monks following the Rules of Lerins.

[210] Prince of the Apostles which saw the risen Christ and of those who followed him as Pope.

[211] Op cit Bede p 228.

[212] Loc cit.

[213] Op cit Farmer & Webb. P29.

and martyrs he had brought back."[214] Ecgfrith was so impressed by all this that he gave Biscop seventy hides of land on which to build a monastery dedicated to St Peter. The monastery was built close to the mouth of the River Wear in 674.[215] Then, around 681, Ecgfrith awarded more grants of land and on this latest gift the monastery dedicated to St Paul at Jarrow was built.[216] Ecgfrith attached only one condition to this second grant of land, but it was one of great importance namely that there "always be preserved between the two monasteries a common peace and harmony, a common family spirit and love."[217] Wearmouth and Jarrow were to remain "united in the fraternal companionship of the first to Apostles"[218] Bede himself was no less devoted to Roman saints, especially St Peter, than was Biscop himself. This is demonstrated by the way he wrote in *Lives* about Biscop's love of the Apostle. It may be then that what we have here is a "reading in", a transference of Bede's devotion to the greater man Biscop. An instance of this might be where, in the fifth chapter, Bede addresses himself to the construction of the abbey at Wearmouth and says that it was as a direct result of Biscop's love of St Peter that it was built so quickly.[219] The possibility of "reading in" becomes greater when we recall that Bede lived at Jarrow while Biscop was still alive and moreover is likely to have been taught by him. It is logical assume therefore that at the very least Bede caught something of Biscop's zeal and enthusiasm for Peter. It is also interesting that Bede says that Ecgfrith wanted the monasteries at Wearmouth and Jarrow to be dedicated to Peter and Paul respectively. Howbeit that as king of Northumbria there might have been many other local saints to attract his attention and compete for this honour. At all events, it is another example of the push to establish European, Roman, practices over anything that might be regarded as local and Celtic.

---

[214] Op cit Bede p 229.
[215] Loc cit.
[216] Ibid p 232.
[217] Loc cit.
[218] Loc cit. This is either naive or ironic because of course there was very little "fraternal companionship" between Peter and Paul. I should make clear that today Wearmouth is known as Monkswearmouth, but that for the purposes of this Chapter I have decided to use the original name as found in the hagiographies we are considering.
[219] Loc cit.

Ceolfrith was appointed Abbot of Jarrow, while Biscop's cousin Eastorwine, was chosen as joint abbot with Biscop at Wearmouth.[220] Bede says that it is not a requirement that a monastery be ruled by two joint abbots but that in the case of Wearmouth it was regarded as being especially beneficial. For example, having an additional abbot enabled Biscop to "bear more easily the burden which he had not been able to sustain alone. Nor should anyone think it out of place for one monastery to have more than one abbot at the same time. It was demanded by Benedict's [Biscop] frequent absence from the monastery, his constant setting out across the sea and the uncertainty of his return."[221] It was while Biscop was away on one of his adventures that disaster struck in the form of plague.[222] Eastorwine died and Sigefrith was appointed abbot instead even though he was still only a deacon. Upon his return, Biscop accepted Sigefrith's position as his partner in authority because he "was a man well trained in the knowledge of the Scripture, graced with the finest qualities of character and possessed of a wonderful power of self-control."[223] Soon both Biscop and Sigefrith became ill, though not from plague. They both suffered from his mysterious illness for years before death finally claimed them, but their illness did not prevent them from instructing and guiding their monks. Biscop began to develop a particular view about the distinctiveness of being a monk of Wearmouth—Jarrow which was that they should learn form and practice something of every monastery he had ever visited, and put in place procedures for the election of future abbots: "You must not think that this institute which I drew up for you was simply the impulsive voice of my heart, without any study having gone into it. What I have passed on to you to be observed to your own benefit, is nothing but a compilation of all the practices I have learnt from the seventeen monasteries, that, in the course of my frequent journeys abroad, I have found were the best."[224] These words are significant because they suggest I think that Biscop may have developed his own monastic "Rule" for the monks of Wearmouth—Jarrow. If so, it did not survive. These words are also intriguing because they show a willingness to teach and accept something *other than* strict Roman monastic discipline. If he was indeed compiling the best of what he had learnt on his

---

[220] Ibid p 232–233.
[221] Ibid p 233.
[222] Ibid p 236.
[223] Ibid p236–237.
[224] Ibid p 237.

travels, then he was teaching something in addition to and different from that which he had learnt at Lerins. Biscop was educated in and supportive of the Roman tradition of Christianity, but he also seems to have been a unique individual who recognised the need to make the transition from Celtic to Roman more acceptable.

He, therefore, acquainted himself with the organisation and management of other monasteries and discovered what was working at these monasteries and what was not. He was quite eclectic about taking the best practices from each monastery and incorporated them into what he knew about Roman monasticism in its Benedictine forms.

In the matter of the future election of Abbotts, Biscop's instructions were that both monasteries should elect one abbot with responsibility for the two houses. The monks were instructed to elect a new abbot according to what they knew *and* the Rule of St Benedict. By implementing the Benedictine Rule, the possibility of the succession becoming a matter of heredity was eliminated. Biscop was obviously adamant about this particular instruction because he worked very hard to prevent the accession of his brother to the abbot's throne:

"I tell you truly, in comparing two evils, if God should decide that all this property on which I have built this monastery should be turned back into the wilderness forever, I would find it much easier to bear than if my brother of the flesh, who we know walks in the way of truth, should succeed me as abbot and rule this monastery. Therefore, always be very careful, my brothers, never to seek a father for yourselves on the principle of who his family is, and never seek an outsider."

"But according to the prescriptions of that great Abbot Benedict of former days, and according to the prescriptions of our own privilege, look for whoever shall be approved by common consent at a meeting of your community as the most capable and worthy by his virtuous life and wise teaching to fill such an office, and for whomever you all shall unanimously and knowingly have selected as the best in an election conducted by all in charity. Then you will summon the bishop and ask that this man be confirmed as your abbot by the usual blessing."[225] Biscop's legacy to his houses was that he made the adoption of Roman monasticism a little easier for his fellow monks to accept. Other monastic leaders were not so fortunate. Cuthbert, for example, met with great opposition on

---

[225] Op cit Bede p238–239.

Lindisfarne and Ceolfrith had greatest difficulty when he ruled Wearmouth—Jarrow after Biscop's death. Perhaps then the smooth transition to Roman monasticism was as much a matter of personality as it was of policy. At all events, Biscop's travels were extremely valuable to the cenobitic life of his communities.

While he was travelling, he was learning more about the nature of monasticism and how, if at all, it could be fused with the prevailing culture and organisation in Northumbria, while other leaders stayed in their monasteries and could not acquire his depth of knowledge or skill at adaptation. Biscop's travels are at the more surprising since wandering monks were regarded as the very worst kind and are explicitly condemned in the opening verses of the Benedictine Rule. Indeed, whereas such journeys may have been encouraged as an act of devotion on the part of every Christian few could have embarked on such a journey far less complete it as many times as Biscop did.

By writing Biscop's story Bede[226] set the standard according to which all other hagiographical writings of the period might be judged.

The Anonymous Life of St Ceolfrith, Abbot of Jarrow

Biscop died in 689 and was succeeded by Ceolfrith who was in charge of both monasteries.[227] The author of the Life of Ceolfrith says that he was "the kind of man whose life of devotion to God should fitly be followed, not only in its ending but also in its beginning and in its whole intervening course, and whose unfeigned faith should be copied for its constancy."[228] Immediately before this statement the author addresses his "dearest brethren", which indicates that one of his chief purposes in writing the *Life* was to specifically instruct his fellow monks in the Roman practices of Christianity. Like Biscop, Ceolfrith was born into a noble family. Like Biscop too he and his family had strong links to the court and retinue of King Oswy. One of the many differences between Biscop and Ceolfrith is that Ceolfrith longed to be a monk from a very early age and, unlike Bicsop, spent no time as a member of Oswy's court.[229] Ceolfrith first entered the monastic life at Gilling, which was ruled by his "brother of the flesh",

---

[226] Op cit head. p xxi.
[227] Op cit Farmer & Webb. p32.
[228] Op cit Albertson SJ p247.
[229] Loc cit.

Cynefrith. The author says that Cynefrith was also "a devout man of God" even though he had been "lured away to Ireland."[230] This indicates that Cynefrith had some firsthand knowledge of the Celtic method of studying Scripture and their strange form of Latin. The author says that Cynefrith was motivated to go to Ireland because of "his strong attraction to the study of Scripture and partly by his desire to serve the Lord in a freer manner with more opportunity for prayer and affectionate devotion."[231] The only other mention of Cynefrith is in connection with his untimely death. It cannot be determined whether this is a literary ploy used by the author as a scare tactic against others who might be tempted to be "lured" to Ireland and the Celts (contact with the Celts causes death) or simply used as a way of discouraging others from making the journey. The physical and religious space left by Cynefrith is in any event a useful device for it allows the author to bring Ceolfrith to the foreground, devoutly pursuing a pure monastic life "giving himself with enthusiasm to the reading and the working and the discipline in all things", but his brother and "others of the Anglican nobility who had gone to Ireland to study Scripture departed for eternal life by the brief passageway of death."[232] While this time, the departure to Ireland is not an explicit death threat, it does not exactly convey a trip to Ireland as being a pilgrimage that would be beneficial to a person's physical and spiritual health!Ceolfrith moved to the monastery at Ripon after he accepted an invitation from its newly appointed Abbot and Bishop, Wilfrid. At Ripon, Ceolfrith "settled into the regular life of the Rule, and after the proper time had passed was chosen for the priesthood."[233] Shortly after 669, at the age of twenty-seven, he travelled to Kent to "satisfy his desire for the fullest possible understanding of the Rules of monastic life and of the priesthood which he had undertaken."[234] He also travelled to East Anglia to learn what he could from Abbot Botulf, a man who was reputed to have an "exceptional life and teaching and a man filled with the

---

[230] Ibid p 248.

[231] Loc cit. My emphasis added because these words are extremely interesting and quite counter intuitive. Indeed, part of the "triumph" of Roman monastic practice over that of the Celts was precisely because it—and not the Celtic way—which provided the very opportunities which Cynefrith sought.

[232] Loc cit.

[233] Loc cit.

[234] Loc cit.

grace of the Holy Spirit."[235] On his return to Ripon, Ceolfrith was regarded as the most educated man in ecclesiastical matters and the keeping of a monastic rule.[236] The author also says that Ceolfrith "could not be enticed away from his humble attitude of mind either by consideration of his state of life, or of his learning, or of his noble name. On the contrary, he endeavoured to make himself subject in everything to the observance of the Rule."[237] Humility, knowledge, nobility and obedience are all good characteristics of a man looking forward to leading others in their monastic lives. It was, therefore, not long before Benedict Biscop himself had "become aware of Ceolfrith's gifts of learning, piety, and devoted application to work.[238] Biscop then asked Wilfrid to allow Ceolfrith to leave Ripon and assist in the foundation of the monastery at Wearmouth. At this point the author makes it clear that although Biscop was seeking Coelfrith's assistance, Biscop still outshone him in knowledge of monasticism.[239] The author illustrates this by reference to the relationship between Moses and Aaron. Even though Moses was chosen by God to lead the people of Israel out of the bondage of Egypt and towards the Promised Land, he still required the assistance of Aaron. In this way, Moses could accomplish a task whose enormous weight of responsibility he might well have feared to bear alone.[240] Biscop, a second Moses, needed the help of the second Aaron, Ceolfrith because "even though he was most learned in all matters of monastic discipline, yet in establishing his monastery he sought the help of Ceolfrith who could strengthen the observance of the monastic life by a devotion to the study of religious teaching equal to Benedict [Biscop] own, and could help with the service of the altar since he was in priestly orders."[241] In the second year of Wearmouth, Biscop left Ceolfrith in charge while he travelled to see his friend, Abbot Torthelem in Gaul. Torthelm had contacts with the building trade and specifically those who knew how to construct stone churches. In Biscop's absence Ceolfrith met great opposition from the community. They did not like or agree with his teaching methods to the

---

[235] Loc cit.

[236] Loc cit.

[237] Loc cit.

[238] Ibid p 250.

[239] Ibid p251.

[240] Loc cit. This is interesting. Is the author suggesting that adherence to the Celtic tradition was a form of spiritual bondage?

[241] Loc cit.

extent that "the office of Prior was becoming a burden for Ceolfrith, and the freedom of the quiet monastic life began to appeal to him far more than the responsibility of the ruling of others."[242] The "quiet monastic life" was that of the Rule of St Benedict which he had learnt at the hands of Wilfrid in Ripon. Wilfrid, as his *Life* indicates, was a man of strict Roman principles making little allowance for anything Celtic in Christianity. Ceolfrith, therefore, was at this time also strictly Roman and, coming from Wilfrid's monastery at Ripon was one of the first Benedictines in Northumbria. In short, Ceolfrith went from Ripon, a Roman monastery, to a monastery that housed former Celtic monks who were resentful of all attempts to force them to adopt Roman (Benedictine) practices. The decisions of the Synod of Whitby were still fresh, being barely twelve years old, and at this point the monastery at Wearmouth was only in its second year. It is highly likely, therefore, that at least some of the monks at Wearmouth had previously been Celtic monks. While Biscop was trained in the Roman tradition and tolerant of Celtic Christianity, he could not have foreseen the degree of difficulty that Ceolfrith had in disciplining the monks of Wearmouth in the proper instruction. This difficulty proved to be so great that, eventually, it would leave him little alternative but to return to Ripon—a departure which, years later, the community mourned.[243] Clearly, he could not command the same respect, and love, as Biscop.[244] The significance of this part of Ceolfrith's story is that it offers an example of the difficult transition the Kingdom of Northumbria faced when it tried to universally impose the Roman model of monastic life. It is apparent that Ceolfrith's education severely contrasted with that of the monks of Wearmouth, and even though the author of this *Life* does not explicitly say to which discipline the monks originally belonged, it is reasonable to assume that it was the Celtic tradition since the author speaks very eloquently against it in a previous chapter. It is also important to note the authors seething anger against the monks of Wearmouth who made Ceolfrith's life so difficult. His words are very expressive of how high tensions could rise during this period of transition.[245] So Ceolfrith returned to Ripon and it took great skill of negotiation and persuasion on the part of Biscop to convince him to return to Wearmouth. The author says that "when Benedict [Biscop]

---

[242] Loc cit.
[243] Ibid p 260.
[244] Ibid p 251–252.
[245] ibid p252.

followed and pleaded with him to come back, Ceolfrith gave in to his loving entreaties and returned to carry out sedulously the duties which he had undertaken with Benedict [Biscop], of establishing the monastery and putting it in order."[246] Ceolfrith did not desire the power or recognition that his new position of abbot granted him, but he accepted it out of the duty of obedience.[247] He still preferred the quite life of contemplation and prayer. We might see in this a parallel between Ceolfrith and Pope Gregory the Great. Formerly a monk, Pope Gregory would have preferred to continue to live inside the monastery rather than becoming the Apostolic Father.[248] He was an "intellectual who had accepted authority reluctantly and as a duty and strove, as best he could, to maintain the joys of the contemplative life while fulfilling the obligations of his office."[249] In this respect, Ceolfrith was not unlike Gregory, and it is not too demanding on the imagination to suppose that the author intended to draw a correlation between the two men so that if Biscop was a second Moses, Ceolfrith (not having proved to be an Aaron after all) could be seen as a second, English, Gregory. It was not long before the abbey church was completed and dedicated to St Peter after which Biscop made plans for yet another foreign journey. This time, however, Ceolfrith joined him on his travels, which meant that they had to leave the monastery under the rule of another, Eastorwine. The main purpose of this journey was that Biscop wanted to get "instructors in the use of the Roman rite who could teach the proper methods of chanting and conducting services in the church he had just founded."[250] This too is important because it shows that Biscop wanted to make sure that his monastery was teaching the "proper" discipline and that he wanted every member of the community to embrace the same tradition. Since the anonymous author never specifies from when the monks of Wearmouth were drawn, it is safe to say that they varied in age and experience and not all of them could have been new to the monastic life. The matter that was most important to Biscop and Ceolfrith was that *all* the monks at

---

[246] Loc cit.

[247] Though one might think that to be appointed (joint) Abbot would surely only serve to worsen relationships between Ceolfrith and the brethren.

[248] See Marilyn Dunn, *Emergence of Monasticism* p133–134.

[249] Richard Ables (1998) *Alfred the Great: War, Kingship and Culture in Anglo-Saxon England*. London and New York. Longman. p 237.

[250] Op cit *Life of Ceolfrith* p252.

Wearmouth needed to be schooled in the Roman instruction whether they had recently received the tonsure of St Peter, or not.

Most attempts to create a monastery in which Celtic and Roman traditions could live happily together had previously failed. Biscop and Ceolfrith would not have wanted to repeat the same experiment. Maintaining a monastery that housed both Celtic and Roman disciplined monks could, especially after the decisions of the Synod of Whitby, only lead to disharmony between the two. In his *Ecclesiastical History,* the Venerable Bede reported that one of the main reasons for discord among the monks at Bishop Colman's joint monastery at Inishbofin was that the Celtic monks "insisted on heading for far places in the summertime while their outraged Anglo-Saxon brethren were left to harvest the crops, which the Irish insisted on sharing when they returned in the winter."[251] With this sort of practical dispute, the potential for disagreement as to monastic discipline and liturgical practice would have even greater. Thus, Biscop and Ceolfrith settled on the view that it was better to have a monastery which embraced only one tradition—specifically that of Rome. It seems that on this particular trip, Biscop and Ceolfrith found that everything went according to plan.[252] They both "learnt much in Rome about the discipline of the church, and they brought back with them to Britain the architecture of the Roman church. John, abbot of the monastery of the Blessed Martin…instructed…fully, both orally and by his writings, in the method of chanting according to the proper rite."[253] Two points which arise from this. First, Biscop was able to persuade Abbot John to return with them to Wearmouth and instruct the community in Gregorian chant.[254] Second, Abbot John was from the monastery of St Martin de Tour. The fourth century *Life of St Martin de Tour* was a key text that helped to establish monasticism in the western provinces (including Gaul, and perhaps Britain) of the Roman Empire. It seems only fitting, then, that an abbot from the monastery dedicated to St Martin would be used to establish the Roman tradition as the proper liturgical instruction in the monastic life. In or around 681 King Ecgfrith granted the land on which the monastery at Jarrow could be built and it was to Jarrow that Ceolfrith removed to establish the hi=use with some twenty-two brothers from Wearmouth, "ten tonsured and twelve still waiting the grace

---

[251] Op cit Albertson SJ p252 and Bede *Ecclesiastical History*. P179.
[252] Op cit *Life of Ceolfrith*. p253.
[253] Ibid p 53.
[254] Gregorian chant differed greatly from the style of the Celts. Op cit Albertson. P253.

of tonsure"[255]—so some were still waiting to be finally accepted into the monastic life. As we noted in the last chapter, tonsure was more than an expression of faith. Receiving it was mandatory and was "prescribed by Canon Law in the very early Christian times; it was imperative for all clerics to be tonsured, and this was very solemnly done before ordination by a bishop in the case of the (secular) clergy, an abbot performing the same ceremony for a monk entering a monastery."[256] In Jarrow, Ceolfrith found it much easier to persuade the monks to accept the discipline he presented to them.[257] That more than half of them were still exploring their vocation may be one possible explanation of this and, after all, during the long journey to and from Rome Ceolfrith had plenty of opportunity to watch Biscop's teaching methods and may well have decided to adopt them. The smooth transition might also have been due to the influence of Abbot John. Whatever the precise reason, the anonymous author makes it clear that at Jarrow Ceolfrith decided to "…observe the very same discipline of the regular rule, and all the same canonical procedures of chanting and reading which they had followed in the first monastery, even though at the moment not all of those by any means who had come knew how to sing psalms, or much less how to read in church, or how to say prayers or antiphons or the responsorial. But they were aided by their love of the religious life and by the example and wise persistence of their earnest superior. For while, they were in the process of planting in the deep root of the monastic life, he made it a practice to visit the church while the brothers were there, often during all the canonical hours, and to take his meals and his rest with them. So that if there was anything that needed correction or if anything had to be taught to the novices, he could do it personally."[258] Ceolfrith's decision to live in common with the brethren seems to have been an important part of his instructing others in the Roman tradition, and the anonymous author seems to be offering Ceolfrith's example to other abbots as a means to help the make the transition to Rome much easier.

---

[255] Op cit Life of Ceolfrith. p253.

[256] Herbert Norris (1950) *Church Vestments: Their Origin and Development*. New York. E.P. Dutton & Co inc. p180.

[257] This raises an interesting question: Did Ceolfrith personally choose the twenty–two from Wearmouth before he set out? At all events it seems very unlikely that they would have agreed to establish a new monastery at Jarrow under Ceolfrith's leadership if they had been resistant to him.

[258] Op cit *Life of Ceolfrith* p 254.

On his death bed, Biscop named Ceolfrith as his successor at *both* Wearmouth and Jarrow.[259] It was clearly a means of preventing his biological brother succeeding him—something which, according to Bede, he most hated. But the anonymous author goes further than Bede and suggests that it was a means of uniting the two houses: "And he decreed that there should be but one monastery in all things, even though situated in two places, and that it should be governed always by one abbot, and guarded by the protection of same privilege which he had received from Pope Agatho and by the rule of our holy father Benedict [of Nursia], an Abbott was never to be sought for the monastery on the grounds of family descent but on the grounds of his manner of life and his devotedness to teaching."[260] This version of Biscop's last request is similar to Bede's version in the *Lives of the Abbots*[261] since both say that an abbot should be selected according to the Benedictine Rule. The anonymous author of the *Life of Ceolfrith*, however, also states that all future abbots should obtain final approval from the Pope, so that the monastery would be assured of the papacy's protection. This indicates that both Biscop and Ceolfrith were successful in establishing two distinctly Roman monasteries in Northumbria in the quarter-century after the Synod of Whitby. Ceolfrith led both monasteries as one for a further twenty-seven years before he decided to retire. He longed to spend the remainder of his days in a more contemplative life by living "as a pilgrim in the home of the Apostles."[262] In parting for his final journey to Rome, Ceolfrith told the monks to "keep the Rule he had taught them."[263] He also told them that it was important to remember that "both Wearmouth and Jarrow are one monastery and must always be ruled by the same abbot lest the inner bond of brotherhood should be sundered."[264] Ceolfrith, like Biscop, in his final message wanted the monks to realise the importance of the monastic Rule they had been taught. Biscop may have made a few adjustments to make the transition a little easier[265] but both, Bede in his *Lives of the Abbots* and the anonymous author of the *Life*

---

[259] In direct contradiction to his previous insistence on election according to the precepts laid down in the Rule of St Benedict.
[260] Op cit *Life of Ceolfrith*. p256.
[261] Op cit Bede p 238–239.
[262] Op cit *Life of Ceolfrith*. p259.
[263] Ibid p260.
[264] Ibid p262.
[265] Op cit Bede *Lives of the Abbots* p237.

of Ceolfrith were keen to point out that the life of the monks of Wearmouth-Jarrow was at least *partly* governed by the Rule of St Benedict.

Life of Wilfrid by Eddius Stephanus

The Life of Wilfrid is unique in that Eddius Stephanus wrote it in defence of the Roman traditions as well as in defence of Wilfrid to his enemies. It is likely that Eddius, like Ceolfrith, studied under Wilfrid for he too was a monk at Ripon.[266] This might explain why Eddius was so keen to portray Wilfrid as entirely innocent of the claims made against him. In the seventh century, Wilfrid of York had accumulated vast land holdings and wealth and exercised a great personal as well as ecclesiastical authority over them. As Wilfrid's power and influence increased, so did the number of his enemies who resented Wilfrid and his prominence. For Eddius, however, Wilfrid was a man innocent of any wrongdoing, and the *Life of Wilfrid* is the story of an innocent and virtuous man—even a Christ-like figure—hounded by his enemies and attempting to prevent his mission to convert the pagans and make a transition to the establishment of the Roman Christian tradition in the north of England. If it is an exaggeration to say that Eddius compares Wilfrid to Christ, there is no doubt that he does compare him to the Apostles, Peter, James, Andrew and Paul and uses their words from the New Testament to describe Wilfrid's life and character. For example, as a boy Wilfrid is said to be "obedient to his parents, beloved by all, handsome, well proportioned, gentle, modest and controlled, with none of the silly fads common to boys but, as the Apostle James says swift to hear but slow to speak."[267] Also, when Wilfrid was considered worthy of holding Episcopal office it was said that he met each of the Pauline criteria perfectly. According to Eddius, it was the "councillors of the realm" who said: "We know him to be such as the Apostle Paul describes to Titus." For a Bishop must be without crime, as the steward of God: not proud, not angry, not given to wine, no striker, not greedy of filthy lucre—but given to hospitality, gentle sober, just, continent, embracing the faithful word which is according to doctrine, that he may be able to exhort in sound doctrine and convince the gainsayers, he has every quality Paul thinks

---

[266] Op cit Albertson SJ p 87.
[267] Eddius Stephanus (1965) 'Life of Wilfrid' in *The Age of Bede* trns. J.F. Webb London Penguin Group p107.

necessary."[268] This style of writing is clearly a literary device by which to cement Wilfrid's praiseworthiness, but it was also used to encourage the Roman tradition. If Wilfrid could be shown to live by the laws and words of Christ's Apostles, it was logical that others should follow his example, and this example placed precedence on the Roman tradition. It was not uncommon for Anglo-Saxon hagiographers to use this method, but Eddius made such references throughout his *Life*.

In addition to comparing Wilfrid to the Apostles, Eddius also compares him to other Biblical figures and events. For example, whereas the anonymous author of the Life of Ceolfrith compared the relationship between Biscop and Ceolfith to that between Moses and Aaron, Eddius uses Biblical references to as more than a "helpful "comparison. His continual use of the words "just as" and "like" when referring to the Biblical text are deliberately intended to suggest to the reader that Wilfrid lived his life in parallel to Scripture—even (like, Jeremiah, Christ and St John the Baptist) before he was born. For example:

"A sign from God proved that he was sanctified while still in the womb of his pious mother, just as clearly as when he announced to Jeremiah: 'before I formed thee in the womb I knew thee; and before thou camest out of the womb I sanctified thee and I ordained thee to be a prophet unto the nations.'"[269] Another example is after Wilfrid witnessed the death of his mentor the Archbishop of Lyons. Wilfrid was prepared to sacrifice his own life to follow his mentor as a martyr, but he was spared a similar fate and this allows Eddius to compare Wilfrid to St John:

"So, Wilfrid in his youth was already worthy to be counted a confessor like St John the Evangelist, who sat unscathed in a cauldron of boiling oil and drank deadly poison without taking hurt. Of him and his brother James the Apostle, Jesus said: 'Can you drink the cup that I will drink?'"[270] It might seem somewhat strange that Eddius would try to portray Wilfrid as a latter-day Biblical character or compare him to respected Roman saints, but it relates, I think, to what D.H. Farmer says in his book "*The Age of Bede*" concerning the place of miracles in

---

[268] Ibid p116–117.

[269] Ibid p106.

[270] Ibid p111–112. This is also interesting for other reasons. Whereas the words of Jesus are Biblical, the idea that St John sat in boiling oil and drank poison "without taking hurt" are certainly not. From whence did these stories come, and why did Eddius think that they were indeed Biblical?

Bede's *Life of Cuthbert*.[271] In a non-scientific world, religious writers, including hagiographers, were expected to show Christianity's superiority over all other forms of religious practice. The simplest way of achieving that was to write about miracles and authenticate divine power at work in the present or very recent past. The difference is, I think, that while Eddius *did* write about miracles for this reason, he did not do so very often. One of the few miracle stories in the *Life of Wilfrid* is that of Wilfrid saving the life of a young stone mason who had fallen from the top of the church at Hexham in the process of its construction.[272] Eddius, unlike the Venerable Bede for example, does not tell one miraculous story after the other. Rather he seems far more concerned to show Wilfrid's superiority over any and all of the local (Celtic?) saints and hence the superiority of Roman over Celtic Christianity. By comparing Wilfrid to the Prophets and the Apostles, Eddius was *not* saying that Wilfrid deserved the same veneration and devotion, or that his teaching had the same authority, but rather that Wilfrid and his teachings were superior to anything else that might be available.

Eddius, like Wilfrid, had scant tolerance for Celtic Christian practice. At one point in the *Life,* Eddius explicitly calls the supporters of the Celtic tradition "schismatics" and said that they were "ignorant", as their *computas* for the dating of Easter demonstrated.[273] Another good example of this intolerance is in Wilfrid's speech accepting his elevation to the Episcopate but before his consecration:"Your royal majesties, it behoves us to take careful thought as to how, with God's help but without criticism from Catholics, we, your candidate, might be raised to Episcopal dignity. Many English bishops are as much Quartodecimans[274] as the Celts themselves. Of course, it is not for me to point the figure at them[275] but I know I am right. The Holy See does not consider the men they ordain to be in communion with her—anymore than she does those whom she calls schismatic. In all humility, therefore, let me beg you to send me, under your protection, across the sea to Gaul where there are many bishops recognised for their Orthodoxy. There, though unworthy, I can be consecrated

---

[271] Op cit Farmer p18.

[272] Op cit Eddius p129.

[273] Ibid p110.

[274] "Quartodecimans" were those who celebrated Easter on the fourteenth day of the month of Nisan, regardless of whether or not it was a Sunday. See DH Farmer & JF Webb. *Age of Bede* p118.

[275] This is, of course, ironic—that is precisely what he is doing!

without the Holy See raising any objection"[276] Thinks raises an interesting question: did Wilfrid actually say this or are they words which Eddius for his polemical purposes would have him say? At this distance the question is surely unanswerable; howbeit that Farmer and Albertson have variously conducted a lively debate on the issue.[277] In any event, this is by no means as important as the clear condemnation of the Celts. Unlike the other hagiographies that illustrate a willingness to make the new monastic changes more acceptable to those who still wanted to hold on to their Celtic faith and practices, *the Life of Wilfrid* shows no willingness to compromise. This rigidity is, I think, the direct result of the account that Eddius gives of the proceedings of the Synod of Whitby in 664, and the surprisingly influential role that women played in Wilfrid's career. The women that Wilfrid encountered in his early years give a good example of the important role they played in his life. The first was his step mother with whom his relationship was to say the least rather turbulent. She is portrayed as being cruel to Wilfrid.[278] It was this cruelty that convinced Wilfrid to leave home and pursue an ecclesiastical life. Wilfrid's father (who apparently had done nothing to prevent the cruelty) agreed to this course of action and sent him first to the court of King Oswy with the intention that he serve Queen Eanfled. The queen put Wilfrid under the supervision of Cudda, a nobleman who had recently devoted himself to monastic life on Lindisfarne.[279] At the monastery of Lindisfarne, "He [Wilfrid] strove humbly and obediently to carry out the rule with sincere devotion [and] made his master and the older monks love him as a son, and his equals to regard him as a brother [of the flesh]. He learnt the whole Psalter and several other books by heart. His head was not yet tonsured but he served God in purity and in circumcision of the heart, deserving a share in the blessing which Samuel received as Eli's servant."[280] At this point in the life, it is important to note certain aspects that would have made Wilfrid inflexible towards Celtic teachings, especially since he was sent to Lindisfarne, a monastery founded by Aidan. Eddius does not specifically say which Rule it was

---

[276] Op cit Eddius p118.

[277] See Farmer and Webb at p118 and Albertson at p 106.

[278] This again is somewhat interesting. Was she really cruel to Wilfrid or is this a standard literary device in which all stepmothers must be cruel—along the lines of the Wicked Queen and Snow white.

[279] Op cit Eddius p107.

[280] Ibid p107–108 Note again the clear Biblical analogy.

to which Wilfrid so devoutly subjected himself though, as we noted above, it is likely that there was more than one available to him. If Wilfrid truly did bring the Benedictine Rule to England[281] this could not have been the Rule he followed on Lindisfarne. If what Eddius says about him in this connection, then it is far more likely that he received the Benedictine Rule from either Archdeacon Boniface in Rome or the Archbishop of Lyons. Since it is impossible to draw any firm conclusions as to which rule it was that Wilfrid followed on Lindisfarne, there has to be another way to explain how Wilfrid developed such rigid attitudes against Celtic Christianity. One possible solution is to compare the monastery of Lindisfarne with the court of King Oswy. The court was divided between the two traditions. On one side there was Oswy, who spent a long period of his youth in exile among the Celts[282] with his brothers. After coming to the throne in 641, Oswy, like his brother St Oswald before him followed the Celtic tradition. On the other side was Queen Eanfled, Oswy's second wife. Eanfled was raised in Kent[283] which was the first kingdom to convert to Roman Christianity after Augustine [of Canterbury's] mission in the sixth century. So, Queen Eanfled was decidedly Roman. The divided situation extended beyond the royal family to encompass the entire court, including the priests who also had conflicting views among themselves. But, more notably it was affecting some of the king's most significant royal duties like the all-important Easter festival during which he was expected to make great show of his piety and devotion. All of this leads to a number of pertinent questions: why would a queen who was so decidedly Roman send her ward to a *Celtic* monastery? Lindisfarne was of course explicitly Celtic, the sister abbey to Iona. It had been founded by Aidan and was currently being led by Colman who was both an abbot and a bishop in the Celtic tradition.[284] Why would Queen Eanfled send young Wilfrid to Lindisfarne and place him in the care of Cudda? Eddius says that "Cudda was one of the king's most loving and faithful companions," who "had also resolved, on account of his paralysis, to give up worldly ambition and dedicate himself to the monastic life on Lindisfarne."[285] Why would the queen send Wilfrid into the hands of those

---

[281] Ibid 156. Though this might be another way by which Eddius promote Wilfrid's importance.
[282] Op cit Albertson SJ p 9.
[283] Ibid p 54.
[284] Op cit Eddius. p116.
[285] Ibid p 110.

whom, presumably, she regarded as "schismatic"? Why did she send Wilfrid specifically to Cudda, who was nobleman turned monk living with a disability, rather than to Colman as head of the monastery? To what extent, if at all, was Colman consulted or involved in her decision? I think that there had to be an important and determinative difference between Cudda and Colman. The question is, what? We know that large numbers of people abandoned their Celtic practices and replaced them with Roman ones. But was it equally possible to move in the other direction, to renounce newly adopted Roman ways and return to familiar Celtic tradition? If so, could Cudda have been one of them? If the answer to this question could be shown to be "yes" then it would have both negative and positive implications. It would be negative in that it would surely make Eanfled's sending of Wilfrid to Cudda far less likely than it already is because she would regard him as a traitor as well as a heretic, the more so because he once knew the "one true faith".

And yet, to give Cudda such grave responsibility for the care of the queen's personal ward might have been offered as an incentive to return to Rome, knowing that the queen could not countenance Wilfrid's upbringing in the Celtic manner. On the other hand, one positive implication might be that it would open up the interesting possibility (and it can never be more than that) that at some time between its foundation in 635 and the year of the Synod of Whitby in 664, Lindisfarne had been—or at the time of Wilfrid still was—a joint Roman-Celtic monastery. If the answer to this question could be shown to be "yes", then I think it would further explain Wilfrid's disenchantment with all things Celtic.

Disillusionment between the two traditions has occupied us for much of this and the preceding chapter. We have seen that the depth of that disillusionment was well documented and that at least one monastic house divided against itself could not stand. I do not believe that the possibility that Lindisfarne was another example of a failed joint experiment to be entirely fanciful, especially as Colman, the abbot at the time of Wilfrid's arrival, had something of a "track record" in creating such experiments. Even though the sources do not provide sufficient evidence to prove the possibility either way the question seems—to me at least— to be central if we are to fully grasp how, why and in what ways Wilfrid's views against the Celts were formed and hardened.

In the light of the paucity of current evidence, all we can know for certain is that under Cudda's tutelage Wilfrid somehow saw the differences between the Celtic and Roman traditions at first hand and that this led, after only two years, to Wilfrid's announcement that his wished to journey to Rome and visit the See of St Peter. It was this journey and his meeting with Archdeacon Boniface that proved decisive and can be said to have eventually changed the future direction of Christianity in Britain for ever.

Wilfrid met Boniface at the shrine dedicated to St Andrew the Apostle where "he [Wilfrid] humbly knelt before the altar over which the four Gospels were placed, and adjourned the Apostle, by the name of God for whom he had suffered, to obtain for him a keenness of mind to learn and then teach the nations the message of the Gospel. His prayer was granted, as many will testify. He passed many months in daily visits to the shrines of the saints, at one of them he found a teacher, sent by God and the Apostle to be his faithful friend, the Archdeacon Boniface…the wisest of counsellors."[286] Thus began a far more entrenched education in the Roman tradition than would have been possible even if Lindisfarne had been a joint community. It set in motion Wilfrid's dogmatic views on the Christian faith that he had no fear of expressing during the proceedings at Whitby only a few short years later. As Eddius explains;

"Boniface made him word-perfect in the four Gospels, taught him the rule of Easter of which the British and Irish schismatic's were wholly ignorant, and many other rules of church law, teaching him as diligently as though he were his own son."[287] Increasingly, and not for the first time, Wilfrid saw his own people as schismatic, as heretics, and himself as the (sole) bearer of the truth to what had become for him an alien land. His burgeoning friendship with the Archbishop of Lyon, and his brother, did nothing to disabuse him of this belief.[288] It was during his three year stay in Lyon that Wilfrid received the Roman tonsure. It was his first visual display of his commitment to the authority of the See of Peter.[289] It was not long after this that the Archbishop was martyred together with eight other bishops. The martyrdom came about because the pagan Queen Baldhild had embarked on a systematic campaign to eradicate Christianity from

---

[286] Loc cit.

[287] Loc cit.

[288] Eddius says that the Archbishop of Lyon who influenced Wilfrid so greatly was called Dalfinus. But Farmer and Webb have shown that "in reality Annemundus was Archbishop; his brother Dalfinus was Lyon's secular ruler." Op cit Farmer and Webb p111.

[289] Ibid Eddius p111.

her provinces.[290] Wilfrid, as noted earlier, wanted to follow his mentor in death, but the dukes who were carrying out the persecution spared him because he was an alien foreigner.[291] On Wilfrid's return to his native Northumbria, word reached Alhfrith[292] that Wilfrid was "a man adherent to the true Easter and an expert in the discipline of the church of St Peter."[293] So Alfrith ordered Wilfrid to appear before him. At their first meeting, Alfrith recognised Wilfrid as *"God's chosen servant"* and the two became firm friends.[294] In 660, Alfrith went so far as to grant Wilfrid ten hides of land that was later increased by another thirty and the monastery of Ripon.[295] Eddius says that Ripon was a "great opportunity for worldly aggrandisement—given by the Lord through the prayers of St Peter—Wilfrid used as a means of alms giving."[296] Ripon was the first monastery given to Wilfrid, and knowing this helps further explain the situation mentioned earlier in this chapter about the difficulty Ceolfrith experienced at Wearmouth early in his career as abbot. Ripon could probably be considered one of the first completely Roman monasteries in Northumbria. The monks at Ripon lived entirely under Wilfrid's guidance. They celebrated Roman Easter and received the Roman tonsure, and Ceolfrith lived his early life among these brothers. Benedict Biscop recognised Ceolfrith as the wise and holy man that he was, but the transition from Ripon to Wearmouth was surely too great.

In 663, three years after Alfrith gave Ripon to Wilfrid, he told the Bishop of Wessex that Wilfrid was "humble, peaceable, given to prayer and fasting, kind, temperate, discreet, compassionate, full of the power and grace of God, modest, prudent, no wine-bibber, pure and open of speech, willing to learn and a good teacher."[297] Accordingly, he asked the bishop to ordain Wilfrid as priest of

---

[290] As usual Eddius is able to draw a Biblical comparison. He compares Baldhild to Jezebel who *"killed the prophets of old."* Loc cit.
[291] Loc cit.
[292] Sub-King of Deria ruling alongside his father Oswy.
[293] Op cit Eddius p112.
[294] Loc cit.
[295] Wilfrid seems to have received many such grants and built up a substantial land holding. At this time land was measured in "hides", one "hide" being roughly equivalent to 120 acres.
[296] Op cit Eddius p 113.
[297] Ibid p 114.

Ripon.[298] Oswy called the Synod during the following year. Among those present with Oswy and Alfrith were "abbots, priests and clerics of every rank gathered at Whitby Abbey in the presence of the most holy Abbess Hilda, the two kings and Bishops Colman and Agilberht,[299] to discuss the proper time for celebrating Easter."[300] An important aspect of the Synod is that Bishop Agilberht was *not* the person who spoke for the Roman side of the argument. Agilberht chose instead to let Wilfrid, now newly ordained, to speak in his place because, perhaps, Wilfrid was the more eloquent speaker. Farmer and Webb suggest, however, that though this might have been true, a far more decisive factor was that Wilfrid was a native of Northumbria whereas Agilberht was not.[301] Agilberht was from Gaul. It seems to me that the chapters on the Synod of Whitby in the *Life of Wilfrid* must be considered the high point in this *Life*. Eddius actually wrote a condensed account of what was written by Bede in his *Ecclesiastical History*. He chose to highlight the importance of the debate over Easter and the reasons why the Roman tradition eventually won the day. At the Synod, Bishop Colman, arguing for the Celtic tradition opened the debate:

"Our fathers and theirs before them, clearly inspired by the Holy Spirit, as was Columba, stipulated that Easter Sunday should be celebrated on the fourteenth day of the moon if that day were a Sunday, following the example of St John the Evangelist who leaned on the Lord's breast at the Last Supper, the disciple whom Jesus loved. He celebrated Easter on the fourteenth day of the moon as did the disciples, and Polycarp and his disciples, and as we do under their authority. Out of respect for our fathers we dare not change, nor do we have the least desire to do so."[302] Next, Wilfrid opened for the Roman side:

"The question has already been admirably treated by a gathering of our most holy and learned fathers, three hundred and eighteen strong, at Nicea, a city on Bithynia. Among many other things they decided upon a lunar cycle recurring every nineteen years. This cycle gives no room for celebrating Easter on the fourteenth day of the moon. This is a rule followed by the Apostolic See and by nearly the whole world. At the end of the decrees, the fathers of Nicea come to

---

[298] Loc cit.
[299] Agilberht was Bishop of Wessex.
[300] Op cit p 115.
[301] Op cit Farmer and Webb. *Age of Bede* p 114.
[302] Op cit Eddius p115.

these words "let him who condemns any of these decrees be anathema."[303] Colman and Wilfrid's words bring into light the main reasons for the differences between the two traditions with startling clarity. In the previous chapter, we noted that Ireland was never conquered by the former empire, and was, therefore, never under Roman control or influence. The clerics in Ireland who had learnt Latin taught themselves by studying the sacred texts that were available to them. As a result, they developed a huge respect for Saints Columba and St John the Evangelist and followed their teachings, whereas "nearly the whole world" that had been conquered progressed in a different direction. The Council of Nicea, to which Wilfrid referred, played an important part in that division. Ireland, situated in its own small corner outside the empire, missed some of the great changes that were brought about by that council.

The differences between the Celtic and Roman traditions, and the "Celtic ignorance" (as Eddius calls it) of the laws passed by the church since St John seems to be one of Wilfrid's main arguments against the Celtic tradition. They did not follow the "Rule" passed down by the Apostolic See, which Wilfrid viewed as something less than respectful not only to Rome as the centre of mainstream Christianity, but also to St Peter, the chief of the Apostles, and therefore greater than even the disciple whom Jesus loved.

After the Synod, Wilfrid became famous and won the deep respect of both his peers and his superiors. He was elected Bishop of York towards the end of 664.[304] An interesting aspect of Wilfrid's consecration was that he did not want to be consecrated in Britain. He instead chose Gaul. This request came at the end of his acceptance speech, which was previously quoted in its entirety. We should return to it here because it raises two significant points. The first is that Wilfrid found Britain's Orthodoxy to be too chaotic to want to be consecrated here! The second reason is that though he claimed to be "unworthy", Wilfrid wanted to make sure that Rome would accept his consecration. In short, Wilfrid wanted to be consecrated in a place where there was no confusion, or even a fusion, between competing traditions. This pointed to a consecration in *southern* Gaul, especially Lyons, with its rich tradition flowing from the time of Iranaeus, geographically nearer Rome and the place where Wilfrid received the Roman tonsure. While the first portion of the *Life* offers much evidence that is in favour of the Roman triumph over the Celtic tradition, the remaining portion is, for the

---

[303] Loc cit.

[304] Ibid p115–117.

most part, Eddius' defence of Wilfrid against his enemies as well as a detailed account of Wilfrid's struggles once his fame and reputation grew. Wilfrid's troubles began shortly after his election as Bishop of York. In 666, while Wilfrid was returning from Gaul, King Oswy let Chad, a Celt, be placed over Wilfrid's See and it was another three years before he could begin to exercise Episcopal authority.[305] This was not, however, the end of his problems. Through the years Wilfrid gained a vast number of monasteries, in addition to Ripon, a number of buildings including a church at Hexham, and what appears to have been a private army "armed like a king's retinue".[306] There were other followers too: abbots and abbesses who gave him their possessions and monastic land holdings, and nobles of high position who sent their sons to be educated by him.[307] Wilfrid's popularity and influence was so widespread throughout Northumbria that resentment towards his wealth and power made him the enemy of his peers and kings. His two great antagonists were King Ecgfrith of Northumbria (Oswy's son and successor) and Theodore, Archbishop of Canterbury. The remainder of Wilfrid's *Life* concerns itself not with Wilfrid's determination to capitalise on his success at Whitby in defeating the Celts, but with his political efforts to wrest York from the hands of Chad and so it is that we move now to the next hagiographical work that concerns this study.

Life of Cuthbert by Bede

There are two surviving "lives" of St Cuthbert. The first was written in about 700AD by an anonymous monk at Lindisfarne.[308] According to Albertson it is the "earliest surviving piece of written literature" produced by the English for the English.[309] Bede's version was written in 716AD and he used the earlier Lindisfarne manuscript as his base text.[310] Bede's purpose, like that of all the hagiographers studied here, was the veneration of Cuthbert as a holy man and saint so it should not surprise us that Bede's *Life of Cuthbert* is a catalogue of Cuthbert's teachings and the miracles that he performed, howbeit that it

---

[305] Ibid p 120–121.
[306] Ibid p130.
[307] Ibid p 128.
[308] Op Cit Farmer *Age of Bede* p 16.
[309] Op cit Albertson *Anglo-Saxon Saints and Heroes*, p 31.
[310] Op cit Farmer p 16.

somewhat contrary to the method employed by Eddius Stephanus in writing the *Life of Wilfrid*. Eddius was, as we have seen, mainly interested in defending and "proving" Wilfrid to be a man of great piety and virtue. In the case of Cuthbert, however, Bede had nothing to prove in this respect and a comparison of the *Life of Wilfrid* and the *Life of Cuthbert* shows that the crowning difference between the heroes was their choice of lifestyle. It was this that ensured that Wilfrid had as many enemies as Cuthbert had friends. While Wilfrid was willing to accept authority over a number of monasteries throughout Northumbria, Cuthbert was content with a more eremitical life. The point at which Cuthbert was happiest was while he was living as a hermit on the small island of Farne.[311] He dreaded the day on which Abbot Boisil's prophecy about him becoming bishop might be fulfilled.[312] Cuthbert would have preferred to remain a hermit because he feared the power that came with the position of bishop.[313] Wilfrid, on the other hand, was the exact opposite of Cuthbert. While Wilfrid chose to fight for and hold on to his bishopric (which forced him to petition Rome on several occasions and look for aid in his cause),[314] it took some heavy convincing on the part of the Synod that appointed Cuthbert to persuade him to accept the bishopric of Lindisfarne.[315] Bede's respect and admiration for Cuthbert is obvious enough even though Cuthbert was originally taught in the Celtic traditions of Christianity. A major problem with Bede's *Life of Cuthbert* is that this aspect of Cuthbert's Christianity is almost passed over in silence so that anyone reading this *Life* who is also unfamiliar with the surrounding history might be left with the impression that Cuthbert had always been a supporter of the Roman rites and traditions. Cuthbert, however, was an adult when he began to live according to Roman monastic principles, probably sometime after the death of his mentor, Abbot Boisil.

In order to consider the nature of Cuthbert's transition from one tradition to another and his reasons for doing so, it is important to look at this *Life* from the beginning. As a boy, Cuthbert had already exhibited holy qualities. He devoted himself to God at a very young age, but did not immediately enter the monastic

---

[311] Bede. *Life of Cuthbert*. P66.
[312] Ibid p 72.
[313] Ibid p 54.
[314] Op cit Eddius Stephanus *Life of Wilfrid* p 136–137 & p159–160.
[315] Op cit Bede *Life of Cuthbert*. p75.

life.[316] It was not until after the death of Aidan that Cuthbert decided to do so. On the night of Aidan's death, Cuthbert was out tending a flock of sheep when he witnessed Aidan's direct reception into heaven. It was this visionary experience that convinced him to go to a monastery.[317] An interesting aspect of both the incident and Cuthbert's decision is the symbolic meaning behind them: with Aidan's death Cuthbert's new monastic life would begin in the same way as Elisha followed Elijah. For Cuthbert, the mantle of Aidan's holiness and leadership had fallen upon him. Even so, Cuthbert did not go at once to Lindisfarne but instead decided first to gain a theological education from Boisil who was then a priest at Melrose. Both Melrose and Lindisfarne began as Celtic monasteries, but Bede scarcely mentions this and certainly shows no antagonism towards the communities there. Indeed, Bede is very keen to point out that Lindisfarne was "well adorned with holy monks, under whose example and teaching he [Cuthbert] might make good progress, but the reputation for sublime virtue enjoyed by Boisil, priest of Melrose, led him to enter there."[318] At Melrose, Cuthbert received the tonsure at the hands of Eata, Abbot and Bishop of the monastery. It is surely significant that Bede chooses not to tell us whether this was a Celtic or Roman tonsure but I think that what evidence we do have suggests that it was the former rather than the latter. Farmer and Webb have shown that Eata was a strong supporter of Celtic monasticism and was deeply disturbed by and unwilling to accept Roman rites and practices and so the likelihood that he would give Cuthbert a Roman tonsure is extremely slim.[319] Moreover, for purposes of his own Bede would not have wanted to openly state that the man he was venerating had, at one time, received a Celtic tonsure. Whereas it is specifically stated in the other Lives that Wilfrid, Benedict Biscop and Ceolfrith received the "Roman tonsure of St Peter", Bede's *Life of Cuthbert* says only that Cuthbert "gained permission…to receive the tonsure and become one with the community."[320] It was at about this time[321] that Eata was granted land on which to establish the monastery at Ripon. When the monastery was completed, Eata sent some of the monks from Melrose to Ripon and Cuthbert

---

[316] Loc cit.
[317] Ibid p 46.
[318] Ibid p50.
[319] Op cit Farmer and Webb. p 51.
[320] Op cit Bede p 50.
[321] Sometime around 661.

was among them. These monks had only been living at Ripon for a few years when the control of the monastery was taken away from Eata and given to Wilfrid.[322] Eata, along with Cuthbert and the other brothers were thrown out of the monastery they had built because Eata refused to accept *any* Roman practices there.[323] According to Bede, King Alhfrith, a Roman Christian and the one who endowed the monastery for the safety of his immortal soul, wanted the monastery to be organised according to the Roman tradition.[324] Eata, was clearly not the man that Alhfrith needed after all so Ripon was passed on to someone more willing to enforce Roman monastic and Wilfrid was, of course, well placed to fulfil such an undertaking.[325] The impact of the forced departure from Ripon clearly put Cuthbert in a position where he questioned some of the assumptions and practices he had held and to try to determine where the future lay. Only a few chapters later on Bede shows Cuthbert preaching the Roman version of the faith to his fellow monks as well as in the surrounding villages.[326] In Cuthbert's *Life,* Bede does not tell us when the moment of Cuthbert's "conversion" to Roman ways arrived. Perhaps it was a gradual process. Nor does Bede specifically tell us whether and to what extent the decisions of the Synod of Whitby influenced Cuthbert's decision. This is an important and deeply disappointing omission because even if the Synod was not the determinative factor it must have had a crucial impact on Cuthbert's life and practice. For Bede, it is the Ripon incident and Boisil's death that were the triggers that persuaded Cuthbert to accept monastic life under the authority of the Roman Church either before or immediately after the Synod of 664. The best evidence in the *Life*[327]

---

[322] Op cit Eddius Stephanus p 101.

[323] And this strengthens the view that Cuthbert did not receive a Roman tonsure from Eata.

[324] If this is in fact the case, it is difficult to see why he should have granted the monastery to Eata in the first place.

[325] Op cit Eddius p13.

[326] Op cit Bede p 54. This surely cold not have endeared him either to Eata or to his fellow, Celtic, monks. But once more Bede chooses to gloss over any potential antagonism.

[327] If I am right about this, then it puts Cuthbert in a rather darker light than Bede would have either desired or intended, because it carries with it a suggestion that full conversion to Rome was a cynical ploy on the part of Cuthbert in order to gain power. This places him alongside Wilfrid in terms of avarice. Just as Paris was, according to Henry of Navarre, "worth a mass", so too was Melrose.

suggests that Cuthbert may have fully embraced the Roman tradition on his appointment as Prior of Melrose: "On Boisil's death, Cuthbert became prior, an office which he carried out for many years with holy zeal. Inside the monastery, he counselled the monks on the religious life and set a high example of it himself, and outside, in the world, he strove to convert people for miles around from their foolish ways[328] to a delight in the promised joys of heaven"[329] It may be however that there was nothing sinister or cynical in this "conversion" at all and that Cuthbert's preaching both inside and outside the monastery simply conformed to contemporary practice. In seventh-century England, it was not at all uncommon for priests and other clerics to wander around the countryside to bring not only pagan worshippers, but also schismatic people back into the fold. A priest would often go from village to village and the whole population would gather and listen to him, and Cuthbert was always eager to preach to ordinary people.[330] Preaching to the masses about the mass was something that Cuthbert considered to be a *"labour of love"*[331] despite his apparent preference to remain in meditative isolation. It was important to Cuthbert because he was preaching to those who "…had forgotten the mystery conferred on them in baptism and had fled to idols, as though incantations or amulets or any other diabolical rubbish could possibly avail against a punishment sent by God the creator. To bring back both kinds of sinners he often did the rounds of the villages, sometimes on horseback, more often on foot, preaching the way of truth to those who had gone astray."[332] It is significant that Bede points to two specific types of sinners in this passage, the ones he says have "gone astray". There are those people who had "fled to idols", or fled to paganism, but there were also those who followed "other diabolical rubbish" or more specifically those who followed something other than strictly Roman ideals—like the Celtic Christians. As we have already

---

[328] It is not obvious what Bede means by "foolish ways". Are they the "foolish ways" of sin, or the "foolish ways" of the Celts? The ambiguity is, I think, deliberate and leads the reader to the view that the "foolish ways" are sinful Celtic practices.

[329] Op cit Bede p 54. The phrase "promised joys of heaven" is also interesting, especially if Bede is indeed suggesting that the "foolish ways" of the Celts are sinful, for Bede would then be announcing his allegiance to the view "*extra ecclesiam non salus est*" Outside the Church (of Rome) there is no salvation.

[330] Ibid p 55.

[331] Loc cit

[332] Ibid p 54–55.

noted we need to ask why Bede would classify both Celtic Christians and pagans as "sinners". A reliable answer would be to consider the incompatible relationship between the two traditions. At a time when there could only be one main authority over all of Christianity, there would be instances when *anything* that contradicted it would be regarded as inferior and heretical. In this instance, Bede was giving Celtic monasticism both of these negative connotations just as he was giving them to paganism.

After leaving Ripon, Cuthbert spent many succeeding years at Melrose until Eta ordered him to Lindisfarne.[333] According to Farmer and Webb, Cuthbert arrived not long after Colman departed with thirty of his brethren.[334] In addition to being Abbot of Melrose Eata became Abbot of Lindisfarne and either unable or (as I think) unwilling to teach the Roman version of the faith to the monks still living at Lindisfarne, he sent Cuthbert in his absence as prior "…to teach the true Rule of monastic life in his capacity as prior and to illustrate it by his own example."[335] Also the Bishopric of York had recently been out under the authority of its new Bishop, Wilfrid. Under Wilfrid and his temporary replacement, Chad, York became the main ecclesiastical centre in Northumbria, which left Lindisfarne without a bishop from 664 to 678.[336] As Prior, Cuthbert had the task of instructing the monks of Lindisfarne but most of them seemed to have preferred to continue the monastic life they had learnt from Aidan.[337] They were not interested in conforming to the new Rule they were expected to follow. An important aspect of this section of the *Life* is the information it provides about how Cuthbert was able to work with his brethren and convince them to convert to a monastic life in the Roman tradition. Like Biscop, Cuthbert realised that it was not going to be an easy task and that it would take more than a little ingenuity. While Biscop chose to incorporate all he had learnt into the education of his brethren, Cuthbert preferred to lead by personal example. As the following

---

[333] Op cit Bede Life of Cuthbert p 63.

[334] Op cit Farmer and Webb, *Age of Bede* p 19.

[335] Loc cit Bede.

[336] Loc cit Farmer and Webb.

[337] Here we should recall that Cuthbert had such a close spiritual relationship to Aidan that he received a vision of Aidan's assumption into heaven. But now as Prior of Melrose, translated to Lindisfarne Cuthbert is teaching in direct opposition to everything that Aidan stood for—in Aidan's own monastery too.

quotation shows, it took Cuthbert years to gain the trust and the obedience of the monks on Lindisfarne:

"Some of the monks preferred their old way of life of the rule. He overcame these by patience and forbearance, bringing them round little by little through daily example to a better frame of mind. At Chapter meetings, he was often worn out by bitter insults, but would put an end to arguments simply by rising and walking out, clam and unruffled. Next day he would give the same person exactly the same admonitions, as though there had been no unpleasantness the previous day. In this way, he gradually won their obedience."[338] This is an excellent example to show why this transition period had to take place. The Roman Easter may have won at Whitby, but it was much harder to force conformity in other areas of Celtic culture and religious practices.

Bede does not tell us which of the many possible Rules it was that Cuthbert wanted to establish on Lindisfarne, but it may have been the Benedictine Rule especially since, as Peter Brown has argued Pope Gregory the Great (himself the hagiographer of Benedict in the *Dialogues*) had once been "*a great devotee*" of the life the monks (of Lindisfarne) were living.[339] There were many monastic Rules available both at this time and that of Gregory, but what struck Gregory about the Benedictine Rule was its "unfailing sense of measure and insight".[340] Benedict was an abbot who was able to "lead his tiny flock of monks through every spiritual and material emergency" and he had done this by exacting absolute obedience.[341] Cuthbert too, as shown in the above quotation, managed to eventually gain the obedience of those monks who found themselves under his spiritual guidance. The other and probably more decisive factor which suggests that it was in fact the Benedictine Rule that Cuthbert wanted to establish on Lindisfarne, is Wilfrid. In 666, King Oswy contravened Canon Law and appointed Chad to York even though Wilfrid was returning from Gaul to take up this position. During the years in which Chad was stationed at York, Wilfrid was travelling around Northumbria looking for support for his cause. His main accomplishment during these wanderings was his ability to introduce the Benedictine Rule in the communities he visited.[342] While Wilfrid was travelling

---

[338] Loc cit.

[339] Op cit Peter Brown, *Rise of Christendom* p 210.

[340] Loc cit.

[341] Loc Cit.

[342] Op cit Eddius Stephanus, *Life of Wilfrid* p 120.

around, Northumbria Cuthbert was on Lindisfarne. It may not be documented that Wilfrid visited Lindisfarne at the time, but it seems logical to suppose that Lindisfarne would have been one of the main monasteries to convert not only to Romanism but to the Benedictine Rule as well. When Colman lost at Whitby, he was both Abbot and Bishop of Lindisfarne. Lindisfarne was also the sister monastery of Iona, which was proving to be the most difficult community to convert. Cuthbert began to pursue the eremitical life in 673.[343] By this time, he had won the respect and affection of his fellow monks and although he had more recently enjoyed teaching them, he longed for a more contemplative and solitary life in his old age. "He was delighted that after a long and spotless active life he should be worthy to ascend to the stillness of divine contemplation."[344] He found a secluded place on the island of Farne that was located "in the outer precincts *of* the monastery"[345] Once there, he closed himself off from the outside world, leaving only one small window through which to pronounce blessings or address other important needs.[346] It was during these years on Farne that Cuthbert's reputation for miracles began to grow and these attracted visitors from all over Britain. His fellow monks from Lindisfarne ware also frequent visitors seeking counsel, even though they had long rejected it and even though he had separated himself from them. A typical but central piece of advice he gave them was to marvel at their own monastic lives and not his miracles:

"It is the monastic life in which you should stand in awe. In that life everything is subject to the abbot; the times of prayer, fasting, vigils, and work all governed by his will. I have known many abbots, who for purity of mind and depth of prophetic power have far surpassed my poor self—Boisil for example, a man to be named in honour and veneration."[347] Cuthbert's words reflect those of Benedict in the suggestion that the coenobitic life under the single rule of an abbot is the best possible form of the monastic life. Cuthbert is also suggesting

---

[343] Op cit Farmer and Webb p 19.

[344] Op cit Bede p 65.

[345] Loc cit.

[346] Ibid p 68.

[347] Ibid p 73. It is not clear who these "many abbots" might have been, Cuthbert's personal monastic experience having been limited to only three houses, Ripon, Melrose and Lindisfarne. Perhaps this is knowledge by report rather than acquaintance—but at all events it is a phrase full of hyperbole designed to ensure that his fellow monks regard this as coming from his wise experience and not merely a personal opinion.

thereby that many might think that they are called to the eremitical life but few have the discipline and the ability to handle it. This was and is a widely held monastic principle. This was the main reason why so many people throughout the ages looked upon the hermit with such deep respect, but as far as this hagiography is concerned one of its main purposes was to encourage monks to embrace the monastic life in the form understood and approved by the Roman Church.

As Cuthbert makes clear in the above quotation, every aspect of a monk's life in a monastery was (is) subject to the abbot. The abbot was more than a father figure for these monks. He was also their spiritual and material adviser on a number of different levels and in every matter. Hermits, however, though living by a Rule were (are) subject only to themselves. The Roman Church, and Cuthbert himself, would not have wanted to encourage just anyone into pursuing the eremitical life; it was far safer to keep the majority under the authority of a man approved and appointed by a bishop.

Cuthbert did not stay long in his hermitage. In 685, a Synod led by Theodore Archbishop of Canterbury (the opponent of Wilfrid) and King Ecgfrith of Northumbria elected Cuthbert to be the new Bishop of Lindisfarne.[348] The purpose of this Synod was another attempt to decrease Wilfrid's power and wealth as well as fragmenting his ever increasing Episcopal domains into smaller ones.[349] Cuthbert was at first reluctant to accept the bishopric and leave Farne but eventually agreed because "*...the decree of the Supreme Ruler cannot be escaped, no matter where one might flee to.*"[350] He was consecrated in the winter of the same year. As bishop, Cuthbert resumed his preaching and teaching ministry. He taught by "example first and precept later."[351] Cuthbert, however, was only bishop for two years before he understood that his life would end and that he must return to Farne.[352] "Once free from material worries he might give himself undividedly to his prayers and psalms, to prepare himself for death, or

---

[348] Ibid p 75.

[349] Op cit Farmer and Webb. p 20.

[350] Op cit Bede p 75.

[351] Ibid p 77.

[352] Bede suggests that Cuthbert now suffered from a fatal illness. Although the illness is unnamed the symptoms were obvious for all to see and caused a rapid deterioration and death after only a few months.

rather, for eternal life."[353] His request was granted and, in 687, Cuthbert returned to his secluded place on Farne.[354] He was again frequently visited by his brethren from Lindisfarne who were this time more concerned about Cuthbert's health than seeking his advice. Cuthbert lived for only a few more months and then died of an unnamed but terminal illness.[355] It was in these few short weeks that Cuthbert gave his most famous and eloquent discourse in which he instructed his brethren on how to uphold the monastic life that he had spent years teaching them. He warned against schism and tells them that the best and only way of avoiding such divisions is to remain faithful to the Roman tradition. It is worth quoting at length: "Preserve among yourselves unfailing divine charity, and when you have to hold a council about your common affairs let your principle be to reach a unanimous decision.[356] Live in mutual concord with all the servants of Christ; do not despise those of the household of the faith who come to you seeking hospitality.[357] Receive them, put them up, and send them on their way with kindness, treating them as one of yourselves.[358] Do not think yourselves any better than the rest of your companions who share the same faith and follow the monastic life. With those who have wandered far from the unity of the Catholic faith, either through not celebrating Easter at the proper time or by evil living, you are to have no dealings.[359] Never forget that if you are ever forced to make a choice between two evils I would much rather you left the island, taking my bones with you, than that you should be party to wickedness on any pretext whatsoever, bending your necks to the yoke of schism.[360] Strive then to most diligently learn the Catholic Statutes of the fathers and put them into practice. Make it your special care to carry out these rules of the monastic life which God

---

[353] Op cit Bede p 85.

[354] Op cit Farmer and Webb p 20.

[355] Op cit Bede p 89.

[356] Unlike the bickering that had caused him to remove himself from Chapter meetings worn down by their insults.

[357] Unlike their attitude towards him when he first arrived on Lindisfarne.

[358] Again, unlike their hostile attitude towards him which for many years made him a stranger in his own house.

[359] Thus, radically unlike his own earlier attempts to win them back by preaching in the villages.

[360] It seems that Cuthbert was afraid that the monks might revert to Celtic ways after his demise.

in his mercy has seen fit to give you through my ministry. I know that, though some might think my life despicable[361] none the less after my death you will see that my teachings are not so easily dismissed."[362] A significant aspect of this quotation is that Cuthbert is making a marked distinction between the Celtic and the Roman traditions and tells the monks how the adherents of each are to be treated. He considers Roman Christians to be "servants of God", and they were to give their brothers mutual respect. The teachings of Rome were so central that Celtic Christians were to be rejected as outcasts. The monks could have no dealings with them at all. These are extremely strong words coming from a man who was reportedly patient and non-confrontational when teaching others about the joys of heaven.

For this part of the *Life,* Bede tells us that he has taken as his primary source the information he has from Herefrith who was both abbot and priest on Lindisfarne when Bede was composing his work. Even though we may, as a consequence, allow for both Bede's hyperbole and Herefrith's rhetorical defence of Rome over the Celts in what is supposed to be Cuthbert's last speech it is important to note what the essential message is. These words that supposedly come from Cuthbert clearly outline the central concern of Anglo—Saxon hagiography with which we have dealt in this and the previous chapter. Here Cuthbert is speaking to his brethren, telling them what they need to do in order to ensure the salvation of their souls once he has died, while still managing to place an ultimate emphasis on the Roman tradition and its practices, thus distinguishing it from all other orthodoxies.

The hagiography which has been considered here reveals how Northumbria, a kingdom divided both culturally and ecclesiastically over its Christian ideals, was eventually brought under the authority of the Roman Church. The Synod of Whitby passed the rule that said that Easter was to be celebrated universally according to what had been decided at Nicea, but the Synod itself had no means to ensure its acceptance or stability. The transition took many years and even in places such as Lindisfarne, where great efforts were made to establish

---

[361] Perhaps Cuthbert had not won all the monks of Lindisfarne to Roman ways, or at the least he thought their commitment was somewhat shallow. If so, it would increase his fear of their lapse into Celtic Christianity and make his life seem worthless.

[362] Op cit Bede p 93. This last phrase "teachings not so easily dismissed" is rather dark and has something of a threat about it. What did Cuthbert have in mind and who, if any one, did he think would bring about this retribution?

conformity, allegiance may always have been fragile. The argument of these chapters has been that the transition did not begin at all until the saints, whose *Lives* have been analysed here, began preaching in favour of Rome. Each Life considered here offers a glimpse of how these saints dealt with the problem of convincing others to follow Roman monastic principles. They had to find a great variety of ways to combat Celtic beliefs and loyalties.

One feature of the period in question that cannot be shown in the hagiography is how much of the Celtic tradition remained in Northumbria during the transition and after its completion. As Peter Brown has pointed out, it is likely there were many aspects of Celtic Christianity that remained in Britain and that this can, at least to some extent, be traced through the religious art of the time.[363] The hagiography, however, was not written to show how much Celtic Christianity still affected Britain, but rather to contest it. The writers of Anglo-Saxon hagiography may have written for the good of their immortal souls as well as for the souls of their readership, but this being a period of change gave them a second purpose to write and provided a motive to use the style they adopted. Since there could only be one authority over all western Christianity, there could only be one representation of the "one true Church". The Roman tradition may have won the battle of Whitby, but the war for hearts and minds of monasticism and the general populace was far from over.

Despite the fact that the Roman tradition had a more widespread influence, Celtic Christianity possessed remarkable qualities that were firmly entrenched in the British psyche and mode of life. For instance, a few of the Celtic saints, like Patrick, Columba, Columbanus and Aidan were well respected in both traditions. The Roman tradition, however, claimed to follow the teachings of St Peter and the other Apostles, who held a much higher standing in western Christendom than any other saint. The difficulties with the transition with which the Roman Church had to contend were far more than the attempt to persuade everyone to accept the authority of the Vatican and the papacy as representative of the one true church. The main problem was persuading those who were completely loyal to Celtic monastic principles and to the memory of the Celtic saints to switch loyalties. The Synod could not contend with these loyalties.

The transition could not begin unless or until men like Biscop, and Wilfrid were chosen to preach all that they had learnt in Gaul and Rome and other places

---

[363] Op cit Peter Brown. *Rise of Christendom*. p 372.

inside prominent monasteries at the heart of the controversies. The hagiography is an excellent resource to show how these monasteries, founded on the basis of Celtic monasticism, were transformed into the leading Roman monasteries of future generations.

Another important aspect of the hagiographies is that each of these saints and their varying backgrounds reveal how the transition affected Northumbria on a number of different levels. Benedict Biscop was raised in the Roman monastic tradition, but he was able to empathise with those who wanted to remain loyal to their Celtic roots. His personality mixed with his education and personal experience made him a unique individual, one well placed to move the transition forward. Only Biscop, of all the saints considered here, experienced a smooth transition when teaching his brethren. Only Biscop, it seems to me, had the ability to persuade others to accept the authority of monastic life under Roman authority. The Pope obviously recognised his ability since he ordered Biscop to return home to Northumbria.[364] Ceolfrith, unlike Biscop, did not enjoy unconditional acceptance from his brethren in the beginning. He was educated in the Roman tradition, but he also spent a good portion of that education living at Ripon, which was the monastery led by Wilfrid and supported by King Alhfrith who were both followers of the Roman tradition. Ceolfrith's first attempt to instruct the monks of Wearmouth in the same manner in which he was taught did not suit the monks, especially as they were used to Biscop's more sympathetic and understanding attitude towards their difficult transition. This episode in the *Life* is important because it shows many of the complexities of the transition.

The outcry of the monks at the end of the *Life of Ceolfrith* is also important because it shows the progression of this transition. It reveals the extent to which the monks of Wearmouth and Jarrow (and perhaps other monasteries in the same situation) had become more agreeable to the Roman tradition over the years. Ceolfrith's brethren had grown not only to accept him as a person, but his teachings as well.

The most significant parts of the *Life of Wilfrid* concerning this transition to Roman monasticism were the role he played at the Synod of Whitby and the recognition he earned as a result. This recognition *may* also have been due to his introduction of the Benedictine Rule into Northumbria. In any event, it was

---

[364] Op cit Bede, *Lives of the Abbots*, p 228.

certainly through his words that Wilfrid changed the face of monasticism, and it was certainly his actions that helped to develop that change. Wilfrid may have acquired many enemies, but he profited from the influence of his powerful friends as well.

Noblemen sent their sons to be educated by him. His fellow ecclesiastics donated their possessions to him when they entered the community, and he had the support of three Popes who favoured his petitions for the return of his Episcopal see. Wilfrid was, in essence, the spokesman for the Roman tradition in England by his own words as well as those put on his lips by Eddius Stephanus.

The special aspect of Cuthbert which distinguishes him from the other three is that he was the only one among them who had originally been schooled in the Celtic ways. Wilfrid spent time at Lindisfarne as a boy, but he was only there for a few short years before he left on his first pilgrimage to Rome. Cuthbert, on the other hand, was an adult when he converted to the Roman tradition. Bede does not mention the moment or progress of Cuthbert's own conversion which may imply that Cuthbert was willing to accept Roman monasticism from the beginning. It may also, as I have suggested, indicate rather more sinister and cynical motives. Cuthbert, like Ceolfrith, however, did not have an easy time convincing others to convert.

As Bede indicates, it took many years before the monks of Lindisfarne were able to accept the new Rule that Cuthbert attempted to impose upon them. In this respect, the monks at Lindisfarne were like the monks of Wearmouth in those first years. The difference between the two monasteries was that Lindisfarne was founded on Celtic monastic principles by Aidan, which meant that the loyalties at Lindisfarne were more entrenched than at Wearmouth, a newly established monastery. The situation at both monasteries, however, may have been symptomatic of houses across Britain.

That the monks of Lindisfarne finally approved of Cuthbert and his new way of organising monastic life was, I think, essential to encouraging acceptance of Roman monasticism throughout Northumbria, as well as the whole of Britain. Lindisfarne was, after all, one of the most prominent monasteries in Northumbria, and it was founded by missionaries from Iona, the monastery that helped bring Celtic Christianity and the Celtic form of monasticism to Anglo-Saxon England. If the sister monastery to Iona could accept Roman monasticism (however reluctantly), other monasteries should be able to follow suit. Thus,

Cuthbert's ability to earn the respect and obedience of his brethren was of paramount importance. So crucial was it, in fact, that it is recorded in the pages of history not once, but twice!

Each work of hagiography selected for these chapters stands alone as a significant record. Their importance to this period in Britain is apparent within these works as well. Written after the (in)famous Synod of 664, each *Life* provides a chronicle of the direction that monasticism took during this period of continuity and change. The Synod could decide what changes needed to be made within the church herself, but it could not initiate that change. It is also important to emphasise that the prominent role played by Roman monasticism in each of these *Lives* reveals the extent to which these saints, their hagiographers, and the church authorities were trying to push this transition. It was an endeavour to gain acceptance that the Roman faith was the truest representation of Christianity; an acceptance that would remain in these islands for much of the succeeding millennium.

Chapter 9
St Augustine of Hippo: Monasticism and the Defeat of Heresy

The best way to approach the monastic spirituality of St Augustine is through the errors he had to combat in his day. To understand the errors is to understand Augustine because sometimes in the history of the church, as here, the heresies are so great as to produce such a reaction that a large body of systematic truth in the face of which the errors cannot stand. The Augustinian opus must, on any account, rank alongside that of the Apostle Paul in providing a body of truth which would ensure that the church survived not only the internal strife of heresy but also the collapse of the Roman Empire and beyond.

But first it is important to remind ourselves of some of the main stages in the life of St Augustine because, like the Apostle Paul too, they have an immense bearing on what he had to say and on how he said it. He was born to a Christian mother, Monica, and a pagan father and until the age of thirty-three lived a morally reckless, even sordid, life. For nine of those thirty-three years, he had been a Manachaean. The reasons for his conversion were, as he says himself in "*Confessions*"[365] twofold: first the prayers and tears of his mother and second the patience and wisdom of St Ambrose under whom he studied in Milan. Monica saw his conversion and died shortly before he became the great man we know. Her death affected him profoundly and it may well be that he never resolved the suffering of this bereavement. Augustine's writings are numerous and extensive but there are three that are especially important for lives lived on the edge "*Confessions*"[366] "*De Civitatae Deo*", or "City of God"[367] and "On the

---

[365] St Augustine of Hippo: *Confessions.* At Last Accessed March 2024.
[366] Loc cit.
[367] St Augustine of Hippo: *City of God.* At Last Accessed March 2024.

Trinity".[368] The last two in this list are much harder reading than the first but only by taking them together do we have the essence of his thought and show how he was able to make a major contribution to the defeat of heresy. What then were the principal heresies he confronted and through which he gave us the doctrines that have become embedded in the foundations of Christianity and the religious life ever since? They were Donatism, Manichaeism and Pelagianism and his writings can be divided into separate attacks on each of them. His sermons are different, for although they too contain passages which attack these heresies they were given to the faithful as commentaries on the Scripture and, like all sermons, not intended to be systematic works of theology.

What was it about each of these heresies that, he thought, undermined the very existence of monastic communities?

The problem that gave rise to the error of Donatism was both human and tragic. As the persecution of Christians became more intense, many of the faithful renounced their belief. This could be done in a variety of ways. For example, one way was to surrender the sacred writings that Christians held most dear. Another was to step or spit on a cross or pronounce a blasphemous phrase that included the name of Christ, or make a sacrifice to one of the pagan Roman gods. In any event, out of fear of imprisonment and death many Christians apostatised. Among them was a North African bishop, Donatus.

Persecutions came and went. One result was that, often, after the persecution those who had renounced their faith wanted to come back. So, what was to happen in such a case? A bishop would apostatise, repent and want to go back to practising his Episcopal office, so some of the bishops said in effect. "Sorry, this is not possible because an apostate loses everything. You have denied the very presence of Christ within and around you. You have denied the very thing that makes you a Christian. You have lost the effect of the sacraments and of your Confirmation. You have denied your priestly character and as shepherd you have thrown the flock to the wolves. How then can we trust you? How then can you remain part of the household of faith—depart from it."

That in a nutshell is the heresy of Donatism.

Augustine fought against this idea and in the process, he helped develop the church's understanding of who belongs to the church, because what the Donatists were, in effect, saying was that the church of Christ is a church exclusively of

---

[368] St Augustine of Hippo: *On the Trinity*. At Last Accessed March 2024.

saints. They were saying that when a person sins, commits apostasy or some other grave crime, that's it. A person might once have been a Christian, but no more. If a person enters the church by baptism, they leave it through sin.

Clearly this is not the church we know today. Some are scandalised, especially in the matter of homosexuality, because they regard the church as going too far towards the other extreme, but it is thanks in large measure to the work of Augustine that we now know the church to be composed not of saints but of sinners saved by grace, sheep and goats living together. Throughout the Gospel, Christ could not have made it plainer that his church is, indeed, the home to many potential saints but also to a lot of actual sinners.

That is why it is interesting to note that when Augustine had to defend the church as being composed not only of the holy but the unholy too, he was clear that those who stood in judgement of their fellow Christians were not so holy themselves. This was, in fact, one of the main arguments that Augustine used: "Who, exactly, is calling whom a sinner?" This is a timely question that we may do well to ask ourselves in the current debates that unsettle the church.

What then is the significance of Augustine's teaching in the controversy with Donatism that has a direct impact on the development of monasticism? I think the answer is to be found at many different levels. Here I shall mention three.

First, because of that controversy and Augustine's response to it the church now teaches with unmistakeable clarity that the admission to the sacraments does not depend on the holiness either of the person who administers them or on the part of the person who receives it—*ex opera operatum*—the work, works. It was Augustine who was responsible for that beautiful phrase. The benefits of the sacraments we receive, the Eucharist's we pray are effective if (but only if) the one administering has the power and the minimal intention to do what Christ wants. That is important because with Donatism the whole sacramental system was at stake.

Secondly, as Augustine made such effort to emphasise, Christ calls sinners to repentance. The very hope of perfection assumes that the one who wants to become a saint is a sinner! To make progress in our spiritual journey towards final unity with God is to make progress against our sinful appetites and passions. The sins to which we are most prey indicate the equal and opposite virtues in which Christ would have us become specialists. So, the church is always and everywhere a church of sinners striving to become saints and accordingly, unlike the exclusive club desired by the Donatists, everyone qualifies for membership.

The third profound insight that Augustine had in his battle against the Donatists and which remains with us to this day is that the efficacy of Grace depends on Christ and not on us. If Grace depended on us no one could even aspire to be saved. St Paul had, of course, said exactly this but Augustine knew from personal experience that God actually wants to be glorified by sanctifying the most unlikely scoundrels so that to him alone might be the glory, honour and praise. Augustine knew that though grace might be defined by theologians a variety of ways: it is total reliance on Christ or it is nothing at all.

The second major heresy against which Augustine argued was one which he knew well because he had been a prominent member of it: Manichaeism. Manichaeism originated with an oriental who became a Christian whose name was Manichios. After becoming a Christian, Manichios decided that what he had been taught about the faith was less than true. It is no longer clear as to how many of the false doctrines flowed from Manichios himself or his followers but by the time of Augustine the heresy was plain enough: the only way to resolve the theodisic problem (= if God is so good, how come evil exists) was to posit the existence of two gods, one who is benign and providential, and the other who is malicious producing all that is evil.

The world in general and human beings in particular were, he thought, caught up in an eternal war between them. So, if good things occurred it was because the good god was winning and if evil things occurred it was because the strategy of the other evil god was more successful. The struggle was eternal because both gods were thought to be equal in power and strength.

In essence, the Manichaeian dilemma was this: either evil is real or it is illusory and all the evidence points to the former rather than the later. So, if evil is real, and it is, then defied Christians had to explain why their omnipotent and benevolent God would allow it to continue. The choice was clear, either the Christian God was all powerful and would end evil as an expression of his power, or he did not in fact have the power to do so and so could not be God.

Moreover, if Christians were to argue that God imposed a self-denying ordinance on his power so that evil was a matter of permission rather than a deliberate act then, the heretics would argue such a God was not worthy of human allegiance, adoration or worship. Manichios knew that there is no more incisive objection to faith that the human mind can conceive than this, because it touches on the deepest mystery on earth—the presence of evil.

Augustine knew this too. Having been a Manichaean for nine years he knew the system and the specious arguments only too well. Even so, it took him a long time to see the errors of Manichaeism in general and his own involvement with it in particular. But when he did so what he discovered, if I may be permitted to paraphrase, was this: if you look at the Manichaean explanation of evil—especially moral evil, sin—through the supposition that there are two gods at war with each other, what does this say? It says, in so many words that all evil is due to an evil god, an evil deity that is outside of you.

How convenient! How useful! It is like a small child when caught disobeying some rule saying to a teacher, "It's not me, Miss, and it was him. He *made* me do it." In short, Manichaeism denies that we have any moral responsibility for the wickedness we create and reduces human beings to mere playthings of the gods.

"Once it dawned on me that the same Augustine who is sinning had the power (with God's grace) not to sin: that was a great discovery."[369] A great discovery indeed because it meant that Christianity was the champion human freedom, of our ability, within limits and in cooperation with the grace of God, to make what we want of our lives. In other words, Augustine saw that Manichaeism was a philosophy of determinism. Manichaeism as a religious error might have been defeated but determinism has not. Indeed, it may be reasonably argued that it is one of the greatest heresies of the modern world—heredity, environment, education. Billions of pounds are spent each year on this illusory hypothesis; that virtue is in the suburbs and vice in the inner cities, that if people are born to virtuous parents, they will automatically be virtuous too, that provided people. Not so. it is likely that most British citizens have never heard of Manichaeism but fewer and fewer of them seem to want to take moral responsibility, or make up their own minds, for themselves blaming their wickedness instead on factors external to themselves and so for all practical purposes are followers of Manichios. Consequently, the church's teaching on free will and its power is in large measure due to the impetus which Augustine gave it in his conflict with Manichaeism.

The third heresy which Augustine confronted was Pelagianism and that too had much to say about the relationship between free will and determinism. Pelagianism is the one great heresy for which Great Britain, specifically the

---

[369] Op cit Augustine; *Confessions*.

English and Welsh, can take credit! Pelagius, or Morgan, was a Welsh monk in England. He made the mistake of travelling beyond these shores and became subject to many whims and fancies. During his travels he saw much wild and immoral behaviour especially among bishops, priests, monks and nuns which scandalised him.

The only explanation that Pelagius could find for this behaviour was this: they are not using their will power. So it is that Pelagianism may be thought of as the polar opposite of Manichaeism. He went around thinking preaching and teaching and gaining a large following as a result. In the end, he altogether denied the need for any grace from God. All one needed was moral fibre, a strong backbone and lots and lots of will power. What is the mark of the Christian? Simply to be moral. How is morality obtained and exercised? By innate will power. What is the church? A self-help group. Who are the saints? Those who exercised more will power than anyone else!

When Augustine first heard about Pelagianism, he found it extremely hard to believe and thought it may be some form of practical joke because its errant teaching was so obvious. He thought, as Bertrand Russell said about Benthamite Utilitarianism, that *"it was so false, it is difficult to see how it might have been regarded as credible in the first place."*[370] By this time, Augustine knew exactly what sort of will power he had! When he realised that this was indeed no joke but a pernicious illusion he decided to enter the list against Pelagius. One of the problems in doing so was that Pelagius was no fool. He was widely read. He wrote and spoke effectively and well. In appearance, he was a bag of skin and bones—which made him appear all the more holy. He ate little and fasted much. He was, all things considered, the very picture of sanctity—and he was popular. So, during the period of his "ministry" he misled thousands. The heresy lasted for at least four hundred years and it has infected parts of the church ever since.

Augustine was at his best here because he could be autobiographical. He seldom resorted to sarcasm, but with Pelagius he did. Augustine explained, as he knew from experience and as the Gospel of John makes abundantly clear, without God's grace we can do nothing and make no progress[371] in the spiritual life or in any other respect. It was Pelagianism that forced the church, through the genius of St Augustine, to clarify its position on the admixture of the two

---

[370] Bertrand Russell: *History of Western Philosophy. London. Routledge Reprinted Edition. 2001.p 580.*
[371] John 15:5.

lives we lead; the natural life and that hidden in God. From the conflict with Pelagius, Augustine produced the first systematic theological treatment of Grace; Grace as divine life, Grace as invitation and Grace as the remedy for our fallen sinful nature. It is important to be clear about what Augustine meant by grace as the remedy for our sinful nature because it is this that John Calvin, took up, wholly misinterpreted and reapplied with all the harshness that only his brand of Puritanism could provide in Geneva and beyond during the reformation. Augustine did *not* mean (as Calvin thought) that human beings are so utterly depraved that we cannot exercise any free will at all.

He did *not* mean that for to have done so would, after all, have pressed too close to Manichaeism.[372] He *did* mean that if we are to make spiritual progress in our lives, we need to ensure that our wills are saturated by the grace of God, keeping the words of John 15:5 always in our minds and in our hearts. He also meant that we cannot acquire virtue without grace and that neither this, nor progress in the spiritual life is possible without prayer. It was this combination of our natural free will, the gift of divine grace and prayer that earned Augustine the title of *doctor gratiae—the teacher of Grace*. No one had written so eloquently about the indispensable necessity of Grace in our lives as Christians and in our aspirations towards sanctity. He is also the *doctorations—the teacher of prayer*. His writings on the link between Grace and prayer are among the most beautiful in all Christian literature and in which he, yet again, reasserts his arguments against Pelagius. If we are still in any doubt as to his teaching, it is this: There is no salvation without Grace. There is no grace except that which God gives each and every one of us. There is no progress in the spiritual life or in the acquisition of virtue beyond a combination of the exercise of our own free will, divine grace and prayer.

The ways in which Augustine defeated the heresies of his day is important for this history of the development of monasticism because we find that much of his teaching against them is embedded in his Rules. There are really two Rules of St Augustine, one for men and the other for women. That for men was devised for the clergy of his diocese. He decided to organise his clergy and priests-in-training into a religious community. The rule for women was much more detailed and has set the standard of for women religious in the Catholic church ever since.

---

[372] This raises an interesting thought: Is Calvinism, especially in its "strict and peculiar" variety a reworked version of the Manachaean heresy?

Both Rules assumed that all those who lived by them would be contemplatives, or at least aspire to the mystical life. Describing the structure of his religious communities emphasised the importance of not denying free will. It is by the exercise of free will that a person becomes a monk or a nun—however strong the compulsion to do so as a result of the "call" of God, in the first place. Indeed, the decision to enter the monastery is a prime example of the ways in which free will, divine Grace and prayer work together in the life of the Christian. The same is true of placing oneself in obedience to the Rule.

II is instructive to compare the Rule of Pachomius with the Augustinian Rules, both of which were, of course, written for African Christians. When we do so, we see a mildness and compassion in Augustine which is lacking in the former because of Pachomius' military tendencies. The compassionate mildness is surely the direct result of Augustine's personal knowledge of human frailty and his teaching on Grace and free will. And so it is that perhaps Augustine's greatest and most lasting contribution to the Christian life in general, and that of monks and nuns in particular, was to realise that the most important sacrifice that a human being can make to God is not of the body (important as that may be too) but of the spirit, the mind and the will.

Chapter 10
St Augustine of Hippo: Monastic Friendship in the Cloister and Beyond

In the Uffizi Gallery in Florence, there is a painting by Botticelli called "*St Augustine in his Study*". It depicts the early church father with thinning hair writing in a book or journal with a quill pen. At his feet are many tattered and torn pieces of parchment, presumably ideas and words that Augustine had written but discarded. What is striking about the picture is that Augustine is alone, which, judging from what we know of his life, was surely a rare occurrence. Besides the pastoral duties and administrative responsibilities which took up so much of his time as priest and bishop (about which he frequently complains in his *Letters*), Augustine hardly ever spent time without a close friend nearby[373] perhaps because of his poor health. Even his dramatic conversion at the age of thirty-three in a Milanese garden took place in the presence of his close friend, Alypus, who is holding the book that Augustine takes up to read. When Alypus himself is also immediately converted the two friends rush off to Augustine's mother, Monica, who is similarly close by.[374] This, I will argue, is one of the predominant patterns of Augustine's monastic life: the constant

---

[373] J.H. Baxter, trans, *St Augustine: Select Letters*. Cambridge. Harvard University Press. 1980 in which there are numerous references to the burden of his [Augustine's] duties as bishop as well as to his poor health. In 410, for example, he addresses a letter to his "*dearly beloved brethren, the clergy, and all the laity*" in which he laments "*the weak state of my health [which means that] I cannot adequately cope with all the attentions required from me by the members of Christ, whose love and fear of him compels me to serve.*"

[374] Augustine (1963) *Confessions VIII*. 182–183 trans by Rex Warner. New York. New American Library.

presence of friends, and his obvious love of them. It contributed to his becoming one of the great pioneers of western monasticism who, according to Brian McGuire, "took the lead in forging attitudes towards friendship" which influenced later western culture and theology.[375] That is why Peter Brown has said that "no thinker in the early church was so preoccupied with the nature of human relationships."[376] This chapter will examine the many intimate relationships which influenced Augustine's understanding of monastic friendship. My primary source will be the *Confessions* which contains Augustine's clearest statements on friendship. As we will see, Augustine closely identified those relationships and interpreted them through the image of fire.

Women, Sex and Children

From his youth, Augustine was filled with the longing for union and the yearning of wisdom. Writing *Confessions* at the age of forty-three, some ten years after his dramatic conversion, he describes his adolescence and the natural growth of puberty in the worst possible light. In Book II, he tells his readers that "in the sixteenth year of my flesh…the madness of lust…held complete sway over me."

It is at this point that he introduces the image of fire: "For in that youth of mine I was on fire to take my fill of hell." He goes on to associate that fire with a quality, though disparaged, that stayed with him throughout his life.

"And what was it that delighted me?" he asks, and immediately answers, "Only this—to love and be loved." He then links the fire imagery with the love of friendship and the friendship that comes from love; "But I could not keep that true measure of love from one mind to another mind, which marks the glad area of friendship."[377] In Book III, Augustine uses the same imagery and make the same connections. At the age of eighteen, he says, "I came to Carthage, and all around me in my ears were the sizzling and frying of unholy loves. I was not yet in love, but I loved the idea of love…It was a sweet thing to be loved, and still sweet still when I was able to enjoy the body of my lover."

---

[375] Brian Patrick McGuire (1988) *Friendship and Community: The Monastic Experience 350–1250*. Kalamazoo, MI. Cistercian Publications. p32.
[376] Peter Brown (1950) *Augustine of Hippo: A Biography*. Berkeley. University of California Press.
[377] Op cit *Confessions* II, 40–42.

The very next sentence, after this reference to the body of his lover, is telling: "And so, I muddied the clear spring of friendship with the dirt of physical desire and clouded over its brightness with the dark lusts of hell."[378] This sexual relationship with a woman who remains unnamed throughout the *Confessions* lasted for thirteen years, from 372 to 385AD, and as early as 373 it produced a son, Adeodatus, who emerges in Augustine's autobiography, *The Teacher*, as an exceptionally precocious child, but a close friend.[379] Although Augustine equates his relationship with this unnamed woman with an inability to control his sexual appetite, it is clear from the short description of its ending how much they loved each other: "My heart, which clung to her, was broken, and wounded and dripping blood. She had returned to Africa after having made a vow to you [God] that she would never go to bed with another man..."[380] It is also clear that although the classical culture that had shaped Augustine believed that only men could be friends in the truest sense[381] Augustine applied the term *friend* to his female lover, the mother of his child.

Cicero: The Friendly Mentor

The imagery of fire appears again shortly after Augustine's move to Carthage. Augustine's father died when Augustine was seventeen, and now at the age of nineteen and a student of rhetoric, he discovered a copy of Cicero's *Hortensius*. As a result of reading this book, he tells us, "...my spirit was filled with an extraordinary and burning desire for the immortality of wisdom...I was on fire then, my God, I was on fire to leave earthly thinks behind and fly back to you, not did I know what you would do with me; for with you is wisdom. But that book inflamed me with the love of wisdom (which is called philosophy in Greek)."

This discovery of Cicero's writings had a significant effect on the course of Augustine's life; it was in fact a turning point in which his heart was profoundly changed:

---

[378] Ibid III. 52.
[379] Joseph Colleran. Trans. (1950) *St Augustine: The Greatness of the Soul and The Teacher*. New York. Newman Press. P115–186.
[380] Op cit *Confessions*. VI. 132–133.
[381] According to classical culture friendship presupposed the full mutual equality of those involved—and only men were equal.

"I was urged on and inflamed with a passionate zeal to love and seek and obtain and embrace and hold fast to wisdom itself, whatever it might be."[382] Although another twelve years would pass between the discovery of Cicero's writings and his Christian conversion, the mentoring of Augustine received from Cicero had a lasting effect on his life and thought, not only in terms of his continued passionate quest for wisdom, but in his understanding of the nature of friendship.

In *De Amicitia*, written about 44BC, Cicero had described a friend as an *alter ego* (another self), and succinctly defined the nature of friendship as the "complete identity of feelings about all things in heaven and earth; an identity which is strengthened by mutual goodwill and affection." He says that, "with the single exception of wisdom" friendship is the "greatest of all the gifts of the gods" and the "finest thing in all the world". As such it is the source of all happiness, and, he writes, "the significance of friendship is that it unites human hearts."

Cicero's book on friendship takes the form of a dialogue whose main character is Gaius Laelius Sapiens, and the occasion for these reflections is the untimely death of Scipio Africanus, his close friend. Cicero has Laelius say at one point:

"Without affection and kindly feeling life can hold no joys. Scipio was suddenly snatched away…We shared the same house, we ate the same meals, we ate them side by side. Together we were soldiers, together we travelled and together we went to our country for holidays. Every minute of our spare time…we devoted to study and research, withdrawn from the eyes of the world but enjoying the company of one another."[383] As we will see, Augustine uses similar language in the *Confessions* describing his own friend who died suddenly, as well as the sort of activities with other friends that helped to assuage his extreme grief at that loss. The influence of Cicero, who lived over four hundred years before Augustine, reveals how friendship is *not* limited to contemporaries. Along with Plato, Plotinus and Porphyry [384] Cicero was a significant teacher and mentor for Augustine. He obviously admired the great Roman orator and statesman, and wrote on the same subjects as Cicero, such as

---

[382] Op cit *Confessions* III 56–57.
[383] See in this order of quotations Michael Grant, trans, Cicero: *On the Good Life*. New York. Penguin Books. 1984, p187–188, 227, 218, 221, 226–227.
[384] Op cit Brown. Pp88–100.

friendship and the happy life, using the same dialogic approach.[385] He also quotes Cicero's definition of friendship in a letter to Marcianus, who he describes as "my oldest friend" whom he hopes will join him in baptism, so that their friendship will be as all true friendships are, united in Christ.[386] Writing at the age of seventy, he echoed Cicero's words again when he is reflected on the profound happiness and support he had received from his friends during his long life: "There is no greater happiness and consolation than the unfeigned loyalty and mutual love of…true friends."[387]

Soul Friends and Playmates

Book IV of *Confessions* contains Augustine's fullest explanation of what friendship is, and by implication, what it is not. Again, he uses a story from life to explain the theology, and again he begins this section of autobiography with reference to those desires that he had earlier described under the image of fire:

"So, for the space of nine years (from my nineteenth to my twenty-eighth year) I lived a life in which I was seduced, deceived and deceiving, the prey of various desires."[388] We find him, at the beginnings of his manhood, living with his lover and young son, teaching rhetoric, attracted to astrology and the "vanity of the stage". In 375, he moved to Tagaste, his birthplace, to continue teaching. It is there that he introduces his readers to a friend whom he has known from childhood:

"We were both of the same age…he had grown up with me as a child and we had gone to school together and played together."

This early friendship was, he says, "…sweeter to me than all the sweetness that in this life I had ever known." From a contemporary viewpoint, this relationship might be associated with a youthful infatuation, a co-dependency,

---

[385] See Grant pp49–116 for Cicero's *The Tusculans* for the essentials for a happy life. Augustine wrote *De Beata Vita* the same year as his conversion in Milan and retreat at Cassiciacum.

[386] Op cit Baxter. Pp491–499.

[387] Augustine. (1950) *De Civitatae Deo* (the City of God) Ed. Vernon Bourke. Garden City. New York. Image Books. P447.

[388] Op cit *Confessions* IV 69–73. It seems that since he has now established a settled relationship with his friend and lover, the mother of his child, the cravings are more intellectual than physical.

even with homo-erotic tendencies for as Augustine acknowledges, "my soul could not do *without* him" and *"we depended too much on each other"*.

He goes on to say, with the hindsight of Christian conversion and his own developing theology, that this young male friend was not, however, "a friend in the true meaning of friendship."[389] This friendship was not caught by *"the true meaning of friendship"* because neither of them was Christian. As Augustine explains: "…there can be no true friendship unless those who cling to each other are wielded together by you [God] in that love which is speared throughout our hearts by the Holy Spirit which is given to us."[390] But that is clearly not what he thought or felt at the time! Then Augustine valued this friendship above any other. It was one that had "ripened in the enthusiasm of the studies which we had pursued together." He identifies it with much happiness, and he was obviously devastated when this friend suffered from an uncontrolled high fever and died. This was a tremendous personal loss evidenced in the way Augustine wrote about it:

"My heart was darkened over with sorrow, and whatever I looked at was death. My own country was a torment to me, my own home a strange unhappiness. All the things which we had done and said together became, now that he was gone, sheer torture to me. My eyes looked for him everywhere and could not find him. And as to the places where we used to meet, I hated all of them for not containing him."[391] This is somewhat reminiscent of the stories of the young Buddha and his encounter with an elderly man on the road. It is like the story of Gilgamesh at the death of his friend Enkidu.[392] Augustine is, as are we all when a loved one dies, confronted with his own mortality. Augustine was beside himself with grief: "I became to myself a riddle…tired of living and extremely frightened of dying." He found only tears, tears that *"had taken the place of my friend in my heart's love…I was a misery and had lost my joy."* And then he adds, quoting the poet Horace: "I agree with the poet who called his friend 'half his own soul'. For I felt that my soul and my friend's had been one soul in two bodies, and that was why I had a horror of living, because I did not

---

[389] Ibid. IV ch.4.
[390] Ibid IV 73.
[391] Ibid IV 74–75.
[392] Michael Carrithers (1986) *The Buddha* in Keith Thomas. Ed. *Founders of Faith.* Oxford. OUP. And N.K. Sandars, trans (1972) *The Epic of Gilgamesh* Baltimore. Penguin Books.

want to live as a half being, and perhaps too that was why I feared to die, because I did not want him, whom I had loved so much, to die wholly and completely."[393]

Heretical and Saintly Friends

Still in the depths of his grief, "for my heart could not flee away from my heart, nor could I escape from myself," Augustine returned to Carthage in 376. At this point of his writings, he returns again to the image of fire—associating it no longer with sexual desire, or with intellectual pursuits, but with the ties of friendship. The comfort he found among these other friends in Carthage "helped most to cure me" of his grief. Echoing the words of Cicero, Augustine described the many joys of these friendships:

"…to talk and laugh and do kindness to each other; to read pleasant books together; to make jokes together and then talk seriously together;…to be sometimes teaching and sometimes learning…These and other similar expressions of feeling, which proceed from the hearts of those who love and are loved in return, and are revealed in the face, the voice, the eyes, and in a thousand charming ways, were like a kindling fire to melt our souls together and out of many to make us one."[394] It was at about this time, according to Book V of *Confessions*, that Augustine became a follower of the heretic s Manes and Faustus. Moving eventually to Rome and then to Milan he met Ambrose, someone who "welcomed me as a father". It was, of course, to Ambrose that Augustine poured out his heart;

"I began to love him at first not as a teacher of the truth[395] (for I had quite despaired of finding it in your church), but simply as a man who was kind and generous to me."[396] Alypius and Nebridius.

Augustine was increasingly impressed by the *lived* example of the Christian life which he saw in Ambrose. The preaching of Ambrose had converted his mother, Monica, and two friends Alypius and Nebridius. So it was that the moment for Augustine's conversion intensified. Alypius and Nebridius were to remain his friends throughout his life.

---

[393] Op cit *Confessions*. IV 75–77.
[394] Ibid 77–78.
[395] By this time Augustine was a firmly convinced Manachae.
[396] Op cit *Confessions* V 108.

Alypius had been born in the same town as Augustine, was younger than he and indeed Alypius became a student of Augustine in Cathage. Despite the differences in age and education, mutuality was a key dynamic of their relationship:

"He was very fond of me because he thought me good and learned, and I was very fond of him because of his natural tendency towards virtue which was something really remarkable in one so young."[397] They shared a love of learning and, according to Augustine, "…together with me he was in a state of mental confusion as to what way of life we should take."[398] They were eventually baptised together and lived a monastic lifestyle in Tagaste from 391–394. Some months before Augustoine became Bishop of Hippo, Alypius was consecrated Bishop of Tagaste where he remained until his death in about 430. Years after his Christian conversion, Augustine described Alypius quite simply as "the brother of my heart" and in a letter to Jerome, written in 394 or 395 he states that "anyone who knows us both would say that he [Alypius] and I are distinct individuals in body only, not in mind; I mean in our harmonious and trusty friendship."[399] The imagery of fire returns when Augustine tells his readers about the other close friend, Nebridius, whom he had first introduced in Bok IV, just before describing the death of his other close friend. He there referred to Nebridius as "a dear friend" and "a really good and really pure young man, who used to laugh at the whole business of divination" which Augustine was pursuing at the time.[400] This wealthy young man had left his family estate near Carthage and journeyed to Milan in order, Augustine says, "to live with me in a most ardent search for truth and wisdom. Together with me, he sighed and together with me he wavered. How he burned to discover the happy life! How keen he was and how close was his scrutiny of the most difficult questions." And so, there were "the mouths of three hungry people sighing out their wants to one another."[401] Others made plans to join them in a communal life in which all possessions would be shared, but the plans were quickly abandoned as being impractical, primarily due to the objections of their wives! But the ideal remained and, along with Augustine's communal lifestyle with friends both before and

---

[397] Ibid VI 121.
[398] Ibid 126–127.
[399] Op cit Baxter p57.
[400] Op cit Confessions IV, 73.
[401] Ibid Book VI 127.

after his Christian conversion, contributed to his writing his *Rule*. Rule 11 proposes an ideal of monastic friendship that would be expressed in the sharing of property, living together in godly harmony and being "of one mind and one heart".

Alypius and Nebrisdius continued as intimates of Augustine in that process he refers to in Book VIII of *Confessions* as God's "setting in front of myself, forcing me to look into my own face."[402] As we have already noted, Alypius was with Augustine in the garden of conversion and heard his anguish, and his tears, and was present when "it was as though my heart was filled with a light of confidence and all the shadows of my doubt were swept away."[403] The two friends were baptised together with Adeodatus, by Ambrose—with Monica in attendance. Augustine describes the scene: "And we were baptised…What tears I shed in your hymns and canticles! How deeply was I moved by the voices of your sweet singing church! Those voices flowed into my ears and truth was distilled into my heart, which overflowed with my passionate devotion. Tears ran from my eyes and happy I was in those tears."[404] Augustine returned to the subject of his friendship with Nebridius in Book IX of Confessions: "Not long after our conversion and regeneration by your baptism you [God] took him from this fleshly life; but by then he too was a baptised Christian" Augustine's love and affection for this friend is plain, as is his belief that friendship in Christ survives death:

"And now he lives in the bosom of Abraham…There he lives in a place about which he used often to ask questions of me, an ignorant and weak man. Now he no longer turns his ear to my lips; he turns his own spiritual lips and drinks from your fountain and drinks his fill of all the wisdom he can desire, happy, without end. And I don't think that he is so inebriated as to forget me; since it is of you, Lord, that he drinks and you are mindful of us."[405]

Augustine's Understanding of Monastic Friendship

Having now traced some of the most important relationships in Augustine's life we are now in a position to see how, why and in what ways they might have

---

[402] Ibid VIII, 173.
[403] Ibid 183.
[404] Ibid IX 193–194.
[405] Op cit Confessions IX 187–188.

influenced his idea of monastic friendship. For we have, in a sense, come full circle round: from the sudden loss of his unnamed first friend with whom his soul was intertwined to that of his dear Christian friend drinking his fill of divine wisdom. We have passed from tears of anguish from his young friend's death to tears of joy at his own regeneration in baptism and of his friend baptised with him. We have turned from a fear of dying when he first confronted his own mortality to a strong Christian faith that our friendships made in this life live on for eternity, united in a God who is mindful of us.

We have moved from a wayward life chasing many physical and intellectual pursuits to the life of a soul at rest in God alone. Augustine went on to become both priest and bishop, to start a monastery and write a Rule, but it is only because of these early friendships, remembered in that "great harbour of memory",[406] that he was able to do so at all. It is my contention that for Augustine, human friendships were increasingly important because he became increasingly convinced that they were a model and example, a sign and token, of our friendship with God. What then is true of friendship for Augustine? True friendship is nothing less than the binding together of two or more souls who seek the same goal. It is nothing less than two or more hearts united by the Holy Spirit of God and it is this that lies at the heart of a well-organised, disciplined and harmonious monastic community.

This understanding emerges from Confessions and other writings, especially the letters. It is to no small extent a Christianisation of some of the views put forward by Plato, Cicero, Plotinus, Horace and other classical writers who rated friendship and dialogue with friends as the highest calling of humankind. For them, it was a means by which "the good" could be contemplated and known. But as a Christian theologian, Augustine differed from them in one crucial respect. While friendship for classical writers is a mutual search for beauty, truth and wisdom for their own sake, Christian friendship leads friends to the *source* of all Beauty, Wisdom, Truth and Love. This source is God who, far from being remote is personal and makes himself known in love, including the love of friends. God abides in love and insofar as and in the degree to which friends share love, they abide in God.

But what is the source of Augustine's own great passion to love and to be loved? What is the source of his yearning for truth and wisdom, his all-embracing

---

[406] Ibid X 210.

desire to be united with God? How does God work to lead him[407] to his true self? What accounts for Augustine's obvious ability to form deep and intimate friendships and find such overwhelming joy in them? There is, I think, but a single answer: his mother, Monica. Peter Brown has argued that Augustine's inner spiritual life was "dominated by one figure—his mother"[408] and according to Augustine's own accounts she is there at the most important turning points of his life. He mentions Monica in Book I of *Confessions* and says that even as a neonate he "was welcomed…with the comfort of woman's milk." In Book II, he says that during his puberty Monica privately warned him "not to commit fornication and especially not to commit adultery with another man's wife." [409] In Book III, Monica has a dream, or vision, of a "very beautiful young man with a happy face" who promises her that her son will be converted to Christianity and telling her that "Where you are, he is too." In Book V, her bitter tears for Augustine "daily…watered the ground" when he announced that he was about to travel to Rome. In Book VI, she joins him in Milan, and plays, Augustine says, "a large part" in breaking up his relationship with his lover, the mother of his child, so that he could be properly married.[410] In Book VIII, it is to Monica that Augustine and Alypius run after their conversion, and then in Book IX she dies at the age of fifty-six.[411] Augustine describes her death, however, only after he summarises her life and one of their last meetings.[412] Here, in this one scene, Augustine most clearly paints for us the meaning and direction of Christian

---

[407] As Augustine believed God does in all conversions.

[408] Op cit Brown p29.

[409] Pre-marital sexual relations and masturbation (= fornication) are to be avoided but adultery, being specifically mentioned in the Ten Commandments, is to be avoided at all costs.

[410] It is not clear to me why Augustine could not have "properly" married his lover. Was the illegitimate child an impediment? Had Monica's advice to the pubescent Augustine gone unheeded so that this relationship was adulterous? Or was it simply that Monica the matriarch thought that this woman could never be good enough for her son? No doubt Monica thought that she was acting from the best and most pious of motives but it seems a rather cruel (and un-saintly) act even if the end result might be viewed as having been "for our good and the good of all his church." Fr Terence Kordong simply says that the impediment was one on unequal social status.

[411] Op cit *Confessions*. I, 6. II, 3 III, 66–67 V, 101 VI, 131.

[412] The passage in question, *Confessions* X 200–201 is so well known that it need not be quoted in full here.

friendship: two or more souls, two or more hearts united in one vision of eternal wisdom. In this scene too, we see his paradigm for monastic friendships, spiritual friends, transcending the ages, mutually helping each other to discover and feel God's infinite love. It is no wonder then that after this encounter with Monica at Ostia and after a life time of memories, Augustine says that at the death of Monica his soul "was wounded and my life was, as it were, torn apart, since it had been a life made up of mine and hers together"[413] and that as a result Henry Chadwick could claim that Monica was Augustine's "supreme friend".[414] In Augustine's friendship with Monica, we find not only the source of his adult Christian convictions in general[415] but the origins of his idea of male and monastic friendship. Judging from references to his father Patricius in *Confession,* Augustine had very little personal affection for him.[416] As a result, Augustine searched throughout his life for a suitable male role-model and father-substitute. Besides Ambrose there was his wealthy patron, Romanianus, who sponsored his early education, and remained a friend for life. For nine years, the Manichaean Bishop Faustus, served as a kind of long-distance mentor until Augustine actually met him and was disillusioned because of his great ignorance. Simplicianus, originally a mentor of Ambrose, became an important guide for Augustine especially when, in 386 he told Augustine the story of the conversion of a man called Victorinus.[417] Augustine also felt close to those of a bygone age such as Plato and Cicero and those he heard about, such as St Anthony of Egypt acted in a mentoring capacity. Despite the cold relationship with his father, or perhaps precisely because of it, Augustine grew exceptionally close to Monica, and she to him.[418] The depth of their relationship might, from a more contemporary viewpoint be regarded as psychologically unhealthy. The description in *Confessions* V, 102, "She loved having me with her, as all mothers do, only she more than most," gives some weight to this view. The Swiss psychologist, Carl Jung has called this a "mother-complex", and although it can be associated with psychological illness, in its wider connotations it can have

---

[413] Op cit Confessions X 205.
[414] Henry Chadwick (1986) *Augustine*. Oxford OUP. p69.
[415] Peter Brown calls these the "religion woven into our very bones as children". Op cit Brown. P105.
[416] At least not until after his death, *and* that of Monica.
[417] Op cit *Confessions* VIII 167.
[418] Ibid V 102.

very positive results: "Thus, a man with a mother-complex may have a finely differentiated Eros…Thus give him a great capacity for friendship, which often creates ties of astonishing tenderness between men and may even rescue friendship between the sexes from limbo of the impossible. He may have good taste and an aesthetic sense which are fostered by the feminine streak. Then he may be supremely gifted as a teacher because of his almost feminine insight and tact. He is likely to have a feeling for history, and to be conservative in the best sense and cherish the values of the past. Often, he is endowed with a wealth of religious feelings which help him to bring <u>ecclesia spiritualis</u> into reality, and a spiritual receptivity which makes him responsive to revelation."[419] All these attributes can be discerned in the life and work of Augustine, and, with this Jungian interpretation we may, finally, have a clue to the meaning of the imagery of fire that is so prevalent in Augustine's *Confessions*.

According to Jung, fire is a symbol of transformation and of Eros, that powerful human yearning for wholeness, freedom, and wisdom. This "fire" is a spiritual force, a passion and enthusiasm for what and whom we love deeply that ultimately leads us beyond ourselves to the deeper self that lies within (and from thence to God). While Augustine could and did acknowledge that spiritual side of the flame on an intellectual level, it is precisely the bodily aspect of it which caused him so much anguish, both personally and theologically.

Personally, he struggled with a passionate nature that had difficulty in accepting limitations of any kind—whether sexual longings or limits on work. Theologically he was influenced by the Neo-Platonists who, though acknowledging the importance of Eros in the spiritual quest, ultimately distrusted it and the affective side of human life in favour of pure reason. Augustine shared this belief, immersed as he was in that philosophical and cultural tradition. In *De Civitate Deo* (City of God) he describes how Socrates believed that "…only…a mind purified from passion" could comprehend "the origin of all things," including "the will of the single and Supreme Divinity." As a result, Augustine failed to fully appreciate the goodness of passion itself, denigrating and condemning his own sexuality, but almost every form of sexual expression too.[420] Many modern writers, even Christian ones would, happily, profoundly

---

[419] Carl Jung 1969 *Collected Works*. Vol 9. Princeton. University of Princeton Press p86-87. Emphasis in the original.

[420] Op cit Augustine *City of God*. p146ff. It is, in my view, a matter of great regret that many Christians have continued to do so ever since. Its consequences are plain to see in

disagree with him in this respect. C.S. Lewis, for example, points out in *The Four Loves* that the so-called "highest" loves cannot stand without the lowest. Jungian psychologists, and I hope sensitive and sensible modern Christians, would advise Augustine that *all* human relationships, including our friendships, have a bodily and sexual aspect to them, and that if there is no emotion, no affect or attraction between people, there will be no depth of intimacy either. Rosemary Houghton, among other contemporary theologians, such as Adrian Thatcher, would point speak to him of how the Christian doctrine of the incarnation makes holy all materiality and bodiliness, and how sexual passion can, and so often does, lead us to greater self-giving. The mythologist Joseph Campbell would warn Augustine, as he would all of us to: "Be careful lest in casting out the devils, you cast out the best that is in you too."

Even Socrates's mentor, the priestess Diotima, believed that Eros is a great force which acts as a mediator between the human and divine.[421] If Augustine had perhaps taken that message from Plato's *Symposium* more seriously, and listened more closely to his feminine side, he might have been a little more trusting of his own Eros and appreciated it more genuinely as a vehicle leading him to the wisdom, holiness, and friendship of God he desired so much. From these perspectives, we can now see that references to fire in Augustine's writings are in fact references to Augustine's own Eros, and that, despite his own denigration of that passion when expressed sexually, Eros—in all its

---

all denominations and especially in the current debates in the world-wide Anglican Communion and which threaten the strength and unity of local parish congregations too. It can also split members of a family. I was once invited to a house party in the Herefordshire countryside where the sleeping arrangement became quite absurd simply because some guests could not accept the idea that unmarried single people (even those related to each other) could share a bedroom. It is astonishing that one set of Christians can seek to legislate the morality of another in this way and feel that they have "traditional Christian values" on their side for doing so, and in the belief that they were somehow "witnessing" to them and to the truth of Christ. The effect of course, was precisely the reverse. Those most affected by the absurd sleeping arrangements may well have been finding a way towards faith but were effectively turned away from it because the joy of faith and religion had been reduced to mere morality and disapproval. And so, it is on a local, national, and international ecclesiastical level. Indeed, I would go further. If salvation depends on what does, or does not, take place behind the closed doors a person's bedroom—then I suspect that we are all in serious trouble!

[421] Plato (1986) *The Dialogues of Plato*. Ed Erich Segal. New York. Bantam Books. p7.

manifestations—made him the person he was and the saint he was to become. Truly, his life, to use the poetic language of TS Elliot, was "tongued by fire",[422] and the directions it took and the important relationships he made were touched by that fire. Of course, Eros, like fire can have a destructive power; but it is also the place where the Holy Spirit dwells. This spiritual presence, as Augustine knew from his own lived experience, manifests itself in numerous ways, from the voice of a child in a garden to a kindling fire whose warmth and power unites human hearts in the cloister, in the church and beyond. That spiritual power, in fact, most often seems to be manifest in the heart, and it is intriguing to note that whenever Augustine, in his *Confessions* uses the imagery of fire, the image of the heart is near at hand. That is where Augustine locates monastic friendship for, according to him, friendship is simply a sharing of the counsels of the heart.

This chapter on Augustine's view of monastic friendship, then, has been about Augustine's own erotic passage to ultimate wisdom, and how, through his many friendships, he was led to the God who unites souls and hearts (and bodies!). As his life story clearly shows, it is true that a person can be known by the friendships he or she makes, or perhaps, more accurately, that he or she is given. Monica was a significant part of that process; she did what Augustine in his writings considered one of the chief duties of friends: that of drawing each other closer to God. Because of her love, prayers and persistence the dream and prophecy of her son's conversion came true.

In one of Augustine's letters, he says this:

"When you have read this letter, use it as an invisible bridge to cross over and proceed in through my heart, and see what goes on there concerning you. There will be laid open to the eye of love that inner chamber of love, which we close against the troublesome trifles of the world when we adore the Lord. There you will see the ecstasy of my joy in that good deed of yours, which I cannot utter in my speech or express with my pen, burning and glowing as it is in the sacrifice of praise by Him by whose help you carried it. Thanks be to God for his unspeakable gifts."[423] If love is a shared vision and the heart its resting place, a dwelling place for our friends, as Augustine suggests here, then we can perhaps

---

[422] TS Elliot (1971) *The Complete Poems and Plays.1909-1950 Little Gidding.* San Diego. Harcourt brace Jovanovich. p139.
[423] Augustine. Epistle 58.2 in Adele Fisk (1970) 'St Augustine: Stages of Friendship' In *Friends and Friendship in the Monastic tradition.* Cuernavaca, Mexico. Centro Intercultural De Documentacion. p 2–5.

conclude that the original interpretation of the painting by Botticelli of an ageing Augustine seated at his desk is somewhat misleading. For even in Augustine's rare moments of solitude, he was really not alone. He was probably thinking of his friends, developing an even greater intimacy with them in his memory and in his heart. Knowing what we know of him it is not hard to imagine him stopping writing for a moment, putting down his pen, smiling and then praying for them to the god who had been revealed in his life as a God of friendship, a God of fire, a God of eternal Love."

Part 4
St Benedict Then and Now

Chapter 11
The Quest for the Historical Benedict: The Man, the Myth and the Rule[424]

In 580AD, the Benedictine monks of Monte Cassino, Italy, were overcome by wandering warlike bands of Lombards. It was in the latest of a series of invasions by disaffected Teutonic tribes against the crumbling power of the Roman Empire. The Lombards attacked the monastery during the night and plundered as much as they could. But, as Pope St Gregory the Great reports, no monk was harmed in the attack: "They had no power to lay hand on any man. But Almighty God fulfilled what he had promised to his faithful servant, Benedict, that although he gave their goods into the hands of Panynims, yet he preserved their lives."[425] The monks scattered far and wide finally reaching Rome some eighty miles to the south taking with them the few remaining important things such as "the book of the Holy Rule…some other books, the weights for bread and the measure for wine, and what other furniture they could get away."[426] No doubt, Paul the Deacon lists the items in order of importance, the most valuable of which was the original manuscript of the Rule of St Benedict (RB). While a few copies of RB were already in circulation, the survival of the original autograph

---

[424] Much of this chapter was first presented as a paper given to a gathering of Anglican Lay Readers in the Diocese of Southwark in 2013.

[425] Pope St Gregory the Great: *The Life of Our Most Holy Father Saint Benedict. The Second Book of the Dialogues.* Grand Rapids. Christian Classics Ethereal Library. P61.

[426] Paul the Deacon: *Historia Langobardorum* IV.7 as cited in Abbott Justin McCann (1958) *St Benedict: The Man and his Work.* Garden City New York. Image Books. It is interesting to note that Paul the Deacon was himself a Lombard. He lived from 725–799AD.

which Benedict had written some fifty years earlier, was a token of inspiration as the monks tried to re-establish themselves in Rome.

Today, many thousands of monks, nuns and lay people live according to the spiritual life laid down in the RB and even more draw inspiration from it. Whether we know it or not, whether we are prepared to acknowledge it or not, the plain fact is that much of western culture and civilisation is derived from the RB. The fact that the RB, written over 1,500 years ago, is studied and read by so many people and communities may be interesting enough, but when we consider the modest origins of RB in the light of its endurance through the Gothic wars, the collapse of Rome and the beginning of the so-called Dark Ages (which as we will see in later chapters were nothing of the sort) its survival takes on a truly remarkable status.

The RB has many antecedents in earlier monastic literature and rules, including those of Pachomius, Basil, Cassian, the Rule of the Master (RM), The Rule of Colombanus and that of Augustine of Hippo to name but a few. Benedict's Rule not only subsumed these other rules and writings, it eclipsed them. Paradoxically, however, the RB is somewhat archaic and according to many modern minds, even authoritarian. Yet it is enjoying a great popular resurgence and the number of thoughtful commentators and interpreters of it are growing. This leads to two obvious questions: Why? What exactly is it about this relatively short work and the life it enjoins that makes it so influential both historically and now?

In every country of Western Europe, the Benedictine's (or "Black monks" as they were popularly known) gradually established themselves as landowners, administrators, writers and artists as well as clerics and bishops. In England, for example, more than half of all the pre-reformation Cathedrals were of Benedictine foundation.[427] But as A.G. Dickens points out it is perhaps precisely because of these things that it is possible to overestimate the numbers of Benedictines in England[428] and he goes on to explain that by the time of the Henrician dissolution, many monasteries were woefully under populated. Dickens believes that for this reason alone the monastic influence on church and state has been consistently overrated by historians and those interested in monastic spirituality ever since. The problem with Dickens' argument is, of

---

[427] Ester de Waal (1984) *Seeking God: The Way of St Benedict*. Minnesota, The Liturgical Press Collegeville pp20.

[428] AG Dickens (1996) *The English Reformation*. London Fontana Press. p80.

course, that he confuses numbers with influence. History—monastic history in particular—is replete with examples of one person having a huge and lasting influence over thought and practice. So, the paucity of numbers which Dickens claims to have identified does not at all disprove the overall phenomenal influence of monasticism in general and of Benedictines in particular, over church and state. Indeed, Ester de Waal has persuasively argued that to write a history of the Benedictines before the reformation would be not only to write an exhaustive history of the church in the period, but of society and its economics as well.[429] In the light of these arguments, it is more than a little ironic to note that from the first, Benedictines never intended to exercise any influence beyond the cloister at all! In short, there is no evidence that Benedict ever intended his Rule to be anything other than a guide for spiritual and practical conduct of those who were already, or were intending to be, Benedictine.

This complete lack of intentionality concerning any form of notoriety beyond the cloister makes the historical person, Benedict, somewhat elusive. Benedict, unlike others in monastic history never wrote a spiritual journal of his soul, never composed essays or commentaries on scripture and never sent letters. His *only* writing appears to be the RB. It is for this reason that the historical Benedict is "an enigma for the historian, or at all events, one of those brilliant figures whose very radiance prevents his individual features from showing through very clearly."[430] This is a problem since to try to grasp the essence and perennial persistence of the RB we are compelled to ask about the person and character of Benedict. Recourse to the writings of Pope St Gregory the Great only adds confusion to the quest for the historical Benedict. To say that Pope St Gregory is Benedict's biographer is intensely misleading for his *Dialogues* are not to be thought of as a straightforward account of Benedict's life and work. As Gregory's favourite term for Benedict, *"man of God"*, indicates he was not concerned with facts and times and places but with the action of God in a person's life. To this extent, Gregory's Benedict is not an actual person at all, but rather an ideal type, a paradigm, of a holy and virtuous person and thus an example to which all that live by the RB may aspire.

The paradigm is strengthened by stories which are explicitly mythical in form and in content especially where Gregory tells of Benedict's many miracles,

---

[429] Ibid de Waal p20.
[430] Henri Daniel-Rops (1962) *The Church in the Dark Ages*. **Volume 1**. Garden City New York Image Books. p 348.

prophecies and moral virtues. Yet the few facts that Gregory does include are tremendously important. He tells us that Totila, King of the Goths, visited Benedict and that Benedict reproached him and prophesied against him. On one level, this looks and feel like yet another myth, but it can be historically verified to the extent that it may also help date Benedict's death.[431] All the other details of Benedict's life in the *Dialogues* can be taken at face value *and* interpreted allegorically. Pope Gregory tells us that Benedict (and a twin sister, Scholastica), was born "in the province of Nursia of honourable parentage and sent to Rome to study the liberal sciences"[432] and that Benedict quickly became sickened by the moral decay and corruption of Roman society. He abandoned his studies, *"skilfully ignorant and wisely unlearnt."* [433] Quite how Benedict's father reacted to this "dropping out" of college Gregory does not record, but relationships with Scholastica, at least, seem to have been maintained. Benedict went first to Affile with his either his old nurse or a handmaid (the text is not entirely clear) who served him.[434] He then went to the mountains around Subiaco, some forty miles from Rome, and lived in a cave. It is at this point that his "nurse" fades from view. From his vantage point in the cave, Benedict could see most clearly the ruined arches of Nero's palace, its overgrown fish ponds and the broken

---

[431] The visit took place in 543 and Benedict died in 547. For more on how these dates are linked and their historical importance see Hugh Edmond Ford *The Catholic Encyclopaedia* **Vol 2** Copyright 1907 by Robert Appleton Company. New York.

[432] Op cit Pope Gregory. p10.

[433] Loc cit.

[434] There are a number of interesting points of speculation here. Some traditions about the sojourn in Affile tell us that his old nurse was very wise and that her name was "wisdom". This, in my view, reinforces the suggestion that Benedict is more of an ideal type than a historical character. If so, three things are at work here. First a clear clash between Christianity and Roman culture. Second that Christian wisdom is not defeated by that encounter and indeed survives in such a way as to "serve" the man of God". Third the departure to the Italian countryside is a metaphor for monastic withdrawal from the world generally. If, on the other hand, we again take all this at face value and if Benedict's companion is a handmaid and not some old crone from childhood, then we might speculate as to whether it was really Benedict's distaste for Roman society that caused him to leave Rome or some personal scandal. Even this might be regarded as symbol, however, as it would place Benedict firmly in the traditional of Evagrius of Pontus, and possibly of St Jerome too.

aqueduct.[435] Benedict lived in his cave, with occasional visits from a hermit called Romanus for three years.[436] His isolation was then broken by the arrival of a great many visitors whose numbers appear to have been so great and their demands for advice so persistent that Benedict had no choice but to alter his lifestyle.[437] "By this means his name began to be famous throughout the country, and many did resort unto him, bringing with them necessities for his body, while they received from his lips the food of life."[438] Then, like the first apostolic community after Pentecost, many of these people decided to stay on and soon, twelve small monasteries were formed on the mountainside, each containing twelve new disciples.[439] Soon Benedict left Subiaco and went to Monte Cassino.[440] We are not told why he did this, especially since he was now fifty years old and so of great age for the times. The only reason that Pope Gregory gives is more than a little cryptic and is a report of what a monk called Mark had to say about it: "But Holy Benedict, by God called from the desert lone, made pure his port, the statues broke, threw down the sculptured stone.

A temple for the living God this idol fane is now.

Let not the faithful soul delay to pay his pious vow."[441] It is not at all clear to me what this means and, in fact, it may not mean very much at all except as a

---

[435] Esther de Waal describes these as symbols of Rome's broken society, *Op cit Waal p16* and so they are. Some of these ruins can still be seen today. But there is, of course, more to the symbolism than this. Many of the symbols are about water, or the lack of it. Their ruined state suggests that they are waiting for Benedict to fill them with the water of life springing up in fountains of eternal life, to paraphrase St John's gospel.

[436] Again, the cave and the period of time spent there can be interpreted allegorically. Three years in a cave might put us in mind of the three days that Christ spent in the cave of the tomb. The name of the hermit Romanus (of Rome) might also be symbolic, meaning occasional visits to and from the "outside" world from which "Benedict" as monk and paradigm of virtue has withdrawn.

[437] Yet again we might think of parallels between this and the enormous growth of Christian converts reported in the Acts of the Apostles which eventually forced the Apostles themselves to change their life style so that they no longer waited at table etc.

[438] Op cit Pope Gregory. p15.

[439] This too may be symbolic: twelve tribes of Israel > twelve disciples of Christ > twelve monasteries > twelve Benedictine disciples. Each gathered in, or around, *one* location itself a symbol of Christ.

[440] Is this too symbolic of the mission of the early church—a missionary journey?

[441] Op cit Pope Gregory p31.

piece of early Benedictine doggerel! The best interpretation we can place on it, I think, is this: Benedict began an eremitical life, moved to a coenobitic one and now felt called to develop new monastic communities in places which had previously been devoted to pagan worship.[442] Or perhaps the move from Subiaco to Monte Cassino was one of simple necessity. The site of the former temple to Jupiter, Venus and Apollo would provide more living space for the new community and the building materials with which to enclose it. Whatever his motives for removing to Monte Cassino, it was this that would become his principal establishment in which the final version of the RB would be written. So thus far St Gregory's account of the life of Benedict leaves us with far more questions than answers and to go any further with the *Dialogues* is to pass from history and myth into fiction and legend. No doubt "Contemporary historians are embarrassed by these legends as they do not carry the force of historical information"[443] but to dismiss them out of hand, as Byrne would seem to wish to do, would be to miss a dimension of Benedict's life that finds some parallel in the RB. There is a particular quality to Gregory's legends that asks for a particular kind of attention which may yield a particular kind of information. It seems to me that the more legendary parts of Gregory's *Dialogues* operate in much the same way as some Biblical stories, (especially those of the prophets in the Old Testament) and are reflected in the role and purpose of the RB. So, for example, when the *Dialogues* speak of Benedict's journey from Rome via Subiaco to Monte Cassino it does so from a somewhat narrow perspective of obedience, labour and suffering to delight and intimacy with God and his kingdom. The journey comes to a climax with Benedict's vision of the whole world contracted to a single ray of light.[444] In the same way, the RB is also an invitation to journey towards the light of God by throwing off the sloth of disobedience and running towards it through obedience, labour and prayer. This spiritual journey "…is bound to be narrow at the outset. But as we progress in

---

[442] If I am right about this then my speculation that Benedict's time in Rome can be interpreted as a clash between Christian virtue and Roman decadence (howbeit that Rome tolerated Christianity) gains more weight. At all events we seem to have another direct parallel between Benedict's life and the expanding mission of the primitive Church in to the pagan, gentile world.

[443] Lyvinia Byrne (1998) *The Life and Wisdom of Benedict*. London Hodder & Stoughton p6.

[444] Op cit Gregory p99.

this way of life and faith, we shall run on the path of God's commandments, our hearts overflowing with the inexpressible delight of love."[445] This was, as Gregory sees it, Benedict's personal journey—and it is this journey, offered in the RB, that gripped Gregory so firmly. There is then no doubt that Gregory's devotion to Benedict is genuine, but as Pope Gregory also understood the importance of a saint like Benedict to sixth century Italy, beset as it was by war and apparently without hope. Gregory's overarching motive in this respect is made clear in the very first Chapter of *Dialogues*: "…that the life of Benedict should be manifest to the world for an example for all…that the candle wet upon the candlestick might shine and give light to the whole Church of God."

So, although in some respects, Gregory leaves us with a featureless Benedict allowing only a few personal facts, he bestows on succeeding generations a model pilgrim, a man of god, a heroic figure worthy to be followed and to become an object of personal and corporate devotion. As we will see below St Benedict's importance to Gregory is only eclipsed by St Gregory's importance to the Benedictine movement and the RB itself, for it is to the Rule that Gregory directs his readers:

"Only this I would not have you be ignorant of, that the man of God, among so many miracles wherewith he had shined in the world, was also eminent for his doctrine, for he wrote a Rule for Monks both excellent for discretion and eloquent in style."[446] He also points to the RB for any who wish to know more of Benedict the man:

"Of whose life and conversation if any wish to know further, he may in the institution of the Rule understand all his manner of life and discipline, for the holy man could not possibly teach otherwise than he lived"[447] It is the last phrase "…could not possibly" etc that causes difficulty to the modern historical and theological mind. But it is precisely that phrase which, in the eyes of St Gregory at least, makes Benedict the saint that he is.

If Benedict's life and teaching are one and the same "text", that is, if Benedict "could not possibly teach otherwise than he lived," the RB becomes, as Gregory intended, a compelling resource for any Christian intent on the quest for holiness.

---

[445] St Benedict: *The Rule of St Benedict in English.* Ed Timothy Fry OSB. Collegeville Minnesota The Liturgical Press. p19.
[446] Ibid p103.
[447] Loc cit.

It also guarantees the longevity of the RB and this desire for God, this holy longing, found in the RB again mirrors something of Scripture.

It is not surprising then that even a cursory reading of the RB will show that it contains any number of scriptural references and quotations. As Columba Stewart has shown in great detail how the RB can be divided into four main sections, the call and spiritual formation, the structure of liturgical prayer, the common life together, and the basic theology of monastic life, every single one of these sections is underpinned by scripture and at nearly every point within them,[448] so that its very breath and life-blood is scripture—especially the Psalms and the Gospels. According to Stewart the seventy—three short chapters of the RB contain one hundred and twenty-six citations of scripture, fifty-three of which are from the New Testament and seventy-one from the Old Testament. But to see Benedict's use of scripture as merely "proof texts" would be mistaken. There function, especially in the opening chapters, is to carry the narrative line[449] so that the RB becomes *lectio divina*, sacred and meditative reading. This narrative use of scripture is a key feature of the Benedictine spiritual tradition. For all his use of scripture, Benedict was not a systematic theologian. He was a practitioner of scripture and an interpreter of it. It was his belief that all Christians should be saturated in scripture because scripture leads to and is accompanied by prayer. Scripture and prayer together form the key elements of the *opus dei,* the work of God. From RB chapter eight to chapter twenty, Benedict outlines the number and arrangements of the choral recitation of the psalms and other Biblical readings:

"What page, what passage of the inspired books of the Old and New Testaments is not the truest guide for human life?"[450] The RB is not therefore an end in and for itself. Rather Benedict's intention was that it always point away from and beyond itself and this is, on my reading at least, something which Benedict shared with the anonymous author of the Rule of the Master (RM).[451]

---

[448] Columba Stewart (1998) *Prayer and Community: The Benedictine Tradition..* Maryknoll. New York Orbis Books p 20.

Loc cit.

[450] Op cit RB Fry. P95.

[451] The Rule of the Master (RM) is much longer than the RB. In fact, it is three times as long. This led scholars to debate two opinions. First that the RB is a part copy, paraphrase or "handy guide" to the RM. Second that RM is a longer more detailed "worked up" edition of RB. The debate was still being fought as late as 1958 in which year Justin

While Benedict shared RMs high view of scripture and its uses, Benedict did not follow it slavishly. He edits and frames his primary source with a commentary of his own and to it adds his own unique wisdom, learning, discretion and inspiration. The RB is a harmony of his allegiance to the wisdom and learning of the past—including the classical period—his existential understanding of humanity and his own vision of monastic life. Compiling and editing was Benedict's great strength but he also had creativity, originality and foresight in abundance.

This becomes obvious in some of the differences between the RB and RM. In RM, the monk's expectation of "reward" is only spiritual and never in this life but only in the next. Benedict, however, insists that spiritual rewards are not only possible but to be expected in this life too. In the last chapter of RB, he chronicles a high hope with "heights of perfection" for those having made a start towards holiness through his "little rule for beginners".

There is another feature that sets the RB apart from the RM, and indeed all other preceding Rules and that is Benedict's understanding and encouragement of Christian altruism. This is an altruism based on empathy and chapter 72 of RB shows how this is derived from the writings of St Paul, especially Romans 12:10. Benedict says that the good zeal of his monks is about "…supporting with the greatest patience one another's weaknesses of body or behaviour, and earnestly competing in obedience of one another. No one is to pursue what he judges better for himself, but instead what he judges better for someone else."[452] The French Benedictine scholar, Andre Boras has made a detailed study of chapter 72 of RB in which he surveyed many of the preceding rules and speculated as to why it was that Benedict gave altruism such importance.[453] Boras wondered whether altruism was all part and parcel of the smooth running of the community and therefore of great assistance to the abbot. But in the light of Benedict's humility and loyalty to scripture, together with this insistence that the abbot must be

---

McCann argued that RB was the primary source for RM. (see Justin McCann (1958) *St Benedict: "The story of the Man and His Work* Garden City New York. p102.) Fortunately, the matter has been settled in modern scholarship. Benedict used the RM as a primary source. (See Kardong et al *Benedict's Rule: A translation and a commentary.* Collegeville Minesota The Liturgical Press.)

[452] Op cit Fry pp 94–95.

[453] See Kardong et al *Benedict's Rule: A translation and a commentary.* Collegeville Minnesota. The Liturgical Press p 600–602.

obeyed in all things this speculation is clearly false. It seems that Boras goes on to say that most other monastic rules are orientated towards the individual and are concerned about the individual's ascetic growth and behaviour. He concludes that even though altruism is not entirely absent from other rules[454] it is not, as here in the RB, regarded as *both* a moral precept and the distinguishing feature of monasticism. What we have here then is a major shift in monastic thinking and a new turn in the path towards holiness. The RB was written over many years and, more importantly still, its mode of life was lived before ever it was codified. Consequently, the RB shows an awareness and overarching concern for the individual monk *within* the monastic family. Its aim is to provide an achievable ascetic. As a result, the RB is an antidote to the harsh asceticism of the earliest Christian ascetic communities in general and those of the Desert fathers and mothers in particular. It is also an antidote to the other rules circulating at the time[455] "…when set against the other rules such as that of St Columbanus, that of St Benedict was so infinitely more humane, more moderate, and less excessive, that favourable comparisons swiftly resulted, and it attracted large numbers of postulants."[456] In fact, we can go further and say that the RB's radical paradigm shift towards humanising the Christian ascetic life has made it an instrument of general Christian appeal.

Another important aspect of RB is that while St Gregory points to it as a source of information about Benedict an examination of it yields no information about Benedict the man at all. What it does achieve however is to give a clear indication of the virtues that Benedict promoted and this alone leads me to suspect that the RB is influenced by Aristotelian ethics, something I will explore in the next chapter. For the moment, it is enough to say that the RB includes no information about Benedict's experience or anything like an idiosyncratic theology. There is no information about his "celebrity" status in the earliest Benedictine communities either so that it is not really possible to say with any certainty that Benedictines took his personality as a starting point for its growth. On the contrary, what we find is a "spirit" of Benedict diffused throughout the

---

[454] Citing the Augustinian Rule as a particular example.
[455] Even though Jonathan Wodding argued during the Fourth Monos Annual Conference at Douai Abbey in July 2010 that some communities lived both by the RB and some other extant rule and saw no contradiction or difficulty in doing so.
[456] Op cit Daniel-Rops p46.

RB.[457] Thus, if there was and is a cult of the "personality" of Benedict it is a formation of popular piety and cannot be derived from the RB. This is important because *rules* for community life that contain too much of the author's personality is subsequently bound to the person and so in some sense bound to a particular time and place. Although rules like these may always serve as useful references, they quickly become obsolete and thus irrelevant to monastic life. When the "spiritual father" dies, the followers scatter and the community dissolve.[458] The rules need to be revised and rewritten or the community will wither and die. In part at least this is what happened to the RM, the Rule of St Columbanus and others. More importantly still, since Benedict's personality is absent except by way of virtue, the RB is essentially open to development. The Latin word *regula (= rule)* can also mean model or framework; a framework that can support the growth of a climbing plant perhaps.[459] Benedict saw the importance of structure and stability balanced by context and exception. One clear example of this lies, I think, in Benedict's concern for the very young and the very old: "Since their lack of strength must always be taken into account, they should certainly not be required to follow the strictness of the rule with regard to food, but should be treated with kindly consideration and allowed to eat before the regular hours".[460] If Benedictine communities frequently divert from the RB, it is because there is a freedom and fluidity in the Rule that allows them to do so. Yet there is always conformity to the "spirit" of the RB and so, as it were, to St Benedict himself. It is also worth noting that the RB has been rewritten many times according to a distinctly *feminine* perspective, some of which can be dated to the thirteenth century.[461] It is important, however, not to overemphasise the

---

[457] Daniel Rees, *Consider Your Call: A Theology of Monastic Life Today.* Kalamazoo. Michigan. Cistercian Publications. 1980 p 46.

[458] This seems to be a particular problem for some "new" "secular" monastic communities today. Many dissolve or completely cease to exist on the death of the founder(s) has not been sufficiently diffused throughout the community. Their personalities have remained too strong. They have not sufficiently seen their individuality as being *within* the "new" monastic family rather that a focal point around which the members can gather.

[459] This is a useful image or trope by which to think of the way the RB has been thought of and used by Benedictine communities down the ages and by many lay Christians today.

[460] Op cit Fry p60.

[461] See http://www.osb.org/aba/rb/feminine/index. Last Accessed March 2024.

consolations and assurances of the RB at the expense of some of its more stringent and demanding aspects. While Benedict calls his rule a "little rule for beginners", and while towards the end of the RB he assures his monks that he is setting down nothing "harsh, nothing burdensome", it is after all and when all has been said and done, a rule for monastic living in a structured, hierarchical community in which each stratum has its own unique authority. Some modern minds which insist on the building of a big society based on fairness rather than justice might find this unedifying, especially when they find that at least eleven chapters of RB concern themselves with the penalties to be handed down if the rule is breached either through negligence, through weakness or the monks' own deliberate fault.

Throughout the RB chapters often end with a threat of punishment. In chapter 65, for example, where Benedict discusses the final authority of the Abbott, Kardong says that "…it should be admitted candidly that Benedict can become quite furious in the face of what he perceives to be a challenge to monastic authority"[462] Nevertheless, Benedict ends this chapter with an entreaty to the abbot to recall that he is also under obedience and must give an account of the use of his authority to God. As we have come to expect, Benedict is progressive and conciliatory in comparison to other rules; where the RM is concerned with retribution, the RB is concerned with reconciliation and where Cassian uses expulsion from the community as punishment, Benedict uses internal sanctions such as exclusion from meals. Whereas St Columbanus allows for six physical beatings with birch rods for simple misdemeanours, such as not saying "Amen" or singing out of tune, and thirty for more serious offences, Benedict restricts all physical punishments to an absolute minimum—and then mostly for the disciplining of children.

In comparison to these other rules the RB is no less orderly, procedurally based as it is on Mtt.18:15–16. "Moreover, if your brother sins against you go and tell him his fault between you and him alone. If he hears you then you have gained your brother. But if he will not hear you take with you one or two more, that by the mouth of two or three witnesses every word may be established."[463]

---

[462] Op cit Kardong. p377.

[463] Church and monastic discipline is based on mutual correction in three expanding stages. Sin and correction are to remain completely private unless the offender refuses to repent. All correction must be done with great pastoral care and humility, with the highest concern being to preserve the spirits and the salvation of the offender (see also 1 Cor 5:5

All this contributes to the reform of the role of the abbot. Benedict seems to have in mind a kind of communal model reflecting Christ's relationship with his disciples. While maintaining and even reaffirming traditional abbatial authority Benedict displays a new sense of respect and even empathy for the great responsibility placed upon the elected superior, and enjoins that the abbot respect those in his charge. What is unique about this, I think, is that the RB makes this a distinctive aspect of leadership and a special duty of the abbot and as Adalbert de Vogue has pointed out the abbot, although a teacher and interpreter in many things the abbot is never above the Rule.[464] Indeed the abbot is the physical embodiment of the Rule and organically linked to it.[465] This is a movement towards a more integrated, if not yet collegiate, form of authority. There is no question that a hierarchy is assumed but Benedict has purposefully created a tension between those who in authority and those who obey—<u>and</u> *vice versa.* Or rather his method balances the positions of those in the upper echelons of the community with those below and includes within it a stark recognition of the abbot's own poverty and human fallibility. This recognition, this way of seeing the office of abbot is distinctive of the RB and an enduring hallmark of the Benedictine movement.

Taking a somewhat broader view, the other body of material in RB, beyond the detailed descriptions of communal organisation is, of course, spiritual teaching. At the heart of this teaching, and arguably at the heart of the whole of the RB and the later Benedictine movement is prayer. Benedict imposes a daily and seasonal rhythm and pattern for prayer. Monks were to pray without ceasing and in this way develop their unassailable devotion to Christ. It is clear to Benedict that in this way of prayer not only is there a personal transformation, but also a time a place and an entire cultural social arrangement can be reconstituted and made over to Christ as well. An example of this is Benedict's Christianizing of Roman allegiance to civil rule, order and devotion to emperors. In her commentary on the RB, Joan Chittister has interestingly observed that the times set for the monastic offices exactly coincide with the times for the changing of the Imperial Guard. So, while Rome (as the centre of the world) was revering

---

and Gal 6:1). Nevertheless, admonition and correction must take place so that the contagion of sin does not spread throughout the community.

[464] Adalbert de Vogue. *The Rule of St Benedict: A Doctoral and Spiritual Commentary.* Kalamazoo. Michigan Cistercian Publications. 1983. p72.

[465] Op cit Rees p90.

and providing protection for its secular leaders, St Benedict was teaching his community to return that homage and reverence to God and to seek divine protection.[466] As far as Benedict is concerned, this is simply Christian common sense! There is no doubt that a "common sense" approach to spirituality is a key and eloquent part of RB and has contributed to its survival and dispersal. According to Dom John Chapman that dissemination across Europe was rapid. His argument rests on the contention that Benedict was *commissioned* by Pope St Hormisdas to write the RB as a permanent code of monastic law and that it was this imprimatur that gave the rule an unparalleled head start in its adoption by monastic communities.[467] Part of Chapman's theory is based on the structure, symmetry and phraseology of RB. He believes that it finds its parallel in the canons and laws of the era and he cannot believe that Benedict would undertake such an elaborate study of monastic, ecclesiastical and secular civil law simply to govern his monastery.[468] But why should he not do so, especially if the dialogues are correct and Benedict had at least a rudimentary interest and training in law as a student? While we might agree with Chapman that the RB shows that Benedict was aware of other monastic rules and communities, especially those in Rome itself, there is surely no secure reason to suppose that he considered a larger audience when writing RB. Indeed, everything we know about Benedict, some of which we have considered here, would resist that conclusion. Obviously, we too can only speculate as to the audience Benedict had in mind as he wrote but it seems much safer to assume that he was concerned primarily and specifically for his own monks. To think otherwise is a beach of the philosophical principle enshrined in Occam's razor. With respect to Benedict's use of language, it is true that the RB is framed in legislative and legal terminology. It has even been used in the study of Roman law as an example of brevity and efficiency, but that this document is an excellent example of legal language and therefore proof of Benedict's extra attention due to a papal request is far from necessary.

The other part of Chapman's *"papal request"* theory is his further speculation that "the Holy Rule was famous at Constantinople in 530, in Gaul in

---

[466] Joan Chittister osb. (2000) *The Rule of Benedict: Insight for the Ages* New York Crossroad Publishing. p85.

[467] Dom John Chapman OSB (1971) *St Benedict and the Sixth Century*. Westport Connecticut Greenwood Press. pp 194–204.

[468] Ibid p203.

534, in Africa at the same date, as well as in Italy."⁴⁶⁹ For proof of this he claims that Ferrandus, Cassiodorus and Dionysius Exigus and the Gothic Emperor Justinian all quote from and make copious use of the RB. Well, perhaps, but Chapman's argument succeeds or fails at this point on the very point he is trying to establish, namely the rapid dispersal of RB. Plainly then Chapman needs to show how, where and in what ways these men of prominence did indeed use the RB as a *direct* source for their own writings. He does give the example of Cassiodorus, a contemporary of Benedict, a Roman of noble birth, grandson of a general and son of a diplomat who accepted service under Theodoric the Arian Goth and who eventually founded his own monastery using his own Rule. Chapman alleges that Cassiodorus knew RB intimately and attempts to demonstrate this by marshalling an impressive list of supposed comparisons showing what he believes to be a family resemblance between the two rules.⁴⁷⁰ If this is true, Chapman must then explain why it is that when Cassiodorus came to establish his own community and rule, he thought it necessary not only to fail to adopt the RB but to depart from it so markedly in his own writings too. Chapman does not do so because, I suspect that if he did so, his theory would be seen to be the house of cards that it otherwise seems to be. It seems to me that even before checking with other Latin scholars the difficulty of Chapman's argument here is immediately obvious, especially when we recall that Benedict himself used all of the available monastic literature in compiling RB, and McCann has argued that the resemblance to which Chapman points is much more likely to be attributable to Cassian and other monastic sources and not to the imperial sources which Chapman uses to strengthen his argument.⁴⁷¹ The final defeat of Chapman's "papal request" theory is that more recent scholarship has shown that the dispersal of RB was anything but rapid. Sarah Foot believes that the RB was quite unknown in England until a late date in the Anglo-Saxon period⁴⁷² and Jonathan Wooding has persuasively argued⁴⁷³ that even then it sat quite comfortably alongside other existing rules and was not necessarily to be

---

⁴⁶⁹ Ibid p195.
⁴⁷⁰ Ibid p88–110.
⁴⁷¹ Op cit McCann p149.
⁴⁷² Sarah Foot: Monastic Life In Anglo-Saxon England c 600–900 (2009) Cambridge. Cambridge University Press. First Paperback Edition.
⁴⁷³ Jonathan Wooding; Unpublished paper to Fourth Annual Conference of Monos. Douai Abbey July 2010.

preferred to that with which the monks were most familiar. Columba Stewart agrees and says that abbots, much like Benedict himself, felt free to use many rules available to them in a quite pragmatic way and that as a result the RB was initially only a source and not a norm in most monasteries.[474] McCann has gone a further still and claims that the popularity and widespread adoption of RB was entirely dependent upon the widespread interest that was shown in Pope St Gregory's *Dialogues*: "It may be said with justice that he [Gregory] was the greatest and most powerful influence in the propagation of Benedictinism, and may even be regarded as its co-founder."[475] This claim is, in many ways, just as remarkable as Chapman's failed theory and so deserves to be examined in a little detail. Gregory's education was the best available given the degenerated state into which it had fallen in his day. But more importantly, his family contained many examples of Christian piety. He was a direct descendant of Pope St Felix III, his mother, Sylvia, was canonised as a saint and so were two aunts. It is not surprising then that Gregory should have a strong sense of vocation and became a monk. His desire was to live out his life as a simple and humble brother dedicated to study and prayer. This was not to be. His gifts of diplomacy, administration and leadership were everywhere evident. As a result of the momentous upheaval in the church of his day it was not a question of whether he would become Pope, but when.

Gregory was a reluctant Pope, but in 590, having once accepted the mantle he set about his work with unparalleled imagination and vigour. Henri Daniel-Rops says that Gregory's pontificate was "…certainly the most outstanding in the whole period covering the centuries between the invasion and the Middle Ages."[476] He concludes that Gregory's was the pontificate in which the papacy assumed its leading position, a position it maintained throughout the centuries that followed and so laid the foundation for the role of the papacy in more recent times. St Gregory nevertheless remained a monk at heart and his attraction and obedience to the RB was total. His "curia" was staffed by monks and he used

---

[474] Op cit Stewart p21.

[475] Op cit McCann p8.

[476] Op cit Henri Daniel-Rops p291–292. By "invasions" he means those of the disaffected Teutonic tribes at the decline and fall of the Roman Empire.

monks in all his endeavours and enterprises.[477] He was convinced that the monastic system was of very special value to the church and its proclamation, and so he did everything in his power towards its propagation. Gregory spent his entire patrimony in founding religious houses and abbeys and urged the wealthy to endow and support them.[478] While Gregory knew of the existence of other rules for him there was only one which had the capacity to grow monasticism in the way he intended. That rule was, of course the RB. He called it the *regula monachorum.*[479] So the influence of an essentially Benedictine pontificate set the stage for the RB to become, after the Bible, the most widely circulated text of the Middle Ages. St Gregory was also well known for his compassion and humanity. He vigorously defended the right of Jews to maintain and worship in their synagogues. He loved and cared deeply for the people of his oppressed country and this pastoral care extended even to the invading barbarians. His great concern was to evangelise the Lombards and the Byzantines. His missionary zeal also drew his attention to distant horizons, including England. IN this way Gregory not only planted the RB into the hearts and minds of subsequent generations of monks, he was the catalyst that established and propelled the RB into the Middle Ages and it was Gregory's initiative that transformed the style and manner of education throughout Europe and so transformed its cultural life certainly until the reformation, if not to our own day. We will deal with this in far more detail in three later chapters under the title "Revival and Reform", but for the moment we can say that there is much merit in McCann's claim that Gregory is at least as important to the spread of the Benedictine movement as Benedict himself.

Even today, books and commentaries on the RB, Benedictine spirituality and ITR history continue to be written by those who have found in the RB a wellspring of wisdom, spiritual direction and a tool for practical Christian living. The RB has been adapted for parents, families, managers and corporate executives. John Macquistion, a lawyer, has adapted the RB to the circumstances of a busy

---

[477] Including, of course, the sending of St Augustine and his companions to Canterbury, though Sarah Foot has questioned whether those engaged in the first mission to England were monks at all.

[478] Catholic Encyclopaedia. At http://www.newadvent.org/cathen/06780a.htm Last Accessed March 2024.

[479] Op cit *Dialogues* p103.

legal practice. He calls the RB a way of learning the art of living,[480] and he is surely right about that. The ancient practice of (Benedictine) monastic association and attachment through Oblation is also becoming more popular now than for some time. It is interesting to speculate whether and when there will come a time when the numbers of oblates and those using the RB in their private spiritual practices will far outstrip those who are professed. Perhaps that time is already upon us. In her very popular and critically acclaimed book, the poet Kathleen Norris describes her own journey as a Benedictine Oblate as a kind of homecoming.[481] Through St Benedict and the RB she has discovered a way of living in harmony and balance with herself, with others, with her environment and with God. This short account of the quest for the historical Benedict shows, I think, that we must disagree with the idea, promulgated by Chapman, that the RB is no more and no less than an example of Canon Law or for those leading a coenobitic life alone.[482] But we can agree with his conjecture that Benedict "…produced a rule which was so practical and moderate that it could be enforced as a minimum, and so wise and holy that it could lead saints to perfection."[483] Writing about this very point, Regina Goberna puts these words in the mouth of Saint Benedict:

"If I gather a set of laws, either they will serve to increase the dust of the archives of people who will not even want to look at them, or they will wither up those who want to follow them. No, at the heart of the Rule I shall insert the *l*ove of a family. Love is the *f*undamental rule applicable to everyone. Strong minds will not be disappointed nor weak minds bewildered."[484] Timothy Fry believes that this manifest direction and discretion, more than any other qualities, are the prime reasons for the longevity of the RB.[485] Certainly it is discretion that allows for its flexibility and unique malleability. The Rule's discretion opens the door to the un-heroic and ordinary monk or a lay person. It allows entrance and provides pastoral direction for contemplative and active Christian life for the

---

[480] John McQuiston II (1996) *Always we Begin Again: The Benedictine Way of Living* Harrisburg Pennsylvania. Morehouse Publishing p 3.
[481] Kathleen Norris (1996) *The Cloister Walk*. New York. Berkley Publishing.pp 5–9.
[482] Op cit Chaman p196–197.
[483] Ibid p204.
[484] Regina M Goberna (1983) *Our Father Saint Benedict.* New York. New York City Press. P114.
[485] Op cit Fry p11.

whole people of God. If we were to conclude from these and other attestations the RB itself argues most persuasively for its record of endurance we would, I think, be mostly right. But as we have seen there were people such as Pope St Gregory and concomitant events, in the absence of which the RB might not have had such a lasting legacy. Perhaps it might even have been lost. As it stands, we can say with some certainty that the RB survived because of a benign conspiracy of accidents and that it endures through its inherent pragmatism and simplicity and its intrinsic spiritual insight.

The RB is then a great spiritual work because it is subtle and humble. Occasionally it is mundane in its prescriptions but always bold in its demands. It is a great spiritual work because it sets out a way of life, a balance and moderation, a prayerful focus and a Christocentric approach to life that speaks to our innermost need for commitment, coherence and community. I let Columba Stewart have the last word: "The genius of Benedict was to situate the individual search for God within a communal context that shaped as well as supported the quest."[486] Perhaps in the end, this is still the richness that Benedict offers to all of us through his Rule.

---

[486] Op cit Columa Stewart p15.

Chapter 12
Shared Virtue? The Possibility of Aristotelian Influences on the Rule of St Benedict

Even the dullest student of philosophy can usually recall that Aristotle was born in Thrace in or around the year 384 BC and that by the year 368 BC he was already an established and respected member of Plato's Academy in Athens. Following Plato's death in about 348 BC Aristotle left Athens to set up a new branch of the Academy at Assos, and it was here that he began to develop his own distinctive systematic philosophy. After many travels and a time spent as private tutor to the young Alexander the Great, Aristotle was again in Athens and founded his own school of philosophy, the Lyceum in 355 BC. Despairing at the news of Alexander's death in 323, Aristotle again left Athens and settled in Chalcis in Euboea where he died of an incurable illness the following year.[487] The extensive writings of Aristotle are often grouped into three periods of composition. It is to the third period, the time when he was leader of the Lyceum, that his most famous works on ethics and politics belong. Supreme among these is still *"The Nicomachean Ethics"* ("Ethics") named for Aristotle's son, Nicomachus who, by tradition, is said to have edited this work after his father's death.[488] It is Aristotle's belief that virtue is the goal and end (*telos*) of all human action that will occupy us in the first part of this essay. In the second part we will examine how the Aristotelian notion of virtue may have influenced the development of the early Christian idea of the heroic martyr and some forms of

---

[487] Frederick Copleston SJ (1993) *A History of Philosophy* **Vol 1**. New York. Doubleday. P269.
[488] Ibid p274.

pre-Benedictine monasticism. This will necessarily demand a brief and hasty review of some material examined on previous essays from a different viewpoint. The third and final part of this essay will examine certain aspects of the Benedictine monastic tradition in the light of Aristotle's ethical system. We will see two great schools of thought separated by time and outlook but which share a number of similar themes and values. It is these that might shed valuable light on what is I think an area which has received little scholarly attention; the philosophical influences at work on Benedict as he composed his *Rule* for those who would join his "school for the Lord's service".

Theme 1: Aristotle's "Ethics"

Aristotle believed that ethics is not a theoretical science, but a practical lived reality that holds meaning not only for the individual but also for the community, the city-state. Politics, he thought, was the "master art", the key to understanding that lived reality because it takes as its main object that which is "good" for man.[489] While the city-state and the individual share the same "good", this "good" as it exists in the community is ultimately nobler and greater.[490] The first task, however, is to identify what is "good" and defines its contents:

"Now fine and just actions, which political science investigates, admit of much variety and fluctuation of opinion, so that they may be thought to exist only by convention, and not by nature."[491] It is according to the knowledge of each man that one can judge what is good for man (and by extension the whole community of the city-state). Aristotle recognises that, "…both the general run of men and people of superior refinement say that [the good] is happiness."[492] Thus, while there is a general consensus that happiness is the ultimate goal of human actions, individuals disagree as to what happiness really is.[493] So it is that "all knowledge and every pursuit aim at some good"[494] with some identifying

---

[489] Aristotle (1094) *Nicomachean Ethics* Trans. W D Ross. London. Oxford University Press.1966. (hereafter cited as NE) p29.
[490] Ibid 1094a-1094b. See also Copleston p332.
[491] Ibid 1094b p14–17.
[492] Ibid 1095a p17–20.
[493] Ibid 1095a 20. See also Kelly J Clark (2003) *The Story of Ethics: fulfilling our human nature,* Upper Saddle River New Jersey USA Pearson Education Inc. P24.
[494] NE 1095a p13–14.

happiness as pleasure, others wealth and still others honour.[495] Different people will understand happiness differently according to their differing life situations. Commenting on precisely this points the philosopher Kathleen Wilkes wrote: "A good or happy life becomes, in part at least, one that works, and works over time—a life wherein the minimum is missing and the least inner conflict is found. To achieve this man must analyse his amorphous notion of what a good life would be; this involves a reflective assessment not only of his own short-term and long-term needs and interests but also of whatever other desiderata society in general…find important."[496] It is probably worth noting at this point that for Aristotle "man" does not refer either to individuals or to human beings as a species. It has a very restricted meaning and refers only to those males who can claim to a good "all round education".[497] Manhood is not something we are by nature but rather something we acquire and grow into according to our knowledge and learning. Those who cannot lay claim to an "all round", or have had no education at all, are not really men at all but an underclass fitted for manual labour or slavery but little more. So "man" is an elitist term referring only to middle class Greek males whose learning has also endowed them with property and so wealth and leisure and the ability to maintain good health. Only they are capable of leading a "good" life and that is why the purpose of the "*Ethics*" is not to persuade or show one how to live, but to "…give people who are already living a happy, virtuous life insight into the nature of their own souls."[498] This insight is, according to Aristotle, impossible without a certain level of material possessions and social influence:

"[Happiness] needs external goods as well; for it is impossible, or not easy, to do noble acts without the proper equipment. In many actions, we use friends and riches and political power as instruments; and there are some things the lack of which takes the lustre from happiness, as good birth, goodly children, and beauty."[499] So it is that Aristotle distinguishes between having and leading a good life and he maintains that a person who is lacking in material goods cannot

---

[495] Ibid 1095a p22–23. See also Copleston p334.
[496] Kathleen Wilkes (1980) *Essays on Aristotle's Ethics. "The Good Man and the Good for Man"* Berkley. University of California Press. p 341–342.
[497] NE 1095a 3.
[498] Jonathan Lear (1999) *Aristotle: The Desire to Understand.* Cambridge. Cambridge University Press. p 157 my emphasis added.
[499] NE 1099a 31–1099b 3.

be happy. It is in having these certain goods that we are able to lead a good life and count ourselves happy.[500] Even so, a happiness that is based on pleasure or wealth or honour alone cannot be an ultimate "good". Aristotle argues that pleasure is the "good" only of vulgar men.[501] Wealth cannot be an ultimate "good" either, for wealth is only a means to other ends,[502] and the pursuit of honour is so superficial that Aristotle can hardly bring himself to explore the idea that it might be an ultimate "good". It is the last refuge of the weak who mistakenly believe that honour recognises their own merits whereas it is, properly speaking, a demonstration of the merits of those who bestow it.[503] All of these so-called "goods" are ultimately subordinate to the highest goal: *Eudaimonia*. *Eudaimonia* has been variously translated but can be thought of as "human flourishing", "proper and full human functioning" or "inner peace".[504] This is the ultimate goal and end of all human activity. Human activity arose from it and returns to it. Only in the pursuit of *eudaimonia* can a man be happy and fulfil his human nature.[505] The realisation of man's nature is the virtuous life and it is this knowledge that allows one to direct the actions of one's life. As Copleston notes "Happiness [Eudaimonia] is an activity and an activity of man"[506] In order to understand this more fully, we must discern this activity of man, that is, the *function* of man.[507] It is, thinks Aristotle, quite dangerous to suppose that contemplation of sensory experience and of that which is common to all living things can yield such discernment. It cannot because the objects of such contemplation are external to man whereas the function of man is internal, "an activity of the soul which follows or implies a rational principle"[508] Aristotle goes on to say:

"Human good turns out to be an activity of the soul in accordance with virtue and if there is more than one virtue, in accordance with the best and most

---

[500] Op cit Clark p27.
[501] NE 1095b 14.
[502] Ibid 1096a 5–7.
[503] Ibid 1095b 23–25.
[504] Op cit Clark p24.
[505] Op cit Lear p156.
[506] Op cit Coppleston p334.
[507] NE 1097b 23.
[508] Ibid 1098a 8.

complete."[509] This means that the active use of reason is man's special function. This is not simply the use of reason, but the excellent use of reason, which is virtuous activity.[510] This is the goal to which all other "goods" are directed and tend and since human happiness and fulfilment are a unique human function it is this that constitutes the ultimate, universal good. We noted that Aristotle thought that human good is the active soul working in accordance with the most complete virtue, and now we see that virtue is "a state of character concerned with choice, lying in a mean, i.e. the mean relative to us, this being determined by a rational principle, and by that principle be which a man of practical wisdom would determine it."[511] Here we have an indication of what was to become Aristotle's doctrine of "the golden mean".[512] The doctrine of the golden mean is based on an intermediate sate between excess and defect within an action or object.[513] All good actions have a certain proportion and virtue which is found between the two extremes.[514] This can be illustrated by our feelings of anger. An excess of anger is a short temper and its opposite (lack/defect) is apathy or total indifference. In discerning the golden mean, we see that gentleness would stand between a shortness of temper and the defect of apathy. A gentle person can be said to respond appropriately to a tense of abrasive situation; restraining or acting according to each instance of them. That a gentle person will judge how to respond to circumstances which might lead to anger on a case-by-case basis shows that when Aristotle writes about a mean, he is not thinking in terms of a mathematical formula for seeking a balance or finding the middle ground. Rather, Aristotle makes it quite clear in his definition that the mean is *"relative to us"*. So much depends on the feeling or action in relation to specific circumstances or situations. "In some cases, it might be preferable to err on the side of excess rather than on that of defect, while in other cases the reverse might be true."[515] "For in everything it is no easy task to find the middle, e.g. to find the middle of a circle is not for everyone but for him who knows; so, too, anyone can get angry—that is easy—or give or spend money; but to do this to the right

---

[509] Ibid 1098a 16–17.
[510] Op cit Clark p25.
[511] NE 1106b 37–1107a 2
[512] Op cit Clark p25.
[513] NE 1106a 26–32.
[514] Ibid 1106b 6–8. See also Copleston p336.
[515] Op cit Copleston p337.

person, and to the right extent, at the right time, with the right motive, and in the right way, that is not for everyone, nor is it easy; wherefore goodness is both laudable and noble."[516] How then is virtue acquired? Through *praxis*. By repetition, virtue becomes a habit—it becomes part of our character[517] and this supposes a rational choice. Our natural inclinations have no intrinsic moral value. An act becomes a virtue or a vice only when a rational choice is made; this means rational control and deliberate surrender: "The virtue of a thing is relative to its proper work. Now there are three things in the soul which control action and truth—sensation, reason, desire. Of these sensations originates no actions; this is plain from the fact that the lower animals have sensations but no share in action…since moral virtue is a state of character concerned with choice, and choice is deliberate desire, therefore both the reasoning must be true and the desire right, if the choice is to be good, and the latter must pursue what the former asserts."[518] This kind of understanding is practical wisdom. The origins of our actions is our choice and reasoning with a view towards an end. So it is that choice cannot exist without reason and intellect.[519] Aristotle's emphasis on a *practical* understanding in the formation of habit leads him to believe that true moral training involves more than merely learning to distinguish between right and wrong actions.[520] Moral education and learning must also develop the right likes and dislikes, attractions and repulses and appropriate feelings and in this way develop character.[521] Our desires and feelings must be brought into line with right reason so that when we pursue virtue we will take pleasure in it and increasingly experience an aversion to wickedness. These feelings are an expression of reason.[522] For Aristotle then, the highest use of reason lies *beyond* the discovery of the mean between excess and defect in actions, this, while it is a proper function of man's reason, is not the highest use of reason. Here Aristotle's thoughts turn to contemplation. It is both the possession of material goods (having a good life) and virtuous habits (leading to a good life) that allow

---

[516] NE 1109a 25–29.
[517] Op cit Clark p27.
[518] NE 1139a 17–26.
[519] See Ne 1139a 32–1139b 3.
[520] See Amelie Rorty (1980) *Essays on Aristotle's Ethics*. "*The place of contemplation in Aristotle's Nicomachean Ethics*" Berkeley. University of California Press. p380–381.
[521] Op cit Clark p27. See also Copleston p339–341.
[522] Ibid.

leisure and right orientation for this act, both of these having been shown to be necessary for human flourishing and inner peace.

Human activity is "intensified by its proper pleasure, since each class is better judged of and brought to precision by those who engage in this activity with pleasure."[523] With these words, Aristotle points out the relationship between activity and pleasure. The logical extension of this idea is that pleasure will always accompany the things we love and the more we love virtue the more pleasure we will have. We will pursue it and eschew evil.[524] If the highest expression of reason is man's contemplation of unchanging (eternal?) truths, then contemplation has as its ultimate end a god who is unchanging.[525] It is therefore in the exercise of reason concerning the noblest objects that man's complete happiness is to be found. Since this life expresses the divine element in man it follows that we ought to put off our mortality and do all we can to live the live to which the highest element in us points.[526] The ultimate happiness for man, man's fulfilment, demands a life given over to philosophy and the contemplation of the unchanging god as based on the possession of material goods and the life of virtue.[527]

Theme 2 Early Christian Monasticism and Heroic Virtue

While there are obvious implications in Aristotle's ethical system for the scholastic theology of the Middle Ages, particularly in the work of St Thomas Aquinas (d 1274) this system did have a direct impact on the origins, values and ideals of Christian monasticism. This, as we will see, was especially true of the Benedictine tradition that developed in sixth century Italy.[528] As we have seen, a desire to grow, to conquer human nature, lay at the heart of early Christian monasticism. The structures, theologies, philosophies and traditions of monasticism invited the monk to rise above pride and personal ambition, excessive curiosity and unrestrained concupiscence.[529] Within the Benedictine

---

[523] NE 1175a 29–32.

[524] NE 1099a 7.

[525] NE 1177 12–18 and 1177b 1–5.

[526] Op cit Copleston p349.

[527] Op cit Lear p 172–173.

[528] Op cit Copleston p350.

[529] See 1 Jn 2:15–26.

tradition the vows of obedience, stability and conversion of life,[530] as well as wearing the habit, community rank the hours of prayer and a spirit of sacrifice and penance, all serve to facilitate the practical lived experience of God.[531] They combined to compel the monk to live for something beyond himself: God. In their search to understand the nature and meaning of sin and its consequences, early Christian monasticism began to develop an ideological system that sought to combat man's self-preference and misdirected actions as it had come to be understood by the light of faith and relying on sacred Scriptures. The ascetic tradition in Christianity, on which the monastic movement is built, can, of course, be traced back to the New Testament. Of particular importance was the tradition of virginity and celibacy that was grounded in the teachings and example of Jesus (Mtt.19:12) as well as in the writings of St Paul (1 Cor, 7). What distinguishes the monastic movement from the earlier tradition of asceticism within Christianity—is the withdrawal from society. The New Testament had a profound effect on the early monastic movement and the relationship of the church to society also played a major part in the development of the movement.

The persecutions preceding the astonishing acceptance of Christianity in the Roman Empire prompted many Christians to flee to avoid red martyrdom and some of these may have banded together to form religious communities. There is, as we noted earlier, much scholarly debate about this—especially since according to Athanasius, St Anthony deliberately went to Alexandria in the hope of achieving martyrdom! It seems that Origen's mother hid his shoes to prevent him from the same desire to die for the faith. Whatever may be the case about the formation of earliest religious communities, there is no doubt that the privations of living in the desert greatly contributed to the ascetic practices of those living there.

Conversely, the cessation of hostilities and persecutions against Christians has also been offered as an explanation of the rise of early monasticism:

"The monk came to replace the martyr as the hero of the early church in its new triumphal condition. When the triumph of the church drove the demons from the cities, the new heroes of the faith pursued them to the desert, there to engage

---

[530] Benedict of Nursia. (1981) RB 64:1 in *The Rule of St Benedict in Latin and English with Notes.* Collegeville. MN.USA The Liturgical Press. (Hereafter cited as RB1981.
[531] Charles Cummins OCSO (1986) *Monastic Practices*. Kalamazoo. MI. USA. Cistercian Publications P3.

in single handed combat."[532] While the martyrs undoubtedly held first place as heroes of the church, they were soon joined by virgins who were also held in high regard so that, by the end of the third century one wrrither refers to the virgins as martyrs and even Athanasius in his *Life of Anthony* refers to virgins *and* martyrs as "testimony to the faith and teachings of Christ".[533] Very soon, monastic profession came to be seen as a second baptism, a place previously held by red martyrdom:

"Martyrdom had earlier been seen as a substitute for baptism or, for those already baptised, as a second baptism. When the monastic life came to be equated with or placed on the same level as martyrdom, it was but a short step to compare monastic profession with baptism…Just as baptism was held to forgive sins, so now monastic profession came to be held to forgive sins…Since the opportunity for martyrdom no longer existed for those who wished to respond fully to the teaching and example of Christ, the development of monasticism may well have been in compensation for this, to provide an outlet for those not satisfied with mediocre Christianity."[534] But, of course, the notion of retreating or withdrawing from the world was not unique to Christianity. It can be found in numerous ancient philosophies and schools of thought. Writers such as Cicero, Seneca, Marcus Aurelius and Plotinus all recommend it for the sake of contemplation and inner peace. For example, in his life of Plotinus, Prophyry portrayed his master as loving to withdraw from the city. It has been suggested that Athanasius had precisely this work in mind when he composed his *Life of Anthony*.[535] With these pagan influences, the Scriptures offered other numerous precedents.[536] In the writings of Clement of Alexandria, for example, we find the presentation of the ideal Christian man that was consistent with the Hellenistic ideal of one who has achieved contemplation of and unceasing union with God.[537] In the *Stromata*, Clement stresses the importance of detachment from the world and this detachment is the fruit of knowing and contemplating the "good". "Knowledge is purifying; it begins with repentance, separates from the passions

---

[532] RB 1980 14.

[533] Ibid 15.

[534] Ibid 15–16.

[535] Ibid 17.

[536] See Mtt.14:13. Jn 6:15 and Mtt.4 2–10.

[537] Mayeul de Druille (1999) *Seeking the Absolute Love: The Founders of Christian Monasticism* New York. Crossroads Publishing Company.p 4.

and from what is purely pleasurable and leads to a life of virtue."[538] He continues by saying that exercising control over one's passions and the desire for good culminates in *apatheia:* a moderation and perfect calm.[539] Praise and self-oblation are the highest expression of love. *"We glorify Him who gave himself as a sacrifice for us, and we, in turn sacrifice ourselves."*[540] The essential value in martyrdom is not the heroism of the act but the perfection of charity. By the end of the fourth century, the religious life came to be understood as the recovery of the divine image in human beings.[541] "A man's intention to live as a monk was the result of a personal decision." [542] Monastic writers, building on Clement's system, such as Pachomius, Basil the great, Gregory Nazianzen, Gregory of Nyssa, Isaac of Syria, Athanasius of Alexandria, Origen. Evagrius and John Cassian, all developed the idea that the death within the monastic life, the search h for *apatheia (*later called "purity of heart by Cassian"), and the common life of obedience, was the most effective and the most authentic expression of the Christian life.It was within this spiritual and theological climate that Benedict of Nursia wrote his Rule; though it may seem more appropriate to say that Benedict "anthologised" his Rule since Benedict pulled together writings from numerous earlier monastic rules, relying most heavily on the "*Rule of the Master".*[543] Laid out in seventy-three relatively short chapters and a prologue Benedict's vision is of a strong monastic community, based on the idea that a man is not called to live for himself, or by himself: "Listen carefully my son to the master's instructions and attend to them with the ear of your heart…The labour of obedience will bring you back to him from whom you have drifted by sloth of disobedience. This message of mind is for you, then, if you are ready to give up your own will, once and for all, and armed with strong and noble weapons of obedience do battle for the true King, Christ the Lord."

Is there anyone here who yearns for live and to see good days? What dear brothers is more delightful than this voice of the Lord calling to us? We must then prepare our hearts and our bodies for battle of Holy Obedience to his instructions. What is not possible for us by nature, let us ask the Lord to supply

---

[538] Ibid 5.
[539] Ibid.
[540] Ibid 5–6.
[541] Rule of St Benedict 35.
[542] Ibid 437.
[543] Ibid 69–73, 79–90.

through grace.[544] Here Benedict writes as a father to his children. He lays out his vision of the monastic life. It is through the obedient performance of good works that a monk can conquer pride and rely on God's grace to attain eternal happiness, contemplation and union with God.

Theme 3. Shared Values

Having given a very brief overview of Aristotle's understanding of virtue, and an even briefer note about how this noble notion might have been shared by the very earliest founders of monastic communities we now turn our attention to the extent to which later monastic traditions, specifically that of Benedict, can be said to have developed a system closely akin to that of Aristotle's ethical system as found in the *Nichomachean Ethics*. It is quite beyond the scope of this essay to offer an exhaustive evaluation of each element in the Benedictine religious life in relation to Aristotle's system and attempts only to note certain points of instruction offered by St Benedict in his *Rule* which, in my view, make this comparison possible.

Immediately in the prologue, as quoted above, Benedict questions the prospective monk as to his motives for seeking God within the context of the religious life.[545] Benedict begins from the view that a man must be formed in the practice of virtue. Only through education in virtue and the constant practice of it can a prospective monk acquire the ability to discern virtue in relation to his end (*telos*) as a Christian monastic. Benedict believed that the monastery is a "school for the Lord's service"[546] where one might learn virtue. His prime concern was not the good of the individual soul alone (though he is concerned for this too) but all the souls in the monastic community. As with Aristotle's system, Benedict's ultimate concern lay on the health of the entire community and this was based on the virtue and fulfilment of the individual's life. In the case of Aristotle, the focus was on the end of life, for Benedict this concern is on the monk fulfilling his Christian vocation alongside others doing exactly the same thing and for exactly the same reasons and from the same motives.

But Benedict realised that the members of his community were not necessarily virtuous men. He most certainly believed in the moral frailty, indeed

---

[544] Ibid. Prol 1–3 15, 19, 40-41.
[545] Ibid.
[546] Ibid Prol 45–47.

the fallen nature of his monks. This is a point of *dissimilarity* with Aristotle's system. As we noted earlier, Aristotle wrote for people who were already leading a virtuous life, hoping only to help them gain an extra insight on their life of virtue and the nature of their own souls.[547] Benedict, however, believed that "as we progress in this way of life and in faith, we shall run on the path of God's commandments, our hearts overflowing with the inexpressible delight of love."[548] So while they are faulted creatures, Benedict ultimately believed that virtue and ultimate happiness, the fulfilment of their monastic vocation (the beatific vision) is possible for his monks. In various chapters of the Rule, Benedict lays out his own version of the golden mean, emphasising moderation in all things, good and bad. There must always be a balance in the life of the community[549] and this is something that Benedict repeats with regularity. The monastic life of Benedict's Rule is not one of extreme asceticism, or of self-denial. Rather, like Aristotle, Benedict recognised the need for material security with regard to food, drink, time, recreation and so on. Those who are in need of these things are not able to fully live out their commitment to seek God above all things.[550] This is the monk's vocation of which Benedict writes in Chapter 7 of the *Rule,* the monk "having ascended all these steps will quickly arrive at the perfect love of God which casts out fear."[551] It is in the realisation and contemplation of this love, through prayer, that the monk finds the pleasure and consolation that compels him to perform those actions which once he might have dreaded but he "will now begin to observe without effort, as though naturally, from habit, no longer out of fear of hell, but out of love for Christ, <u>good habit and delight in virtue</u>."[552] As the Benedictine Abbott of the Cistercian reform, William of Saint-Thierry says: "…they arise from their own ethics to a sort of physics, from the creatures of this world to the invisible things of God."[553] For Benedict, this constant living awareness of God's beauty, presence and gentleness and his action in the life of the monk is the ultimate end and

---

[547] Op cit Lear 157.
[548] RB 1980 58:7.
[549] See RB1980 chapters 4,5,6,27,31,33,34,37,39,40,49,53,55 and 72.
[550] RB1980 58:7.
[551] Ibid 7:67 see also 1 Jn.4:18.
[552] Ibid 7:68–69 my emphasis added.
[553] William of Saint-Thierry (1981) *On the Nature and Dignity of Love.* Kalamazoo. MI Cistercian Publications. p103.

consolation of the monastic life. As in the case of Aristotle's ethics, this contemplation is the result of a conscious decision to choose virtue over vice, the middle-way over excess. Finding pleasure in the divine presence, the monk is compelled and encouraged to continue and deepen his own dedication to his monastic calling and to an ultimate union with the divine in the beatific vision, that is, Christ inviting the individual soul *and* the community to share his everlasting life.[554]

---

[554] RB 1980 72:11.

Chapter 13
Benedictine Spirituality Then and Now

Let us begin with a story told by Pope St Gregory the Great in his enthusiastic hagiography containing details of the life and work of St Benedict:

"There was a hermit called Martin, who had chained himself to a rock inside a narrow cave not far from St Benedict's monastery. When Benedict heard about this, he sent word to him, "If you are indeed a servant of God then do not chain yourself with chains of iron. But rather let Christ be the chain that binds you."[555] There are, of course, clear parallels here between this supposed incident in the life of Benedict and Plato's analogy of the cave and it may be that Gregory devised this story to demonstrate the enlightenment of learning that Benedict and his order brought to the beginning of the so-called "dark ages" after the collapse of the Roman Empire. Be that as it may, for the importance of the story for this study of the history of continuity and change in the development of monastic spirituality is that it shows us that Benedict's prime aim and goal was simply to introduce people to Christ.

The spirituality that came out of his particular way of doing so offers a means of binding his monks in freedom to Christ. This might reasonably be said of all "mainstream" Christian spirituality but, as we will see, what Benedict offers is a unique means to reach for Christ, to grow in Christ and to be freed by Christ. It is a way so consonant with the Gospels that we might already think of Benedictine spirituality as a distillation of their teaching the short booklet format that became Benedict's "Rule" and which is so familiar to many Christians both professed and lay today.

---

[555] St Gregory the Great (1988): *Dialogues* Bk.3. Ed and Introduction by Edmund G. Gardner. Chrisitan Roman Empire Series Volume 9. Place Unknown. Evolution Publishing and Manufacturing.

Like the Gospels, what Benedict offered was revolutionary because he departed from the means of spiritual growth most commonly available in his day. By the time of Benedict bodily austerities and complete solitude were, as they had been with the desert mothers and fathers, believed to be essential means of making progress in the journey of faith.

This was exactly the sort of spiritual method that Benedict practised as a young man but found to be wholly inadequate. In place of a sort of spiritual competition to see who can put up with the harshest spiritual lifestyle or physical beatings, Benedict offered a common mode of life made up of a round of positive duties and tasks. Mortification of the body was out and more adequate and an encouraging system of physical, emotional and spiritual support was in. Thus, Benedict lays down in his "Rule" that his monks are to have sufficient supplies of food, ample sleep in their own beds (a luxurious innovation!) and clothes appropriate to the changing of the seasons. As he wrote in the Prologue to the "Rule": "We are going to establish a school for the Lord's service in which there is to be <u>nothing harsh, nothing burdensome</u>."[556] In this school, there was to be no isolated detachment from affections either. Indeed, when speaking of the degrees of humility much later in the "Rule",[557] Benedict said quite openly that it is only through love and affection that people will be attracted to Christianity and the cause of the Gospel. The sort of loving affection he had in mind is analogous to that which exists between members of a family. The love and affection we find in a family draws us out of ourselves and into active communion with one another. It gives us a key element in our personal identity and gives us the confidence and encouragement to be of service to one another, the community in which the family is placed and the wider world too. So, according to Benedict, it must be with the community of Christian faith in general and in religious communities in particular. At this point, Benedict wanted to see ordinary human affection as a God given gift. Without human affection there can be no truly humane or Christian community and so, while Benedict certainly wanted to say that the marks of the Christian church are that it is one, holy, Catholic and apostolic, he would also claim that these things are true if, and only if, the church first understands itself to be a community, a fraternity, a family.

Just as there was to be no detachment or renunciation of affections in this school so it was not to be run with military precision. After all, Benedict's

---

[556] St Benedict: Rule. Prologue. V. my emphasis.
[557] St Benedict. Rule. Chapter 7.

generation, like ours, had been torn apart by invasions and defensive actions of one sort or another with all the human cost that they always entail. So unlike Pachomius, and the later St Ignatius of Loyola, Benedict completely rejected the military mind and lifestyle in favour of the free discipline of a well-regulated family—including all the mess, turmoil and difficulties that run along with them. As a consequence, if someone is looking for a spirituality or method that is precise, systematic, hierarchical and entirely cogent and clear and well set out, this is not it.

Benedict believed that Christians can (and should) make our everyday tasks and the natural world into stepping stones towards the holy, and that it is by the careful ordering of the normal and the natural we nurture a life that gives the greatest possible response to God's providence and Grace.

If Benedict did not intend his "Rule" to be mortifying, purgative, detached or systematic, what did he intend? He saw it as nothing less than the means by which ordinary people doing ordinary things and struggling to do those ordinary things well could be united to Christ. Benedict was not interested in killing the will or denying its very existence, but, like his great predecessor Augustine, in using the will in such a way that it can be united to the will of God. The best way of doing that, thought Benedict, is to love and desire everything that is noble, true, good and beautiful so be united to what God's heart truly loves too. *Cor ad cor loquitur*, as Blessed John Henry Newman's motto has it—heart speaks to (or with) heart. Benedict offered a means to this end; family life in religious community, building stability, converting our ways of life in obedience as worked out in his Rule—and it is to each of these special features that we must now turn our attention.

First, stability. Benedict knew that individuals need to be at home, to be grounded in a specific place. He knew that this not only provides actual and psychological security but that the mutual interaction between a person and his or her environment makes us the people we are, the people which by Grace we might become. For him, a life voluntarily limited to one place, one community and one specific group of people forces us to face ourselves and, what is more, to be sanctified through that commitment.

God is in *this* place. God is in *this* community. God is in *this* (local) church and in individual families. If all this is true, and for Benedict it is, then his monks would already begin to glimpse the virtue of steadfastness. Through steadfastness we are given a sense of belonging, the very antithesis of the anomie and alienation that so many people experienced in his day and in ours.

For Benedict, stability meant not only committing oneself to a physical place and community but also to the demands of a settled interior state. Benedict saw that the two are intimately connected. A monk can hardly develop a settled interior state if he is constantly dropping out, starting again, doing different things somewhere else. So, in his "Rule" Benedict offered those who live by it a variety of ways through which they might be stable.

There are two aspects of Benedict's concept of stability that we should emphasise here. The first is contentment. In his communities, there was to be no striving to have more, better or different. A monk was given what was considered necessary for spiritual and physical health—and no more. The clothing which varied with the seasons was to be adequate but not extravagant. Food was to be sufficient to meet the needs of the body but not to excess. No one was to take on unusual spiritual practices or austerities that could not be equally followed by the weakest and most fragile member of the community. Complaining and grumbling and always wishing that things could be different, either as they were (often wrongly) thought to be in the past or in some future utopia, could not be tolerated. Such things represent restlessness, an agitated spirit, a lack of imagination and creativity. Thus, Benedict asked all who wanted to go to school in the Lord's service to be at peace with the way things are, what has been given, with what they have been asked to do and with those who guide them.[558] For Benedict, true freedom of the will does not come from controlling, or having, or knowing everything or even from the possibility of doing so, but from seeking God in the present circumstances. This is an extremely valuable and important message for our own time.

How often do we find ourselves saying that we do not have the time to do the tasks we need to perform or the things we would like to do, as though our being constantly busy were a measure of our virtue. Being busy has become the excuse for not engaging in the lives of people at all, or if we do, only at a very superficial level even with those who should be most dear to us. And then we wonder why marriages break down and end in divorce or, alternatively, persist but in a way that lacks love or even interest between husbands and wives. We wonder too why the offspring of such relationships often develop psychotic

---

[558] St Benedict; Rule. Chapters 34 and 68.

tendencies, engage in drug taking and petty crime, or that others are confused about their sexual orientation. We look about us and lament our broken society in much the same way as the Prophet Jeremiah laments over the fall of Jerusalem in the remarkable painting by Rembrandt.[559] For Benedict and the spirituality that he developed to identify ourselves with the intensity of our business is not funny, something to be proud of, or a playground game. Rather it is a scandal, a shame and a disgrace. It is something of which we should be deeply ashamed. It is evidence of a perversion of the individual human will and of a corrupt society which has lost sight of the goal and purposes of life. That is precisely why it is a disgrace, a denial and refusal of the Grace that God gives. There is simply no virtue in having no time to pray, to read the scripture, meet with fellow Christians. For Benedict is not healthy to take on anything with a zeal that absorbs all of our time and energy and which burns out our strength, our health and, whether we know it or not our very souls.

To be busy in the way I have described is the very opposite of Benedict's concept of stability that he enshrined in his "Rule". The character of stability is a certain restfulness, a contentment, not in doing nothing but in doing the familiar, even the monotonous and the routine things in life as well as we can and *ad majoram deo Gloria*—to the greater glory of God. Stability means to remain physically unmoved and emotionally unexcited.

The second aspect of stability that is worth noting is commitment. We have already noted that the members of his communities were to regard themselves as a family in enduring love. This meant that his monks were not to seek sanctification as isolated and anonymous individuals but as a member of a community, knit together by a common life, with common interests, duties, work and prayer. The completion of these duties and tasks is not for the reasons of the personal satisfaction of a job well done but for the good of all. In living out this commitment to one another, Benedict's monks were to exercise an influence over their local communities, again not as individuals but as one whole community influencing another.

An essential element in creating a stable Benedictine community was the *opus dei*, the work of God, common worship. There was work to be done and it was to be done together. It was to follow a pattern and a rhythm, the same day after day, year after year in a fixed order like the changing of the natural seasons

---

[559] Rembrandt: Jeremiah Laments the Fall of Jerusalem. A painting. Rijksmuseum Amsterdam.

and the tides of the sea. Benedict intended that this pattern of prayer would unite the hearts of worshippers with the Spirit of God as expressed in the psalms especially. The whole community was to be bound up in the common eternal praise of the communion of saints both militant and triumphant and with all the hosts of heaven.

But the creation of stable monastic communities is, Benedict rightly thought, quite impossible without Holy Obedience. Simply to write these last two words in our day is likely to raise not a few eyebrows. It may even be regarded as something of a contradiction or an oxymoron. After all, in an age obsessed with personal rights and freedoms and in which even the merest suggestion those same rights and freedoms might be bounded by equal duties for the sake of the common good, is likely to be met with outrage. Even in some churches, the very notion of Holy Obedience is likely to conjure up the spectre of a forelock tugging subservience to a priestly caste, or otherwise dismissed as an anachronism.

As we will see, nothing could be further from the truth of what Benedict had in mind but, for the moment, let us think of Holy Obedience as Mutual Faithfulness. Again, we have here faint echoes of what it means to be a member of a loving family and of the relationship between spouses who take their vows of faithfulness completely seriously. While that is so, the more important context that Benedict had in mind is explicitly associated with the redemptive faithfulness of Christ to the will of God through which Jesus' own self-giving gives way to his exaltation.[560] For Benedict, like the Apostle Paul, this is the paradox that lies at the heart of Christian faith. Through humility we will be exalted and by obedience we will be free. Following the Apostle who saw the cognition between the obedience of Christ and Christ's humility, Benedict described the movement towards the holy as an ascent through humility. Like John Climacus before him, Benedict used the metaphor of a ladder, the first rung of which is obedience. Obedience, for Benedict, was faithfulness to one another. Whether out of holy fear or of good things to come, a monk adopting Benedict's notion of Holy Obedience commits themselves to listening[561] and to faithfulness. Then the ladder is climbed rung by single rung throughout the religious life. Moving from one rung to another demands a constant turning over of the will to God, always seeking the best for the other members of the community. Step by painful step, through mutual faithfulness, the false layers that hide our true selves

---

[560] Philippians 2: 5–11.
[561] The first words of the prologue to Benedict's "Rule" are "Listen my Son…"

that keep us from one another and from God, are stripped away. As a monk ascended the ladder of humility outward obedience was supposed to become one with the stable inner state. It was to become an obedience of the heart. How a monk, indeed how all Christians live is an expression of how we see ourselves in relation to Christ. Holy Obedience, mutual faithfulness, comes from the heart and is the expression of what is truly desired in the depths of a person's being. And finally…when the top of the ladder is reached, the soul is embraced in welcome by divine love. Total humility through a life of Holy Obedience, faithfulness to one another, leads to the perfect love of God. There will be no fear in this union, only joy in knowing God and in being known by him.

By offering the metaphor of a ladder, Benedict created a practical means to deal with what I call "the enthronement of self". We saw something of this a moment or two ago when I wrote of the disgrace of being constantly busy to the exclusion of everything and everyone else that should take our attention. Such busyness derives from the "enthronement of self"—the idea that the individual is the measure of all things, always and everywhere more important than any community, and that his/her needs must always be met come what may. For Benedict the goal of every Christian, full union with God in Christ, means that our human will must be one with the will of God and Holy Obedience is a practical means to this end. Holy Obedience takes "the enthronement of self", takes our supposed unbounded freedom to do as we please, and consecrates it to God so that it becomes our path, our ladder to true freedom.

So, for Benedictine monks, Holy Obedience could never be thought of as a theological construct or abstract concept. Rather it had to be a lived experience. Members of his communities were to be obedient to one another and generous in their dealings. This is not the servile submission that some might suppose, but rather the recognition that the Christian life is one of service to one another and that we are all responsible for each other's spiritual formation and growth in Christ. So, insofar as Holy Obedience can be thought of as submission it is only the submission of a child to its parents—and we are always both parent and child! Benedict insisted that that in serving each other his monks served the image of Christ embedded in every human being, through grace, and so obedience to one another must be as strong as our individual relationship with him.

Just as his monks were to be obedient, mutually faithful to one another, so each individual in a stable community was to submit to the will and the Word of God. Submission to the Word of God could be expressed in a variety of ways in order to develop a particular community's common purpose in seeking God in the way that suited them best. Mutual faithfulness enabled the communities to fulfil its calling and through submission to the Word of God Benedict asked his monk's to be obedient to all the precepts governing the life of the community.

Once again, murmuring, complaining and forming little groups of alliances as a defence against other little groups could have no part in this. For Benedict, the Word of God was fully inclusive or it was nothing at all. So murmuring and such like threaten to undermine the joint submission to the Word of God as well as the stability of the community. So it was that Benedict, insisted that any complaint or wrongdoing should be brought into the open so that there is at least the possibility of dealing with it honestly as it affects the whole community.[562] Stability, Holy Obedience and submission to the Word of God were the first three stepping stones to the holy that Benedict put in place in his "Rule". But these stones could not be crossed without a monk committing himself to a continual conversion of life and openness to change.

For Benedict, the degree to which a monk was open to change was the measure of the extent to which he was prepared to persist in the quest for sanctification. Even now, professed or lay people attempting to use Benedict's "Rule" as a guide in their spiritual journey commit themselves to change; a change of heart, a change in behaviour, a purification of intentions. Benedictine spirituality demanded then, as it demands now, that Christians constantly welcome and embrace change, and the necessary first step in doing so is the desire for a personal transformation.

Benedict opened his "Rule" by calling his monks to arise from their spiritual slumbers and not delay. He called all who were considering using his spiritual method to "…run while you have the light, lest the shadows of death come upon you"[563] This is almost an exact quotation from the Gospel of John,[564] but with a subtle variation. Where St John has "walk", Benedict has "run", making the whole phrase more emphatic and suggesting urgency. Benedict's monks must always be moving on or the shadows of death will overtake them. This does not, of course, mean a physical movement. The principle of stability is primary. But it does mean that Benedict's monks must not be content to remain in the green pastures where they might idly rest and play, but should tread the rugged

---

[562] St Benedict. Rule Chapters 34 and 46.
[563] Benedict Rule chapter 25.
[564] John 12:35.

pathway, rejoicing, in their ability to strike the living fountain from the rocks along their way. In short, just as Benedict recommends stability so he also demands an on-going openness to change as a necessary prerequisite and condition of growing in Christ.

The progress to which Benedict invites his monks is not something they could do on their own. On the contrary, Benedict reminds them that they could only make spiritual progress through their total reliance on God and on each other. God's grace evoked their acts, supported and fulfilled them so that, by Grace, they could be transformed.

Benedict's "Rule" is full of acts that, he thought, would aid the sanctification of his monks. In Chapter 4, for example, he lists some of these acts and some modern readers find this list somewhat hard going. But this is to miss the point. By listing acts which aid sanctification Benedict is trying to find a balance between spiritual and physical works because he is acutely aware of the intimate connection between what a person does, how they think and the prayers they make. Such a balance is essential in communal religious life because, again according to Benedict, where there is excess in one aspect their must necessarily be a lack in another.

The roots of this idea may be grounded in St Paul's sporting metaphor. St Paul tells[565] how the athletes of his day ran the race that was set before them in a balanced way and according to the rules governing that activity. So they did not run aimlessly but in such a way as to increase the possibility of winning. That meant that they ran in an orderly, balanced way. For Benedict's monks, the balanced order of their spiritual journey was achieved first by stability and then by living out their lives in obedience to each other, the Gospel and to Christ. One result of engaging in the acts of sanctification that Benedict lists is that they transform a person's relationship to material objects. Similarly, the more a person is able to transform his or her relation to material objects the better he or she is to engage in acts of sanctification. There is a clue to how this might be achieved in Chapter 31 of Benedict's "Rule" in which he suggests that his monks attempt to see the tools and objects of their daily tasks as though they were the consecrated vessels of the altar—equally filled with the body and blood of Christ. Whereas before Benedict many Christian writers had seen nature as filled with the glory of God, his special insight was to see that this might also be true of

---

[565] Phil 2:16, Gal. 2:2 and 5:7. The metaphor also appears in the non-Pauline Letter to the Hebrews at 12:1.

man-made objects too. Indeed, for him every material object could be a sign and symbol of Christ's sacramental presence with them and around them. For Benedict every material object, created or made, revealed something of the creative power of God and continually at work in and through women and men.

This attitude to material objects, which I describe as "sacred materiality", is in stark contrast to the tendency to think that progress in the spiritual life is possible only on the condition of separating the material and the spiritual and elevating the latter to a higher plain so that the former is debased and regarded as an impediment to union with God. In Benedictine spirituality, that is only necessary where material objects are regarded as things in themselves, as idols, and where the accumulation of objects (or their cash value, wealth) is a measure of a person's worth. The concept of sacred materiality as suggested by Benedict overcomes that idolisation and cuts it out at source.

If sacred materiality changes attitudes to ordinary objects, regarding them as holy, how much more might that be true of the women and men who created them? One implication of sacred materiality is that human beings are holy. It is not that they will become holy, or might enjoy that state in some far-off future state, say, in heaven. No. They are holy, here now, at this time and in this place. They are icons of Christ. They carry not only the image but the sacred presence of Christ to each other and to the world, not in their spirits or minds only—but in their physical bodies too. Thus, Benedict insists[566] that people be treated not *as though* they were Christ, but with the understanding that they *are* Christ. If the claims of sacred materiality seem outrageous it is only because it is easy to overlook the full force of the fundamental Christian belief that God has poured out his love on *every* person. That is everyone has been blessed by God and is loved by God—whether they are consciously aware of it or not. At any given moment when a fellow human being stands before us, that person *is* Christ. In that moment, Christ is to be found in that person and nowhere else.

If sacred materiality helps us see everyday objects as sacred and human beings as holy it follows that they must not only be treated with respect and love but as that which is adored by God, for they are the very stepping stones towards him and the means by which he reveals himself to us. With this in mind, for Benedict, his monks and those who find his "Rule" useful in their spiritual lives there is no such thing as a "mere object" or "just another person". In Benedictine

---

[566] Benedict Rule Chapter 53.

spirituality in general, and in Benedictine monasticism in particular there is no such thing as a "mere" anything, far less can objects or people be treated with disdain. Any relationship to a material object or a human being is a relationship with Christ and the quality of that relationship determines our ability to grow, or wither, in our relationship to Christ.

Sacred Materiality might still seem a counsel of perfection to the modern world caught up as it is in so much hurly-burly and busyness, and perhaps it is. But if it is we need to hear and heed Benedict's warning against taking on anything that is likely to absorb all our time, energy and emotion to the exclusion of everything else. In any case, Benedict is not likely to let his monks or us off the hook so easily for he gave a means of remembering the proper relation to things, and people and Christ which he called "Recollection".

This is was not intended to be some high-flown spiritual practice for an elite. He had, after all, established that no spiritual practices should be introduced into his communities that could not be easily followed by the weakest member of them. Rather it is a simple act of remembering and remembering simply. More simply still, the means of "Recollection" is to stop one thing before embarking on another. In this way, we are fully conscious of what we are doing and of how, why and in what ways the sacred materiality of the task draws us further into the presence of God. Sister Joan Chittister OSB describes this stopping and starting as the "virtue of presence".[567] An example of "Recollection" in the midst of busy secular life might be as follows. There you are at work, head down, meeting deadlines, solving problems both routine and extraordinary. You really do not want or need to be disturbed, but the telephone rings…Now Recollection, the virtue of presence kicks in. You can either moan and groan and think to yourself, "Oh, for God's sake not now, leave me alone…" *or* you can think to yourself, "Oh for God's sake" (quite literally for the sake of God) "now I am about to speak to someone upon whom the fullness of God has been poured out."

The second response is what "Recollection" is all about. In short, it is a reminder of the truth about everything we do and everyone we encounter. Once upon a time, church bells used to ring out to call people outside to lift up their hearts in prayer with the church, and likewise our modern ringtones, faxes, emails or a simple knock on the door call us to stop what we are doing, recall the

---

[567] Sister Joan Chitister OSB; Wisdom Distilled from the Daily: Living the Rule of St benedict Today. San Francisco. Harper San Francisco.

truth of what it is we are about to undertake and pray for the grace to serve Christ through it.

Sacred materiality offered Benedict's monks an opportunity to change the way in which they related to objects and to people and in so doing gave them an opportunity for the conversion of life. Stability rooted and strengthened them. Humble obedience (mutual faithfulness) gave their will over to Christ, and openness to change compelled them towards the next stage of their pilgrimage. All three aspects of the life which Benedict offered his monks are interrelated and inseparable. Together they brought a sense of the perfect love of God.

Chapter 14
Benedict and Work in a Time of Recession

This chapter takes up and extends the comment I made in the previous chapter that the contemporary quest to keep constantly busy and to value the intrinsic worth of a person according to the extent of their busyness is blasphemous. Not only do these things seem to run counter to the whole Judaeo-Christian tradition, they have no place whatever in any spirituality that claims to take seriously the Rule of St Benedict and the insights that might be gained from monasticism and what they may say to us today.

This chapter is then an excursus away from our primary concern with continuity and change in monastic spirituality. But it seems important to revisit this theme now in view of the increasing impact of the current economic recession in which women and men are encouraged to be busier and busier in order to keep their jobs and enjoy "the better days ahead".[568] If people refuse to engage in this quest for busyness they will be regarded as refusing to play their part in the process of economic and social recovery. An ascription of moral weakness will necessarily follow, with the further risk to their continued employment which that implies. So, although this chapter may be a departure from our main theme it is intended as a brief examination of how Benedict's monastic spirituality might impact on a sphere of life and audience far distant from those for whom it was originally intended. This chapter might also be a small contribution to what is grandly called the "spirituality of work".

This chapter will concern two central questions. First, can the Rule that St Benedict framed for his monks provide an ethical framework with which to develop a spirituality of work on a time of recession? Second, how can lay

---

[568] David Cameron in a rather optimistic speech concerning social policy in the recession at the Conservative Party Conference. Manchester 5 October 2009.

Christians who adopt the Rule in their spiritual practice and journey use it as a tool in the workplace so that they can offer a prophetic witness both of critique and comfort to those most at risk of suffering the great effects of the economic downturn?

The answers to these questions must be set against those developments in the last twenty years or so which have generated a renewed interest in the theology and spirituality of work. Many organisations, both "for profit" and "not for profit", have embraced the concept of the spiritually friendly workplace. This might be viewed with some cynicism, as another attempt by employers and businesses to maximise the potential of their workforce to work harder thus improving profitability or output and so improve "the bottom line". Perhaps too it is all part of a dangerous slide into a more emotional "touchy-feely" culture that prefers to wear its heart on its sleeves rather than roll them up and get on with a hard day's work.

Perhaps both or neither are true. But that is hardly the point, for is it not for Christians engaged in the workplace to ask why it is that the spiritual dimension of work now seems to be taken much more seriously? So, I begin by making some observations about the workplace which I hope will begin to answer that question and which will, in turn, have an impact on what I have to say about the theology of work from a Benedictine perspective.

It need hardly be said that the British economy is built on the generation of profit, increased market share, the maximisation of return on investment and efficiency. It is equally axiomatic that the economic growth that these things have brought about has resulted in increased prosperity for the vast majority of people with the further result that their secular and material needs are increasingly met as a result of their work. Greater prosperity is also alleged to have brought about an increase in leisure time and holidays.

Yet despite all this, many people are neither happy in their work nor do they feel fulfilled because of it. We might well ask why it is that when people reach the top, they so often hit rock bottom if not financially then emotionally, in their personal relationships and in their relation to God too.

One answer, I think, is that much of our work is now mechanistic, mere routine. Even managers and directors are now doing the tasks which used to be performed by the typing pool thirty years or so ago, simply tap-tap-tapping away at their key boards all day every day. They are controlled by their computers, spread sheets and word processing facilities and all sorts of technical paraphernalia rather than controlling them.

This is evidenced by the widespread panic and despair they feel when things go wrong, or "crash", if only for an hour or two. Even where this is not the case many people feel that their job has no tangible or positive outcomes and that their role is simply to meet the targets, tick the boxes and fulfil an agenda set by other people and about which they have not been adequately consulted. In short, the work of many people is devoid of all individuality, creativity, meaning and purpose.

A second answer might lie in a prominent feature of our so-called "post-modern" society. Many people have lost confidence in all the major world religions, preferring instead the fanatical and despairing nihilism we see in the works of radical atheists. There is also general lack of confidence in the political and social institutions to which we traditionally looked for encouragement and support because they are regarded as self-serving, elitist and corrupt—and as repeated the UK parliamentary financial and sexual scandals show they often are.

We have only to look at the statistics on declining church attendance[569] and those who bother to vote in Local, National and before Brexit European elections to see the effects of this lack of confidence at work church and state. In other words, the lack of confidence that institutions can, or should, maintain their authority at this super-structural level might, *mutatis mutandis,* be evidenced again at a smaller, local and more immediate level in a rejection in the assumed power and authority of the employer. If this remains unconvincing then perhaps, we should ask what effects the changing patterns of family formation and relationships are having on society. There are areas of the country in which, for good or ill, the majority of children are born to lone teenage mothers who are almost wholly isolated and without the support of friends, parents and extended family—or even professional social care. If we no longer care and protect our nearest and dearest and the most vulnerable members of our society, what possible motive could we have for showing more than a passing interest in our employers, our colleagues, or in the work we undertake?

---

[569] Howbeit that attendance at evangelical and charismatic churches such as Holy Trinity Brompton Road, Hill Songs, the New Wine Movement, New Frontiers and Black led Churches all seem to be moving in the opposite direction.

So, there is a growing crisis of trust and suspicion in all spheres of life and our work is by no means exempt. Increasingly we are faced with legislation, codes of conduct and practice, watchdogs and guidelines all of which contribute to the restriction on individuality and creativity at work by enforcing universal standards and impose an acceptable but conformist ode of moral behaviour. These things have largely replaced a climate of reciprocal trust and respect. In my experience, trust and respect are vital in the workplace because employees feel so vulnerable. People want a workplace in which they can be affirmed and nurtured as the people they are and might become—and as far as Christians are concerned the people God created them to be too. In the absence of a community traditionally built around home and family, local neighbourhoods and friends within a reasonable distance many people long to recreate community in the workplace.

Then there is the whole question of the change in work patterns and practices. A host of factors enter here. We have moved to a post-industrial economy in which rapid, complex technologies supporting our second order or "service industries" put us under increasing pressure. With its emphasis on efficiency and effectiveness, fewer and fewer people are responsible for more and more while millions remain unemployed. Whereas a trainee government auditor in 2007 might have been a member of a team of four or five people now she is very likely to carry not only her workload but those of her former colleagues as well entirely alone l with no commensurate improvement in pay or conditions. The same is likely to be true in commerce and manufacturing just as much as it is also true in charities and voluntary organisations too.

Even if we allow for the present tendency towards self-promotion and boasting about how busy we are and even if we set aside the view that to judge a person's worth by her busyness is blasphemous this is surely a shameful state of affairs. We have invented so many "labour-saving devices" in the workplace—so why is it that people are working harder for longer than ever before?

The culture of what I call "Presentism", (the polar opposite of sacred materiality which we looked at in the last chapter) is having its effects too. "Presentism" is the convention that it is necessary to be seen to be at work as early as possible, take as few breaks as possible, eat lunch while working "aldesko" and refuse to leave the workplace before the boss—whether the time thus spent is productive or not. Rats can longer be seen to leave the sinking ship before the captain! If even the smallest part of this new convention is believed to be contravened the person concerned may fall under suspicion as semi-detached, not being fully committed, more interested in home and leisure than the company, not a company man, professionally unreliable and so on.

Is it any wonder then that work related stress causes absenteeism, burnout, depression and even suicide. These pressures inevitably and unsurprisingly have adverse effects of the psychological, physical and emotional health of people and, equally inevitably the quality of their life suffers too. But more than this, their spiritual health suffers too and, left unchecked may well have consequences for their immortal soul too.

The current instability in the job market and the economy has caused people to be much more independent. This may be positive if it leads people to take greater care and responsibility for themselves, their friends and their family but often, as we have already noted, it does not. The UK is no longer the workshop of the world. Much of our production base either no longer exists or has been transferred abroad to high-output-low-wage economies such as the Far East. Around 70% of employed people now work in second order, service industries so that no almost no one stays with one employer for their entire working lives.

In the charity sector, for example, a full-time professional fundraiser with a specialist ability to raise money from charitable trusts and foundations now rarely stays in post for more than eighteen months. So, the former expectation, which was still possible even twenty years or so ago, that a person would carve out his or her career in one organisation has now long gone to be replaced with a "portfolio career" combining a number of jobs in a life time—and sometimes in order to make ends meet, even at the same time.

Insights gained from the behavioural sciences are important here. Psychology and psychotherapy indicate that we need to pay much more attention to all aspects of human development. Over the last two decades this has led to a far greater emphasis on the emotional and spiritual dimensions of work and their importance in our personal transformation. This interest has manifested itself in a number of ways so that whereas we formerly believed that IQ told us a very great deal about a person we now recognise that its value is quite limited and so we accompany it with EQ ("emotional quotient"). Both IQ and EQ are increasingly used when appointing people to senior positions of responsibility, and indeed even Licensed Readers in the Church of England are now *required* to take a Myers-Briggs test at the end of their training!

So, more and more people are becoming acquainted with the spiritual dimension of work and some are beginning to see work as ministry. This is accompanied by a desire that it be encouraged and fed howbeit that they often want to be nourished in rather unconventional ways. What is desired is a church (sometimes even a monastery) "without walls"[570], a faith stripped of much of its drama and divine mystery but which is nonetheless practical and effective.In these circumstances Christians in the workplace might well need to think of themselves as spiritual mentors or coaches for every level of the organisation's "organogram". In order to do that, it seems to me, Christians must have knowledge of "virtue ethics"[571] as set out, say, in the works of Alistair Macintyre. They must, of course, also be able to apply them. But "virtue ethics" alone are not enough for they are not distinctively Christian and it is for that reason that they must, in my view, be underwritten by the Beatitudes.It is possible to make connections between my arguments in this chapter so far and the Rule of St Benedict. I am not the first, and doubtless will not be the last, to observe that many of our contemporary social, economic and political circumstances are not unlike those of the sixth century in which Benedict composed his Rule.

Then, as now, community structures including traditional patterns of family life were believed to be breaking down. Then, as now, many Christians believed that they were living in a "broken society". Those crushed by work in the sixth century were suggesting that it was simply impossible to sustain the frenetic pace of change and activity. Something was going to have to give. Preoccupied as they were with their own survival and war, many lost sight of a broader, global and even Christian perspective but it was precisely this that Benedict addressed in his Rule and curiously it was these circumstances too that allowed it to flourish.

The Rule is, of course, about many things but from a somewhat oversimplified ethical perspective it directs our attention to what is good and what it is to be called good. It studies activity, whether personal or institutional and their significance for character and human flourishing. It extends the Aristotelian concept of *eudaimonia* to Christian thought and endeavour. Broadly

---

[570] John Main (2006): *Monastery Without Walls – The Spiritual Letters of John Main OSB. The Complete edition* Ed. Lawrence Freeman. World Community of Christian Meditation. Norwich. Canterbury Press.

[571] A Macintyre (2007) *"After Virtue A Study in Moral Theory.* Part of Bloomsbury Revelations Series. Notre Dame. University of Notre Dame Press. Third Edition.

speaking Benedict takes, I think, three approaches as he reflects on Christian ethical behaviour and thus on the relationship between reason and revelation.

The first places great emphasis on the recognition that moral arguments are open to natural reasoning. That is, the findings of our natural processes of reasoning are confirmed by revelation. But this does not mean that revelation is "nothing but" a *post hoc* justification of those findings for revelation brings insights of its own. But for the most part reason and revelation complement each other and need each other to be truly themselves. By their interaction, they bring about our concepts of both natural law and natural rights.

It is interesting and surprising to note that Benedict's naturalism has influenced more secular writings especially in the field of jurisprudence. They help us to understand Benedict's first approach. John Finnis,[572] for example, took himself to be explicating and developing the views of St Thomas Aquinas[573] and William Blackstone.[574] Like Brian Bix[575] Finnis believes that the naturalism of Aquinas and Blackstone should not be construed as a conceptual account of the conditions under which laws exist, but rather as a practical account of the *moral force* of law. "…the principles of natural law explain the obligatory force (in the fullest sense of obligation) of positive laws, even when those laws cannot be deduced from these principles."[576] Like Benedict's Rule, Finnis's naturalism is both a theory of ethics and a theory of law. Whereas Benedict had identified the traditional triad of monastic disciplines and discernment, prudence, temperance in speech and action as primary Christian virtues, Finnis distinguishes a number of other basic moral goods: life, health, knowledge, play, friendship, religious faith, and aesthetic experience. For both Benedict and Finnis each of these goods has intrinsic value in the sense that it should, given our human nature, be valued for its own sake and not merely for the sake of some other good it can assist in bringing about. Moreover, each of these goods is universal in the sense that they are common to all people in all cultures and throughout history. The point of

---

[572] John Finnis (1980) *Natural Law and Natural Rights*" Oxford University Press.
[573] St Thomas Aquinas (1988) *On Law, Morality and Politics*, Indianapolis. Hackett Publishing Company.
[574] William Blackstone (1979) *Commentaries On The Laws of England,* Chicago. University of Chicago Press.
[575] Brian Bix (1999) *On Description and Legal Reasoning* in Linda Meyers: (ed) *"Rules and Reasoning"*. Oxford. Hart Publishing.
[576] Op cit Finnis. pp 23–24.

moral principles, according to both Benedict and Finnis, is that they enable us to select among a competing complex of goods and to define what a human being can (and must) in pursuit of these basic goods.

On Finnis's view, the conceptual point of law is to facilitate the common good by means of authoritative rules that solve the problem of the competing demands of the individual and the group.[577] This, it seems to me, clearly echoes one of Benedict's driving motives for writing the Rule in the first place. The solution is to inculcate the notion that a balance between all competing demands must be struck and maintained at all times.[578] This is something that for a Christian might appear obvious and is, of course, a central feature of Benedict's Rule. But it is probably worth noting that Finnis has held this view consistently since 1966, the point from which it is often popularly believed radical secularisation began.[579] To what extent he was able to do so because this was precisely the moral stance taken by the church at the Second Vatican Council[580] will almost certainly never be known. The second approach that Benedict takes to the relationship between natural law natural rights and human dignity arises from his belief that Christian faith in general and membership of a monastic community in particular changes the natural reasoning process. That is, for Benedict the reasoning of a Christian can never be divorced from the specific communal context in which it takes place and the tradition in which it stands. Thus scripture, liturgy, and the prayerful reading other narratives (such as the Rule itself!) not only guide our ethical thinking they directly influence our actions in relation to the pursuance of a particular moral good. That is why it is essential for members of a religious community to maintain a constant dialogue concerning its moral shape and direction. This is a prime example of the way the Rule maintains its relevance. Through this constant moral dialogue, it is constantly reviewed, renewed and re-launched.

For those of us working in a bureaucratic organisation, say, a school, university, government department or even a charity Benedict's idea of "calling the brethren to council" on a regular basis might be a very useful practice to

---

[577] Op cit. pp276.

[578] Op cit. pp 278 and 351.

[579] John Finnis (1969) *The Truth of Logical Positivism* in Robert P. George; *The Anatomy of Law,* Oxford. Clarendon Press pp 195–214.

[580] The document *Gaudium et Spes* is a pertinent example of this. At Last Accessed March 2024.

adopt—especially the practice of listening to all the views present in the community before arriving at a major decision! His emphasis on the spiritual as well as the physical dimensions of hospitality might also encourage our organisations to change their approach to personnel management, customers and clients.

His third approach is prophetic. Benedict recognises that whatever consensus the continuing moral dialogue might bring about there will always be those who feel hard done by and disgruntled and wish to find the support of a third party. In the modern workplace, these are often referred to as "whistle-blowers". Would be whistle-blowers either in a monastic community or in the workplace, do not tend to analyse their situation as thoroughly, calmly and rationally as those with much to lose as a result of their critique believe. Often whistle-blowing is a spontaneous knee jerk reaction to an event or series of events made in the white heat of the moment arising from anger or frustration. Whistle-blowers blow whistles not because they want to inflict the maximum amount of damage to another person or an organisation in the shortest possible time (although this may also be the case) but, more often, because they think that they are the ones who are hurt and have lost. In either case, whistle-blowing is an act of revenge.

That is why the chapters of the Rule concerning the role and leadership of the abbot and other officials in the monastery are so important for staff relations in the workplace. These together with the chapters about the importance of maintaining good order and discipline in work and worship provide, *mutatis mutandis*, an important lesson. They speak of justice as a virtue, a moral good to be pursued for its own sake. This is at the heart of Chapter 48 of the Rule which Benedict devoted entirely to work.

It is well known that, for Benedict, work is far more than an economic necessity or religious duty. It is an aesthetic and prayerful practice too. Chapter 48 makes this clear in a great number of ways but two immediately take our attention.

First it establishes a timetable to ensure that no one in the community is idle. This is not at all the same as our present quest to be busy, or our desire to define ourselves by the amount and nature of the work we do. Rather it is what it says it is; a timetable which allows the many and varied parts of monastic life to be kept in constant balance with no one area dominating another.

Second "...when they live by the labour of their hands, as our fathers the apostles did, then they are truly monks". This is clearly a reference to the Pauline teaching that Christians should take care not be a burden on the society of which they are part and that it is by work that we earn the means of helping those less fortunate through almsgiving and hospitality. It is also a reference to Paul's personal example of returning to his craft of tent making when times were hard and to the ability of Peter, Andrew, James and John to return to their fishing fleet during their period of discipleship even though they left their fishing nets and boats along the shore with Zebedee.

Important and useful as all these insights are, the Rule of Benedict can provide only part of the foundation of our contemporary reflection on the spirituality of work. We need to look at other monastic resources as well, especially those that influenced Benedict. Not least of these might be our knowledge of the Pachomian monasteries, the ways in which the desert mothers and fathers organised their labour and ensured that their goods penetrated the urban markets nearby. It would also be interesting to see if the learning Benedict's near contemporaries Botheius (480–541) and Cassiodorus (485–577) is able to contribute to this discussion.

Here in the UK a great deal has been written about the history of industrial mission and the rise of worker-priests. Those who are, or have been, involved with this ministry often remark on the need for a systematic theology of work and while there are many well placed to write it none appear to have done so. Perhaps they are all too busy working!

Another most valuable insight would, of course, come from those who are oblates or tertiary members of a monastic order and especially those who have are part of the so-called "new" monasticism.

This is research that should in my view be undertaken and completed with some urgency if we are to reflect more deeply on the place of work in our lives and its impact on our spirituality especially in a time of recession. It might also be an innovative way of letting the Christian voice be heard amidst the hubbub and clamour for the reform of society and institutions in ways which would accord no place to religious dialogue of any kind.

Part 5
Medieval Monasticism

Chapter 15
Revival and Reform (1): New Orders

When Charlemagne came to the throne in 768, he achieved what the hordes of barbarians which had vanquished the old Roman Empire had failed to do: create a unified Europe. It was not, as the title Holy Roman Empire suggests a re-establishment of ancient glories of the successors to Romulus and Remus but it did, nevertheless, bring the Germanic and Frankish people together with the Latin people to the south under the temporal power of the emperor and the spiritual authority of the Pope. During Charlemagne's long reign (768–814) the liturgy was stabilised, the Biblical text was unified and confirmed, Gregorian chant was promoted and new hymns and prayers were introduced. The monasteries played a central role in all of this renewal and reform. In fact, Charlemagne desired to see all monasteries united under one rule but the first serious attempts at this were made only after his death.

Sixteen years after Charlemagne became emperor, the first great monastic of this period, Ambrose Aupert, died. He had been abbot of a monastery in southern Italy. His doctrine was fully in accord with the ancient view that the monastic life was one of spiritual combat and personal sanctification achieved by separation from the world and a loving meditation on the mysteries of Christ. He was also Benedictine and while the Rule kept prayer and labour in balance, Aupert put much greater emphasis on the former rather than the later. As we will see this became of increasing importance later on.

The man selected by Charlemagne to begin to work for the desired unification and renewal of the monastic life was Alban Flacco, who is better known as Alcuin. He died in 804. Alcuin was also steeped in the Benedictine tradition and made a major contribution to it by developing a series of liturgical devotions for every day of the week. In this way, he contributed as much as anyone to the numerous additions to the prayer life of monks, thus extending the hours of community prayer and, like Aupert, interfering with manual labour and holy reading.

Charlemagne also called upon the services of a Spanish intellectual, Teodulfo (died 821) and an Italian, St Paulinus (died 802).in his writings, Paulinus praises Charlemagne extravagantly but he nevertheless had the courage to defend the rights of the church when he perceived that they were, or might be, under threat from the temporal power.

When St Benedict of Aniane appeared on the scene as a reformer, he endeavoured to restore the strict observance of the Rule of St Benedict, but at the same time he imposed lengthy ritual prayers in addition to those of the divine office and he extended the *lectio divina* to the works of Origen, St Jerome, St Augustine of Hippo, and St Gregory the Great. That Origen should be included in this list is somewhat surprising since Pachomius had refused to hear Origenists when they came to his monasteries on the grounds that their theology was heretical and indeed Origen was finally condemned by the Fifth Ecumenical council in 553. By the time of Benedict of Aniane, many people had come to believe that this condemnation was erroneous but, even so, there were many who still regarded Origen's writings with great suspicion.

Born in 750, Benedict of Aniane became a monk at the age of twenty-four and later founded his own monastery at Aniane, near the Pyrenees. At the outset he was greatly attracted to the monasticism of Pachomius, considering that the practice of the Rule of St Benedict had, in his experience, become far too lax. Eventually, however, he changed his mind and adopted the Rule of St Benedict as the *only* practical solution to the problems of living n community. Benedict of Aniane was convinced that the only way to prevent monasteries from falling into laxity was to discover a basis for constant renewal and reform and a form of central organisation to which separate monasteries might be federated.

When Louis the Pious became Emperor in 814, Benedict of Ariane became a kind of visitor to all the monasteries in the empire, sending out monks from his own monastery to reform them. In this way, he began to form the federation he had envisaged with himself as the central authority, an "abbot primate". It was in this role that he composed two documents, the *Codex Regularum* which was a compendium of existing monastic rules, and the *Concordia Regularum* which was a commentary on the Rule of St Benedict with synoptic parallels from other rules.

These works influenced the Synod of Aix-la-Chappel in 816 and 817 which drew up legislation governing the lives of clerics and discussed the ways in which monasticism might be reformed. Unfortunately, the findings of this Synod were largely ignored and when Benedict of Aniane died in 821 the whole empire was torn apart by factional squabbling in the imperial family and the threat of invasion both from the disaffected Nordic tribes in the north and the Muslim Saracens to the south. So monastic reform was delayed but when it did begin to emerge, it was largely on the basis suggested by Benedict of Aniane.

Benedict of Aniane was one of the most important figures in western monastic history because what he envisaged or something very like, it became the pattern for monastic living for much of the Middle Ages and which is familiar to us today. This does not mean that Benedict of Aniane wanted monks to return to some golden age by creating a Disneyland version of Subiaco or Monte Casino but it did mean that the Rule of St Benedict would once again be more prominent than the other numerous layers of tradition that had accumulated in the monasteries of the empire. These other traditions were many and varied; the monasticism of Cassian, of St Martin de Tour, the traditions of Lerin eclectically mixed with contributions from Celtic and Anglo-Saxon Christianity and all held to be equally valid.

Similarly, Benedict of Aniane intended that monasteries should become very large establishments indeed housing several hundred monks and a number of boys to be educated in the monastic school. Hitherto, monasteries had usually been in somewhat remote places following the precedent set by the desert dwellers, Anthony, Pachomius and the great Benedict himself. But Benedict of Aniane thought that monasteries should be near, or preferably in, large centres of population. He thought that the population should both serve and be served by the monastery.

The monastery should be supported by large tracts of land worked by serfs and that the abbot would fulfil a temporal as well as a spiritual obligation to them as their overlord. By delegating agricultural labour to the serfs, the monks would be free to live an ever more ritualised life. Many more prayers and hymns were added to the Benedictine *opus dei*; private masses, altars and churches multiplied with frequent processions and expositions of holy relics. Now the life of a monk was indeed a perpetual seeking after God—and little else.

In short, a monastery was to become a mirror to the medieval state. The abbot was to be the major political functionary and the abbey itself was to be a major economic power. Thus, the state was quick to claim the right to appoint abbots not for their holiness so much as for their management skills. This was, of course, to have dire consequences which may indirectly have contributed to the fury stirred up against the monasteries during the sixteenth and seventeenth centuries.

In an effort to achieve greater uniformity of monastic life and observance, a series of "customaries" or statues began to appear in the eighth and ninth centuries. These were necessary because, of course, the Rule of St Benedict was not a code of law. Particular matters of discipline and regulation had been reserved to the abbot but, after three or four centuries this system had become reified and somewhat anachronistic. Benedict of Aniane had already set the pattern for communities of monasteries under one head and eventually the Benedictines would receive official (papal0 recognition as a religious order.

At the same time, a more intensive study of the Rule of St Benedict was beginning to be made and this led to the composition of a number of commentaries. One of these was ascribed to Paul the deacon, but by far the most important in terms of its lasting influence was written by Hildemar sometime between 840 and 845.

Hildemar argued that the Rule of St Benedict allowed a monk to pursue his vocation either as a hermit or as a member of a community, but he emphasised that the value of living in community lay in its insistence on each individual being part of the same mystical body: one Church, one faith one Lord. Most monks, he believed, were simply not able to maintain the life of a hermit and that such a life was a distinct vocation reserved only for a few.

According to Hildemar, the monastic life should be characterised by a profound sense of the divine found in the ordinary mundane things of the everyday. It was this, he thought, that produced an intense love of Jesus, the desire to pray unceasingly and provided the sole motivation for total renunciation. Renunciation in turn produced the monastic virtues of holy fear, obedience and patience. In order to have a rightly formed conscience and grow in humility, a monk should in the same way be faithful in confessing his actions and thoughts, either to the abbot or to a spiritual director drawn from one of the brothers. For Hildemar, as for St Benedict himself, the life of a monk should be divided between contemplation and labour. Physical labour was essential. While labour should not be delegated to a peasant underclass, neither should it dominate the monastic day.

Hildemar had a number of interesting things to say about prayer, which he believed to be the primary function of a Benedictine monk. Since preoccupation with the things of this world tends to destroy the simplicity of one's reliance on God, the monk should give himself to the divine office and the singing of the psalms with great zeal and fervour. The words of the prayers come from God himself and in the psalms a monk should enjoy God's presence in a direct manner.

Hildemar thought that private mental prayer was often beyond the capacities of most people because the human mind cannot fix its attention on silent prayer for a long period without being distracted by external thoughts and concern. Periods of mental prayer, like the prayer itself should, he thought be brief. Hildemar recommended that when a monk is engaged in mental prayer and becomes distracted by external thoughts, he should give it up! A monk should replace it with reading, psalmody or labour and then return to meditation.

For Hildemar, to persist in mental prayer while distracted by external thoughts is a waste of time and of spiritual energy. Indeed, he thought that it was to act against the spirit, if not the letter of the Rule. However, this did not give monks a licence for abandoning mental prayer on the grounds that they were just not up to it. Rather they should pray to be given the grace of persistence and make every possible effort to receive it.

Hildemar was also aware that some monks might be graced with the desire and ability to engage in mental prayer without distraction and that the desire for prayer could come at any moment when engaged in other tasks such as holy reading or manual labour. If a monk feels this desire then, thought Hildemar, it is better for the monk to stop what he is doing and run to the oratory. But this again should not be used as an excuse to avoid other duties, for such a sudden desire would come only rarely even to a most practised and experienced monk and there is always the danger of illusion. So for Hildemar, the psalmody was the normal prayer for a monk and this should be followed by a brief period of silent prayer; but some—and they are always few in numbers—will also practice mental prayer for longer periods.

By gradually moderating the practice of monasticism through returning to a proper balance between work and prayer, Hildemar's reforms issued in a flowering of the liturgy and of holy reading in the monastic life. This, in turn, increased the influence of Benedictine spirituality on the life of the church at the dawn of the Middle Ages, especially in understanding the Scriptures and in liturgical practice. It was in this period that a great number of revisions of the Latin Bible and Biblical commentaries began to appear. Their purpose was eminently spiritual, namely, to equip Christians with the truths of revelation as a basis for their own holy reading and meditation.

It was in this period too that new hymns were written and monks restored the chant to its original purity. New feasts were introduced into the church calendar; prayers, invocations and other devotional material were interwoven with the existing structure of the liturgy. The "secular" diocesan clergy were now obliged to say the Mass and the choral offices in their parish churches every day, although there was no similar obligation imposed in terms of a private recitation of the other parts of the daily office. In this period, liturgical themes gathered around the titles of Christ—King of Kings, Lord of Lords, the Holy Cross and around the Virgin Mary.

The use of the Saturday votive Mass in honour of the Virgin Mary was already a widespread and common practice but there was now a marked increase in the number of hymns in honour of Mary to accompany it. Two doctrinal questions that attracted the attention of theologians at this time concerned Mary's perpetual virginity and her bodily assumption into heaven.

The Mass also and unsurprisingly received a great deal of attention. It was seen as a perpetual memorial of Christ's passion and death and the means by which Christ communicates with human beings the fruits of that victory. Great insistence was placed on the spiritual and bodily dispositions required for the worthy reception of communion.

These then were the chief characteristics of Christian and monastic spirituality during the Carolingian period. When that period came to an end, the church suffered the effects of the destruction of central authority in civil government and the seizure of church power by the laity. It suffered schism and scandals in the papacy, confiscation of church property, simony and lax sexual morals among the clergy. During the tenth and eleventh centuries, the church and her monk would oscillate between decadence, revival and reform, but eventually under the clear leadership of Pope Gregory VII (1073–1085), renewal would prevail.

Amidst all the turmoil there were, however, pockets of reform the most influential of which was the monastery at Cluny founded in 910. This monastery had a glorious history not just in terms of its influence on spirituality but on western literature as well. What had been started by Benedict of Aniane was carried forward and brought to fulfilment by the monks of Cluny, namely, the establishment of a federation of monasteries under the guidance and control of Cluny itself. The need for federation was plain for all to see and was thought to be the only way a monastery could escape the interference from the bishops and high-ranking laymen who had been appointed by the secular powers. By engaging in federation, it was much easier for individual monasteries to be placed under the protection of the Holy See. Cluny was one of them.

What developed at Cluny was quite extraordinary and lasted for more than two centuries. Cluny enjoyed a series of abbots whose piety was greater than their strong administrative abilities. The monks themselves were discrete and disciplined and faithful to Christ and the Rule of St Benedict. But the reforms at Cluny were not just a matter of strictly observing the rule in a literalist or fundamentalist way. Rather, the monks at Cluny had the insight to see that the rule could not and should not be preserved in some sort of ecclesiastical aspic but had to change and adapt according to prevailing conditions both with the church and in the world while preserving an essence that was both faithful to the past and recognisably Benedictine.

The reforms at Cluny centred on a uniformity of liturgical practice and monastic living that would be common throughout the federation. This demanded an enormous development in ritual and a monastic culture based upon the study of the Bible and the wirings of the church fathers. It demanded a genuinely contemplative orientation, far reaching charitable activity among the most disadvantaged and vulnerable people, and serious (though limited) work.

Many other monasteries found these reforms very attractive and adopted them. Although they differed in some local detail, they all observed the Rule of St Benedict in its Cluniac interpretation. So it was that the reforms quickly spread to other parts of France and into Belgium. The reforms came to England in the tenth century and to Italy, Germany and Spain in the eleventh. The effects of the Cluniac reforms extended far beyond the cloister and greatly contributed to the reforms of the diocesan clergy and in the lives of ordinary lay folk.

Unfortunately, the structure of these reforms also demanded a great deal of travelling and visitations from Cluny to the members of the federation and this took its toll on the contemplative aspect of monastic life. Increasingly the monks saw their serious work as being confined to the production and copying of manuscripts in the *scriptorium* and manual labour was neglected. This resulted in the formation of oblates to which the monks entrusted the manual work and the upkeep of monastic property and the division between "choir monks" and "lay brothers".

In the eleventh and twelfth centuries, monasteries became more and more prosperous and fervent in religious observance, but nevertheless a reaction was developing. Whereas monasteries had, perhaps, once stood over and against the world as a sign of contradiction, they were now firmly part of the economic and religious establishment. While the reforms at Cluny had tried to keep pace with the changes in society in the end, those changes came at such a pace and with such transformation that the reformers were largely unable to match them. It was for this reason that some desired a monastic life that would be much simpler, less institutionalised, more solitary and far less involved in the social and political fabric of society. In short, they wanted a return to the monastic origins. It is not surprising, then, that it often led to the reintroduction of the eremitical life. This movement which sprang up all over Europe brought about a revolution in monasticism and produced a perplexing range of new "orders" and observances alongside the more established houses.

Western monasticism remained Benedictine at heart but it moved in two different directions. So, St Romauld founded the Camaldolese in 1010 in order to foster a strictly eremitical life under the Rule of St Benedict. St Robert of Molesmes, on the other hand founded the Cistercians in an effort to promote the cenobitic life of greater separation from the world in poverty and in strict observance to the Benedictine rule. Two men worked tirelessly for further reform in the church and in monastic life; John of Fecamp and St Peter Damian.

John of Fecamp was an unassuming man who often referred to himself a "poor john" (*misellus Johannes*) and for many years, his writings were variously attributed to Cassian, St Ambrose, Alcuin, St Anslem of Bec or St Bernard of Clairvaux. John was, in fact the author of the *Summe sacredos*, which is still used as one of the prayers before Mass. Until the widespread popularity of "*The Imitation of Christ*" By Thomas A Kempis, it was the works of John of Fecamp that were most widely read in Christendom.

John was born near Ravenna. He lived as a hermit until he entered the monastery of St Beingnus at Dijon. In 1017, he transferred to the monastery at Fecamp and after travels that took him to Italy, he died in 1076.

The spirituality of John of Fecamp is intensely Christocentric. He loved to dwell on those aspects of Christ's mission and ministry that show most clearly God's love for human beings. John longed for mystical union but he did not find the existing methods of contemplative prayer either useful or effective. So, he provided a sort of *lectio divina* that could expose contemplative souls, such as his own, to a direct encounter with the divine. Indeed, it could well be argued, as Sitwell has done[581] that John's exposure to holy reading in the monastery led directly to the writing of his spiritual manual; the *Confessio theological.* To some extent, John's descriptions of prayer which we find in that book are a refinement and advancement on those of Hildemar. After chanting the divine office or engaging in holy reading, the monk may be inspired to engage in affective silent prayer which will sometimes blossom into genuine infused contemplation. "There are many kinds of contemplation in which the soul is devoted to thee O Christ, takes its delight, but in none of these do I rejoice as in that which, ignoring all things, directs a simple glance of the untroubled spirit to thee alone O God. What peace and joy does the soul find in thee then! While my soul year for the divine vision and proclaims thy glory as best it can, the burden of the flesh weighs less heavily upon it, distracting thoughts subside, the weight and misery of our mortal condition no longer deaden the faculties as usual: all is quiet and peaceful. The heart is inflamed with love, the spirit is filled with joy, the memory is powerful, the mind is clear, and the whole soul burning with desire for thy beauty is ravished by a love of things invisible."[582] This passage is surely the equal of anything we find in the later writings of Catherine of Siena or St John of the Cross, but it clearly shows the importance of (contemplative) prayer in the early Middle Ages. However, John of Fecamp, like St Benedict himself, while recognising the validity of a purely contemplative life, believed that it was better to live in monastic community and thus combine the contemplative with the active life—*ora est labourare.*

St Peter Damian was born in 988 and educated in Ravenna. He entered the monastery founded by St Romuald at Fonte Avellana where he became the Superior in 1044. He was created a cardinal and dedicated the rest of his life to the much-needed reform of the church in three distinct areas: reform of the "secular" diocesan clergy, the renewal of the monastic life and a readjustment in the relation between church and state. In addition to all this, he also composed a treatise on the interpretation of scripture, *De fide catholica,* and a work concerning the interface between philosophy and theology, *De divina*

---

[581] G Sitwell (1961) S*piritual Writers of the Middle Ages.* Hawthorn. New York, p26.
[582] Quoted in J Leclerq and J Bonnes (1946) *The Materials of the Spiritual Life in the XII century,* Paris p182.

omnipotentia, in which he coined the expression so familiar to students of systematic theology of my generation, "philosophia ancillia theologiae".

The regulations of St Peter Damian for monastic reform were often severe to the point of harshness, and yet when writing about Jesus or the Virgin Mary he could be as tender, loving and entirely devoted. As John of Fecamp. Like St Augustine of Hippo before him St Peter Damian believed that ascetical practices—which were at least as difficult for hermits in the Middle Ages as anything experienced by the desert dwellers—were not to be thought of as an end in themselves but as a means of attaining spiritual perfection, charity and divine wisdom. But this view did not prevent him from advocating the use of physical punishment to instil discipline in the life of monks and the recommending that severe bodily mortifications (such as whipping the back with cords) should accompany monastic prayer. In addition to a fidelity to the divine office and night vigils, he imposed an almost continual fast and a strict observance of poverty.

His concept of monastic life was one of total separation from the world to concentrate only on the things of God; a life of perpetual penance and prayer. In some cases, his advice was met with fierce resistance and resentment. After all, had not the great Benedict explicitly said in so many words that his Rule would not impose anything harsh or difficult on those enrolled in the school of the Lord's service? How could these recommendations be consistent with that promise?

In short, while in theory advocating the cenobitic life, in practice St Peter Damian enjoined the life of a hermit on his monks. And there were Christian hermits at this time. We noted earlier that St Romauld founded the Camaldolese order in 1010. They followed the Rule of St Benedict as adapted to the eremitical life. The Constitutions for the Camaldolese were composed by the Blessed Rudolph between 1080 and 1085, and they list the following as occupations of the Camaldolese hermit: prayer, *lectio divina*, bodily flagellations and prostrations and all to be accompanied by the recitation of specified prayers. Somewhat unlike St Peter Damian, however, the Constitutions urged great caution and discretion in the use of mortification and penitential practices. They were to be used only in due to proportion to an individual's bodily health and strength, personal need, or the inspiration of grace. The life of a Camaldolese hermit was therefore almost totally contemplative and silent. Chanting was to be reduced to a minimum and solitude was safeguarded as a means of death to self and voluntary exile from the world.[583] Camaldolese spirituality was, then, characterised by separation from the world and asceticism. This was partly a reaction against the abuses and excesses in the diocesan churches of the time. Many Christians, ordained, monastic and lay, felt the need to do penance and to flee from, the world. It is well known that the passions of men in the early Middle Ages were extreme and violent, so it should not entirely that their religious practice would be equally extreme, and sometimes violent. It was not unusual for monks to leave the monastery to live as hermits. Nor was it unusual for bishops to renounce their dioceses in order to become monks.

Amongst the laity, members of the aristocracy and peasant sought admission to the monastic life. Sometimes husbands and wives separated by mutual agreement in order to enter a cloister or a hermitage. Others remained in the world and attempted to pursue the religious life within it. They could flee from the world on a temporary basis by going on pilgrimages to the holy places. Or they remained at home and made use of the disciple of self-flagellation.

The Constitutions of the Camaldolese give a detailed description of the progress of a person from first seeking admission to the order to their life as a hermit. A candidate was first subject to close questioning, even interrogation, as to his past life and his ability to accept the rigours of the eremitical life. This questioning could last for some time, but certainly no less than four or five days. He was made to understand that once he had made his profession there was no way back. His vow of stability was indissoluble and absolute.

Once the candidate was found to be suitable and following his profession, he was led out to his hermitage carrying a small bundle of clothes that he would wear henceforth. He entered the cell alone and the presiding abbot together with a bishop made sure that the door was permanently sealed from the outside. The cell had only two other openings. One was a small window opening onto the church from which the hermit could view and pray the Mass. The other opened onto a small garden with very high walls (so high that he could not escape over them!) so that the hermit could neither see no be seen by the other hermits. In that garden, he could take fresh air and grow vegetables. Whereas the original Rule of St Benedict made no special provision for priests who became monks,

---

[583] Several eremitical communities were founded at about the same time. Valloombrosa in 1038, Grandmont in 1076, Fontevrault in 1101—a double monastery of men and women rule by an abbess, and intriguingly a congregation of Scottish monks in Germany in 1075.

priest-hermits of the Camaldolese were allowed to have a consecrated oratory of their own in which they could not only pray but also give spiritual direction to any who needed it.

In many respects, the life of a Camaldolese hermit was not dissimilar to that of the Carthusians to whom we now turn.

The Carthusian order was established by St Bruno of Cologne in the valley of La Chartreuse, near Grenoble, in 1084. St Bruno's vision was to provide for an eremitical way of life within the framework of a primitive Benedictine *cenobium*. They did not, however, follow the Rule of St Benedict, but that provided by Bruno himself. Bruno's intention was to take the Benedictine Rule and extract from it only those things which he thought were absolutely essential for the religious life. To this, he added his own material which would direct the sort of eremitical life he had in mind.

Bruno wanted to replicate the way of life of the desert dwellers but make it somewhat more severe. So, whereas the desert dwellers had some, though limited, contact with the world, Carthusians were to have none at all. Whereas the desert dwellers were productive in making mats and baskets to be sold in nearby towns and villages, Carthusians were only to labour contemplatively for God. Whereas, the desert dwellers also cultivated small plots of land for the growing of vegetables, Carthusians were only to cultivate their relationship with God making it fertile, not with springs in the desert but with holy tears, prayer fasting and strict observance.

Typical of all Carthusians, who are extremely reticent about the nature and content of their spirituality, St Bruno left only two letters both of which were written towards the end of his life. One was addressed to the lay brothers of the order and makes it plain that the "key and seal" of all monastic discipline is obedience lived in humility and patience and accompanied by a chaste love of the Lord expressed in true charity.[584] It remained for Bruno's fifth successor, Guigo 1, to formulate the Carthusian "*Book of Customs*" sometime between 1121 and 1128.In his prologue, Guigo 1 refers both to St Jerome and to St Benedict but he does not make extended use of them. Rather, throughout the book his emphasis is on utter simplicity of life, moderation and peace. This simplicity is to be reflected in the liturgy which is to be austere. Poverty is to be observed with great diligence. As hermits, Carthusians were to observe strict (almost total)

---

[584] Op cit J Leclerq pp 150–156.

silence and to maintain the solitude of their cells in which they are to study only the scriptures and approved spiritual texts.

There were, and are, two classes of Carthusians, monks and lay brothers. All are hermits and all have their residence in a hermitage of Charterhouse, not a monastery. The use of physical discipline and other instruments for mortification was, and is allowed but only and always with permission from the Prior.

Everything that a Carthusian needed for health, work and prayer was provided for him so that he never needed to leave his cell for any reason whatever. Everything in the cell was to be conducted with solitude and prayer, and perhaps the only reason for prescribing community prayer and liturgy (and in modern times the weekly walk!) was for the sake of balance and moderation as envisaged by St Bruno. St Bruno did not, I think, intend his Carthusians to be the recluses they became, but hermits living in a communal setting.

In a strict sense, there has never been a distinct "Carthusian spirituality", or if it has it has always remained firmly sealed behind the Charterhouse door. But from the little we know of it, and certainly as again the film "*Into Great Silence*" makes clear, we can say that it is made up of extreme austerity and simplicity, constant care, purgation, contemplation and an overwhelming love for Jesus and his Blessed Mother—and the all too rare appreciation of each other's company as companions on the same spiritual journey. The elements of this spirituality are also to be found in the writings of Guigo 2 (the second prior of that name to rule the Grand Chatreuse (1114–1180)). His letter on the contemplative life, known as the *Scala Claustralium*, or *Scala Paradisi* was more widely read and more highly praised than any other of the period. In it, he describes four interrelated stages of the spiritual life of the contemplative: reading, meditation, prayer and contemplation. The last three are not synonyms. Reading, quite obviously, was *lectio divina*, the careful study of scripture, concentrating all one's powers upon it.

Meditation was the busy application of the mind to seek the help of reason for knowledge of the hidden truths buried in the scriptures that have been read. Prayer is the turning of one's entire being towards God, the total renunciation of evil and a commitment to all that is good. In contemplation, the mind and the soul are lifted up into the heavenly places held, as it were, above themselves in order to taste the divine sweetness that is sweeter than honey and to be preferred to the honeycomb.[585] Using a similar analogy to that of John Climacus, Guigo 2 sees these stages as rungs on a ladder leading to perfection. Hence reading words on a page without meditation makes them dead letters. Meditation without careful reading is liable to error. Prayer without reading and meditation is Laodicean, lukewarm and half hearted. Meditation without prayer is unfruitful. Prayer when it is fervent produces contemplation—but to obtain contemplation is a rare event, so rare that it is miraculous. The third reform of monasticism in the Middle Ages, and by far the most popular, was the Cistercian Order, founded by St Robert of Molesmes at Citeaux in 1098. After making the foundation, the Pope directed St Robert to return to Molesmes but other members remained at Citeaux, living in great austerity under St Alberic and St Stephen Harding. St Bernard arrived at Clairvaux with thirty companions in 1112, and so great was the expansion of the Cistercian order that when St Bernard died in 1153 there were 343 monasteries of "the strict observance" running on a chain from Western Europe into the Balkans and beyond to the Holy Land.

Stephen Harding laid down the regulation of the Cistercian Order in 1114 and his *Carta caritatis* (the charter of love). He moved the Cistercians away from the centralisation of the Cluniac system and introduced government by General Chapter, the pattern which is now followed by most, if not all religious order to this day. The Cistercians succeeded in adapting monastic life to the needs of the times with the result that whereas other orders appeared, blossomed and quickly withered and died, the Cistercians have prospered and continue to do so now even at a time when monastic vocations are scarce.

Essentially the Cistercians did not differ from the Benedictines, certainly as regards the concept of monastic living. What they sought to do was to restore the primitive observance in all its original simplicity and austerity—but without the harsh rigours associated with the Camaldolese and the Carthusians. Consequently, they reduced the additional lengthy prayers, restricted the activities in the scriptorium and returned to manual labour. This, says Sitwell, constituted the fundamental difference between the "black" monks of Cluny and the "white" monks of Citeaux.[586] It was a difference that sprang from two distinct understandings of the Rule of St Benedict. But there was, I think, another subtle but important difference between the black and the white monks. The Cistercians desired to seek the eremitical life, not in the manner of the Camaldolese or the

---

[585] Psalm 19:10.
[586] Op cit Sitwell p 43.

Carthusians, but as a community living together, interacting with each other and observing the Rule of St Benedict not in strict isolation from each other but nevertheless as literally as possible. As we have just noted, this literalism did not prevent them from adapting their observance to the needs of the time and to suit their purpose. Consequently, they tended to subordinate everything else to the ascetical life and contemplative prayer, while the Cluniac interpretation gave the primacy to liturgy and *lectio divina*.

For the Cistercians then, separation from the world was a complete as that of the desert dwellers and it was for that reason that they sought out more remote places for their monasteries and observed a strict cloister. Their asceticism consisted in the restoration of the importance of manual labour and an austere mode of life in order to embrace the cross of Christ without mitigation. In order to safeguard their contemplative recollection, they withdrew all forms of apostolate and priestly ministry, observed perpetual silence and avoided the accumulation of wealth. To those who would ask, "How then did the Cistercians obey the command to love one's neighbour?" they could reply with the teaching of St Bernard who stated that the practice of fraternal charity was evident in the community life of the monks themselves.

I doubt whether we can speak meaningfully of a distinct "school" of Cistercian spirituality rooted and grounded as it is in that of St Benedict. But nevertheless, there are certain characteristics that distinguish the monks of Citeaux from other branches of the Benedictine tradition. First, in accordance with the monastic axiom *solo Deo* (=God alone), there was an eschatological quality to Cistercian life. Their gaze was, and is, firmly fixed on eternal realities and of the goal of life in glory. They considered themselves as pilgrims on a road to heaven and in order to prepare themselves for the coming of Christ they divested themselves, as far as possible, of all earthly possessions, interests and attachments.

Second, and somewhat paradoxically, the Cistercians had a profound appreciation for all created things and a delicate sensibility to human needs. They cultivated the fields and became experts in animal husbandry. They even became renowned for their production of domestic items such as wool, bread and cheese. In ecclesiastical architecture, they did away with the ornate characteristic of so many monasteries and abbeys and returned to the pure beauty of simple lines. In the area of human relationships and following the example of St Bernard,

William of Thierry and especially St Aelred, they gave an example of spiritual friendship in the monastic milieu.

A third characteristic of Cistercian life was the prudent adaptation of monastic observances. While holding fast to the beneficial traditional practices, the Cistercians did not hesitate to abandon or change those elements that no longer served the purpose for which they were intended. When they did make such changes, however, they always did so with the intention of preserving the original monastic sources. This was important in order to prevent rampant individualism or differences between one Cistercian house and another. The same pattern was strictly observed by all monasteries, while allowing individual communities to make necessary adjustments as regards implementation.

Two other dominant features of the Cistercian pilgrimage to the heavenly places were poverty and manual labour. For the Cistercians, poverty went far beyond an intellectual adherence to the concept or an interior detachment and the expiation of a possessive spirit as required by all monks. The Cistercians practised poverty as a means of privation and asceticism as a community witness. They did not go to the extremes of the mendicant friars would propose in the thirteenth century, but they did add a new interpretation of monastic poverty.

As for manual labour, they saw it as the logical consequence of their concept of poverty. St Benedict had stated in his Rule[587] that monks should not get distressed if the local conditions of their poverty made it necessary for them to do their own harvesting, *"for when they live by the labour of their hands, they are truly monks"*. The Cistercians, desiring to be "truly monks" made manual labour a required element of their life and became as important as prayer and the *lectio divina.* With the emergence of the lay brothers, or *conversi,* however, a certain imbalance was created in this threefold division of Cistercian monastic activities. Finally, and as a direct result of all these characteristics Cistercian life was marked by complete simplicity united with discretion. Doing away with any possibility of pomp and ceremony and avoiding any trace of ostentation or triumphalism, the Cistercian monks desired nothing more than to live the Rule of St Benedict with as much fidelity as possible and to devote themselves entirely to prayer and to manual labour.

In order to understand these characteristics and the impact of Cistercian monasticism in this period, I think that it is useful to discuss the teachings of

---

[587] Rule of St Benedict Chapter 48.

three of their most influential writers: St Bernard of Clairvaux, William of St Thierry and St Aelred of Rievaulx. St Bernard, whom Sitwell describes as "the last of the fathers" is one who "towers over the whole of the first half of the twelfth century"[588] so he justly deserves a chapter of his own.

---

[588] Op cit Sitwell p44.

Chapter 16
Revival and Reform (2): New Liturgies

"Concerning the mode and order of Divine Services, the monks of Citeaux decided right at the beginning to observe in everything the traditions of the Rule (of Benedict), cutting away entirely and rejecting all appendages to the psalms, orations and litanies, which were added (to the Office) arbitrarily by less considerate fathers. Aware of human frailty and infirmity, after sagacious consideration, they found (these additions) to be more dangerous than salutary for monks, since their multiplicity results entirely tepid and negligent recitation, not only by the slothful but also by the diligent."[589] The Cistercians rejected the elaborate liturgical practices of contemporary religious orders, in particular the Benedictine monks of Cluny, which was notoriously excessive and occupied almost the entire monastic day allowing little, if any, time for manual labour. The Cistercians sought to impose a liturgy that was simple and faithful to the Rule of St Benedict, and so stripped away appendages that had steadily accumulated over the centuries. They introduced a liturgy that was greatly reduced and centred on the eight canonical hours and a daily conventual Mass— a second Mass was soon added on Sundays and on feast days. The psalmody of 150 psalms was recited over the course of a week and not, as at Cluny, during a single day.[590] The Cistercians' concern with liturgical simplicity rather than excess extended to singing and music. T Shrills, trills and frills, which were dismissed as frivolous, distracting and vain. The General Chapter prescribed that monks should sing in virile voices and avoid extremes, to ensure gravity and

---

[589] From the Exordium Magnum, cited in L Laki, *"The Cistercians: Ideas and reality"* Ohio 1977 p249.

[590] The Cluniacs recited up to 210 psalms each day, and some of their houses even organised shifts to ensure that this was sustained.

devotion:[591] "It behoves men to sing with manly voices and not imitate the lasciviousness of minstrels by singing with shrill voices like women, or, in common parlance, falsetto. And therefore, we have decreed that extremes in singing be avoided so that the singing may be redolent of seriousness and devotion preserved."

Aelred of Rievaulx vehemently denounced musical embellishments, and in colourful invective he criticised the swelling and swooping of voices, the din of bellows and the humming of chimes. He argued that far from enhancing religious observance, these histrionic displays and "saucy gestures" made a mockery of worship: sound was of secondary importance and should merely augment the meaning. The Cistercian monk Idung of Prufenings' twelfth century *Dialogue* criticised the Cluniacs for taking expensive liquorice cordials to help them reach the high notes while singing the Office,[592] and in the fourteenth century, an English Cistercian, John Anglicus, debated the legitimacy of choir monks sucking lozenges in an attempt to improve their vocal range. Further attempts to pare down the Cistercian liturgy included reducing the number of feasts and processions.[593] Over the years however, new feasts replaced them and others rose in importance. The increased number of feasts meant that an *Ordo* was now needed to ensure that there were no clashes. But these reforms did not escape reproach. The theologian and philosopher Peter Abelard was a particularly harsh critic and claimed that the reforms were a liturgical scandal.[594] Of all their reform, it was the Cistercian celebration of Lent which provoked the greatest reaction from their contemporaries, for, in stark contrast to the practice at the

---

[591] *Institutes LXXV.* in C Waddell (1999) *Narrative and Legislative texts* p489 Citeaux.

[592] Idungus (1977) 'Dialogues', *Cistercians and Cluniacs; the case for Citeaux—a dialogue between two monks, an argument and four questions.* ed and translated J O'Sullivan and J Leahey. Kalamazoo, 1:41 p44.

[593] While the Cistercians accorded few saints feasts, they commemorated many more; the earliest extant calendar of the Order shows that only fifty-seven saints were granted feast days though over one hundred were commemorated. The calendar is included in the earliest Cistercian breviary which dates from circa 1130 i.e. during the abbacy of Stephen Harding.

[594] It should be remembered however that Abelard's criticisms were, in some respects, a reaction against Bernard of Clairvaux's modifications of the recitation of the Lord's Prayer by the nuns of the Paraclete. The words "daily bread" had been changed ironically on Abelard's own recommendations to "substantial bread". This had prompted a somewhat surprised response from Bernard.

time, the white monks recited the office without any alterations until Easter. That is to say, they did not stop singing the Alleluia after Septuagesima Sunday, and even during Holy Week chanted the usual hymns and concluded the psalms with a "Glory be..."[595]

The Monastic Hours

So the monastic day revolved around the seven canonical hours[596] during the day, and an eighth night office of Vigils. The exact time of each office varied depending on the season and the time of the year, but the sequence remained the same: the night office of vigils was followed by lauds at daybreak, and thereafter the daily office of prime, terce, sext, none, vespers and the concluding office of Compline. While the Cistercians were increasingly known for the brevity of the divine office, their decision to forgo the customary pre-lauds nap attracted much attention. Traditionally monks rose at midnight to celebrate vigils and in this way observed the saying of Psalm 119 v 162: *"At midnight I rose to give thanks to thee"* and then returned to bed until lauds. The Cistercians were sterner and stricter with themselves, dispensing with the nap, so that they could remain in prayer and vigil until lauds was sung at daybreak. Their intention was noble but overly ambitious, so in order to sustain their prayer they rose later—and were noted for their tardy start.

The monks celebrated all of the offices in the church, except at harvest time, when they were recited as they worked in the fields. The lay brothers, by contrast, only celebrated some of the hours in their choir, reciting the others as they worked; in summer, when the lay brothers rose earlier and the working day was longer, they said vigils, lauds and prime in church. In winter, when the time for work was greatly reduced, they left the church after vigils, but generally returned for Compline. On Sundays and the great feast days when the lay brothers had no work, they participated in the full liturgical day—but celebrated the offices in silence.

Certain monastic officials, such as the porter, were excused from attending the hours on account of their duties, but during the times when the rest of the community were singing in the choir these officials were instructed to draw up their cowls and observe silence. Otherwise, attendance was mandatory and

---

[595] Op cit Lekai p250.
[596] Psalm 119:164.

punctuality expected. Latecomers were punished. They were not allowed to enter the choir until they had atoned—the penitent faced the altar at the chancel step and knelt until the abbot gave a signal that he could return to the choir, where the penitent took the last place. On Sundays and feast days, the penalty was greater and more physically challenging. The offender bowed, extended his hands until they reached the floor and remained in that position until the abbot signalled that the penance was complete.[597] In theory, but not always in practice, anyone who was not a member of the Order was prohibited from attending the offices. This applied as much to other Benedictine monks as to laymen and this, of course, bred considerable resentment provoking complaints of Cistercian exclusivity, lack of charity toward others in the religious live and secretiveness.

At the start of every liturgy, the sacrist struck a bell to summon the brothers to the church. Occasionally, as on Good Friday, the bell was replaced by a *tabula*, a wooden clapper, to mark the solemnity of the day to be commemorated. Each office began with the Lord's Prayer and consisted of hymns, psalms and canticles. The offices of the lay brothers were much simpler and shorter and essentially consisted of a series of recitations of the Lord's Prayer. The monks prayed standing up and not prostrate[598] and even stood for vigils—perhaps to ensure that the brethren stayed awake! The monk appointed as priest for the week led the office, while the precentor stood to the right of the choir and led the chant. The Cistercians were greatly concerned with the quality of worship and sought to prevent sloth, boredom and negligence. Psalms were not to be rushed. Words were not to be slurred or clipped, and monks who did not sing with devotion were beaten.[599] The precentor and succentor (the sub-cantor) were charged with the tasks of encouraging singing and ensuring vigilance; the latter was especially important during vigils and a number of anecdotes warn of the dangers of falling asleep during this office.[600] Measures were also taken to minimise all distractions

---

[597] Op cit C Waddell p477.
[598] Loc cit C Waddell P49.
[599] C Harper-Bill (1980) 'Cistercian Visitations in the late Middle Ages: the case of Hales Abbey', *Bulletin of Historical Research LIII* pp103–114.
[600] The Cistercian monk, Caesaruis of Heisterbach tells of a monk who fell asleep with alarming regularity. On one occasion, the monk nodded off while the psalms were being sung at vigils and in his sleep, he dreamt that he saw before him a tall and misshapen man holding a whiff of straw—the kind that grooms used to rub down horses. The man came closer and leered at the monk. He angrily asked him why since he (the monk) was

and disruptions, including how to deal with a brother who showed signs of illness during the office and no visitors were to be announced to the abbot until the office was complete.

The Mass

The *Rule of St Benedict* makes no prescriptions for a daily High Mass, though increasingly this became an integral part of the monastic day. In Cluny, the monks celebrated Mass at least two or three times every day, but the Cistercians who advocated simplicity and brevity reduced this to one. Over time, however, a second "low mass" was introduced on Sundays and on feast days and even more were added for deceased members of the community, for benefactor, and on days associated with the Virgin Mary.

In times of crisis, more masses still could be included in the monastic day and in 1194, the General Chapter ordered that masses be said for the recovery of the Holy Land from the Infidel.[601] But the multiplication of masses did not stop there. There were also corporate masses and private masses said by monks at side altars and specific times were set aside during the day to accommodate them. These masses were especially labour intensive as the priest had to be accompanied by at least two witnesses—a fellow cleric who served the priest and a layman to light and extinguish the candles—in order for the Mass to be "valid". The celebration of all these extra masses was not obligatory, but was generally observed and was indeed necessary with communities receiving a growing number of requests from donors and benefactors willing to pay handsomely for this privilege. By 1192 however, the number of masses was becoming so great as to demand regulation and approval by General Chapter. But the way in which these additional masses were performed is a mark of continuity with the earliest forms of western monasticism. Following the custom of the communities founded by St Augustine of Hippo the priest always faced northwards to read the Gospel. St Augustine, in turn, thought that to do so was

---

now the "son of the great lady" (the Virgin Mary) as a consequence of his monastic vows, he slept on. The man struck the monk over the face with the filthy straw. The monk immediately woke up and instinctively drew back from the perceived blow and in doing so painfully banged his head against the wall, much to the delight and amusement of his fellow brethren. See Caesarius of Heisterbach (1929) *On the Dialogue of Miracles* 1. Ch XXXIV, p231. Translated by H von E Scott and C.C.S. Bland 2 volumes London.
[601] Op cit Waddell. P477.

enjoined by scripture: "Go and proclaim these words to the north…" (Jeremiah 3:12).

The daily conventual Mass was celebrated by all choir monks. Officials, such as the porter, were allowed to be absent on account of their work, but on feast days two such masses were held. This meant that their deputy could take over during one of them, thus ensuring that the whole community had attended Mass that day. Lay brothers did not attend Mass, other than on feast days, either. But on Sundays and on feast days, they participated in the full liturgical office. If work was to be conducted on feast days, then the lay brothers were expected to attend the first conventual Mass, leaving them free to work for the remainder of the day. Officials and lay brothers were expected to attend every burial Mass.

The distinguishing mark of the Mass was its liturgical simplicity—even allowing for subsequent modifications. Like each of the liturgical hours it began with the Lord's Prayer and the Sign of the Cross. This was followed by an abbreviated version of the *"Confiteor"*, rather than Psalm 42. A priest acted as deacon, but wore the stole around his neck and not, as we might expect from a "deacon" across the shoulder. The celebrant was the monk appointed as priest for the week, and it was his duty to sing all the parts of the Mass until the offertory, when the altar was censed. This was one of the few times when the Cistercians allowed the use of incense. It was usually regarded as a luxury and a quite unnecessary expense. Other parts of the Mass were sung by the servers and, of course, the choir.

The *"Gloria"* was intoned at the Epistle Side of the altar and the *"Creed"* at the Gospel side. At the beginning of the *"Gloria"*, the chalice was prepared; it was not covered by vellum or a pall, but by a corner of the corporal that was folded over for protection.[602] The celebrant broke the Host, (which was made of pure wheat) into three pieces, two large pieces and a smaller piece which was placed into the chalice.[603] Originally the Host was not elevated, nor did the community genuflect. The Cistercian Statutes only allowed for the Host to be elevated after the amendments of 1152 and the elevation of the Chalice did not come about until after 1444. Interestingly, however, in 1210 it was decided that candles could be raised and lowered so that those in the choir could get a better view, and a small bell was struck so that all who heard it could genuflect and pray. The Kiss of Peace was exchanged only with those who were about to

---

[602] Op cit Lekai *The Cistercians* p254.
[603] Op cit Canivez *Statutes* 1:1191; 92.

receive their communion.[604] Cistercian monks received communion more frequently than other Benedictines. Whereas the "black" monks of Cluny communicated only once each month and on special feasts and solemnities, the Cistercians received communion every Sunday and on every feast. In the early days of the Cistercian Order, this only included Christmas and Easter, but other feasts were soon added. Originally too, all the monks received communion under both kinds. The monk received the Host at the right side of the altar and then processed behind the altar to the left side where the chalice was given.

In 1261, however, the General Chapter expressed a curios concern at the danger of taking the blood of Christ from the chalice[605] and decreed that from henceforth the chalice would only be received by those who had actually officiated at the altar.[606] Communicants now only received the Host, although cleaning the mouth was retained.[607] At the end of communion, the celebrant returned to the altar and completed the ritual cleansing of the sacred vessels with wine; the use of water was not permitted until the thirteenth century. The Statutes made no provision for a final blessing, which was only introduced as part of the renewal of the Cistercian liturgy during the counter-reformation. When Mass was ended, all the altar cloths were removed: these were generally made of linen, although silk hangings were permitted after 1256. In the early days of the order, the lay brothers received communion twelve times a year. This was later reduced to seven, which was still unusually frequent, since the laity generally received communion only up to three times a year. The "*Laybrothers Usages*" explained in detail how the Kiss of peace that preceded communion should be administered. It was a complex process. The most senior lay brother processed to a door that connected the two choirs and received the Kiss of Peace from one of the servers of the Mass. He then processed to the stalls and gave the Kiss of

---

[604] Op cit Ecclesia official p169 57:1 translated by D Choisselet and P Vernet. Reiningue. 1989.

[605] It is not at all clear to me what was feared, or why, but at all events their decision seems to have been congruent with contemporary practice elsewhere.

[606] Op cit Canivez *Statutes* 11 1261:9.

[607] See Miri Rubin (1991) "*Corpus Christi: the Eucharist in Late Medieval Culture*" Cambridge. Cambridge University Press. Revised Edition. p 48 where it is explained that a sip of unconsecrated wine often replaced the consecrated wine to give a symbolic symmetry, and also, for more practical purposes, to help with swallowing the Host.

Peace to the Lay brother who was next in seniority. So, the peace was passed down the line—rather like a Mexican wave, or a Chinese whisper.

The *"Laybrothers Useages"* does not make clear where they were to receive communion. I somewhat doubt whether, being lay, they would have been allowed to join the choir monks at the High Altar, and if this is the case then it is relatively safe to assume that communion was received at the much smaller altars to the west of the rood screen. If I am right about this then, almost certainly the lay brothers saw little, if anything of the proceedings in the eastern part of the church even if the door in the rood screen had been left open. In this way, the inherent division between the choir monks and the lay brother would have been preserved and the "mystery" of the Mass increased. At all events, they would have had no access at all to any liturgical text.

Texts Old and New

"And since we receive in our cloister all their monks who come to us, and they likewise receive our monks into their cloisters, it therefore seems to us opportune, and this also is our will, that they have the Useages and chants and all the books necessary for the day and night hours and for the Mass according to the form of the Useages and books of the New Monastery, so that there may be no discord in our conduct, but that we may live by one charity, one Rule, and like Useages." [608] The Cistercians initially followed the liturgical texts of Molesme, which Robert had brought with him on their departure from the abbey. In 1099, Archbishop Hugh of Lyons agreed that the community should keep the *capella*[609] they had brought with them from Moleseme but return the *brevarium*[610] - after having made a copy for their own later use![611] It is not clear how long the early Cistercian community continued to follow the Molseme texts, but it seems that it was not long before their quest for authenticity and accuracy prompted them towards revision. This seems to have started with Stephen Harding's

---

[608] *Carta Caritas* clause 3 in Waddell, *Narrative and Legislative Texts* p444.
[609] This probably consisted of a collection of both liturgical texts and appropriate vestments.
[610] Perhaps copies of the text for the night office and a lectionary.
[611] C Waddell; "*The Molseme Cistercian Hymnal*", p79. For a copy of Archbishop Hughe's Letter, see "*The New Monastery: Texts and Studies on the early Cistercians*" pp 29-30. For a much more detailed study of it see Waddell "*The pre-Cistercian background of Citeaux and the Cistercian Liturgy*".

critical edition of the Bible and followed by a revision of the Hymnal and the Anitphoner.[612] The correction of these texts underpinned the Cistercian's desire for unity and uniformity of practice as in the quotation at the head of this section. To prevent irregularity and to ensure that every Cistercian house was united in a common observance, the corrected works were declared exemplars so that no new community could be founded without them. Thus, a monk visiting another abbey in the Order might take his place in choir and follow the worship there exactly as though he were doing so in his own house.

The process of revision took three stages which began with Harding's revision of the Vulgate. He believed he had discovered discordance among various texts and this prompted him to consult a number of Jewish Rabbis to determine the most accurate translation from the Hebrew.[613] He was especially concerned to remove certain so-called superfluous passages in the Book of Kings and intended that his new amended version of it should become the official model for further copies. To ensure this, he banned all further alterations and revisions. Harding's work shows his great zeal for authenticity and uniformity, but today his Bible is usually appreciated more for its beautiful illustrations rather than the text. The next stage of revision was the hymnal, particularly the hymns for Vigils, Lauds and Vespers. The original Rule of St Benedict had spoken of hymns for these offices, but it was commonly thought that the hymns actually used in these offices had had their origins with St Ambrose and that they survived in Milan in their pristine form. It is not surprising then that when the Cistercians came to revise the hymnal it was to Milan that they turned.

The first revision was again begun by Stephen Harding in or around 1108–1112:

"By the common consent of our brothers and our decision, we have ordained that henceforth these and no others are to be sung by us and those who come after us. This is because in his Rule—which we have decreed shall be kept with zeal in this place—and our blessed father and our teacher, our blessed Benedict, directed that these Ambrosian [of Ambrose] hymns be sung."[614] A second

---

[612] Antiphoners were especially large and unwieldy manuscripts that were shared between the brethren. They were often divided into seven volumes, one for every day of the week (=temporal) with a supplement for feast days (=sanctoral).

[613] Given the entrenched animosity, indeed endemic anti-Semitism, of Christians towards Jews at this period this was a highly unusual and radical step to take.

[614] *The New Monastery: Texts and Studies on the early Cistercians.* p78.

revision was begun in or around 1147 because the difficult Latin was found to impede singing. Greater simplicity and clarity were needed and Bernard of Clairvaux was appointed to supervise the task. Bernard retained al the hymns which he thought had their roots in Milan, but corrected some of the alternative readings and divided the longer ones into shorter passages. He introduced eighteen hymns which he selected from the Molesme hymnal. He suggested that these be sung at Compline and the so-called "lesser" hours of Terce, Sext and None. He revised seven melodies and rewrote several more so that in the end his revised hymnal contained some fifty hymns. It remained largely unchanged for the next five hundred years.

The third stage of revision was to the antiphoner. We have already established that the Cistercians were greatly concerned with the musical qualities of the liturgy, and given the diversity of anitphonaries it was crucial to establish a single standard and authoritative version. Stephen Harding sought to impose the purest form of Gregorian chant, one that was free from all superfluities. As Metz was considered to be the home of authentic Gregorian chant, he sent two monks to obtain copies of their antiphoner and gradual. When they arrived, however, they discovered that the chant at Metz was nothing at all as they, or Harding, had imagined. It was very elaborate indeed, corrupt and "contemptible from every point of view". It was lax, negligent and soiled by errors.[615] Those who used it were at best bored by it and at worse indifferent to it and so it gave rise to slovenly worship. A change was needed and the General Chapter ordered a revision of Harding's work. Under the leadership of St Bernard of Clairvaux a committee was set up whose members had skill in both the theory and the practice of chant so that they could devise rules for the use of the chant. Among the members of this committee were Abbot Guy of Cherlieu and Gut d'eu; Richard of Vauclairs and William of Clairvaux later first Abbot of Rievaulx.[616] It was already clear to them that Harding had relied on manuscript evidence and tradition alone to corroborate authority, but given the great diversity of manuscripts, Bernard's committee had little choice but to look to theoreticians for whom music was the science of singing correctly, nothing more and nothing less. They sought authenticity through reason and advocated, as we might expect

---

[615] See C Waddell: "*Monastic liturgy; prologue to the Cistercian antiphonary*". pp161–162.

[616] William and Bernard seem to have engaged in an almost constant correspondence and discussion about the issues of liturgy in general and the chant in particular.

by now, simplicity and unity. The revised texts, therefore, reduced the number of feasts, imposed modal unity, restricted melodies to a specific range of ten notes and avoided unnecessary repetition.[617] The committee decided that their new antiphoner was "irreproachable in both music and text" and the first draft was presented to the General Chapter before 1147. A few minor modifications were made and then it was promulgated as the official text to be used throughout the Order. So it was that the Cistercian Gregorian Chant remained unchanged until the seventeenth century at which time the General Chapter had to quash many attempts to introduce innovation and new musical styles. Inevitably there was often a gap between the idea of uniformity and simplicity and what actually happened in practice. Throughout the twelfth century, for example, the General Chapter had to deal with those houses that persisted in theatrical trill and shrills and repeated Bernard's thoughts on the matter. In the fourteenth century, this had to be repeated yet again because many houses had adopted syncopation and polyphony. While these were expressly denounced, it was to little avail and the new musical styles persisted, so that by 1486, even the General Chapter had to concede that organs could be used to enhance the liturgy. In the nineteenth century, attempts were made to restore the Cistercian Gregorian Chant to its original form. While the monks of the strict observance continued this work, it was really a matter of too little too late.

Perhaps there were always variations and deviations from Bernard's original strictures for in religious reforms and revolutions, just as much as in political ones, it is one thing to create a framework to create uniformity and quite another to ensure that it is always and everywhere observed.

---

[617] For an interesting, if complex, discussion of this see C Maitre (1994) "*Authority and Reason in the Cistercian Theory of Music*" Cistercian Studies Quarterly. 29:2 pp 197–208.

Chapter 17
Revival and Reform (3):
From Monastery to Marketplace

This chapter will show how, in the twelfth and thirteenth centuries, the understanding of how monastic spirituality shifted from monastery to market place and, (potentially at least) became available to far more people—especially the laity.

At the beginning of the twelfth century, Rupert (d.1130), abbot of a monastery at Deutz wrote a book on the monastic life which he called "*De vita vere apostolica*", or "The Truly Apostolic Life".[618] In it, he claimed that *only* the monastic life can be considered to be the true life and pattern of life for the church as an institution and for individuals in particular. Unsurprisingly many Christians then and now have found this a hard teaching especially since Rupert said that, "If you desire to consult all the testimonies of Scripture, they seem to say nothing other than that the church originated in the monastic life."[619] He also wrote. "It is evident that monks, insofar as they are monks, take their form [of life] from the apostles; therefore, all apostles were truly monks."[620] But Rupert's view was not always and everywhere accepted even in the twelfth century. Writing only a few years later, Gerhoh of Reichersberg (d.1169) argued that:

"Whoever has renounced at baptism the devil and all his trappings…even if that person never becomes a cleric or monk, but nevertheless has definitely renounced the world…Whether rich or poor, noble or serf, merchant or peasant, all who are committed to the Christian faith reject everything inimical to this name…Every order and absolutely every profession in the Catholic faith and

---

[618] PL, CLXX p609–64.
[619] *De vita vere apostolica.* Iv. 4. PL, CLXX p644.
[620] Ibid. iv. 11 pl CLXX p648.

according to apostolic teaching, has a rule adapted to its character; and under this rule it is possible, by striving to achieve the crown of glory."[621] Both Rupert and Gerhoh offer a description of the Christian life, but what is striking about them is their dissimilarity. While Rupert championed the life of the monk as the only true vocation, Gerhoh heralded a change in Christian awareness that was to mark the twelfth and thirteenth centuries.

It was a change which would see the early development of "inner space" through which the life of lay Christians would emerge as the sphere in which grace was active and in which salvation was to be worked out, (sometimes literally *"with fear and trembling"*—Philippians 2:12b–13. As James of Vitry (d. 1240) wrote, not only monks but "all the faithful of Christ who serve the Lord under the Gospel's rule and live by the orders of the single greatest Abbot or Father of all [Jesus Christ]" participate in the Christian life.[622] This expansion of the Christian life from the monastery to the market place signalled a new understanding of the laity in the medieval church. In order to fully understand the extent of this change and just how radical it was we need to remind ourselves of the extent to which the church after the death of Augustine of Hippo to, say, 1050 had been increasingly influenced by the monastic life and its ideals.[623] It was in the monasteries that the old Roman virtues of order and stability were continued. Through the monasteries, these virtues were legitimated and promoted for the external good of the gradual evangelisation of Western Europe and for the spiritual welfare of those now embraced by the arms of mother church. However, it is one thing to suggest that the monastic life was the inspiration of Christian life in the west, and quite another to imply that the two were synonymous. Nevertheless, from the viewpoint of some monastic writers, life in the monastery was, indeed, the pinnacle of the realisation of the Christian life. As Rupert of Deutz contended, being a Christian meant being a monk.[624] Was this simply a form of hyperbole or religious arrogance? Certainly, in the

---

[621] *Liber de aedifico Dei*, xliii Pl CXCIV, p1302, quoted in M-D Chenu (1968) *Nature, Man and Society in the Twelfth Century*. Ed and trans J Taylor and L Little. Chicago. University of Chicago Press. p222. *My emphasis added.*

[622] Douai (1597) *Liber duo quorum prior orientalis…alter occidentalis historiae*. P357 quoted in ibid Chenu p221–222.

[623] Marc Bloch (1964) *Feudal Society*, trans L A Manyon. Chicago. University of Chicago Press p60 calls this period the "first feudal age".

[624] Op cit De vita vere apostolic. Iv. 4. Pl CLXX p644.

eyes of many monks it was not. Rupert himself made this statement as the result of a particular understanding and interpretation of history that promoted the notion that monastic life was the direct descendant of the primitive Christian community described in the Acts of the Apostles. Unity of heart and soul, common property, renunciation of the world—these were the spiritual and material values which writers like Rupert regarded as the true marks of the Christian life which the monastery continued to preserve in critical periods of political, social and economic instability. By the abandonment of private property in favour of a common life of prayer, the monk imitated the life, the inner space, of the first Christian community.

This position suggested that the monastic life manifested what the church was really all about: the holiness of God mediated to human beings, but holiness separated from the world: "The monk leaves the world. Like every Christian, he detaches himself from it. But even more, because of special vocation, he separates himself from it."[625] However, what St Augustine of Hippo had envisaged as the necessary tension between the City of God and the City of Man gradually collapsed as the earthly city (the secular world) was either absorbed into, or forgotten by, the City of God (the monastery). In the sacralised world of the monastery, paradise was restored so that the monk, through prayer, could surrender himself to the delights of heavenly contemplation.[626] As LeClerq has argued, medieval monastic writings clearly nourished the desire and yearning for the heavenly life: "Everything [in monastic culture] is judged according to its relationship with the whole consummation of the whole reality…The present is a mere interlude."[627] As a consequence, the development of an inner space, an apostolate, among the laity was, for all practical purposes, as pointless as it was unnecessary. If the monastic experience was, indeed, the locus of grace (and nowhere else) what need remained for active ministry in secular society? Moreover, if the Kingdom of God had *already* arrived on earth as it is in heaven in the shape of a monastic community and its practices, why should women and men work to create the conditions under which it might come? By emphasising so strongly the inner experience of grace to the exclusion of it social dimension, the marks of the church's holiness would not be found in preaching, or

---

[625] Jean LeClerq (1960) *The Love of Learning and the Desire for God* trans Catherine Mishrai New York. Fordham University Press. p70.
[626] ibid LeClerq p68.
[627] Ibid p83. My emphasis added.

catechesis, or the celebration of the sacraments, nor in practicing the works of mercy, but only in the liturgy and routine of the monastery.[628] It is not surprising, then, that the eleventh century reform of the clergy advocated by Pope Gregory VII (himself educated in a monastery school) was based on an austere penitential code inspired by monastic discipline. Having recognised the bonds between the monastery and the church we should also recognise that the bonds between the monastery and secular culture were just as strong. Indeed, it was their strength which led to a crisis of spirituality which shook Western Europe between about 1050 and 1300 AD.[629] Although monastic writers such as Rupert promoted a view of the world as being entirely sacred monasteries were actively involved in education, administration and missionary work of all kinds. Many monks served not only the church but also became intimate advisors to kings and secular officials. Monasteries also established a variety of charitable institutions which cared for the sick and the dying, distributed clothes and food and fuel to the needy as well as shelter for pilgrims and travellers.[630] In addition, tax systems, juridical structures and the execution of legal decisions were often administered by monks. In short, monastic life existed in a symbiotic relationship with the simple and fixed order of vassalage, an order represented by the traditional Trinitarian structure of society: the knight (who held the sword of temporal power), the priest (who held the sword of spiritual power) and the monk (who shed tears of constant prayer)!

Three factors began to tighten all of these bonds. First, throughout Western Europe, especially in England, France and Germany, population density had declined both in cities and in rural areas and this resulted in low productivity. Second, because of the chronic disrepair of the infrastructure communication between the rulers in their political centres and the ruled, especially in more rural areas was extremely difficult. Third, though some trade existed, it was rather small in volume and increasingly dealt only in luxury goods beyond the reach of many even among the ruling class. Economic historians have shown that, at this time, there was a crisis in the money supply and that a long-term flow of currency

---

[628] *"It is not preaching, baptizing, and performing miracles that makes the apostle, but being virtuous, and, as it was taught, to make themselves humble towards others."* Op cit Chenu p211.

[629] Op cit Bloch who calls this period the "second feudal age".

[630] D Knowles and D Oblensky. (1969) *The Middle Ages*. In *The Christian Centuries* **Vol 2**. *Ed,* Louis Roger New York. Paulist Press pp 117–128 and 184–197.

to the east drastically reduced the circulation of money in Western Europe.[631] So, most societies in Western Europe at this time were marked by a lack of movement and mobility. They were conveniently ordered into a vertical and paternalistic system dependent on agriculture and fidelity to oaths of vassalage. We should note, however, the spiritual colouring of medieval Christianity inspired by a monastic vision whose temporal success was rooted and grounded in the feudal structure and whose spiritual effectiveness lasted as long as the Christian life could be identified as the monastic life.

However, as new currents in religious thought and in secular life began to emerge in the eleventh and twelfth centuries, the permanent value of monastic spirituality as the sine qua non of Christian spirituality was called into question.

This questioning was as great and as radical as anything which brought about the end of the Cold War some twenty years or so ago. Like the end of the Cold War too, it brought about a commercial revolution and the possibility of the flowering of a new culture. The emergence of technical skills, intellectual vigour, commercial wealth and deep spiritual yearnings among ordinary people gave birth to systems on which we still rely in the twenty-first century. By comparison with the social rigidity of the times, the eruption of new life in the west during this cultural springtime was truly remarkable.

Here we should note several socio-economic factors which influenced the life of the church and, thereby, the spirituality of the laity. First, the population began to increase steadily throughout what Bloch has called the second feudal age. New villages and towns were created as land was reclaimed from marshland and as forests were cut down to facilitate greater agricultural output. The infrastructure was gradually repaired.

Second, centres of political power became centres of commercial activity too with a corresponding increase in the circulation of money and the beginning of the banking system. This growth in trade produced a new social order, the merchant classes and at the same time trade guilds not only regulated independent services they imposed restrictions on vassalage.[632] With the change in social and economic conditions, new educational opportunities also appeared. Monastic intuitions which had for so long exercised a virtual monopoly on

---

[631] Lester Little (1978) *Religious Poverty and the Profit Economy in Medieval Europe.* Ithaca. Cornell University Press. p3–18 and 19–41.
[632] Jill N Claster (1982) *The Medieval Experience 300-1400.* New York. New York University Press. pp213–246.

education, suddenly found themselves in competition with the secular clergy and the initiatives undertaken by the new mendicant orders of friars. Thus, another force entered into the social history of the period: civil servants and intellectuals schooled in thriving urban centres.[633] Third, with the expansion of commercial life, new trade routes opened between the west and Byzantium and further afield. This produced an influx of new commodities as well as ideas and methods in science and philosophy. [634] These socio-economic factors—increasing population, land reclamation, urban growth, expansion and educational opportunities, new trade routes and an emerging merchant class—shaped a new consciousness which strongly influenced the religious spirit. It was a spirit which prompted the expansion of the Christian life from the monastery to the market place.[635] In this environment, the identification of the Christian life with the monastic life began to crumble. Though movements of monastic reform had used the model of the apostolic life as an ideal which would govern the renewal of monastic culture, the success of such efforts did not, in the end, greatly influence the religious experience of the laity. As the secular world bubbled with unprecedented activity in thought, commerce, and art, monastic writers tended to be more puzzled and confused than tolerant or welcoming of this new vitality.[636] As European culture moved away from the stability of vassalage and monastic forms of life, the rigid cohesion of feudal life began to disintegrate. It began to crumble and disintegrate, but it did not collapse. On the contrary, enthusiasm for the monastic life as the primary model for the Christian life did not diminish. Rather, its attractiveness as *a way* of Christian life was grasped, at least intuitively if not consciously, by those women and men of the church who, in desiring to live the Gospel intently and experience Christ's love tangibly, became promoters of lay religious movements independent of the monastery and,

---

[633] Colin Morris. *Medieval Christendom* in *The Christian World.* Ed. Geoffrey Barraclough. New York Harry Abrams inc. 1981, p134.

[634] Op cit Little. Pp29–34.

[635] M-D Chenu (1964) *Towards understanding St Thomas*. Trans. A-M landry and D Hughes. Chicago. Henry Regnery Company. Pp31–39 Op cit Cenu *Nature Man and Society* p228 and 232.

[636] See for example Anselm of Havelberg in *Dialog: De unitate fidei et multiformitate Vivendi ab Abel usque ad novissimum electrum.* PL CLXXXVIII p1141, defends the evolution of "a Chrisitan religion subjected to many variations, altered by so many innovations, and upset by so many new laws."

at times, removed from all ecclesiastical control.[637] The process of formation of these new lay movements was, generally, twofold. First, they were based on the *universal* nature of the call to live a Christian life. Such a call could not be confined by or limited to the monasteries. *Everyone,* laypeople, monks, clerics and friars—were called to imitate Christ and his disciples. Thus, Christian life in the secular world could be lived as a fully-fledged vocation and one in which all the fullness of grace was operative.[638] As James of Vitry also insisted, all Christians by virtue of tier baptism and adherence to the rule of the Gospel participate in the way of Christ.[639] The second feature which marked the formation of the lay movements was a circumvention of existing religious institutions. Through their pursuit of the apostolic life, popular movements offered an alternative to the traditional dependency of the laity on a diluted form of clerical or monastic spirituality, such as the Lay Cistercian brothers, for example. As participants in this ideal, emphasis was placed on those aspects of the Christian life which had been cherished in monastic culture but which could now be promoted in the secular world: fraternity, charity, voluntary poverty and the active proclamation of the faith by living a faithful and virtuous life.[640] This circumvention was not without its problems. It could, and did, lead to heresies such as that of the Cathari or a reawakening of Gnosticism such as that seen in the Albigensians.[641] Despite these errors, we can have no doubts that all new popular lay movements represented a fundamental yearning of the Spirit. Margaret Aston has argued that these movements amounted "to an endeavour to live with the inexplicable and intolerable".[642] The members of these movements therefore lived on the edge. In the face of the unknown, popular belief was attached to the concrete and the tangible, not because lay spirituality was necessarily materialistic (it was not), but because visible and literal forms could more readily express the presence of the divine and a personal commitment to it. It is not difficult to see, then, why such popularity was accorded to the mendicant orders and to Saints Francis and Dominic as individuals. By their devotion to the

---

[637] Margaret Aston. '*Popular Religious Movements in the Middle Ages*', The Chrisitan World. Op cit. p157–170.
[638] Op cit Chenu, Nature p219.
[639] See footnote 604 above.
[640] Op cir Chenu. Nature. P239–269.
[641] Op cit Knowles and Obolensky pp365–371.
[642] Op cit Aston p158.

humanity of Christ,[643] they channelled the popular preference for an affective spirituality in a direction which, based also on preaching and knowledge of scripture, was both fully Orthodox and meaningful. The imitation of Christ, proclamation and a willingness to serve the needy and the most vulnerable— these were the ideals which shaped the lay movements of the Middle Ages. Once the radical break with monastic spirituality had begun, the ministry of the word among the people could rightly become an experience and a project in which a wide variety of people could participate. It would be wrong, however, to assume that the laity emerged as leaders in the church as a result. They did not. But, by the same token, it would not be incorrect to suggest that whenever the church "seeks to find its proper theatre of activity in the world, it has proper recourse to laymen, who are familiar with and inhabit the world, and not first to the clerics who have more or less abandoned it."[644] That the Christian life was planted nourished and came to fruition in a variety of forms attests to the extraordinary hunger of the medieval spirit and the desire of so many people to translate that yearning into a visible form of life and devotion. That these lay movements turned, not to the established monastic life but to the rule of the Gospel, testifies to the enduring strength of the Word of God to serve as a source of spiritual renewal in every age. We know that the spirituality of the laity which emerged in Western Europe during the Middle Ages heralded new appreciation of the activity of grace present in every order and profession of the Christian faith, an activity bound not by the social sluggishness of cloister or church, but present in the encounter between grace and nature, Christ and culture, the Gospel and secular life.

---

[643] Seen especially in the creation of the Christmas Crib and the Rosary respectively.
[644] Op cit Chenu Nature p222 and 254–255.

Part 6
Monasticism and the Heralding of God's Kingdom

Chapter 18
St Bernard of Clairvaux and the Sufficiency of Love

In the last chapter, we made a brief excursus into the reasons why the monastic movement of revival and reform became so embedded in the secular world and popular imagination through its visible presence in the built environment. We concluded that female patronage of religious houses was an outward and visible expression of the developments taking place in the inner space of their souls—and at the time when the question as to whether women had souls at all could be asked and then answered negatively! We now return to matters directly concerned with the inner space through the monastic (Cistercian) theology of St Bernard of Clairvaux and his notion of love.

Bernard was born in Burgundy, very near the Swiss border, in 1090. He entered the monastery at Citeaux with four of his brothers, an uncle—and twenty-five friends. After three years of spiritual formation, Stephen Harding sent Bernard to make a new foundation at Clairvaux, if only to ease the now overcrowded conditions at Citeaux! So great was the influence of Bernard in attracting people to the Cistercian life that he might almost be regarded as the second founder of the Cistercians.

Bernard was clearly a highly motivated and extremely active man engaged in all sorts of work and activities. Today, we would say he was "driven". He composed an *Apologia* in defence of the Cistercian reform. He worked for the reform of diocesan clergy and in the life of the laity. He helped to end the schism in the church by defending the rights of Pope Innocent III against the usurper Anaclete II. He argued against the theology of Abelard which he regarded as erroneous and heretical. He obliged Gilbert of Porree, Bishop of Poitiers, to retract similar ideas during the Council of Rhiems. Bernard preached against the insidious influence of the resurgent Manichaeans in southern France. He went on missions as a peacemaker between warring factions and notoriously preached the Second Crusade. In addition to a vast number of works,[645] towards the end of his life he wrote the treatise *"De consideration"* which he sent to Pope Eugene III. Unfortunately, Pope Eugene III died in July 1153, almost certainly without having read it, and Bernard died a month later. Throughout his life and in accordance with the tradition and practice of the Rule of St Benedict, St Bernard drew on the inspiration of scripture for his spiritual doctrine. He regularly meditated on passages of the Bible and on the writings of St Jerome, St Augustine of Hippo, and St Gregory the Great. For Bernard, "…the Bible contains no other mystery than that of Christ, for it is he who gives us the Scriptures, their unity and their meaning. It is Christ who is the principle of that unity for he is everywhere present, pre-figured in the Old Testament and revealed in the New."[646] As a result, the St Bernard is profoundly Christocentric. The individual Christian is perfect insofar and in the degree to which he or she assimilates the mystery of Christ. This, in turn, can be affected only by participation in the doctrinal, sacramental and liturgical life of the church because scripture—which reveals the mystery of Christ—can be understood truly and only in and by the church. St Bernard had no doubt then, that extra *ecclesiam non salus est*, (apart from the church there is no salvation)

Again, and as we would by now expect of a Cistercian, St Bernard's theology had the words of St John at it's very core: *"God is Love; he loved us first, his love was revealed when he sent his Son into the world so that we could have life in him."*[647] Asking, then, how God is to be loved, St Bernard replies: "The reason for loving God is God himself; the measure of loving God is to love him without measure."[648] In this, St Bernard can be regarded as the spiritual descendant of St

---

[645] Including a series on the Song of Songs. His first spiritual work was entitled *"The Degrees of Humility and Pride*. In 1125 he wrote his *Apologia* and between 1126 and 1141 composed *"The Love of God"*, *"Grace and Free Will"*, *"The Customs and Obligations of Bishops" "Conversion"* (a work calling for reform of diocesan clergy*)* and *"Precepts and Dispensations*, to name but a few from the vast number of books and tracts he also composed.

[646] W Yeomans "St Bernard of Clairvaux" in *"Spirituality through the Centuries"*. Ed. J Walsh & P J Kenedy. New York. 1964. p109.

[647] I John. Chap.4.

[648] St Bernard: *De diligendo Deo* This phrase was also used by Severus of Milevum and is attributed to St Augustine of Hippo. Last Accessed March 2024.

Augustine and the precursor of the style of spiritual writing more often associated with St Francis de Sales.

This quotation about love does not at all permit us to think of Bernard's theology in terms of sentimentalism. Rather, his teaching here is realistic and demanding. It begins with humility which Bernard thought was a product of self-knowledge that reveals to a person the nature of the sinful condition and the need for grace.[649] St Bernard then develops a psychology of asceticism in which he demonstrates that free will is the key to conversion and progress in spiritual perfection. Whether speaking of the degrees of humility (and its shadow side opposite, pride) through which the soul must pass in its conquest of sin, or the grades of love that ultimately climax in a mystical union with God, the priority of emphasis is always given to the will, though never divorced from intellect or memory.[650] Although Bernard repeats that there is no end to the love of god in this world and that a person cannot attain the fullness of perfection in this life, he nevertheless stresses the obligation of every Christian to strive for it constantly; "No one can be perfect who does not desire to be more perfect. And he shows himself to be more perfect in the measure that he aspires to yet greater perfection."[651] Indeed, "One who refuses to be better is certainly less good; as soon as you refuse to become better, you cease to be good."[652] The love of God, therefore, should grow constantly in the Christian who desires perfection and in doing so it passes through four stages that St Bernard describes as the carnal, the mercenary, the filial and the mystical. Carnal love is natural and instinctive. It is the love which we have for ourselves and for one another and at first sight does not seem very spiritual at all. But if we allow it to be infused by grace, this carnal love leads us to concentrate on the sacred humanity of Christ and the mysteries of his life on earth. Mercenary love is servile. It occurs when people love God, not for his own sake, but only because of the benefits that might flow from it. But at least it arises from an awareness of the need of God, howbeit at a rather

---

[649] St Bernard; *De grandibus humilitatis*. At ww.newadvent/cathen/02498d.htm Last Accessed March 2024.

[650] Cf. W Yeomans. *Art cit. p 117.*

[651] St Bernard. *Letter 34. Trans. Bruno Scott (1953) The letters of St Bernard of Clairvaux. Washington DC. Henry Regney Company.*

[652] St Bernard: *Letter 91.* In the light of this quotation, it is somewhat surprising that Alastair McIntyre in "*After Virtue*" wishes for a second Benedict. Perhaps the coming of a second Bernard might have been more appropriate to the agenda of Virtue Ethics.

superficial level. Filial love is the last of the four loves, Bernard thinks, are possible in this life.

It is the disinterested love of God as our Father and it enables us to taste the sweetness of the Lord. The fourth and highest stage of love is a pure love of God which can only be glimpsed, and that rarely, in this life. It is a love which is totally devoid of self-interest. It is a love in which the person no longer lives for himself but only for God. This is the love which is expressed in the key line of the Lord's Prayer; "Thy will be done on earth, as it is in heaven."

Simply to state the stages of love is, of course, not sufficient. So, scattered throughout his many writings, St Bernard lists the means by which we might pass from one to the other. They include; grace, the humanity of Christ, Mary as co-redemptrix and mediatrix, meditation and contemplation especially on the life of Christ, prayer, the conscious control of thoughts feelings and affections (in much the same way and for the same reasons as recommended by Cassian) and the advice given by spiritual directors. It is probably worth noting that this list, and the teaching of the four stages of love, greatly influenced Richard of St Victor, the Franciscans, Thomas a Kempis, the Rhineland mystics, St Ignatius of Loyola and St Francis de Sales to name but a few.

That the life of a Cistercian monk could lead to the fourth stage of love is found in his treatise on the Song of Songs which was delivered as a series of homilies to his monks at Clairvaux. He begins by identifying the bridegroom with Christ and the church as his bride. This is an identity with which we are now very familiar, and St John of the Cross followed exactly the same pattern in his work on the same Biblical book many centuries later. According to Bernard, the love between the bride and groom begins in carnal love. It focuses on their very humanity and on the passion arising from the events, experiences and emotions they share. Indeed so! Although this is a great gift of the Holy Spirit, it is, says St Bernard, "nonetheless carnal as compared to that other love which is not so much related to the Word made flesh as to the Word as wisdom, the Word as justice, the word as truth, and the word as holiness."[653] When St Bernard speaks of the love which glimpses and becomes mystical union, he speaks of the love which passes all understanding but which keeps the heart and mind in the

---

[653] St Bernard; *In cantica.* See also the authoritative work by E Gilson, "*The Mystical Theology of St Bernard*" trans A Downes. Sheed and Ward. London. 1940 in which he persuasively argues that although, for Bernard, the highest form of love might be rare in this life it must nevertheless be striven for with unceasing effort and prayer.

knowledge and love of God and of his son, Jesus Christ. It is therefore a love which, understanding Christ to be fully a person and fully God, passes from his humanity to concentrate on his divinity. Still in his work on the Song of Songs, he says this; "Be careful to think of nothing corporal or sensible (=open to the senses) in this union of the Word with the soul. Let us call to mind what the Apostle Paul says, 'He who is joined to the Lord is one with him.'"[654] "The upward contemplative gaze" of the love of the now pure soul towards God, or the loving descent into the soul by God, (the direction is at the fourth stage is entirely unimportant since it is a union) can only be expressed as best we can by analogy, but always striving to simply let it be, allowing it to be embraced by and absorbed into great silence.[655] Since the Cistercians had, as we noted earlier, almost completely eliminated the active apostolate from their way of life, it may be surprising to find that St Bernard promoted it as an outpouring of the loves he described and the interior life of prayer. In the same homilies in which he described the nature of the fourth stage of love - mystical union—he often refers to a ministry of preaching and teaching.[656] To preach and to teach is a specific vocation which comes only to those who have begun to make progress in the spiritual life, to glimpse the stages of love and to understand its language. Those who receive the call respond "by works of love and piety".[657] From then on, preaching is not so much what a person does as what they are. Preaching is at the core of their Christian identity and this should be honoured by the community. St Bernard also speaks of a pastoral ministry, though this does not seem to have captured his imagination or to have been as important to him as preaching and teaching. Since grace and divine love come to the soul at a time of communing with God, those who have a role in pastoral care and the practical cure of souls should be especially devoted to meditation on divine truths. Then, and only then, it is possible to pass from meditation to action. Indeed, Bernard insists that no

---

[654] Loc cit. Bernard (also quoting 1 Cor 6:17).
[655] Loc cit St Bernard *In cantica*. When trying to describe this mystical union, St Bernard always refers to God as object and to the soul as subject. This has a long and honourable tradition which, perhaps, begins with Pseudo-Dionysius and is certainly common to the writings of St Augustine of Hippo. The role of the *humanity* of Christ in the mystical experience was discussed by Cassian, the Rhineland mystics, Thomas a Kempis and most famously, of course, in the writings of St Teresa of Avila.
[656] Loc cit. St Bernard: *In cantica*. See Sermons 9. 20, 23, 25, 33, 41, 42, 56, 57, 76, 78.
[657] Loc Cit St Bernard *In cantica* and especially Sermon 79.

one should engage in pastoral ministry without having first pursued their own sanctification and made sufficient progress in obtaining it.[658] Not to do so would be a classic case of the blind leading the blind to mutual destruction. To avoid this, he offers some practical advice and observations to those who would engage in a pastoral ministry. From a modern perspective, one of the remarkable features of this advice is that while it is addressed to a male audience, Bernard uses feminine imagery. That is because we have now politicised our theology to take account of gender and sexual roles. Bernard would not have understood this. For him, it is not a matter of gender so much as the manner in which pastoral care is given. His aim throughout is to preserve the monastic virtue of humility by preventing his monks from notions of self-aggrandisement and power. At all events, for Bernard, the use of feminine imagery is all of apiece with his notion of the love of God giving sustenance to the whole of creation:

"Know that you must be mothers to those that are submitted to you and not masters. If, from time-to-time severity must be employed, let it be fatherly and not tyrannical. Show yourselves to be mothers of encouragement and fathers in correction."[659] Zeal without knowledge is insufferable. When love is very ardent, discretion, which regulates charity, is especially necessary. Zeal unenlightened by knowledge always loses its force and sometimes becomes harmful… Discretion indeed, regulates all the virtues, and thus makes them moderate, beautiful and stable. "…It is not so much a virtue itself as the chastener and guide of all the other virtues…Take it away and virtue is turned to vice."[660] According to Yeomans, "Bernard is led through Christ to the Trinity. His devotion to the saviour fructifies into consciousness of the presence of the three divine persons in his soul and in the whole of creation."[661] It is true that the mystery of the Trinity is at the heart of Bernard's teaching of his monks at Clairvaux and elsewhere, as it must be for all Christians, but my reading of the Sermons referenced above[662] would suggest that Bernard was far more conscious of the presence of Jesus and Mary than the Trinity. In my view, Yeoman fails to fully understand the overriding importance of contemplation on the earthly life of Christ for Bernard and for the whole of the Cistercian movement. In my view,

---

[658] Ibid. Sermon 41.
[659] Op cit. Sermon 58.
[660] *In cantica.* Sermon 49.
[661] Cf. W Yeomans. *Art cit.* p116.
[662] See footnote 91.

the Cistercian theologian who concerned himself with the mystery of the Trinity was not Bernard but rather William of St Thierry, who now claims our attention. Until relatively recently, the works of William of St Thierry were ascribed to St Bernard and other medieval mystical writers[663] but in the last thirty years or so scholars have vindicated the claim that William is one of the most important monastic writers of the period.[664] William of St Thierry (1085—1148) was abbot of the Benedictine abbey near Rheims for fifteen years. In 1135, he transferred to the Cistercian abbey at Signy, where he remained until his death except for a short visit to the Carthusians at Mont-Dieu. This visit brought about the writing of the *"Golden Epistle"* or *"Epistola ad Fraters de Monte Dei"*. During the course of his ministry, William wrote numerous treatises on a wide variety of subjects including the love of God, the nature of man, the Eucharist, faith, a life of St Bernard and Biblical commentaries on the Song of Songs and the Epistle to the Romans. His masterpiece, however, is *Aenigma fidei* which was written as a defence of the doctrine of the Trinity. He intended it as a response to Abelard. This work, together with the *Golden Epistle* and *De natura et dignitatae amoris,* contain the sum of his monastic, spiritual theology.

Although the writings of William on the spiritual life are practical, it is clear that he was greatly influenced by the thought of Origen, St Gregory of Nyssa, Duns Scotus and St Augustine of Hippo. Sitwell points out that in this regard, "The fact that he had gone back to the Greek fathers is of great significance. It represented a development of interest in the theoretical aspect of contemplation…In calling attention to this purely contemplative ideal, in his appeal to the early Benedictine monarchism, and in the use he made of its theological background, William of St Thierry was looking ahead to a movement which was to come after his death."[665] Like St Bernard, William saw the monastic life as a return or ascent to god. In his golden Epistle, he divides the ascent into three classical stages which roughly approximate to the stages in the career of a monk from the novitiate, through to temporary and then final vows: beginners, advanced and perfect. The beginner, or novice, in whom the animal man predominates, is stimulated to a great extent by his senses and appetites. For that reason, he needs the guidance of a Rule and authority. He responds to this in obedience. He needs the ascetical practice of the mortification of the flesh, an

---

[663] Could this be one of the reasons for Yeoman's error?
[664] Op cit Sitwell p57.
[665] Op cit Sitwell. P60.

examination of conscience, spiritual reading and prayer.[666] In the advanced stage, the rational man becomes more prominent. and in the third and final stage becomes truly spiritual. Since the golden Epistle devotes three quarters of its content to a consideration of the beginners, it is necessary to turn to the *Aenigma fidei* to complete the picture of the other two stages.

In this work, William refers to the stages as degrees of faith; initial faith, reasoning faith and faithful experience. The novice, as described above lives by faith. Since he is particularly ruled by the senses, he is led to the Trinity by that which is perceptible by the senses. Here William stresses the importance of the humanity of Christ and the use of sight, sign and symbol.

The second stage, the period of rational faith (*ratio fidei*), is one in which the monk begins to seek reasons for faith. This may be done through the study of theology or by meditating on Scripture—or both. In writing of this stage of faith, William never lets his readers forget that the goal of the ascent is union with the triune God, howbeit that, unlike the scholastics, he does not concentrate on the metaphysics of that union nor on the metaphysics of the process by which it is achieved. In this second stage, reason is always obedient to faith.

At the third stage, William describes how a monk passes beyond intellectual faith and reasoning to the mystical experience of perfection. At this point, according to William, God the Father and God the Son reveal themselves through God the Holy Spirit. So that the monk is not only united with God but shares in the very life of the Trinity. It is an anticipation of the beatific vision, an apophatic knowledge without understanding, an *amour-intellectus*. This does not mean that that there is no longer a mystery, that the antithesis is now reconciled by reason, so as to see how three and one are compatible. It means that the mind has passed out of the realm of conceptual knowledge, where the questions whether reason can in any way explain the mystery no longer arise.[667] William's concept of the mystical experience of the Trinity involves a change or transition from man as an image of God to man as a likenegative*eitudo*) of God. The difference is subtle but enormously important. Man in his very nature, as a creature, has an imprint of God upon him which can never be destroyed. This innate image gives man the

---

[666] It is interesting that here William seems also to be influenced by Cassian's teaching on prayer. According to Sitwell, "*The different techniques of mental prayer had not yet been worked out, and contemplation was not specifically connected with prayer in the same way as it later came to be.*" Op cit Sitwell. P58.
[667] *Ibid* p127.

capacity to receive the higher types of image which come to him through the virtues and through the indwelling of the Trinity in his life.[668] But if a man is to enjoy the mystical experience of perfection, he must somehow become transformed into a divine likenegativee*itudo*) and not remain simply as an image. This occurs when "We become like him when the image of the Trinity in the soul has been perfected…and brought back to a perfect likeness…the most perfect union with the soul and God compatible with the distinction between creature and creator."[669] But according to William, this union is brought about by the Holy Spirit who is both uncreated and that which unites the father and the Son. So, William concludes: "Through the Holy Spirit the man of God becomes in some ineffable, incredible way…not God exactly, but what God is by nature, man becomes by grace."[670] Hence the Holy Spirit is himself the love by which and through which God is loved (*ipse enim amor noster*)[671] As we will in the following in the following chapters it was the question of how, why and in what ways that interplay of love could be made a practical lived reality that was to occupy much of later monastic theology.

---

[668] *Epistola ad Fratres* de Monte Dei 184, 384.
[669] *Speculum fidei* 393.
[670] *Op cit Epistola* 349.
[671] *De contemplano Deo.* 376.

Chapter 19
Holy Poverty and Holy Preaching

On one level, it is difficult to write meaningfully about St Francis of Assisi because, in recent years, he and his movement have been hijacked and sentimentalised beyond measure. As a result, the foundations of Franciscan theology have been all but obscured. It is the purpose of the first part of this chapter to try to recover some of them.

First, the basis of Franciscan theology rests on that of St Augustine. There is, I think, no direct literary dependence between Francis and Augustine and in any event, Francis was somewhat disinclined to write things down. While he was literate, Francis was no scholar and so the dependence of Francis on Augustine is one of spirit rather than letter; a spirit that Francis seems to have imbibed in three key ways:

Francis, like Augustine is preoccupied with God's sovereignty. This is God's world and not only is he in charge of it, his management is very "hands-on".

Francis, like Augustine, has a profound awareness of human sinfulness and the corresponding need for grace. Now, on this level, Augustine had experiences of which Francis knew nothing whatever. Augustine had drunk deeply from the chalice of lust. So, when Augustine wrote about sin he wrote from personal experience. Francis, on the other hand, was no great sinner, but the few writings that came from his pen and certainly that of his contemporaries give the impression that he was worse than Judas.

This is, of course, a literary device—if Francis in all his sin could repent and be forgiven then anyone can be. But even though it is a literary device it has much to teach us because while Augustine understood sin in a way that Francis never could, (and was better for it, Francis had an awareness of sin and the least deviation from the will of God as an *interior* deviation. It is difficult to think of any great founder of a religious order whose mind and soul was as sensitised to the will of God as was Francis. As a result, he really believed that he was the greatest sinner on earth. Since he believed himself to be a great sinner, he believed he needed grace abounding. For Francis, it is by grace that sins are forgiven. It is by grace that sins are expiated. It is by grace that sins are avoided.

In other words, Francis believed that human beings were totally helpless unless or until they experience the power of the grace of God. It was this that Francis believed it was his duty to reveal to the world but to do so would be complicated. He recognised that human beings are a composite of mind and body, of will, intellect and volition, with a capacity to love and for knowledge, but with Francis all the emphasis lies with the will, the affections and with love. Francis never denied the importance of the intellect but he wanted to keep that importance under control and in balance. The best way of doing so was to give much greater prominence to the will.

What are the implications of this?

First, it matters very little how much I know *about* God. It matters a great deal how much I *love* God. So already we can say that one of the foundations of Franciscan theology is the all-important difference between knowledge by description and knowledge by acquaintance. Now, part of my love of God will be that I will want to know more about God—but only in order to love him more. Moreover, (and this is somewhat surprising for someone so aware of grace) Francis was terrifyingly aware of the power of human freedom. So, a person, a sinner needs grace but even the Almighty cannot save me let alone sanctify him or her unless they want it. They hold their destiny in their own hands.

And this brings us to the third point at which his theology can be said to have at least been influenced by Augustine. By the freedom of the will Francis meant, of course, *internal* freedom. As my experience and that of many others shows, it is possible to be in prison without being incarcerated behind bars as the result of a judicial decision. Internal freedom is freedom from the passions, freedom from unruly desires; freedom from inordinate fears, loneliness and rage. Freedom from myself. Freedom from that part of me which would first enslave and then destroy the better part of me. But why be free? In order that I might love God more. But freedom of the will also implies that it will be beholden to nothing. This is, I think, why Francis placed so much insistence on the need for poverty.

The primacy of poverty is the physical demonstration of the primacy of holiness. For Francis, unless we embrace poverty the pursuit of holiness is the pursuit of a dream. All he knew (and this time he knew it from living in his own merchant family) is that rich people are not free people. They have at least one terrifying fear and that is of losing their wealth. There is no need to dwell on this point, except to state it.

His emphasis on poverty was accompanied by a great devotion to the Blessed Virgin Mary. Both were, I think, a reaction to the heresy of Albigensianism which had seduced the entire populations of over a thousand cities in medieval Europe and which was condemned by the Fourth Lateran Council in 1225. Albigensianism was a form of Gnosticism that believed that some Christians had access to special, secret, spiritual wisdom which was unannounced and unavailable to other Christians. Those who possessed the secret knowledge were the *perfetctii*. But the secret knowledge was available *only* by committing suicide through starving oneself. This did not matter because the essence of a person is his or her spirit which must be freed from the material, the earthy, and the bodily in order to know and love God.

In contrast, Francis' stress on poverty was that we are to use the worlds good because they have been given us in their plenty for our good. But we are to use them according to the will of God. His devotion to the Blessed Virgin was to make sure that no one made any mistake that God became man and was born of a woman. God clearly thought that bodies are important. If God did not deny the body, why should we? Moreover, if God became a fleshy, earthy individual with all that that implies and entails then human bodies are adorable. The humanity of Jesus is imitable. The humanity of Jesus is loveable so that when I love the man Jesus, I love God. Since that is true, the love we have for Jesus can extend to human experiences and the world around us. So Francis was not, as is so often mistakenly believed, the first environmentalist. Francis' "love of nature" was simply a means of insisting on the Orthodox belief in the incarnation of Jesus, fully a person and fully God.

His invention of the Christmas crib was another reaction to the errors of Albigensianism, and a tangible sign and token of this irreducible truth.

The purpose of Franciscan theology is that people may know and love God and be united to God through meditation, prayer and contemplation. It is important to grasp the differences between them it we are to make progress in understanding a little more about the foundation and growth of the Franciscan movement.

For Francis, meditation is thinking about God. So meditation is using the intellect, not much but nevertheless using it. This is quite different to many of our modern understandings and techniques of Christian meditation in which (certainly for those enjoined by John Main and Lawrence Freeman) the mind should be stilled and prevented, as far as possible, from distracting us through thoughts.

Prayer is invoking God and asking for his help.

Contemplation is looking at God in love and knowing ourselves to be loved. It is this that, for Francis constitutes Christian perfection. A Christian is perfect insofar as and in the measure to which he or she loves God. For Francis at least that's it, there is nothing more to be said.

Thus, Franciscan theology does not deny that there is a great deal that we can and should learn about God through study and by dint of our human effort. But the principal source is not study, but prayer and prayer is itself the expression of faith and deepens it. For Francis, faith is light of the mind and the soul and the means by which they live.

As light, faith gives insight, penetration, stages of purification, illumination and perfection. Francis had no doubt that that in the religious life there is a beginning and that though many of his followers were quite well advanced in the pursuit of virtue, nevertheless he realised that every one of them required purification, then enlightenment and then perfection. In short, the journey to the heart of God is long, hard, and often extremely difficult and dangerous. Often it means passing through a dry and barren desert inhabited by the wild beast of our imaginings and our shadow side and in which the paths are far from straight and along which our feet and our souls bleed copiously with every step along the way.

This is, I think, one of the key messages of Francis for our day—but unlike the sentimentalised view that so often surrounds him it is unlikely to make him popular. This message is important at a time when there is a great deal of deception being perpetrated in the spiritual life. There are all kinds of pseudo-holiness, pseudo-mysticism. There are all sorts of alleged means to sanctity on offer most of which hold out the promise that the light of faith can come more instantly than instant coffee. But both are quite ersatz.

What Francis has to say about the light of faith and that there is no substitute for passing through each of the stages of purification might be a useful corrective to some of the more extreme forms of spirituality to be found in the more charismatic or Pentecostal churches or their associated groups.

A few years ago, I was required to attend the annual conference of a Christian charity for which I was then working. During the final closing session, the CEO said this; "…for too long we thought with John of the Cross and Theresa of Avila that to become a mystic you must first be an ascetic. That to reach the gifts of prayer they experienced, you must go through the long process and stages of what they called purification. Well, now my friends, after more than four centuries we know better."

I doubt that we do, in fact, know better and Francis tells us that we either go through all these stages of purification or what we think is mystical will turn out to be nothing of the kind. God, Francis tells us, enters only a purified soul and that means suffering, self-surrender, spiritual pain and personal sacrifice. This was a view proclaimed in the preaching of St Dominic to whom we now turn.

We will consider the contribution that St Dominic and his Order of Preachers made to the religious life in four aspects:

1. The Ministry of the Word
2. Community Life
3. Prayer
4. The Study of the Word.

First the ministry of the Word. Dominic was called by God to the ministry of the Word in a special way—to preach. It was from this call that his whole spirituality, his whole emphasis in the religious life developed and in terms of which it can best be understood. It is important, however, not to misinterpret the term "preaching" as it stands in the title of the order he founded, the Order of Preachers.

The first misunderstanding is to take the term "preaching" too broadly to mean simply "witnessing to the Gospel" in any of the ways it can be witnessed. The whole of the Christian life is a witness to the Gospel and this includes every form of ministry. The Second Vatican Council made this clear when it said that every Christian has a threefold ministry first to preach by word and action, teach, evangelise and (within limits) to prophesy, second to engage in pastoral care, social action and charitable works, and third, to engage in sacramental worship and n prayer. It is confusing to speak of the second and third sort as "preaching", howbeit that they may present opportunities for doing so. Only the first is preaching in a strict and proper sense and it was to this ministry that Dominic was called.

Dominic made a choice of this ministry and was content to let the other charisms be conducted by others. In this, he believed he was following in the footsteps of the apostles.[672] It is a mistake therefore to say that the Dominican apostolate is anything that a Dominican does. To be true to his calling Dominic had to choose the ministry of the Word in preference to any other of the great Christian ministries. A second misunderstanding of the term "preaching" is to take it too narrowly and identify it with the preaching of homilies and sermons. In the early days of the Dominican movement, brothers (even novices) who were not yet ordained were sent to preach in this sense and preaching was often done outside Mass and sometimes outside the church in the open air. In this they were said to fulfil the command of St Paul when he told Timothy to "preach in season and out of season."[673] Neither the place nor the time characterises preaching. Nor was Dominican preaching limited to any one group of people. It was adapted to meet the needs of everyone from the youngest to the oldest, the least educated to the most learned, and dealt with the most simple and most profound topics in the faith. Nor was it limited to one style of preaching or a particular medium. Its aim was to reach people both intellectually and emotionally and in so doing enhance their spirits. The Ielin which Dominic himself understood the term "preaching" was Communication of the Gospel Word in a way that not only moved the heart but also illumined the mind with the light of an understanding of the stages of faith and purification (in a sense similar to that of Francis). Like Francis too, Dominic knew that the true understanding of the faith is not for some supposed spiritual elite, but for every person.

Dominic thought it was strange that although our Lord devoted much of his ministry to instructing the crowds and teaching in parables this aspect of the church had often been neglected. We build churches and beautiful abbeys, we celebrate the sacraments, we engage in works of mercy—but we neglect to instruct the people! It was (and is) this ignorance of their faith which exposed people to heresy and St Dominic's perception of this danger was the founding inspiration of his Order.

The third misunderstanding about the meaning of the term preaching—an error which can only arise in a time and a culture which promotes the cult of

---

[672] Acts 6:2–4.
[673] 2 Tim 4:2.

individualism—is to suppose that if the purpose of the Dominican order is to preach, then all Dominicans must be preachers. Certainly, this was not Dominic's understanding. Even before he founded his brotherhood, he founded an order of enclosed nuns who did not preach. The nuns were no less a part of the Dominican movement just because, as contemplatives, they were excluded from the active ministry of preaching. Moreover, in the brotherhood there were (and are) brothers who did not preach—including some who were ordained priests.

Preaching is the purpose of the Order *as a community,* not of its members simply as individuals. Just as our front-line troops in Afghanistan cannot fight without the support of many other soldiers who may never actually engage in a battle, so in the Dominican movement the cooperative effort of preaching requires many particular tasks other than the actual delivery of sermons. One of the most important of these "backroom" tasks is intercessory prayer and the doing of penance, as Dominic himself so clearly realised. This was, after all, the primary function of his enclosed nuns.[674] The second fundamental feature of Dominic's Order and its spirituality is community life, because Dominic learnt from harsh experience that the ministry of the word cannot succeed as an individual effort but rather requires the teamwork of many. Today, some people seek the religious life primarily because it offers community living. That is healthy, especially when our communities are increasingly fragmented and broken, but it was not Dominic's guiding motive. For him, the ministry of the Word was the primary motive, and the community was the primary resource for performing that ministry effectively. Nevertheless, it is a mistake to oppose these two motives. The Gospel to be preached is the Gospel of the Kingdom of God—true community in the spirit of Christ.

In order to preach that Kingdom, a Christian must live in it so that preaching and living become inseparably joined. Theory and practice become one. Thus, Dominican community was not merely a means to preaching but the very source and well-spring of its authenticity. This implies, of course, that it is a truly Christian community whose unity is founded not just on good human relations but in those relations transformed by faith, hope and sacrificial love.

And here lies a key continuity of the Dominican movement with all the history of monasticism we have considered so far: Christ himself must be the

---

[674] Phil.1:10.

centre and his spirit the binding soul of such a community. Such a community, like every Christian (or monastic) community, is to be rooted and grounded in the baptismal commitment to Christ and achieves its fullest realisation in the Eucharist. If that communion is to be genuine, it must express a readiness to support every member of it in difficulties and to rejoice with each other at times of achievement. It must truly be a *brother*hood and *sister*hood in Christ who is ever ready to listen, to forgive, to help and to love—even at the cost of his own life.

A Gospel community can never be content with the fulfilment of its duties. It seeks to imitate the Lord through evangelical poverty that frees the person from caring for things to loving people and in loving people to love God. Chastity purifies that love and obedience submits individual notions and inclinations to the commonwealth of the community and its mission. St Dominic, again like Francis, put a special emphasis on poverty because he knew that no preacher can be believed when he speaks of heaven when it is all too obvious that he is actually concerned to amass earthly goods and power. But unlike Francis poverty was not, for Dominic, the keynote of his spirituality. Tomas Aquinas (himself a Dominican) wrote that poverty is not to be measured by how little we possess, but by whether what we possess is proportionate to the ends we have in view—in this case preaching and the kind of life that supports it.[675] Like Benedict, Dominic did not want to make obedience burdensome, as is seen from his explicit insistence that the Constitutions of his order should not bind under sin. The obedience typical of his brotherhood was not to be blind, or servile, but a willingness to cooperate in a common task. Part of that was for each brother to admit that he needed to temper his own opinions and impulses by learning to live and work with others. Cooperation is not contrary to creativity, but makes it possible for the gifts of every individual to bear much fruit. Dominic was noted for the chastity of his life, which made him clear-headed and warmly sensitive to the feelings of others. Since his Order was to preach Christ "and him crucified"[676] his brothers were to come to know Christ through contemplation, but he thought that such contemplation was impossible for someone given to lust.[677] For Dominic, life in community was necessarily penitential in that it always demands self-sacrifice. Dominic insisted that the members of his

---

[675] Thomas Aqunias: Summa Theologiae II–IIq. 188, a, 7c.
[676] 1.Cor. 1:23.
[677] Rom.1:31.

brotherhood live a life of penance through "regular observance", that is, through following a pattern of common life which required rigorous discipline of unruly desires for pleasure and comfort, and of a concentration on the mission of the Order. As Dominic's own example shows, however, there was a deeper motive for his own penances which he also wished to inspire in his own followers. Dominic hungered and thirsted after Christ, offering himself in the service of God for the conversion of sinners. He accepted and even sought suffering so that he might preach the passion of Christ more effectively. Of all the great saints and theologians that this order has produced, nowhere is this aspect their theology more prominent than in Dominic himself.

The third aspect of Dominican theology is prayer. Since Christian community life was the source of Dominican preaching, so prayer was the essential source of the spirit of Christ which binds the community together. Dominic insisted that whenever possible the prayer of his Order should be liturgical, that is, it should centre on the Eucharist and on the Liturgy of the Hours, because his whole spirituality was ecclesial. Dominic was always conscious that to be a Christian is to be a member of Christ's body which is the church,[678] and pray always for its safety and advancement. Dominic also gave an example of private prayer, often praying long into the night with groans and tears for the conversion of sinners—much like the Desert fathers and mothers. His own writing called "Nine Ways of Prayer" shows how he prayed with his whole being, including extensive bodily gestures; bowing kneeling, prostrating, processing. Although like the desert ancestors, Dominic often groaned and wept in prayer, he could also be joyful and often sang hymns with his companions as they travelled the long miles on foot in order to preach. He always insisted that his brethren sing the liturgy with enthusiasm. But essentially Dominican prayer was contemplative prayer.

That is, it is not limited to invocation and petition as Francis thought, but expands to include thanksgiving, adoration and praise of the greatness of the Trinity and the glory of the crucified Christ. Thomas Aquinas encapsulated the spirit of Dominican prayer when he wrote that the mission of the Dominicans was "To contemplate and then to share what we have contemplated with others."[679] The dialogues of St Catherine of Sienna, who was a Dominican tertiary, shows how the great truths of the creed cease to be mere formulas and

---

[678] Eph 5:24.
[679] Summa Theologiae II—IIq. 188. A 6c.

become living realities through their use in contemplative prayer.[680] The supreme model for this contemplation of the Incarnate Word was, for Dominic, the Mother of God herself who "treasured all these things [the events of her Son's life] in her heart"[681] Although the legends of its origins in St Dominic's time are unhistorical; the rosary has been associated with the Dominican order since at least the fifteenth century. It combines the Dominican use of physical gestures in prayer in the "telling of the beads" with the contemplation of the events of Jesus' life in the presence of his mother and with her aid. Central to the rosary and to all Dominican contemplative prayer are the Sorrowful Mysteries of the Passion. With St Paul, Dominic wanted to "preach Christ and him crucified"[682] because God reveals himself most perfectly just where he seems most concealed—on the cross. Thomas Aquinas said that he learnt more from his crucifix than from any book, and many saints have made the cross the chief object of their study and prayer. No wonder then that so many mystics have experienced the passion in their own bodies, through the gift of the stigmata. The Joyful and Glorious mysteries cannot, however, be separated from the cross and have been experienced by the saints, some of whom have had visions of Christ the Divine Child and others of the final triumph of Christ in the glorification of his church, and still others visions of the Coronation of the Blessed Virgin Mary as Queen of Heaven. Dominican contemplation came to understand these mysteries not merely in an other-worldly sense but as a way of illuminating the everyday events of our lives ("the signs of the times") and the unfolding of the events of the history of our salvation in the world. These mysteries are all summed up and fulfilled in the sacraments, especially that of Confession (reconciliation) and the Mass. For the Dominicans, Confession completed penance and conversion of life, while the Mass is, as Thomas Aquinas said, "at once a memorial of our Lord's passion, a present renewal of his grace, and a pledge of the glory to come."

Perhaps St Dominic's greatest contribution to the development of western monasticism was his insistence on the study of the Bible not merely as an aid to prayer (the monks had always known that in their practice of spiritual reading, *lectio divina*), but as an act of worship which produces sanctification. In this

---

[680] St Catherine of Sienna: *The Dialogue* The Classics of Western Spirituality Series. Mahwah Paulist Press. 1980.
[681] Luke 2:19.
[682] 1 Cor.1:23.

Dominic was, howbeit unconsciously, renewing an Old Testament theme developed by the later rabbinical tradition, namely that meditation on the Law of God is itself a form of contemplation and worship. For Dominic, it was obvious that without the study of the Bible his brethren could never successfully extend their preaching beyond simple exhortations. What was needed, he thought, was not "milk for babes" but "solid food for adults".[683] If preaching was to meet every class, condition and level of education of people in different times and in different places and it was to deal not just with elementary truths but things of substance, the preacher and teacher *must* devote himself to hard study.

But Dominic was no literalist or fundamentalist. The hard study he had in mind was on the Word of God but as it has been interpreted by the *magisterium,* the teaching Tradition of the Church through the ages, because the *magisterium* develops to meet the needs of every generation. This, of course, meant that the Bible had to be interpreted with the assistance of theology. At the beginning of the Dominican movement, the brethren were forbidden to study any other subjects lest they lose sight of the true purpose and goal of their studies. But St Albert the Great (*Albert magnus*) and St Thomas Aquinas led the way to widening these studies to include the humanities and philosophy (that is "secular" subjects in general), not for their own sake but because they saw that this was necessary in order to develop a theology able to meet the needs of the times. This need for this is all the more urgent in our own day if we are to properly understand what bearing the Bible has on some of the great controversies that beset us in the church, particularly in matters of personal relationships and sexuality.

St Francis had feared that the pursuit of academic knowledge alongside theology would destroy the humility and simplicity of life he so wished his brethren to achieve. He was not mistaken, because experience in his own life time showed that the desire for knowledge and the power and prestige that inevitably accompany it could lead to a real temptation to despise and condemn the ignorant.

Yet St Dominic knew that a similar temptation lay in ignorance and mental laziness, an error of prejudice and the belief that the matters of the heart (faith) are quite separate from matters of the head (reason). Through their wide studies Dominic wanted his brethren to produce a creative dialogue between them. This

---

[683] 1Cor 3:2.

could, however, only be achieved by putting three safeguards in place: 1) the love of wisdom, 2) prayer and 3) on-going communication between all the members of the community. Dominic thought that if his brethren truly loved wisdom they would not be content with superficialities and banal statements. The deeper their studies took them, the greater their awareness of their own ignorance. If they combined their love of wisdom with prayer, God would, Dominic believed, show them how little the brethren knew in comparison to the divine mysteries and this, in turn, should motivate them to submit their ideas to the rest of the community for criticism and questioning.

Having sketched the main features of St Dominic's spirituality we must now ask the question how all this applied in practice to the organisation of the friars of his order. But first, we should note that even from the earliest days there was always a division between the clerics who were ordained, or preparing for ordination, and lay (or co-operator) brothers. The Fundamental Constitution of the Order says very clearly that, "Since, by priestly ordination we are co-workers with the episcopacy, we have as our special charge the prophetic function, by which—with due regard for the changing condition of persons, times and places—the Gospel of Jesus Christ is announced by word and deed throughput the world, so that the divine faith is aroused or more profoundly penetrates the whole of the Christian life and builds up the body of Christ—which work is completed in the sacraments of faith."[684] And, "Since to dispense the Word of God and the sacraments of the faith is a priestly function, ours is a clerical religious community. But the co-operator brothers share in this work in a variety of ways because they too, in their chosen role, exercise a common priesthood."[685] These statements are certainly historically true, because from the beginning Dominic, unlike St Francis, intended his order to have a specifically *priestly* character in order that its mission of preaching might be carried out to the fullest possible extent. The monastic orders in their origin were made up of laity, with only a few members ordained to provide the brethren with the sacraments. This was because, as we have seen, the purpose of the monastic life was contemplation, not active parochial ministry.

Even St Francis seems to have conceived of his disciples as contemplatives, even as hermits, whose ministry to the poor was incidental. Dominic, on the other hand, was already a canon before he founded the order, that is a priest assisting

---

[684] *Fundamental Constitution of the Order of Preachers* (Dominicans). V.
[685] Op cit VI.

the bishop in his ministry and he founded the order precisely for the ministry of the Word. This might explain why, when he founded the order, Dominic relied heavily on the Rule of St Augustine. Augustine had written it (or at least adapted it) for a group of priests he had gathered to live in community and serve his congregations.

Nevertheless, from the beginnings of the Order of Preachers, the movement also included non-ordained brothers. Dominic wanted to entrust the business of the administration of the order to them, but could not obtain the agreement of his fellow priests to do so. Since preaching is the purpose and goal of the order all members of the Order must contribute to it. But not all could do so by themselves engaging in the different acts of preaching. There were many things to be done that did not require ordination. Today, the co-operator brothers share in the work of the order in many ways, including those forms of preaching and teaching for which ordination is not needed. If at any time, they wish to become permanent deacons or to undertake preparation necessary for the priesthood, and are qualified, these ways also remain open to them throughout their lives.

This raises an interesting and important question. Given that the Roman Catholic church, following the supposed example of Jesus himself, has never ordained women (and has justified this on the grounds that, in any event, sacramental symbolism requires different roles for women and men): why did Dominic admit women to the *clerical* order he founded? In fact, many of the early Dominicans strongly resisted the affiliation of women to the order and it was only (somewhat ironically) through pressure from the Pope himself and the advocacy of Hugh of St Clar, that this was accepted as a regular feature of the Order. It has subsequently proved to be one of its greatest glories. St Dominic himself, as we have seen, was convinced that his preaching brothers needed the spiritual assistance of contemplative nuns, and he founded three communities of them during his life and was preparing to establish a fourth at the time of his death. He hoped that these communities might also prove to be centres of learning for women converted from heresy.

At first glance, it would seem that the total dedication of nuns to penance and contemplation excludes them from preaching, but in fact many have engaged in instructing and counselling those who come to them either by letter or other forms of writing or through the production of works of art. Today, such opportunities have increased, provided that they are kept within the proper limits of what it is to be contemplative. It should also be noted that this equally applies to the male members of the Dominican order. There have always been those who have been called to live a more contemplative life and have been left free of external ministry to devote themselves to that life on behalf of the other members of the order.

From a very early period, both Franciscans and Dominicans began to accept the affiliation of Brothers and Sisters of penance, that is, members of a lay (tertiary) movement that had grown up concurrently with the friars. These lay people lived (and live) under a Rule designed for their mode of life by a master of the Dominican Oder, Munio of Zamora in 1285. In 1405, thanks largely to the efforts of one of Catherine of Sienna's disciples, Thomas Caffarini, it received papal approval. Soon women who wanted to be affiliated to the order, but without the restrictions of the cloister, sought admission under this Rule and became not nuns but sisters.

Thus, the so-called "third order" (as distinct from the first order of Friars and Second order of nuns) was divided into the sisters who take vows and the laity who do not. While some attempts have been able to establish communities of Third Order men, they have not succeeded for very long. In recent years, secular institutes have also been founded in affiliation with the Order, whose members live a form of canonically consecrated life, but in the world. Thus, great variety of ways of being a Dominican received recognition in the Revised Constitutions of the Order under the name of "the Dominican family".

Since the middle of the nineteenth century the (lay) sisters engaged in active ministry have become an outstanding feature of "the Dominican family". While such communities were affiliated to the Order by the thirteenth century onwards, the tendency was for them to adopt the cloister and gradually become almost indistinguishable from the nuns. But in the nineteenth century, new needs in the church for teachers, nurses and social workers both in Europe and on the mission field gave rise to many foundations of (lay) sisters engaged in active ministry. It must be admitted, however, that so rapid was this movement that until the new perspectives attendant on Vatican II not a great deal of thought was given to how this form of life conformed to the purpose of the order as a whole.

That is, ministries were undertaken which had no clear relation to preaching, and the form of life of the sisters was often an eclectic mixture of elements taken from the cloistered life of nuns and from non-Dominican sources, and were often in tension with the ministries which the Order officially recognised. Today, Dominican sisters are faced with remedying this situation by developing their own distinctive way of life within "the Dominican family". The key question for them is this: How can Dominican sisters, who are not (unlike the nuns) the contemplative source of the Order's preaching—and who cannot be ordained—share in the work of the Order of Preachers? The answer is important not only for them, but to the entire Dominican laity, most of whom are also excluded by gender or marriage from ordination and who, if single, may not be called to it.

Historically the movements which produced the mendicant orders of Francis and Dominic were preceded by a widespread movement of lay preaching. Since many of these preachers were ill prepared and fell into one-sided, heretical, views Pope Innocent III welcomed the work of Francis and Dominic who were unswervingly loyal to the *magisterium*. The Second Vatican Council, however, emphasised that the threefold basic ministry of the church does not pertain exclusively to those who have been ordained but is shared by all the faithful, by reason of their baptism. Moreover, today many of the laity are theologically educated to a level which allows them to undertake the Ministry of Word. This is recognised in the new Code of Canon Law:

"The lay members of Christ's faithful by reason of their baptism and confirmation are witnesses to the good news of the Gospel, by their words and example of their Christian life. They can also be called upon to cooperate with bishops and priests in the exercise of the ministry of the word." [686] "The laity may be allowed to preach in a church or oratory if in certain circumstances it is necessary, or in a particular case it would be advantageous, according to the provisions of the Episcopal Conference and without prejudice to Canon767#1."[687] "The most important form of preaching is the homily, which is part of the liturgy, and is reserved to the priest or deacon."[688] Obviously in 766 and 767 the term "preaching" is used in a strict and narrow sense to mean preaching in a church and in connection with the liturgy or other pare-liturgical occasions; but in 759 the "ministry of the word" has a much broader meaning in the sense explored earlier in this chapter. It should also be noted that the preaching by the laity, like that of priests, is ultimately under Episcopal control since it is he who is principally tasked with the proclamation of the Gospel.[689] This is in keeping with St Dominic's own great concern to obtain the approbation

---

[686] Canon #759.
[687] Canon #766.
[688] Canon #767.
[689] See Canons #763 and #772.

of the Pope for his Order of Preachers. From these canonical considerations, it follows that a vast field of the ministry of the word is open to members of "the Dominican Family". No doubt many of them will wonder why *"the most important form of preaching"*, the homily, is open only to priestly members of the order who must be male. Nevertheless, the fact that the Eucharistic homily is, in some sense, "the most important form of preaching" does not either imply or entail that other forms of preaching the ministry of the word are unimportant or even, given the circumstances of our times, perhaps more important in their actual power and effect than the brief (seven minutes?!) homily given on a Sunday morning to those who are, for the most part, "good Catholics". It would, in short, be a great shame, if the laudable desire to preach homilies should by its frustration kill the desire to preach in other ways actually open to the non-ordained Catholic layperson.

There may be several forms of preaching in the wider sense that have the possibility of being more effective that preaching the Eucharistic homily. The first of these is religious education from the most elementary catechetical instruction, to examination level in schools and to teaching at a university. Dominican sisters have been engaged in educational work such as this with notable success, and many Dominican laity are teachers. Some may counter this by saying that what they do is teaching *not* preaching. But it is certainly what the canons mean by the ministry of the word, and they have as precedent St Albert the Great, St Thomas Aquinas and Yves Congar to name but three.

The second is through the use of the public media by writing, television, radio, drama, and the arts. Quite obviously in our day more people spend more time before their television sets than before the altar, and are certainly more influenced by it.

A third is by actively engaging in the discussion of current social and political and ethical issues where the prophetic voice of the church is rarely heard or where it is heard ridiculed and dismissed as a cultural remnant of an outmoded (and so useless) form of discourse.

A fourth is through the great variety of extra-liturgical preaching such as retreats, conferences, quiet days, and workshops etc, which provide extensive and direct opportunities to reach people when they are at their most thoughtful.

Finally, there is also evangelisation in a strict sense, reaching out to the unchurched. These and many other ways are open to all who have a talent for them and are prepared to undertake the (sometimes arduous) preparation for them.

As has already been shown, not every Dominican (male or female) must engage in the ministry of the word because there is a need for more auxiliary tasks without which this ministry becomes impossible. Among these is the care for the sick and the neglected which Jesus himself performed as a demonstration of the power of his word.

And yet, in order to be distinctively Dominican members of the Order of Preachers must (on whatever level) be closely associated with its core mission and ministry and it is important that members are not distracted from it. Thus, a distinctively Dominican spirituality leads all members of "the Dominican family" to seek opportunities open to them and not waste energy in dreaming about what they would do in other circumstances and if they were part of another religious order. A salutary reminder of this lies in the life of St Dominic himself. He longed to go on a missionary journey to the east, but he never allowed this to distract his attention away from the people he was given to care for who were immediately near at hand—and this applies equally to those who do, and do not take lifelong vows as they go about preaching the Gospel.

Chapter 20
The Beguines[690]

In the late twelfth century, women began to experiment with a way of life outside the socially endorsed alternatives of wife or cloistered nun. Social conditions were ripe for this new idea, and the Beguine movement flourished, reaching its peak in the second half of the following century.[691] My interest in the Beguines was piqued when I learnt that "they were not bound by vows, were not subject to papal enclosure, and did not totally renounce the possibility of marriage {and that} their piety seems to have centred on the Eucharist and the humanity of Jesus"[692] as this seemed to suggest a way of life which incorporated parts of monastic spirituality and the creation of inner space—fostering a monastic spirit in society—while remaining entirely "secular". It seemed to be congruent with

---

[690] Originally "Beguine" was a pejorative term. It seems to have had almost heretical undertones. (See Ernest W McDonnel (1954) *The Beguines and Beghards in medieval Culture: With Special Emphasis on the Belgian scene* New Brunswick, New Jersey. Rutgers University Press P430.) Early defenders preferred to speak of "holy women" or "religious women". Others used such circumlocutions as *muliers vulgariter dictae beguina*. This reluctance to use the word "Beguine" without further qualification continued until the latter half of the thirteenth century (ibid 4–5, 445). As to the derivation of the name several explanations have been given. The most persistent idea is that they are named after one Lambert le Begue, and *his* name is sometimes taken to mean heretic or one who stammered. Perhaps "beguine is a derivation of Albigensian—a reference to mendicancy—or to St Begga, or to the characteristic grey colour of the Beguine habit.

[691] Ernest W Mc Donnel (1954) *The Beguines in Medieval Culture: With Special Emphasis on the Belgian scene* New Brunswick. New Jersey. Rutgers University Press. p409.

[692] Nathan Mitchell (1982) 'Cult and Controversy', *The Worship of the Eucharist Outside Mass* New York. Pueblo. p174.

my own calling as an Oblate and yet I also vaguely recalled that it was for precisely these reasons that they were charged with heresy! In my research for this chapter, and my visit to the Beguine houses in Amsterdam in 2009, I have become increasingly convinced that the Beguine movement is very important indeed not only for an understanding of continuity and change in the religious (monastic) life, but of how monastic spirituality might be adapted and applied in a secular context today. There are many fascinating connections between the Beguines and other movements, figures and historical events.

In this short chapter, I will attempt to sketch the early history of the Beguines, describe their spirituality and then briefly discuss some implications for us today.

The Social Context

On the eve of the Beguine movement, the independence and authority of women were severely limited, howbeit that hitherto in monastic circles, at any rate, women had been able to exercise a great deal of power and influence. But now, in the twelfth century the male dominated ecclesiastic and civil powers were determined to put an end to that.[693] They thought that women were dangerously carnal, lustful creatures, far removed from the male realms of spirit and intellect.[694] Women might engage in commercial life and manage their husbands' financial affairs[695] but "there was general acceptance of the notion that formal authority was inconsistent with femininity."[696] Accordingly double monasteries were suppressed and religious orders closed their doors to women.[697] The power of the abbess was curtailed.[698] Married women were to

---

Fiona Bowie (1990) *Beguine Spirituality: Mystical Writings of Mechthild of Magdeburg, Beatrice of Nazareth and Hadwijch of Brabant.* Trans. Oliver Davies. New York. Crossroads. p5.

[694] Ibid. p9.

[695] Especially if they were away fighting the Saracens in the Crusades.

[696] Op cit Bowie p5–7.

[697] See variously: Richard William Southern (1970) *Western Society and the Church in the Middle Ages.* London. Penguin. P313Op cit McDonnell p103 and 189–190. And E Ann Matter (1977) 'Innocent III and the keys of the Kingdom of Heaven' in *Women Priests: A Catholic Commentary on the Vatican declaration* ed Leonard Swidler and Arelene Swidler New York. Paulist Press. P150.

[698] Op cit Bowie p 10 and Matter p145-147. Mattter also points out that this may have been a papal/monastic struggle as well as a gender issue.

submit to their husbands as in St Paul and wife beating for the merest infringement of this was condoned and widely practised.[699] Although women were active in many trades, men made the decision even in predominantly female trade guilds.[700] The two options presented to women of the nobility were marriage or the cloister; women of lower social status might enter a trade, and possibly remain single. This sort of choice was highly inadequate to the social reality. In France, Germany and the Low countries there were more marriageable women than men "due to local wars, feuds, crusades…the large number of secular and regular clergy"[701] and guild regulations which restricted marriage to masters.[702] In at least some regions, women may have been in the majority in absolute numbers as well.[703] Suitable marriages could not be arranged for all the daughters of the nobility, yet it was considered disreputable for these women to earn their own livelihood through work of any kind.[704] And what of the religious life? Quite simply, demand exceeded supply. The number of female convents was small.[705] Many women found the monastic reforms and the new mendicant orders very attractive, but the men considered women dangerous distractions and did little to encourage them in their vocation.[706] Furthermore, whatever their original intent, monastic communities had become the preserve of the nobility and the very members rich merchant classes (of which St Francis was one). Economically, Europe was in transition from rural feudalism to urban capitalism- and despite many protests monastic communities charged high entrance fees![707] In short, neither marriage, nor the cloister was attainable for women. I age of which the Beguines were but one manifestation was a time of widespread religious ferment. Some of the religious groups which sprang up at about the same time as the Beguines were the Waldensians, Lollards, Brothers and Sisters

---

[699] Ibid Bowie p6.

[700] Ibid Bowie p7 Op cit McDonnell p85.

[701] Ibid Bowie p14.

[702] Op cit McDonnell p84.

[703] Op cit Southern. p323.

[704] Op cit McDonnell p85. It might also remind us of Luke 16:3 *"I cannot dig: to beg I am ashamed."*

[705] Op cit Southern p 310 and 323.

[706] See variously Bowie p9–11. Southern p310–317 and McDonnell p103–105, 116–19 and 189–196.

[707] See variously Bowie p10. Southern p315 and McDonnell p63, 85, 89–94, and 96–97.

of the Free Spirit, Spiritual Franciscans, Apostolici, Albigensians, Joachimites and flagellants. These protest movements grew more and more extreme and more and more apocalyptic in their views as the thirteenth century wore on. Umberto Eco's popular novel *The Name of the Rose* provides a relatively good picture of the confusion of the mid-fourteenth century, and the Inquisitor Bernard Gui, who appears in Eco's book, specifically persecuted the Beguines. The common thread running through these new religious groups, and to some extent later monastic reforms and the mendicant orders, was the tremendous appeal of the *vita apostolica*. "Liberty" and "Poverty" were the watchwords.[708] The vita apostolic was conceived as a return to primitive Christianity, with zeal for souls and a simple life in common.[709] Ecclesiastical and secular authorities quite rightly saw these ragtag groups as indictments against them. In particular, the idea of voluntary poverty was held up in stark contrast to greed, simony, the corruption of the clergy and the wealth of the church.[710] Though sharing in horror at the wealth of the church, these protest movements took different paths. Some were Orthodox; others were heretical. Some wanted only to purify the institutional church; others would have preferred to raze the entire structure.[711]

The Rise and Fall of the Beguines

The Beguines were a spontaneous women's movement, not an adjunct to any male figure or group. There was no founder, no Rule, no constitution. Each Beguine community was entirely autonomous and there was no General Chapter which supervised or regulated the Beguine houses scattered throughout northern Europe. The Beguines did not advocate a particular doctrine or a particular exegetical method for the interpretation of Scripture. The members of each Beguine community were engaged in various occupations.

All of these characteristics make it difficult to give a brief descriptive history of the Beguines as a whole. Since there was much room for local variation, it is not possible to say that a certain event affected all Beguines in the same way and so there is, even today, confusion as to what might, and might not count as

---

[708] Emile Zum Brunn and Georgette Epiney-Burgard (1989) *Women Mystics in Medieval Europe* trans. Shelia Hughes. New York. Paragon House. xvi.
[709] Op cit McDonnell. p141.
[710] Op cit Brunn xvi and McDonnell pp 73,142,150–151.
[711] Loc cit Brunn. Ibid McDonnell p142.

authentically Beguine.[712] It is for this reason that I think that it is a gross distortion of the truth to suggest the whole movement can be explained by Lambert of Begue's intention to establish a convent in Liege for rich widows so that they could practice charity towards the poor and the ill.[713] Such a view is simply reductionist. There was, however, a general Beguine ethos, which I will describe below when I consider Beguine spirituality. In addition, although there is no universally applicable timetable, at least in Belgium there is a discernible pattern in the evolution and common life of Beguine communities. The Beguine movement began in the diocese of Liege in Brabant (now Belgium) though there is much debate as to which town can claim to be its birthplace. The two most favoured candidates are Liege itself or Niveles.[714] Lambert of Begue, who was a priest in Liege, certainly encouraged women who wished to live religiously. The group of women with which he was associated and inspired, and who were later recognised as Beguines, appeared between 1170 and 1175.[715] On the other hand, according to McDonnell, the first prominent woman to be identified as a Beguine was Mary of Oignies (d 1213) who was a *conversa* of the (male) Augustinian priory of St Nicholas, near Niveles.[716] "While Germany was noted for the proliferation of scattered women and even small convents"[717] it was in Belgium that the Beguinage developed. The end result of the Beguine communities, the Beguinage, comprised of a church, cemetery, a hospital, a public square and streets and walks lined with convents for the younger sisters and pupils, and individual houses for the older inhabitants.[718] A Beguinage was,

---

[712] Joanna Ziegler (1986) 'Some questions Regarding the Beguines in devotional Art', *Vox Benedictina*, p345.

[713] W. K. Fleming (1913) *Mysticism in Christianity*, London Robert Scott perpetuates this myth which reappears in Lucy Menzies book *The Revelations of Mechthild of Magdeberg* London. Longmans, Green and Co, 1953 where she portrays the Beguines as lady bountiful. Care for the poor and the ill is enjoined on all Christians. It is not at all necessary for this to be organised in the way that Fleming and Menzies suggest, even for women in Medieval Europe.

[714] Op cit Bowie p14–15 and McDonnell p7.

[715] Loc cit Bowie.

[716] Op cit McDonnell p10.

[717] Op cit Zigler p352.

[718] As we see in what remains of the Beguinage in Amsterdam.

like the great monasteries, a city within a city.[719] In the Great Beguinages at Ghent and Amsterdam with their walls and moats, there were at the beginning of the fourteenth century, two churches, eighteen convents, over one hundred houses, a brewery, and an infirmary.[720] The question then is this; how did the Beguines become so organised, so institutionalised and so complex so quickly? From the scholarly literature, I think that we can detect a four-stage evolution.

The first stage consisted of individual women living as *conversae,* or in their own home or that of their parents. At this point, they are not bound to their way of life, nor did they need to renounce property, or abandon their trades.

The second stage, which occurred roughly at the beginning of the thirteenth century, was marked by their joining themselves together in disciplined associations. A grand mistress, along with a council of members, presided over each group.[721] There was some clerical influence as well. The third stage came with the *beguinae clausae*. At this point, the Beguines acquired, or built, infirmaries, and settled near them. I agree with McDonnell that this was, and is, an entirely natural development in any community: as community members grew old, they needed more care.[722] Furthermore, the fact that women were encouraging one another to do good works pleased the ecclesiastical hierarchy. In their view that was exactly what women are for! The drawback is that this later development was sometimes seen as the *raison d'être* for Beguines: either that Beguine communities were to aid single women who could not gain admittance to monastic orders, or the idea, that we have seen earlier, that Beguines were mere charitable ladies with time on their hands with a fondness for the poor and the sick.[723] The fourth stage of the Beguine movement was reached in the late thirteenth century with the creation of many Beguinage. In this stage, large Beguine communities were designated as parishes, and sometimes given grants of land "in a more favourable location".[724] This four-

---

[719] That monasteries could be described in this way is plain by many ruins of ancient abbeys in Britain. Those at Bury St Edmonds are an excellent example.
[720] Op cit McDonnell p479.
[721] The Grand Mistress and her Council are not to be thought of as a Mother Superior and a Chapter. It is, in my view, to be thought of as analogous to the relationship between the Master and Members of a Livery Company.
[722] Op cit McDonnell pp 67 and 159.
[723] Op cit McDonnell p6.
[724] Loc Cit.

fold development has been described by Ziegler as "evolution from isolation to claustration."[725] Certain it is that church authorities urged claustration, but I am not at all convinced that the early Beguines were as isolated as Ziegler believes, even if they did not see the need for an organisational superstructure.[726] In fact, I see the four stages as a transition from independence to co-option, from flexibility to institutionalisation, from self-direction to greater formal, sometimes even clerical, control. Clerical attitudes towards the Beguines were often ambivalent. The women's dedication to charity and chastity was greatly admired[727] but their close proximity to clerics and male monastics was considered dangerous for all concerned.[728] The Cistercians were willing to take charge of convents, but not to provide pastoral care. Their *Liber Usum Conversum* of 1235 made the granges off-limits for Cistercian *conversae* and "entailed a denial of ordinary monastic hospitality to women and even to [their] male escorts".[729] The Dominicans were repeatedly warned against associating with Beguines, and reminded that their mission was the intellectual battle against heresy, through preaching, rather than pastoral work. But, on the local level, these attempts to create space between the female and male religious, lay and professed, was often ignored. According to McDonnell the Beguines were often mistaken for lay Dominicans.[730] When the Beguines were pressed to adopt an approved Rule, some inclined towards the Cistercian *Carta Caritas*[731] and others towards the Augustinian Rule for women, but always working closely with Dominican men! Those who resented the mendicant orders often also hated the Beguines such was the level of identification between them. The Beguines never did adopt an approved Rule or become a religious order. They were, however,

---

[725] Op cit Ziegler p353.

[726] Op cit Bowie p13

[727] Op cit McDonnell pp 6 and 137.

[728] Op cit Bowie p16–17 ibid McDonnell p60 and 103.

[729] Op cit McDonnell p112–117.

[730] Ibid. p187–204.

[731] One reason for this may be that the Cistercians were keen to publish their works in the vernacular: "*...while Bernard [of Clairvaux] shared with Gregory the Great the honour of being the first doctor of the Church to be translated into the language of all the people—in this instance French*" Pauline Matarasso ed: The Cistercian *World—Monastic Writings of the Twelfth Century*. London. Penguin Classics 1993 p xiv.—An enthusiasm shared by the Beguines, howbeit that is was for them, if not for the Cistercians, a highly controversial endeavour.

granted some privileges and exemptions which were common to formally professed religious orders such as indulgences, permission to carry out religious services during interdict, and so on.[732] Their status in the eyes of the Vatican ebbed and flowed for a time, but the tide finally turned against them in the fourteenth century. As is well known, the Fourth Lateran Council prohibited the establishment of any new monastic orders. However, one Jacques of Vitry seems to have managed to obtain permission for some Beguine communities to continue,[733] and the Papal Bull *Gloriam virginalem* of 1233 seemed to endorse their way of life.[734] By 1236, however, Aleydis, a Beguine, had been executed as a heretic. This stirred up violent public protest.[735] The Council of Lyon in 1274 reiterated the ban on new orders, and the Council of Vienne 1311–1312, explicitly named Beguines as heretical (though the same document also stated that there was nothing objectionable to women penitents forming communities without vows!)[736] In the years following, the Beguines often, and unsurprisingly, had their property confiscated. They were even forced to marry.[737] In 1318, the Bishop of Cologne demanded "dissolution of all Beguine associations and their integration into Orders approved by the Pope."[738] On the other hand, Pope John XXII distinguished between "*beghini*", who were truly heretical, living in northern Italy, and the northern Beguines living unobjectionable lives. To make this clear he issued his Bull *Raciio recta*, which stated that these northern Beguines should not be hindered but, on the contrary, "permitted to pursue their way of life without diminution of property or rights."[739] In 1421, Pope Martin V "ordered the Archbishop of Cologne to search out and destroy any small convents living under the cloak of religion without a definite Rule"[740] Pope Martin need not have worried; by this time Beguinages were little more than

---

[732] Op cit McDonnell pp 132 and 236–245.

[733] See variously Bowie p17. McDonnell p30 and the *Corpus Dictionary of Western Churches* ed T.C. O'Brien. Washington. Corpus. 1970 p82.

[734] Ibid Bowie p18 and McDonnell p6.

[735] Ibid Bowie p18 and see also Columba Hart (1980) *Hadewijch: The Complete Works* New York Paulist Press. p22.

[736] Ibid Bowie p35–36 and Op cit Southern p330.

[737] Ibid Bowie p36.

[738] Op cit Southern p330–331.

[739] Op cit McDonnell p536. This ruling was reissued by Pope Benedict XIII in 1336.

[740] Op cit Southern p331–332.

work houses, and the Beguines were no longer concerned with theological matters.[741] Such Beguinages as remained were largely dissolved in the Protestant reformation and though some tried to revive were destroyed again during the Napoleonic wars. Despite this, there were in 1969, still eleven Beguinages in Belgium and two in Holland.[742]

Beguine Spirituality

We noted above that the Beguines, like many of their contemporaries, were drawn by the ideal of the *vita apostolica*. Partly through choice and partly through coercion by the hierarchy, the Beguines *did* have a communal life. But they chose to do so with the minimum of bureaucratic complications and fuss; their goals were simplicity and freedom and this applied equally to their understanding of evangelical poverty. Jacques of Vitry maintained that financial success had vitiated the monastic ideal.[743] For the first hundred years or so, the Beguine movement drew many members from the wealthier classes; these women, for religious and political reasons found voluntary poverty very attractive.[744] However the Beguines never made voluntary poverty a condition of membership[745] manual labour was valued in the same way as humility and the willingness to serve those in need.[746] Thus criticisms of Beguines as lazy and opportunistic are inaccurate, but it is true that they did not see poverty as an end in itself.[747] Another element of the *vita apostolica* was the zeal for souls and the defeat of heresy.[748] So, for example, Mary of Oignies wholeheartedly supported the crusade against the Albigensians, and the Beguine communities in Belgium were regarded as bulwarks against heresy there.[749] Critics faulted Beguines for daring to preach, and it may be that some did so, though they themselves would

---

[741] Op cit McDonnell p573.

[742] Op cit Bowie p20 and Loc cit *Corpus Dictionary*.

[743] Op cit McDonnell p90.

[744] Ibid p96–98.

[745] Ibid p 129–130.

[746] Ibid p 143–146.

[747] Op cit Bowie p24.

[748] Op cit McDonnell p414. The explicit desire to defeat heresy was another reason for their affinity with the Dominicans.

[749] Op cit Brunn XVIII and Mitchell 173–175 and ibid McDonnell p415–416.

have seen this as a way of imparting true religion and virtue.[750] One especially controversial practice was the use of the vernacular, which seemed to link them with the Lollards. New vernacular languages had sprung up in Europe in the ninth and tenth centuries and now Latin had become almost unintelligible to the common people.[751] Adherents of the *vita apostolica* therefore endeavoured to provide devotional literature that people could understand.[752] Ecclesiastical officials feared that this played into the hands of heretics and infidels. Many Beguines had a deep devotion to the Eucharist. This could sometimes have very dramatic forms as we see in the case of Beatrice of Nazareth who is said to have longed to make her communion with such ardour that it provoked bleeding and physical collapse.[753] More often, and much less dramatically, Beguines had the common medieval desire to simply *see* the consecrated elements. But they also had a desire to receive communion *frequently*. This was a widespread attitude among them and one which was unusual enough to provoke comment. At this time, most ordinary people were mandated to receive communion only once each year, and monastics three times a year. According to McDonnell, Beguines wanted communion at least weekly and, where practical, more often than that.[754] It is therefore "no accident that the feast of Corpus Christi has its origins in the Diocese of Liege."[755] Juliana of Liege had an intense devotion to the Eucharist, and from 1208 until her death in 1258 tirelessly promoted the institution of a special feast to honour the Eucharist.[756] Jacques Panteleon, while archdeacon of Liege tried to regulate this fervour by writing a rule for the Beguines which, once again, was rejected. But it can be said to have been recognised when Pope Urban

---

[750] Ibid McDonnell p343–344 and 412.

[751] Op cit Mitchell p69–70.

[752] Such an endeavour would, of course, have been totally impossible without the relatively newly invented printing press.

[753] Op cit Bowie p 27 and McDonnell p314–315. There is an interesting synergy here between the case of Beatrice and the reports of many stigmatics down the ages. The case of Catherine Emmerich is an especially close parallel.

[754] Ibid McDonnell p311 and 316–318.

[755] Ibid p313.

[756] Ibid McDonnell p 98 305–308 and Mitchell p175. For Julian's Beguine connections, see McDonnell p300–304. Julian also linked the Beguine to the cult of relics. She visited Cologne (said to house the relics of the Three Wise men of Matthew's nativity story.) She is said to have later parcelled out relics from the bodies of five hundred various saints to her friends and relatives and to a wide assortment of monasteries and convents.

IV established the feast of Corpus Christi as a universal feast of the church in his Bull, *Transiturus* in 1264.[757] Devotion to the Eucharist was accompanied by devotion to the *humanity* of Christ,[758] the heart of Jesus and especially the passion narratives. But sometimes this grew to excess. The phenomenon of stigmata first appeared in the thirteenth century too whereupon it *"became increasingly common, especially among women"*[759] Mary of Oignies may have been the first woman, and certainly the first Beguine to receive the stigmata.[760] Women could, and did, acquire a reputation for sanctity by receiving the stigmata, as well as visions, trances, levitations, and extreme asceticism. Christine of Stommeln, for example, gained a circle of admirers—male and predominantly Dominican—in just this way.[761] These phenomena were, however, generally viewed by much more caution by the majority of the Beguine themselves whose life was, after all, characterised by moderation and pragmatism.[762] When Christine complained of being tormented by attacks of demons "the claim…merely provoked smiles and drew forth from the extra-regulars comments on mental derangement of charges of feigned holiness."[763]

---

[757] Ibid McDonnell p 163 and 306–309 and Loc cit Mitchell.

[758] Op cit Bowie p27 and ibid McDonnell p318. In this way they reverenced Jesus as truly God in the Eucharist and as truly Man in the ways we are about to examine. There is nothing at all heretical in this. On the contrary, it is fully in accord with the Chalcedonian formula.

[759] Ibid McDonnell p319.

[760] McDonnell thinks that Mary received the stigmata twelve years *before* St Francis of Assisi. (p318). If this is indeed the case then Mary's is the first recorded case of this phenomenon.

[761] Op cit Bowie p28 and 33–34 and McDonnell p344–355. For an account of a woman called Sybyl, a woman who claimed to be a Beguine and traded on the credulity of the times and its hunger for miracles and extraordinary signs and wonders see also McDonnell p452–453.

[762] Loc cit Bowie. Ibid McDonnel p349. I would emphasise here that while the Beguine may have been pragmatic, they were *not* opportunistic as their critics, both then and now, would have them.

[763] Ibid McDonnell p445. I find it interesting that the Beguine should *smile* at this. While it is, of course, a natural (and contemporary) reaction to such claims of demonic attack as "feigned holiness" to smile at demons, even to laugh at them, was a tried and tested methods for defeating demons used by the Desert Fathers. Were the Beguines aware of

The greatest exponents of Beguine mystical spirituality are Mechthild of Magdeberg (1212/-1282?), Beatrice of Nazareth (whose devotion to the Eucharist was so deep that she bled,) (1200? -1268), Hadewijch of Brabant[764] and Margarette Poret. (d. 1310). Like many mystics they believed that the individual soul could be directly united with God. As in most genuine Christian mysticism they believed to that love is the only way to that union. What gives Beguine mysticism its special flavour is the *type* of love they envisage: namely a combination of Cistercian asceticism with the medieval notion of chivalric, courtly love![765] Mechthild and Margurite employ and Augustinian style of autobiography, that is a dialogue between the soul and God,[766] or sometimes between the soul and Love. Love takes the feminine in both German and Dutch and "Lady Love is also Divine Love" according to Brunn.[767] Thus under the name of Love, Beguines had a powerful *feminine* metaphor for God. Although still somewhat controversial, their works are regarded as literary and spiritual masterpieces.[768] According to Bowie, the courtly love lyric originated in southern France among the troubadours and from them spread into the culture of Germany with the *Minnesanger* and the proponents of *dolce stil nouvo* in Italy who also thinks that a good case can be made that Dante was familiar with the writings of Mechthild.[769] Brunn goes some way to agreement on this point by suggesting that Dante's character called Matelda who appears in *Purgatorio* might well be Mechthild.[770] Perhaps, but these interesting but purely literary debates can too easily blind us to the fact that Beguine authors borrowed widely

---

this legacy and to what extent, if at all, were their associations (though by no means eremitical) modelled on the desert tradition?

[764] There is no scholarly consensus as to Hadewijch's dates. According to Bowie (p96) her works seem to have been composed between 1221 and 1240, whereas Brunn (p129–30) argues that the "New Poems" are almost certainly by another hand and at a later date, perhaps as late as the fourteenth century. The argument for a later date rests on the view that the "New Poems" are more scholastic and apophatic. Both Bowie and Brunn agree however that, whatever the date, the "New Poems" are also works of distinctly Beguine theology.

[765] Both Bowie (p 40–42) and Brunn (p xxv) agree on this key point.

[766] Augustine used this method most famously in *Confessions*.

[767] Op cit Brunn p99–100.

[768] Ibid Brunn xxii, xxix, 43, 71, 147.

[769] Op cit Bowie p41–42.

[770] Op cit Brunn p49–50.

from many images of courtly love, and used them to describe the relationship between the individual soul and God. Not least of these was Bernard of Claivaux's commentary on the Song of Songs, a distinctly Cistercian work which showed how a monk, whose theology is careful to be Orthodox, could use extremely erotic language! Even more influential than Bernard was the theology of William of St, Thierry, and another Cistercian. Interestingly, he was from Liege[771] and "the most Greek of all the twelfth century theologians."[772] This seems to press the parallel, if any, too far and Brunn can only say this because William, like some of the Greek Fathers, wrote about the possibility of our divinisation. It is true that passages like the following found great favour and repetition with the Beguines: "…it is well said that we shall see him fully as he is when we are like him that is when we are what he is. For those who have been enabled to become the sons of God have been enabled to become not indeed God, but what god is: holy and in the future as happy as God is."[773] But more distinctive of William is his insistence on Trinitarian theology. For him, the goal of human life is to be found in God, and to love God, the love of the immanent Trinity.[774] To this mix the Beguines added their own themes of "over passing" and "the More". Over passing is expressed in negative the *via negativa*. It means that the soul must transcend itself and all things less than God to reach God. The More, is a way of expressing God's transcendence. However close we may come to God, something of God is always (more) beyond our reach and comprehension. That God is therefore inexhaustible should be a cause of much rejoicing.[775] So, were the Beguines heretical?

If they were heretical, it was only because their contemporaries thought that they shared some of the more outlandish beliefs and practices of the Free Spirit sect.[776] The Brothers and Sisters of the Free Spirit were alleged[777] to be

---

[771] Ibid Brunn xvii.

[772] Ibid xxvi.

[773] William of St. Theirry; *The Golden Epistle: A letter to the brethren of Mont Dieu*. II: XV p257–258.

[774] Brunn does acknowledge this at p xxvi.

[775] Op cit Brunn xxxi-xxxiii, and p48.

[776] Op cit Bowie p35.

[777] Some scholars doubt that the Brothers and Sisters of the free-Spirit were an organised group at all. (see Bowie p39). If they are right about this it is difficult to see how the sect could have met the Inquisition's description of it.

pantheistic and antinomian, and to reject the church and her sacraments.[778] They purportedly taught that it is possible for every human soul to consummate its divine nature[779] and for the soul that had come to this enlightenment that it was God and could not sin. Beguines, by contrast, were not pantheists. Perhaps for their contemporaries, the idea of the "More" did look like a consummation of the divine nature; even though it is not. The Cistercian, William of St Thierry, from whose theology the idea of the "More" was derived makes it clear that the union of the soul with God does not make it God, but what God is (like). Although the Beguines were certainly scandalised by the wealth that the church had amassed and the greed and corruption it seemed to entail, the Beguines did not reject it and, as we have seen, the idea that they were anti-sacramental is very wide of the mark indeed. Quite apart from the widespread devotion to the Eucharist it is, as Brunn has explained, important to note that the visions of Beatrice of Nazareth and those of Hadewijch always occur in a liturgical setting.[780] As for the charge that the Beguines recognised no moral law this too can be answered. It is clear that the Inquisition completely failed to understand the dramatic language of the writings of Marguerite Porete's "farewell to virtues", and deliberately so.[781] In context, what Marguerite has to say looks very like St Paul's attitude to the Jewish Law: virtues are good, and Christians must be moral because both are given by, and representations of Love. The error, however, is to reduce faith to morality and substitute the pursuit of moral virtue with the pursuit of union with God in a way which identifies morals and God as one and the same.[782] In short, we are to "Overpass" the virtues, not abrogate them.[783] As in all religious groupings and communities, there were no doubt "good" Beguines and "bad" Beguines but it is far too simplistic to draw an arbitrary geographical line

---

[778] Ibid Bowie p35 and Op cit Corpus Dictionary p109. But the great devotion to the Eucharist that we have noted above gives the lie to this.

[779] Michael Cox (1985) *Handbook of Christian Spirituality*. Rev. ed. San Francisco. Harper & Row. p96.

[780] Op cit Brunn p77 and 103.

[781] Op cit Bowie p39. The provocative phrase "farewell to virtues" comes from the sixth chapter of "*A Mirror for Simple Souls*".

[782] As we noted in the Chapter on St Augustine's notion of friendship both in the cloister and outside it this false identification still has many unfortunate consequences, especially in debates concerning sexuality, even today.

[783] Op cit Brunn xxviii–xxiv, 110, 122–126, 152, 156, 158–159.

between Italy and the north[784] or to suggest that that the difference depends on whether they lived east or west of the Rhine.[785] I agree with both Bowie and McDonnell that it is even more simplistic to suggest that those who resisted exclaustration were thereby heretical.[786] It is possible that scholars might find other grounds on which to condemn the Beguines as heretics, or it may be that I am unjustified in reading admittedly inflammatory texts *as though* they are mainstream and Orthodox, but for all this I find the contention that Beguines were heretical far from compelling.

Some Implications for Today

From the beginning Beguines combined a life of pray, community and service to the needy. They demonstrated that women could be dedicated to God without necessarily retiring to the cloister and I find this encouraging for those of us who struggle to find a way to integrate the insights and practices of monasticism to our daily secular activities. What is depressing, however, is to have to acknowledge that there are still those, especially in the church and in positions of authority within it, who consider any female initiative threatening. There was, and is, great difficulty retaining the integrity of a distinctly woman's movement in the face of those who believe that ordination and Episcopal jurisdiction is as much a matter of gender as of grace and so restrict these functions only to men.

We can trace in the history and development of the Beguines a transition from a spontaneous women's movement, which shattered convention and expectation and was marked by freedom and simplicity, to an institution which more closely fitted the established model and practice. But even as the Beguines reached their "high point" in the establishment of the Beguinage, they were incorporated into the mainstream and thus the vitality of the original model was drained away. It was, perhaps, their very autonomy that aided their downfall. The Beguines did not have any central and authorised support structure and so it was easy for them to be "picked off" and pacified one by one. This does not necessarily mean that they ought to have adopted a hierarchical structure.

---

[784] As Pope John XXII did.

[785] Op cit Ziegler p347.

[786] Op cit Bowie p19 and McDonnell p6 and 412–415.

The Beguines related well to various religious orders, such as the Cistercians and the Dominicans, so it is somewhat disappointing that that they did not attempt to create a more supportive communications network between their own scattered membership through these orders. In my view, the adoption of a simple rule could also have helped them maintain a distinct identity without sacrificing too much autonomy and freedom.

Part 7
Contemplative Love and the Love of Contemplation

Chapter 21
St Ignatius of Loyola:
Spiritual Exercises for All

While Ignatius is most often thought of as the founder of the Society of Jesus (Jesuits), he spent a good part of his life as a lay person. It was as a lay person that he began developing his now famous "*Spiritual Exercises*" and guiding other laymen through them. During his recuperation from the wounds of war in Loyola in 1522, the first pages of the Exercises were written and the bulk of the book was completed by 1524. He continued to refine it until 1540, and the book was finally published for the first time in 1548. Ignatius was ordained in 1537 (although he did not say his first Mass until Christmas day 1538) and took vows with the first members of the Society of Jesus on 22 April 1541. This date marks the official beginning of the Jesuits.

Ignatius was, as we all are, a child of his time. He was born in the year before Columbus arrived in the Americas believing them to be the East Indies. In the same year, Jews and Muslims were expelled from Southern Spain after more than eight hundred years of Moorish occupation. Spain conquered the Aztec empire in Central America in 1521 and then the Incan empire in Southern America in 1533. In 1522 the first ship, under the command of a Basque captain, Juan Sabastian Elcano, finally completed Ferdinand Magellan's expedition to circumnavigate the globe. The Protestant reformation was sweeping Northern Europe and in 1543 Copernicus published his theory of a heliocentric universe.

The Catholic church was itself in crisis. Its priests were often poorly trained ignorant of the Gospels the nature of sacrament and openly disregarded their vows of celibacy. Indeed, one of Ignatius' own brothers was a priest who lived with the mother of his three children. Another of his brothers was married but his mistress regularly visited them at home. The discovery that the earth was round and not the centre of the universe challenged long-held theological beliefs and cosmic views, and in Spain the Inquisition was in full swing.

Into this milieu, Ignatius was born: a Basque, a member of a noble family fallen on hard times, a person of great passion and loyalty, later a soldier but also a romantic, a visionary and a mystic. He had the mystical gift of tears, struggled with scruples and suffered from chronic illnesses. After his conversion, he had the same passion that he had for romancing and fine clothes and being a great soldier was focussed on Jesus Christ as his chief and the Kingdom of God as the territory which must be defended at all costs.

In 1522, Ignatius had a mystical experience by the Cardoner River near Manrersa that was foundational to his spirituality and the later development of the Exercises. He had a sense of being immersed in God. According to Tetlow, "He was given a deep sense of how all creatures emanate from God and, in Christ, return to God; how Jesus Christ completes human nature in taking on our flesh; and how Christ is present in the sacraments. He grasped that God's pain is really a project to which each person contributes and how what God hopes for us rises in our consciousness and, by God's grace, free enactment."[787] As he gazed into the river, Ignatius received the insight that a person cannot, as the old saying is, step into the same river twice: that God's plan is continually unfolding and that all of creation, past, present and to come are one. Moreover, human beings are co-creators in this plan. Like other mystics before him and since, Ignatius experienced that sense of oneness and unity, not just of the human race with each other, not even of all creation as it now exists, but of all things from the beginning of time and into the future. In God, they are all one. God's creative activity is at work in all things. He glimpsed what modern scientists appear to be confirming: everything is relational.

This creative activity, this work, is sacred. If everything is an expression of the divine, then there is no longer a separation of the secular from the sacred. It means too that all human activity—raising families, earning a living, involvement in civic activities, participating in the mission and ministry of the church, taking holidays, meeting with friends and family—are a participation in this work. We are in fact one with the small drops that make up the mighty river that has its own part to play in the unfolding of god's loving desire for the world.

---

[787] Joseph A Tetlow S.J. (1992) 'Ignatius Loyola', *Spiritual Exercises* New York. Crossroad, p22.

This sense of being part of God's great work is especially evident in the end pieces of the *"Spiritual Exercises"*, the Principal and Foundation and the Contemplation. In the first, he introduces the idea of being a uniquely gifted part of creation and in the later he leads his readers to an exercise in both reviewing the experience of the *"Exercises"* as well as helping them make the transition to understanding how they are called to be God's labourers and to love as God loves. Ignatius says "Just as I see the sun in its rays and the fountain in its waters, so God pours forth a sharing in the divine life in all the gifts showered upon me".[788] But even from the opening of the *"Spiritual Exercises"*, participants are called to consider how the sin of one person impacts on the world and how, even in our sinfulness, the world still sustains us. The sun still shines on us, the rain still falls and we are nourished by the fruits of the earth as well as in our relationships with one another and with God. [789] In short, creation is always the visible sign of God's loving activity. Thus each person, religious, ordained or lay has his or her role to play in this great work, through their personal vocation. According to Ignatius, what makes a person's vocation holy is that it is an authentic and individual response to God's desire for him or her. A personal vocation lived within the context of a lay vocation is as holy as a vocation to ordained ministry or the cloister.It was this radical insight that propelled Ignatius to promote vocation and nurture souls. His primary method for doing this was spiritual conversations with individuals and small groups about the spiritual life; about virtues and vices, the Eucharist and, one of his favourite topics, the nature of the Trinity. The fact that Ignatius, as a layman who had no formal theological training, dared to have these conversations and then go on to develop the "Spiritual Exercises" was a courageous activity at the time of the Spanish Inquisition. He was often accused by the inquisitors of being member of a heretical group known as the *alumbrados* who practised a quasi-Christian mysticism which entirely disregarded doctrinal accuracy and theological precision in its teaching. But they could find no errors either in his teaching or in his published work, howbeit that he was prevented from defining the nature of sin and ordered to take a four-year course of studies. Even though Ignatius knew these restrictions were groundless, he obeyed them while within the bounds of the Inquisition's jurisdiction. He prayed long and hard about them and came to the view that these impediments to his work of nurturing souls and

---

[788] Spiritual Exercises 237.

[789] Spiritual Exercises 60.

promoting vocation was just too great to be borne. So, he travelled to Paris to further his studies and, more importantly, to be free to continue his work.

While in Paris Ignatius had to deal with the realities that Christian lay people always have to face: how to balance his studies, his ministry and finding sufficient funds to sustain both. He was often distracted from his studies by his passion to preach the holiness of lay vocation, but finally understood that he needed a systematic theological education if he and his companions were to distinguish themselves from the *alumbrados*.

It was also while he was in Paris that Ignatius shared lodgings with Francis Xavier and Peter Favre, the first of his companions who would later establish the Society of Jesus. Gradually others joined their company and Ignatius led them through the "*Spiritual Exercises*". As they continued to study and pray together, the Holy Spirit led them into a deeper commitment to each other and the church. By 1534, they had adopted a common way of life, adopting vows of poverty and chastity which were to be sealed in a visit to Jerusalem. But this common life was not an end in itself. Rather it was a means of bringing more souls to God and developing a sense of lay vocation. When, for a whole variety of reasons, the trip to Jerusalem became impossible, they placed themselves at the disposal of the Pope for mission assuming that he would know where the greatest need for mission would be and how it might best be met.

The same desire led those of the company who were not ordained to seek it. Ignatius himself was one of them and by 1541 they had formally committed themselves to one another, to the Pope and to God within the context of their new religious order that was quite different from anything that had gone before or currently existed. On the understanding that knowledge of the world could give knowledge of God, they committed themselves to working in the world, working with people, strengthening their souls.

In this way, Ignatius' passion became more focussed and even though his passion took many forms throughout his life it was the touch stone of his decision-making; discovering the best way to encourage ordinary people to live the Christian life in the world with a full sense of the holiness their personal vocation.[790] But Ignatius also knew that vocations are not lived in a vacuum.

---

[790] In his book *"Discovering Your Personal Vocation: the search for meaning through the Spiritual Exercises"* Mahwah Paulist Press 2001. Herbert Alphonso S.J. states that the election of the Exercises is actually discovering a personal vocation and that it should them become the material for the *examen*. The *examen* then becomes, not a tool for

They are shaped by the contexts of our lives: the point of history at which we have arrived, the country, the religious tradition and culture, ethnic origin, families, gender and sexuality, the recent events of our lives, the food we eat and the care we take of our bodies and mind and more. His first mystical experience led Ignatius and his companions to insist that we are always and everywhere being in relationship. On an organic level, we are in a constant exchange with different combinations of earth, air, fire and water—always receiving always releasing. On a spiritual level, we are in a constant exchange with different combinations of spirit, psychology, intellect, aesthetics' and emotions. We are constantly receiving and releasing energy, feelings, perceptions and ideas with the universe. Since we cannot interact with the whole universe all at once, we are nurtured and formed in community—initially in our family, but expanding in ever widening circles. As we mature, we adopt communities that somehow resonate with us and where our personal vocations can most readily be nurtured, explored and expressed.

We shape and are shaped by those communities of which we are a part. Sometimes it is a joyful process, and at others painful and difficult. In a healthy community, there is a diversity of people and of thought and as much as we might try to reverence the divine in others, we so often fall short both in our judgement of the other and in the authentic expression of our own vocation under God.

Ignatius knew the complexities of all this at first hand. His spiritual conversations, public preaching, catechesis and frequent reception of the Eucharist resulted in at least eight ecclesiastical legal proceedings against him between 1526 and 1538. In his role as General of the Society, Ignatius worked directly with various Popes over issues relating to the Jesuits both profitable and conflictual. According to Dyckman et al., "He did not hesitate to pray ceaselessly, convince politically powerful friends to intervene on his behalf, create a paper trail or visit the Pope personally—Ignatius did whatever it took to hold off or reverse a papal decision if he thought it was wrong."[791] In Spiritual

---

examining our sins, but a tool for discernment. If in our *examen* the question becomes "How, if at all, have I fully lived out my personal vocation in this day's events?" then we become more attuned to how we are disposing ourselves to live out our unique relationship with the divine.

[791] Dyckman Katherine SNJM (2001) Garvin Mary SNJM & Liebert Elizabeth SNJM *The Spiritual Exercises Reclaimed: Uncovering Liberating Possibilities for Women*, Mahwah Paulist Press. P315.

Exercises 352–370, Ignatius gives what is commonly referred to as "Rules for Thinking with the church". While there is some scholarly discussion about whether they are really part of the original Exercises, a later addition, or an entirely separate manual intended for use in public ministry they do contain a number of points that are useful for a lay person in approaching the church in general and theology in particular.[792] As Fleming S.J. has usefully pointed out[793] the title "Rules for Thinking with the church" is something of a mistranslation. Rules have the force of law behind it perhaps, whereas what Ignatius intended was closer to the more flexible idea of "Guidelines". This, to enter the scholarly debate for a moment, is entirely consistent with the more usual translation of the word for "Rule" which Ignatius uses throughout the exercises. Moreover, the word "*Sentio*", so often translated simply as "thinking" is not only thinking of an intellectual kind but a form of sensation or a felt-knowledge, an intuition, a "knowing" of the heart. In short, it is as much an affective activity as a purely rational one. In these contexts, these "guidelines" become more of a way of living in the church that is both divine and human with both loving affection and critical loyalty. "In the midst of the confusion and turmoil of the sixteenth century church of his day, he knew the difficulty of maintaining a mature balance, a clear-headed judgement, and a loving reverence for both tradition and change. The guidelines which he proposed were meant to be internalised…just as the guidelines with regard to eating and drinking or the guidelines on the discernment of spirits."[794] Ignatius' experience with the hierarchical church led him to a deep appreciation for the fact that it is an incarnated structure of authority and that individual Christians need to come to terms with this concrete manifestation of power and authority. "Ignatius's church is always relational, and the relationships are always human as well as divine."[795] Ignatius believed that the ironic and somewhat satirical writings of people such as Erasmus and the new "humanists" of his day undermined the morale of the church and its structures and so undermined the very foundations on which those relationships were built. So, his tenth Guideline {362} echoes {22} by advising that those who

---

[792] David L Fleming SJ (1996) *Draw Me Into Your Friendship: The Spiritual Exercises— A Literal translation and Contemporary reading*, Institute of Jesuit Sources explores these in detail using an ecclesiology that is distinctively post Vatican II.
[793] Loc cit p281ff.
[794] Ibid.
[795] Op cit Dyckman et al; p315.

undertake the "Spiritual Exercises" to be more inclined to praise than to blame and to deal privately with those able to consider the problems in the community.

In the modern church, especially perhaps in the turmoil besetting the Anglican Communion and Roman Catholics, this inclination to praise rather than blame and assume that the person acting in this way is doing so from pure motives is much needed. It seems that not only in the church, but in society more generally we are all too quick to find fault and blame. We hardly take time to really listen to what a person is saying or properly examine the facts rather than the heated emotion around a case before having a pre-prepared rebuttal ready to hand. We seem to have forgotten that, as Ignatius consistently insisted, we are all part of a great work, that people are expressions of God's loving presence in the world - even those whose opinions radically differ from ours. They are still expressing some truth and we need to look for the truth and build together on that foundation rather than the differences that tear us apart.

With this in mind, the understanding of the famous and much quoted phrase "black appearing white" in the thirteenth Guideline [365] takes on a different interpretation. Here Ignatius was simply reiterating the fact that there are some mysteries of the church which go far beyond our full comprehension, such as how we are to understand the presence of Christ's Body and Blood at the Eucharist. It is *not* a call for blind and unquestioning obedience as is so often thought and taught. A key aspect of this different interpretation is an equal insistence that within the community of the church there are many separate functions. The function of the institutional aspect of the church is to carry the traditional and provide a structure which, like a skeleton, will support the rest of the body of Christ.

The community aspect formed by the laity is the prophetic and visionary voice of that body. The laity must learn to read the signs of the times and adopt a mode of expression which meets contemporary life and can speak into it. For Ignatius, it is only this that can move the church forward and make it "relevant". So ideally there needs to be a healthy respect and balance between the hierarchical and the prophetic and an understanding that they exist in a creative tension.

But Ignatius also knew that all this demands an on-going discernment in the church of how the Holy Spirit of God is calling each one of us to a new and authentic expression of our faith. The role of the Jesuits he thought was to provide a new praxis which would discern, send, support and evaluate a new way of doing this and in this way ensure that the church continues to create new wineskins to hold the new wine which God yearns to pour out for us all.

Chapter 22
"God's Bees": Carmelite Spirituality in the Inner Space

Let us begin by looking at the supposed origins of the Carmelite order which are twofold and involve both legend and documented history.

At the time of the foundation of the Carmelite order, in the thirteenth century, there was something of a competition among the emergent monastic movements to trace their particular spirituality as far back as possible. Hence, according to the legend they composed for themselves, the Carmelites claimed that the Prophet Elijah became the first Carmelite during his sojourn on Mount Carmel! This was the winning ticket in the competition. How would it be possible to trace the foundation of a monastic spiritual tradition earlier than this? If anyone doubted the truth of the legend, as well they might, they had only to go to St Peter's Rome where, in the gallery of the founders of the great religious institutes, Elijah stands among the famous founders of the more prominent religious orders. Surely Elijah would not appear among the founders of the religious orders if he had no right to be there!

But, of course, this visual "proof" with all the implied approval of the papacy, is nothing of the sort. Elijah appears in the gallery not because he actually founded the Carmelites, but because the Carmelites said that he did. This is a prime example of the ways in which the stories we tell ourselves about ourselves not only colour our view of the past and influence our actions in the present they direct the course of future events as well.

There are obvious additional problems with this legend. Elijah was a Jew and while there is much in the Jewish tradition which is contemplative and mystical it does not have an eremitical monastic or indeed mendicant tradition in the way that the Carmelites claimed for Elijah. It also assumes that long before Christ there was an *unbroken* chain of groups of contemplatives and mystics on or about

Mount Carmel who recognised Elijah as their founder, inspirer and leader. If this is true, as the legend assumes, then it must go on to explain how it is that the lengthy prophesies of Elijah which appear in the Bible do not mention any of this.

The legend cannot do this because there were, in fact, no such groups gathered around Elijah on Mount Carmel or anywhere else. Indeed, one of the main thrusts of his prophecies is that he was a lone voice crying, as it were, in a deserted wilderness of indifference. It was surely that, and his somewhat eccentric lifestyle that caused later generations of Jews at the time of Christ to make a connection between Elijah and John the Baptizer.

The legend was not however without purpose. It was simply to reject dependence on a specific founder, like a Benedict, a Francis or a Dominic and the possible temptation to create a cult of the personality around him. The legend had another advantage too because precisely in rejecting the notion that they had a specific founder the Carmelites could emphasise their view that their mode of religious life and the spirituality that accompanied it as a direct gift from God. By tracing their foundation to the time of Elijah, they also underscored the prophetic aspect of their life and ministry.

Like all legends this one quickly became mixed and muddled with documented history. The earliest documented accounts of what later became Carmelites show that there were indeed men living as hermits on Mount Carmel close to Elijah's well, not at the time of the prophet, but at the time of the crusades some eight hundred years ago.

These hermits seem to have had a chapel dedicated to Mary, the Mother of Jesus and in which they would gather (following the tradition of the earlier Desert fathers and mothers) once a week for prayer, praise and sacrament. Quite obviously the process of change from a band of hermits to a fully formed religious order did not happen all at once. The present Constitutions of the Carmelite order describe the basic steps in the process:

At the time of the crusades to the Holy Land, hermits settled in various places in Palestine. Some of these following the example of Elijah, a holy man and a lover of God and solitude, adopted a solitary lifestyle on Mount Carmel, near a spring called Elijah's fountain. In small cells of a beehive, they lived as God's bees, gathering the divine honey of spiritual consolation.

Later St Albert, Patriarch of Jerusalem, brought the hermits together, at their request, into a single "collegiums", he gave them a formula for living which expressed their own eremitical ideals (propositum) and reflected the spirit of the so-called pilgrimage to the Holy Land and of the early community in Jerusalem. Moved by their "love of the Holy Land", these hermits consecrated themselves in this land to the One who had paid for it by the shedding of his blood, in order that they might serve him, clothed in the habit of religious poverty, persevering in holy penance and forming a fraternal community.

This way of life was approved successively by Honorius III in 1226, by Gregory IX in 1229 and by innocent IV in 1245. In 1247, innocent IV approved it definitively as an authentic Rule of Life, amending it to suit western conditions. These adaptations became necessary when the Carmelites began to migrate to the west to escape persecution, and expressed a desire to lead a life "in which with the help of God, they would have the joy of working for their own salvation and that of their neighbour. As a result of the approval of the Rule by Innocent IV, the Carmelites placed themselves at the service of the church according to the common ideal of the mendicant orders…"[796] It was in these ways that the Carmelites sought to establish a spiritual, if not strictly historical, continuity between themselves and the "Sons of the prophets" and as these paragraphs make clear the foundation of the Order is found not in a person, nor in a book, but in a community of people. By taking Mary and Elijah as their models for inspiration, they were able to develop a unique identity and means of renewing their spirit. They helped them provide integration between the two great streams of the Carmelite tradition—contemplative and active; prayerful and prophetic, reflective and apostolic each of which led to ultimate union with God.

Indeed, the Rule of Carmel was understood to fulfil the school of the prophets and so the spirituality of Carmel (the order not the mountain!) has no difficulty in developing the basic elements drawn from its Biblical origins within an evangelical life of perfection. Henceforth it is in the light of Jesus Christ, and in dependence on him which is made apparent in the opening lines of the Carmelite Rule that the characteristics of Carmelite spirituality must be considered.

From the first, the Carmelites insisted that the chief and most important characteristic of their common life was a thirst to find Christ in silence and in solitude. They were attracted to the desert as the best place for divine encounter and in which prayer becomes a conversation occupying those who dwell there from morning to night: "Let each remain in his cell, or near it, meditating day

---

[796] Constitutions of the Order of Carmelites. At Last Accessed March 2004.

and night on the law of the Lord and watching in prayer."[797] The question posed here is this: can the climate of the interior life and prayer indicated here, be discovered in the Rule of Carmel and, if so, can it help us describe the elements of a distinctive Carmelite spirituality?

So sober is the text of the Rule of Mount Carmel, and so brief, that the answer would, at first sight, appear to be "No". But considered from within, the text becomes much more revealing.

The sobriety itself appears eminently characteristic of this spirit which imposed it. it is an immediate introduction to a spirituality freed from the letter and is utterly detached. The soul realises that it must sell all to acquire the pearl of great price; that the Kingdom of God alone matters.

Again, the sobriety is accompanied by liberation from every spirit of individualism. Just as "the brother hermits who live on Mount Carmel had recourse to the church in the person of the Patriarch of Jerusalem to obtain a Rule…so we see even now that the Rule requires the divine office to be recited according to the freely embraced regulations laid down by the Sovereign Pontiffs and the customs approved by the church".[798] What would men and women, fiercely devoted to spiritual liberty and accustomed to the breeze that comes from the desert, have to do with special forms and complicated methods of community life and the life of prayer? Instinctively they cling to what is most simple and ordinary because it is precisely the simple and ordinary that makes it possible to give themselves to the "one thing necessary". Of course, this does not mean that the principle of authority is disregarded or undermined. Rather it is affirmed, obedience is exacted, as well as silence, work and the renunciation of all property. But this is to be done in the spirit of the Gospels and is to be understood as a simple means to a simple and uniquely necessary end: union with God.

Thus, the Rule of Mount Carmel is extremely simple and supple, not only because everything in it is ordered and directed to a single end but also because it does not hesitate to make use of all means, according to the gentle and flexible leading of the Holy Spirit. For example: "You may…inasmuch as the Prior shall deem fitting…when it can be done conveniently…unless he be lawfully occupied in some other way…taking into account and consideration the age and needs of each one…when that may be done without too much trouble…unless obligated by sickness or the weakness of the body or by some other just cause to

---

[797] Rule of Mount Carmel. At Last Accessed March 2024.
[798] Rule of Mount Carmel.

break the fast, because necessity knows no law…"[799] Here there is nothing cut and dried, nothing narrowly literal but a simple and spiritual means of enabling the friar to advance in the path and power of the Absolute.

The Rule of Mount Carmel is not unaware that a life of union with God rests on the foundation and generous practice of renunciation. But it asks for a renunciation which "without stifling the soul will enable it to be aware of its poverty so that at that very instant it will turn to God."[800] Of course, no progress is possible without effort and so there is a virile note in every part of the Rule. With Job it repeats: "Man's life on earth is a temptation" and "Those who live piously on earth will suffer persecution." "Therefore, set about with all zeal to clothe yourself with the armour of God."[801] At this point, the Rule lists all the parts of the armour of god as described by St Paul and this reminds the modern reader that the Rule was made for "Crusaders" eager to place themselves at the service of their "Lord, Jesus Christ". Crusaders who were faithful to their spiritual ancestors: the desert solitaries whose heroic struggles with the flesh and the spirit were recorded by Cassian and others.

But the ascetic side of the Rule is tempered. Effort, renunciation, work and silence all appear as a means of stripping the soul of notions of "the self", they appear as means of freeing the soul so that as it becomes unhampered it may make even further progress along the path of spiritual union. All that the Rule of Mount Carmel offers along this path are a series of sign posts marked by an ever-deepening longing for God. The path does not consist of a series of didactic lessons, or formulas, or even techniques in study and in prayer. All it offers is a growing dependence of the friar on Jesus Christ, and a dependence which is, largely unaided.

This being the case, we might expect that the Rule of Mount Carmel would have a great deal to say about the person and work and salvation to be found in Christ. But it does not. This is one of the great mysteries of Carmelite life and spirituality. It is not easy to grasp a hidden, half-formulated spiritual reality which is at the same time truly central and profoundly operative.

Beyond doubt there are other monastic Rules and Christian spiritualities in which Christ's role is much more prominent; here is the model, the exemplar and his life which must be imitated, but the Carmelites claim that as contemplatives

---

[799] Rule of Mount Carmel.
[800] Francios De Sainte Marie (1949) *The Rule and Spirit of Carmel* Edition du Seuil. P88.
[801] Op cit Rule of Mount Carmel.

their Rule and mode of living could never be like that. If it is a question of always looking to Christ, it is also more a question of uniting oneself with him and living by him. Christ, who is the way to the Father becomes by this fact the milieu in which Carmelite contemplation develops and the method it uses. In their own understanding the Rule of Mount Carmel *is* Christ and that the written document is only a statement to that effect.

If the Rule of Mount Carmel and Carmelite spirituality is orientated towards Christ, it is also directed and orientated towards the Blessed Virgin Mary. From the time of their first Prior-General, St Brocard, the Carmelites were known as "Brothers of Our Lady of Mount Carmel", so devotion to Our Lady is seen to be one of the distinctive signs of their spirituality and yet the Rule never once mentions Our Lady by name. Why is this? I think it is because in Carmelite theology anything that can be said about Christ can, *mutatis mutandis*, be said about Our Lady and to do so would be mere repetition.

Hence Carmelite contemplative life advances by assimilation and union, much more than by images, examples and models. Preserving in all due proportion what they have said about Christ they repeat about Mary. If the Carmelites do not strive to imitate Mary's life, they do find themselves in deep harmony with her soul and it is in this sense that they may be said to be "completely Marian" and to lead a "Mary-form" life.

It is in this way that Mary becomes, for the Carmelite, not just the Mother of Jesus, but his or her own mother too. That is, Mary represents and expresses the soul's essential attitude before God. She not only sums up the whole of the Old Testament, she represents all humankind. Hers is the soul thirsting for God, longing for him, hoping for union with him. All her strength and all her faculties are turned towards him so that she may receive his communications receive him; respond to him and so fully live by him. Mary is also the place of the divine response, of the divine coming into the world. In Mary, all humankind becomes conscious of God's desire and his fully efficacious will to communicate himself to his creatures. Mary is the place of this meeting; better still, she is the temple in which is consummated God's engagement with human beings, the hidden sanctuary in which the Spouse is united with his bride, and the desert which blossoms in the dew of God.

For Carmelite, spirituality Mary is pure reference to God and to the life of God in the sense that Elijah spoke to Elias: "*As the Lord lives and as your soul lives*". So, from the moment of her Immaculate Conception Mary's soul had no other life than God, no other end than to know him and love him purely and without admixture in order to accomplish in her and through her, his divine will. Carmelites find in Mary the fullness of a spirit which they claim as their own: "The beauty of Carmel will be given to you."[802] Reciprocally, Mary's soul is said connected with Carmel in the sense that she is a daughter of David according to the flesh and the daughter of the prophets according to the spirit. In the Gospel of Luke, Mary is repeatedly said to "ponder" the events of which she is part. Carmelites find in this a mirror for their perpetual meditation on the law of the Lord. So, in order for a Carmelite to advance along the path towards union with God, he or she must intensify their virginal simplicity and pure reference to God. For the Carmelite where God is the end, Mary is the means to mystical union.

So, the reason why the Rule of Mount Carmel does not mention Our Lady is clear. Carmel seeks to gaze upon God and to love him with mind, body, spirit and emotion. What Mary represents is the soul itself. As the soul is united to Christ, so Carmel is hidden in Mary.

This mystical and filial intuition was confirmed in the history of the Order in the centuries that followed. In a critical point in their history, Our Lady was said to appear to St Simon Stock holding in her hand the scapular of the Order and she said: "This is the privilege that I give you and all Carmel's children. Whoever dies clothed with this habit will be saved."[803] In this way, she is said to have extended, in visible form, her special protection over the order which has always called itself her own. Marian appearances occur again in the lives of some of the greatest teachers and saints of the order; St Albert, St Andrew Corsini, St Peter Thomas, St Teresa of Avila, St John of the Cross, St Teresa of the Child Jesus, to name but six. It seems that at Carmel there can be no great servant of God who is not sustained and guided by Mary. Similarly, and as perhaps we might expect, Carmelite authors multiply works which tighten the already close bonds between Carmel and Our Lady.

The Rule that keeps Carmelite spirituality along interior and contemplative lines and gives it its evangelical and Marian character, equally confirms it active apostolate which is traced to the founding legend of Elijah himself. If he pronounced the sentence on which Carmelite contemplation is based: "He lives before whom I am," he also said, "I am consumed with zeal for the Lord of hosts."

---

[802] Isa. 35; 2.
[803] *Viridarium* in "*Speculum Carm.*" 599.

Within limits suitable to the Order, the Rule of Mount Carmel faithfully maintains this apostolic note in its spirituality. The only reason for which a Carmelite is allowed to interrupt his or her meditation on the law of the lord, and leave for a time the silence and recollected solitude of the cell is the salvation of souls. This orientation is clearly marked in the Rule and explains why the Order has often been classified among the mendicants devoted to the care of souls.

It is, in my view, more properly to be classified (if that is an appropriate task at all) among the so-called mixed orders because Carmelites are orientated *both* to contemplation and to action. So, whatever the dangers and attractions of the active apostolate might be, its spirituality will never be that of an exclusively contemplative order. When Carmelites are asked to preach, give missions or undertake good works the invitation will never be refused on the grounds that their vocation is purely contemplative.

On the other hand, contemplation does lie at the heart of Carmel. It is its *raison d'être*, its distinguishing mark and, historically it has been its protection. If there must be some interruption of contemplation by means of the active apostolates as soon as this work is done the Carmelite must quickly return to the primary and direct object of his vocation.

In the "*Arrow of Fire*", one Nicholas the Frenchman recalls with vigour the Carmelite contemplative tradition which he believed to be endangered. Adding example to words, he withdrew to a hermitage. In his turn, Raoul the German who succeeded him, did exactly the same thing. Indeed, the General Chapter of the Order meeting at Montpelier in 1287 took various measures to maintain the order as "the citadel of contemplation". Retreat and solitude were recommended in every constitution in such a way that the active apostolate follow from the contemplative life, as its fruit, and not the other way about.

It was this combination which enabled the order to successfully integrate in the social and intellectual life of Western Europe in the thirteenth century and Paul Marie de la Croix, himself a Carmelite, has argued that, "Had Carmel remained truly faithful to its central precepts of prayer, recollection and a life of union with God and at the same time not given up its apostolate, no Teresian reforms might have been necessary. Perhaps there is no better way than this of showing how essential to Carmelite spirituality is this priority of contemplation over action which alone makes possible the preservation intact of its ideal. For its restoration Saint Teresa 'will live alone with the Alone' and will establish her daughters in strict cloister; and Saint John of the Cross, the great doctor of the hidden life with God, will sacrifice his life. Nothing less than the genius, the efforts, the sufferings of these two great saints was needed so that the pure spirit of its origins could flourish once again in the order of the Blessed Virgin Mary of Mount Carmel."[804] Yet Carmel did reach the period of its reform, and reform was necessary. To consider this reform apart from the whole Carmelite tradition is to fail to link the reformers with their own spiritual family. When this has been attempted, in the more popular and pious accounts of the lives of St Teresa and St John, the result is an incomplete account of Carmelite spirituality and a wholly erroneous understanding of the reform itself. The power of the genius of both St Teresa and St John, made fruitful by their personal holiness, cannot be denied and the light and penetration they gave Carmel can be seen to this day.

Equipped and enabled by God at a moment which was both critical and propitious, they brought Carmel back to its roots—but they did not give it life. Carmel existed before their reforms and one of its chief branches still owes nothing to these saints and yet has continued to flourish.

In view of their relative historical closeness to us, Saints. Teresa and John of the Cross seem alone to represent Carmel and it is now almost impossible for us to think of the Carmelites without simultaneously thinking about them. Certainly, their role cannot be underestimated but they *must be* situated in the line of spiritual men and women who throughout the centuries have formed Carmel. After all, St Teresa seems to say as much in Chapter 13 of *"The Way of Perfection"*:

"The manner of life which we propose is not merely that of religious women; it is more like that of hermits. Let us remind ourselves of our holy fathers, those hermits who in bygone days whose life we long to imitate."[805] Here Teresa is reminding her fellow religious of the tradition to which she longs for them to return. It is, she thinks, a tradition so richly alive, so full of the Spirit of God, that it is essential that they return to it if they are to create something new: *"nova et vetera"*. This, in turn, seems to resonate with the Psalmist's understanding: "When you send your spirit they are created and you renew the face of the

---

[804] Paul Marie de la Croix OCD "Carmelite Spirituality" http://etn.com/library/SPIRIT/CARMSPIR.TXT p14 Last Accessed March 2024.
[805] St Teresa of Avila. *"The Way of Perfection"* Chapter 13. *The Complete Works of St Teresa of Avila* Volume 2. Trans and ed E Allison Peers. From the Critical Edition of P Silvero de sante Teresa, CD. London and New York. Burns & Oates.

earth."[806] The influence of St Teresa on Carmel's spirituality greatly differs from that of St John of the Cross because of the differences in their personality and temperament and because of the very different roles they came to play. Yet they complimented each other perfectly.

That St Teresa was first and foremost a contemplative is axiomatic and it is in fact in the domain of prayer and the mystical life that she deepened and enriched not only Carmelite spirituality but, through them, the whole of western Christendom. But her personality and role went much further than this because it was with her whole being that she gave herself to a life of union with God. Striping herself of all things without repudiating any of them, it is the totality of her aspirations, her heart, her strength and her life that she willed to make subject to God. So, it is not only the understanding of religious life but also of spiritual life that was renewed and refreshed first in St Teresa herself and then in Carmel of which she was the mother and the reformer.

St Teresa's stark realism is so deep and so authentic that, even unconsciously, she strove to make an organic whole and a living unity of the different parts of her existence. Prayer is the source of the life and movement of this organic whole; it is the principle of unitive transformation. But it only attains its end if, and only if, it is able to orientate all the different parts of religious life towards the same end and to give some directive idea to every aspect of daily life and even to the most mundane forms of activity.

St Teresa's contributions to Carmelite spirituality are not found in her writings alone (profound and revealing as these might be) for they were never anything more than occasional pieces of composition which recorded the action of God in her soul and in her life. Her contributions are to be discovered and examined first in her work as a reformer because; in a certain sense she embodied Carmel in her own life. That is not to imply that she pointed her ideal in a new direction but rather that she strongly impressed it with the imprint of her own genius. So, it is in the Constitutions and in the form of religious life that she asked her fellow religious sisters to follow, no less than in her writings, that we should look for the elements which henceforth were to characterise Carmel's spirituality.

In this, Saint Teresa's influence is sharply distinguished from that of St John of the Cross. There can be no doubt, as we shall see, that he was, from the outset,

---

[806] Ps.104:30 (New International Version).

won to the cause of reform. Moreover, he remained a Carmelite only on the condition that the reform be carried out! But even though he worked heroically for its success, he is pre-eminent because it was in this setting that he achieved perfect spiritual liberty, and complete mystical development. While St Teresa first reconstructed the Carmelite heritage by returning the sisters to their foundations and thereby created a climate for the spiritual life, St John of the Cross systematised its principles and described the riches that would follow from what Teresa had begun.

St Teresa's realism meant that she understood that Carmelite life had to be reconsidered as a function of contemplation and that any reform had to serve and encourage it even in the physical circumstances in which the members of the Order lived. Strict enclosure (for the sisters), silence, work in solitude must be restored so that union with God could develop in the most favourable surroundings. But there is equally no doubt that St Teresa had her own unique way of understanding the contemplative life but it was conducted only within the boundaries of Carmelite spirituality, so that the form of life that she restored appears, in the light of her experience, to be the best adapted to the experience and aspirations of other contemplative souls.

It is sometimes claimed, in the more popular and pious modern versions of St Teresa's life theology and works, that she was a feminist thinker. This is simply not the case and would not have understood such a concept. Her thinking about union with God suggests, rather that while the end in view must be the same for both men and women there is no reason at all why it should not be approached differently in order that the unique circumstances of an individual's life and experience be offered to God to the fullest possible extent. So, beginning with a conviction and a deep contemplative and mystical experience, she considers each separate detail of the religious life not only as a function of the much sought after goal but also in terms of what is unique to women. So it was that she recommended moderation, coupled with a penetrating psychology and a profound wisdom—characteristics which were enshrined in the Constitutions of her many foundations.

Above all, St Teresa had no tolerance for vague abstraction. Contemplation had no purpose unless it could become an integral part of the tiniest acts of life. An intimate bond united prayer and life, morality and mysticism, exterior conduct and interior union with God. In contemplative and religious life, as she understood and organised it, an organic unity was realised, not by outward pressure but by an inner principle which was both gentle and strong: love. The soul that contemplates must long to give itself to Him whom it loves. It must long to be one with Him and serve him at the expense of self. If these characteristics are uniquely feminist so, be it, but my own view is that they are, rather, the marks of an organic unity between the individual and God—according to the norms of a much higher wisdom. As Leepe has observed:

"Teresa was able to resolve with classic good sense, let us say Catholic good sense, two delicate problems: that of the requirements of union with God and the requirements of human nature; that of the relations between the framework in which is inserted common religious life and the personal development of the mystical life. If the asceticism which she practised, and on whose necessity she insisted, was always intransigent, it was also always reasonable. The humble realities of life here below are the foundation on which one must build in order that the spirit may ascend to God. Progress is conditioned by these foundations, just as the life of a tree is determined by its root, to neglect the first, to destroy or to paralyse the second would be fatal."[807] It is essentially by prayer that St Teresa believed that this higher wisdom would reign in the soul and would provide organic unity. Everyone knows that Teresa was the great mistress of prayer and on this capital point her contribution is as traditional as it is original. It is traditional because, like all the spiritual men and women who preceded her, St Teresa wanted to orientate contemplatives towards the summits of union with God. She thought that they would find these results and this grace in prayer because God and the soul, although working on separate plains, unite their efforts in prayer. It is traditional too in that, like her predecessors she did not think that the contemplative ideal of transforming union is extraordinary. She believed that it was the integral fullness of spiritual life. So, she aspired to it with humility because infused contemplation always remains an absolutely gratuitous divine gift.

At the same time, Teresa showed her originality in not being satisfied with assigning this goal to the contemplative life; she pointed out the paths that point and lead to this goal. Her teaching was marked by a wealth of experience and a psychological depth that have rarely, if ever, been equalled, as well as a by a singularly noble and profound conception of a life of union with God.

---

[807] M. Leppe cited in De La Croix p17.

As Gabriel De Santé-Marie-Madeline has it; "To love is to surrender one's self without reserve. This means to surrender one's will in such a way to the divine will, however crucifying it may be, that one finds joy in suffering when this is pleasing to the Beloved; and this intense love is a call for His presence. The soul enraptured by God tends spontaneously to possess Him. The ideal of perfect donation corresponds quite naturally in her doctrine with the desire for mystical union. God must be generous to the generous soul…The soul's total gift calls for the total gift of God."[808] In prayer, as Teresa experienced it and as she taught her Carmelite sisters, Christ's position id dominant. This is one of the original points of her spirituality. Admittedly, before her reforms Christ's presence was implicit and active in every part of Carmel's spiritual life but his role was, somewhat surprisingly perhaps, not sharply defined. St Teresa brought Christ to the fore as never before:

"The method of prayer by which all must begin, continue and end, consists in keeping one's self in the company of the saviour."[809] Few theological statements could be clearer than that.

Since Teresa gave such an important place to Christ in prayer, it is essential to understand what he meant to her and the best way of doing that it to trace something of her spiritual evolution to this point. Christ was, quite simply everything to Teresa. She cherished him with the tenderness of a mother, the respect of a daughter and the excitement of a young lover. But in this love, there is "nothing that is not spiritual".[810] In fact, "the spiritual delights that the Lord grants are a thousand leagues apart from the satisfactions enjoyed by two spouses. Here love is united with love."[811] If Christ was able to raise Teresa above the information of the senses, while keeping alive her powers of loving, it is because she realised that he is the eternal, the transcendent. It is also because she understood in very stark terms the ways in which he is also the Absolute, the Infinite, fully a person *and* fully God. It is precisely because God in Christ is both God and Man that, for Teresa, he is able to respond to her human love with divine love. If some people find that the Chalcedonian formula is an obstacle to

---

[808] Gabriel De Sante-Marie-Madeline: "Carmelites". Dictionary of Spirituality. Col 197.
[809] Op cit The Complete Works of St Teresa of Avila Volume 1. "*Life*" Chapter 12.
[810] Op cir The Complete St Teresa of Avila Volume 2: "*Interior Castle*" Fifth Dwelling. Chapter 4.
[811] Ibid.

a relationship with Christ it is because, Teresa argued, that they do not think of him as they should:

"The humanity of Christ could not fail to help the Blessed Virgin, she was too firmly fixed in the faith, and she knew that Jesus was both God and man. The name of Jesus is constantly on St, Paul's lips. I have studied the ways of several great contemplative saints: St, Francis of Assisi, St Anthony of Padua, St Bernard, St Catherine of Siena—and I find that they travelled along no other road."[812] So, Teresa's decision was made. On this road, there are so many advantages of love and faith, that she offered her Carmelite sisters the humanity of Jesus as the path *par excellence* and the ordinary way for all.[813] Yet the evidence of Christ's role in Teresa's prayer is no less revealing than the position he holds. At the beginning, Teresa kept Christ before her eyes, but gradually she began to meditate on the mystery of his person. Soon she saw him most of all as a guide and a loving companion on her journey of faith; then Jesus became the way for her, the path to the father, the light which enlightens everyone full of grace and truth.[814] Teresa united herself to God by the word made flesh. Finally, with Christ's help, Teresa was led to the Blessed Trinity whose importance thereafter never ceased to increase in her interior life. From this we must not, I think, conclude that Jesus was then relegated to a secondary place but rather that he was no longer seen in quite the same perspective. He continued to be man who, being God, reveals God to all people who will listen to him and contemplate him. But he is, above all the Incarnate Word with whom the soul must be united, in order to make some return through him to the father in the unity of the Holy Spirit. This was the way Christ led Teresa to her understanding of the Trinity. He taught her to be aware of God as her last end, absolute omnipotence, the answer to the call of her whole being. He led her to the heart of the divine mystery which is the origin and goal of all Christian living and especially of its mystical forms. It is true that Christ's role, indispensable though it is,[815] is apparently less visible in certain mystics who seem lost in divine darkness; but in St Teresa's teaching he shines a brilliant light from which Carmelite spirituality has always benefitted. Teresa's first intention was merely to found a monastery where she and her fellow Carmelite sisters could, with the help of a more strict enclosure

---

[812] Op cit *Life*. 22.
[813] Op cit *Interior Castle*. Sixth dwelling. Chapter 7.
[814] John 1:14.
[815] John 14:6.

and a more austere life, keep their vows more faithfully. Later, realising the vast needs of the church (especially in countering emergent Protestantism which she regarded as a heresy) and desiring to assist those who were fighting for her, she went still further, indeed as far as it was possible to go. In strengthening the bonds which united her to Jesus Christ and his church, Teresa acted according to the most Orthodox practices and according to the Carmelite Rule. It is to her understanding of the church that we must now give our attention.

It is, as we might by now expect, with Jesus Christ that St Teresa began her deep understanding of the reality of the church. Of course, her submission to the church had always been completely loyal and even fervently joyous and this was to remain until her death. With her last breath she cried, "*I am a daughter of the church.*" Here she was referring not only to the visible church of traditional Spanish Catholicism that was so deeply rooted and grounded in her soul, but above all to Christ as *the* church, militant in his humanity and triumphant in his divinity.

This view of the church and the absolute confidence she placed in it were possible only because of her mystical experiences of Christ as her Beloved. To Teresa, the church is not only an intensely vital reality, it is also an institution established on dogmatic foundations that are sure, certain and rich. It is Christ as the church who asks that our love be real and active and so it follows that the response of divine love never ceases to grow in ever widening concentric circles, just as waves move outward from the centre. Fraternal and supernatural charity is directed first of all to those who live in the monastery, then with the constantly renewed fervour and strength it is transformed into a love for every Christian soul, the whole of Christ's church.

"A soul who aspires to become the Spouse of Christ himself…cannot allow itself a sluggard's rest. The redemptive God gives his life and self-giving love to the soul who gives herself to him".[816] For Teresa, Christ is always at the centre of the church because the church is Christ. Hence contemplation of Christ in his Church is the first practice of virtue, fidelity to the Rule, renunciation of the self and the acceptance of the cross. Then she sees the church as a form of embodied prayer, love in act and an act of love. The more advanced souls become in contemplative prayer, the more they are concerned with the needs of others, especially with the needs of other souls. "With the passage of time…desire grows

---

[816] Op cit *Interior Castle* Sixth Dwelling Chapter 7.

to contribute to the good of souls…and to the exaltation of the church."[817] So it is that the soul must first be concerned about itself as if it and God were alone on the earth. Otherwise, the soul would lose itself in the world. When it is a little more advanced, its faculties being more at rest and accustomed to contemplation, God ripens the fruits in the garden of the soul so that it can draw strength from them. This is, according to Teresa, what god wants of everyone. However, God does not want a distribution of the fruits unless and until the soul in which they have been grown has first been strengthened by them. Otherwise, those who receive the fruits will only taste a morsel of them and not be nourished and fed by them. Indeed, they may even die of hunger.

To speak more plainly, it is only when the soul has attained to mystical union, and God has taken possession of the very depths of the soul that good works are required. Therefore, to engage in any active apostolate the soul must love, love without any reserve, love so much that it gives itself entirely to God. Once again it is at this point that Teresa can be understood to have completely renewed the spirit of her Order and did so to establish two new purposes, one subordinate to the other: contemplation which unites the soul with God and reveals the infinite value of every human soul, which then flows out into an active apostolate.

These are the major contributions that Teresa made to Carmelite spirituality; she rethought and reformed the whole contemplative life in terms of the original Carmelite ideal. She renewed and deepened their life of prayer founded on Christ. She experienced and described the journey of faith in all its stages and wrote about the highest states of pure mysticism. She held broad and safe views of the church which, she believed, would preserve it against external threat and internal dissent. She poured out all these things in a spirit of freedom, fervour and balance and, despite the appalling political and ecclesiastical opposition she faced, in a spirit of expansive and undisturbed joy. So, we see why she continues to be the most important figure in the development of Carmelite spirituality and why too she continues to attract souls to Christ. It may appropriately be said of her, as of the spouse on the Song of Songs, "Draw me and I will run after you".[818] Yet Carmelite spirituality owes just as much to St John of the Cross. At first, sight both his audience and his influence seem to be somewhat restricted. Unlike Teresa, for example, he deliberately did not address himself to "…certain persons of our holy religion of the primitives of Mount Carmel, men and women,

---

[817] Op cit The Complete Works St Teresa of Avila Volume 3. *"Foundations"* 1.
[818] Song of Songs 1:3.

who by the grace of God are on the pathway of this mount…They are indeed already detached from the things of this life and will better understand this doctrine of the detached spirit."[819] Nevertheless, history suggests that the saint's influence was not limited and that it increased and went far beyond the walls of Carmel. No doubt this is to be explained by the fact that St John of the Cross pursued a single objective with clarity of vision that was equalled only by the rigour of his teaching and the heroic fixity of a will focussed on God. What did he actually ask? Nothing else than to go as far as divine union in transforming love. And what does he teach? Nothing else than the spiritual attitude necessary for one who would arrive promptly at the summit of the Mount of Perfection. Now "whatever may be the mountain" in our life, and whatever form it may take, there is one straight path leading to the summit and this is the way which he indicated to souls. Thus, a soul, who is resolved to advance towards sanctity and feels inwardly attracted to St John's abrupt and direct method, will find precious help in this sure and experienced guide.

St John considers the religious life in its essential and complimentary aspects. First, he discusses the work of detachment in a Christian advancing towards god. Then he examines God's direct action in the soul and the spiritual attitude of the person receiving it. He then speaks of the joys and splendours of divine union. In other words, his work embraces the whole question of the transformation of our lives and our way of being under the influence of the Spirit of God.

St John's theology is unique because of its richness and because of his psychological as well as mystical insights, drawn from his own experience. He goes beyond mere speculation because he wants to persuade souls to make the journey along the path to divine union and to show them its many treasures. To do this he makes use of a very rare poetic gift which enables him to communicate the truths he has received and the living flame of his love for God. It is at this point that two questions arise that we must now consider in considerable detail. They are: 1. which path leads to the Summit of Perfection? And 2 how is the soul transformed by the Spirit of Love into full union with God?

---

[819] St John of the Cross: Prologue to *"The Ascent of Mount Carmel"* 1. 6. In *The Collected Works of St John of the Cross*. (1979) Trans. Kieran Kavanaugh OCD and Otilio Rodriguez Ocd with and iNtroduction by Kieran Kavanaugh OCD. Washington DC. Institute of Carmelite Studies. ICS Publications.

With the whole tradition of Carmel and the Gospel of John to support him, John of the Cross unhesitatingly answers that Christ is the way to be followed, the truth to be told and the life to be lived, because Christ is the Word made flesh that dwells among us full of grace and truth. At Carmel, the soul always draws strength from the divine Word. Of course, this means the person and work of Jesus, but it also means the Old and New testaments, for Carmel's roots are deeply fixed in Scripture. John always kept the Bible with him, no matter where he went or where he was—even in prison. He never ceased to meditate upon it. In it, he searched not only for knowledge of revelation but he believed that he could find in its pages the laws that always govern the dealings of the Holy Spirit with human beings. He believed that scripture alone is the rule and measure of progress in interior life and that it enlarges one's own experience, containing as it does innumerable examples from the past.

But John had a special fondness for the Gospels. In truth, "God, who at sundry times and in diverse manners spoke in times past to the fathers by the prophets, last of all in these days has spoken to us by his Son" (Heb.1:1–2) and so John declares that "God spoke but a single word and that word is his Son." And on another occasion, he said: "God has told us everything in his Son; look well at him and you will find everything."[820] St John's teaching, like his life was based on the Gospels. He placed himself before Christ in the Gospels and absorbed the teaching he found there. It is true that his speculative study of the spiritual life seems, at times, not to be Christocentric, but nevertheless he repeatedly affirms that no union with God is possible except in Christ, and this is true both of faith (which is adhesion to God in Christ) and of life. To reach Christ, we must make Christ our beginning, our model and our end. St John thought that because of the incarnation it was possible not only for Christians to be Christ-like but, in practical ways to act like Christ and so in time become, as it were, Christ to others:

"Of what use is this life if it does not give us an opportunity of acting like Christ?" Christ and he crucified is the synthesis of his whole doctrine. "Let Christ crucified alone be enough for you; with him suffer, with him rejoice, never suffer or rejoice without him."[821] On the face of it, this looks very simple and straight forward and almost a definition of what it is to be a Christian, but of course it is

---

[820] Op cit Collected Works of St John of the Cross: *Ascent of Mount Carmel* Book 2 Chapters 7 and 22.
[821] Ibid.

not! For St John it is the highest wisdom possible in this life and takes an eternity to properly understand:

"The soul, being henceforth raised up…above all things, may now make use of nothing to help it or to rise higher, except the Word, the Spouse himself."[822] The spiritual life is nothing less than an immense love of extreme poverty and suffering for the sake of the beloved: "To love is not to experience great things; it is to know great poverty and suffering for the loved one", that is to say, "for our great God crucified and humbled."[823] Renunciation and love encapsulates St John's Christology. Thus, it is within this framework that we must consider the rest of St John's teaching. The monastic virtue of detachment in all things comes about only through attachment to Christ. Renunciation is the practical expression of love. "That you may possess all things, seek to possess nothing." "Desire to be detached from all things, empty and poor for Christ's sake."[824] St John of the Cross spoke of this renunciation and love in a way that no one had employed before and his words continue to have a singular strength. On the path up the mountain, the soul will meet and be tempted by false goods of many kinds. One by one they must be confronted, rejected, conquered and defeated. No-being and nothingness is to be preferred to them. Faced successively with temporal advantages and intellectual riches, virtues of the soul, graces, finally self—the soul must give the same answer: Nothing, nothing, nothing, nothing, and nothing. This is a road that human nature cannot travel. St John of the Cross knows this well so he draws the strength needed for detachment from an impassioned attachment to Christ:

"Do you want to be perfect? Then draw near to Christ be meekness and humility, then follow in his footsteps to Calvary and the Holy Sepulchre."[825] "If a man resolves to carry his cross for God's sake, he will find great refreshment and much sweetness and this will enable him to travel along this road, detached from all things and desiring nothing."[826] To follow Christ does not mean, according to St John of the Cross, that we must in any way withdraw ourselves

---

[822] Op cit Collected Works Maxim 209.

[823] Op cit Collected Works Maxim 235.

[824] Op cit Cllected Works of St John of the Cross *Ascent of Mount Carmel* Book 1 Chapter 13.

[825] Op cit Collected Works of St John of the Cross: *Spiritual Sentences* 176.

[826] Op cit Collected Works of St John of the Cross *Ascent of Mount Carmel* Book 2 Chapter 7.

from a system of human values or deny them by a renunciation of mind and senses. What he asks is that these values be used according to right order: the senses are to pass judgement on things of sense; the intellect is to appreciate things intellectual.

It is only when a person wishes to attain to God and be united with him, that these things must be renounced for the sake of the faith that is henceforth the only source of light in the dark night of the soul, the only right path for the divine quest.

In two of his works, he described the itinerary of the soul journeying towards the summit of divine union long the paths of renunciation; "*The Ascent of Mount Carmel*" and "*The Dark Night*". The first stresses the work of the soul while the second insists on the divine initiative.

St John of the Cross uses the metaphor of the dark night to describe the work that is first accomplished in the sensible part of a person, this is the active and passive night of the senses; then in the spiritual part, this is the active and passive night of the spirit. Here night is a symbol of the renunciation of things, a renunciation that is either voluntarily assumed or passively endured. The necessary role of the theological virtues is evident in the purification of the soul's spiritual faculties; intelligence is purified by faith, memory by hope and will by charity.

The light cast upon the theological virtues, and especially on faith, is one of the most important aspects of St John's teaching and, because of its universal value, goes far beyond the limits of the Carmelite spirituality of which he was part and inherited. What St John is looking for, I think, is the path that leads quickly and quietly and surely to the summit of the mount of perfection and therefore to union with God. From this point of view, the place he gives to faith is better understood. Its mission is to purify the soul's vision of God.

In fact, it alone can remove whatever acts as an obstacle or screen to the possession of God and enable us to see things truthfully. This is because, for St John faith is an interior light derived from the light of God which illumines all things according to his greater light and helps us to glimpse them as he fully sees them.

There are two reasons why this light derived from God is a light of shadows and glimpses. Faith must cleanse the intellect of notions that are simply human and are in no way worthy of God:

"How, in fact, can the divine being be grasped by human intelligence? What man can feel and know about God is infinitely removed from what He is…there is no communication or essential likeness between God and creatures, but there is an infinite distance between his nature and theirs."[827] This affirmation of absolute divine transcendence, as well as the consequences that follow from it, is a keystone of the spirituality of St John of the Cross and of the Carmelites ever since. But if God is infinitely beyond our reason and intelligence the soul cannot "go to Him unless she spares no effort to deny and refuse her natural as well as supernatural knowledge".[828] For the human intelligence must enter into this night. There is another reason why faith is a light of shadows and glimpses; it permits truth to be grasped only in darkness. Faith is a path well suited for union with God but this union is granted only in a mirror and darkly. Yet St John will sing its praises because "even though it be night" it enables us to know God and to embrace him in the darkness. "I know well the fountains which rise and flee though of the night."[829] The grasp of the mystery of God by means of faith is limited only by our generosity. A faith freed from every image, from every representation will give us God wholly and fully. "The soul strays far from the road leading to divine union when it leans too much on its own understandings…not knowing how to release or detach itself from it.[830] So it is that, "The soul must empty itself of all that is within its competency…and remain always detached and in darkness, leaning on obscure faith and taking it for its light and guide and not trusting to anything it understands, tastes, feels or imagines."[831] St John suggests that this faith should be especially exercised at times of prayer and insists on the necessity of making the journey from discursive meditation to "the obscure, general, and loving" contemplation of the mystery of God.[832] It is plain that the faith he has in mind is not theoretical or abstract, but rich in love; a living and lively faith. Here two questions arise. Where does this love come from? How is it strengthened in us?

---

[827] Op cit Collected Works of St John of the Cross The Ascent of Mount Carmel Book 2 Chapter 8.

[828] Op cit Collected Works of St John of the Cross The Ascent of Mount Carmel. Book 3 Chapter 2.

[829] Mystical Poems. In Collected Works.

[830] The Ascent of Mount Carmel Book 2 Chapter 4.

[831] Ibid.

[832] The Ascent of Mount Carmel Book 2. Chapter 13.

It is in attempting to answer these questions that St John of the Cross achieved a magnificent synthesis between the negative and obscure mysticism of Pseudo-Dionysius (Denis the Areopagite) with the teaching that rightly gives priority to the place of Christ in the spiritual life. At no instant does St John of the Cross forget that Christ is "the author and finisher of our faith" (Heb. 12:2). Christ gives us faith and he is the first to benefit from the gift. When the eyes of the soul are fixed on Christ, the Incarnate Word of god, faith enables them to discover him as he is in the mystery of his divine and human being. Before addressing the divine person of the Trinity and acquiring a general, obscure and confused knowledge of God, faith turns first to Christ and through faith in him the soul is, in a certain sense, made like him: "All the wisdom of God which is the Son of God is communicated to the soul in faith."[833] To attain to God it is, therefore, essential to look with eyes illumined by faith *"fe illustratisima"* upon him who is the way: "If you look on him closely, you will find in him all things…You will find in him the wisdom of the marvels of God, as my Apostle said; In the Son of God are all the treasures of wisdom and knowledge of God."[834] Christ considered in faith becomes the door that introduces us into the divine life and its Trinitarian exchanges. To St John of the Cross, as well as to the writer of the Letter to the Hebrews, Christ is at one and the same time the author and finisher of our faith.

The path followed by St John of the Cross in the purification of the intelligence by faith resembles that taken by him in the purification of the memory by hope:

"As to hope, there is no doubt that it renders the memory empty and brings darkness over it as to things in this life and the next; for hope is ever concerned about things not yet possessed, if they were already possessed there would be no place for hope."[835] And in the purification of the will by charity:

"Charity creates an absolute void in the will inasmuch as it obliges us to love God above all things. This can only take place when our affection for things is centred wholly on God." For this reason, Christ says in St Luke: "He who does not renounce all that he possesses cannot be my disciple."

For when the soul is detached from all things and has emptied and detached itself…which is all that the soul can do on its part…then it is impossible that God

---

[833] *The Ascent of Mount Carmel* Book 2. Chapter 9.

[834] *The Ascent of Mount Carmel* Book 1. Chapter 22.

[835] *The Ascent of Mount Carmel* Book 2. Chapter 6.

will not perform His part which is to communicate Himself to it, at least in secret and in silence.

"It is more impossible that the sun should fail to shine in a serene and unclouded sky. For the sun, when it rises in the early morning and shines into your house, will enter if you open the shutter, even so will God, who keeps Israel and slumbers not (Ps.120:4), still less sleeps, enter the soul that is empty and fill it with divine blessings."[836] For St John of the Cross then, union *with* God is the transformation of the soul *in* God, *by* the Spirit of Love. In this way from the very beginning, the religious life is seen to be placed under the motion of the Spirit of Love. Christ does not cease to act in the soul by his Spirit. This spirit purifies the soul along the paths ascending the mountain, detaches the soul during the trials and the nights, until it reaches the sunlit summit where the soul is filled with the light and the love of God himself. Although the soul was not aware of it during the journey, it was the influence of the Spirit that directed it and carried it toward the central heights. On reaching the peak, the soul perceives and knows itself to be entirely submissive to divine inspiration. In short, for St John of the Cross, the Holy Spirit, the Spirit of Jesus, is the great artisan of the religious life. He is the master of the union of the soul with the Word as its Spouse.

Although it is not necessary to have attained to mystical union rare indeed in with God in order to understand what St John now has to say about life on top of the mountain, it is, I think, necessary to have some little experience of the secret action of the Holy Spirit in our lives. This is surely a common experience of all Christians. When we are aware of that experience actions, symbols, sights, sounds and words are profoundly eloquent.

For those who lack this experience, or who are as yet not conscious of it, these same words and symbols might fail to reveal the deep continuity of the action of the Holy Spirit and the unity that characterises a life wholly marked with his seal. No doubt, this unity can be explained, when the same image of divine action that was proposed by St John of the Cross in *"The Ascent"* is repeated in the first stanza of *"The Living Flame"*. And it is only when the soul can look back down the mountain tracks it has traversed and the transformation accomplished in it by the Spirit of multiple activities that it becomes keenly and clearly aware of the power and admirable effects of divine love:

---

[836] Cf *The Living Flame*. Book 3. Chapter 40. In Collected Works.

"It must be known that before this fire of love is introduced into the substance of the soul and is united with it, by means of perfect and complete purity and purgation, this flame, which is the Holy Spirit, wounds the soul, destroying and consuming in it the imperfections of evil habits. And this is the operation of the Holy Spirit, wherein he prepares it for divine union and the transformation of its substance in God through love.

For the same flame of love which afterwards is united with the soul and glorifies it, is that which formerly assailed it in order to purify it. Even as the fire that penetrate the log of wood is the same flame that first of all attacked it and wounded it with its flame, cleansing and stripping it of its cold accident until, by means of its heat, it could enter it and transform it into itself."[837]

In this way, the Holy Spirit enabled the soul to progressively detach itself from all things, buried deep in faith, enlightened its darkness, helped it to go out of itself, brought it into the prayer of union to allow it to die interiorly and in pain cleansed it during the great passive dark nights. Now it is he who touches its most inmost being with luminous and transforming fire. Throughout this whole work the soul never ceased to descend more deeply into its inner depths and to draw near this centre whence it has its origins in God. Now this flame "transforms it into itself and gives it sweetness, peace and light".

"O living flame of Love, with tenderness you wound my soul in its inmost depths. You no longer oppress me. Perfect me now, if you will. Break the web of this sweet encounter"[838]

To describe the action of the Holy Spirit and the infused graces of the soul, St John of the Cross often has recourse to the rich and burning words of the liturgies of his day. In soul whom he is leading to transforming union the Holy Spirit is the "gentle breeze", "the unction", "the fire", "the perfume", "the living water". The Holy Spirit "breathes" through the "garden of the soul", and each time he touches the soul, "He communicates to it most delicately knowledge full of serene and peaceful love."[839] He gives the soul the fragrance of divine sweetness "the amber sends forth its perfume".[840] This is the living flame "…which not only consumes and transforms it in sweet love but burns it and

---

[837] *The Living Flame.* Stanza 1, 16.
[838] *The Living Flame.* First stanza.
[839] *Spiritual Canticle* Stanza 26; see also *The Living Flame.* Stanza 3. In Collected Works.
[840] *Spiritual Canticle* Stanza 31.

covers it with flames. Each time this flame breaks forth, it bathes it in glory and refreshes it with everlasting life. Such is the action of the Holy Spirit."[841]

This divine fire "transforms the soul into itself and becomes a burn of ardent fire". "Yet this vehement and consuming fire does not destroy the soul…It divinises it, on the contrary, according to the measure of its love, fills it with delights, enkindling it with its fire and its sweetest ardours." "O sweet burn…O tender wound! O delicate touch!…O lamps of fire!…In your sweetest breathing, so full of glory and good things, how tenderly you fill me with your love!"[842]

The action of the Holy Spirit is wholly concerned with the union of the soul with the Word, its Spouse. "*The Spiritual Canticle*" first describes the close of this painful night that prepares for the espousals and gives a hint of the coming dawn.[843] Then the espousals themselves are described;[844] and then lastly the spiritual marriage is consummated.[845] It is this marriage that gives the soul a very deep understanding of the inexhaustible mysteries of Christ and, by enabling the soul to live with the life of God himself, draws it into the heart of the Trinity:

"There it breathes to God the same breath of love that the father breathes to the son and the son to the father and this is the Holy Spirit himself whom they breathe into it."[846]

"*The Living Flame*" also sings of "the most perfect and the richest love" that of the soul united to god by love; and it tries to describe the flaming of this love in the soul and it gives an analysis of the state of a soul that has reached this fullness of love. But when St John of the Cross begins to comment on the last stanza of his poem in which he sings of the mysterious awakening of the soul to God, overwhelmed by "all the fragrance of pleasing perfumes of all the flowers in the world", he pauses and is strangely silent. It must be so for here all words finally loose meaning and are consumed in everlasting flame. Just as he has glimpsed the sunlit peak to which he has struggled and journeyed, it too is cast into a shadow and cloud and he finds himself, once more, back at base camp. Perhaps, after all union with god is no more, but no less than an aspiration, a craving of the soul for God.

---

[841] *The Living Flame*. Stanza 1.

[842] *The Living Flame* Stanza 4.

[843] See *Spiritual Canticle* Stanzas 1–12.

[844] See *Spiritual Canticle* Stanza 1 and then 3–27.

[845] See *Spiritual Canticle* Stanza 28–29.

[846] *Spiritual Canticle* 39.

"I would not want to speak of this aspiration, nor am I able to say how full it is of the glory and goodness of God's most tender love for the soul. Because I see clearly that I cannot describe it and if I were to speak of it, men would not believe that such a description were possible..."[847]

Back at base camp he might be, but the progress of his spiritual quest from now on will entirely different and, for the moment at least, he is content to be wrapped and enfolded in the love that now penetrates every fibre of his being. He is, as it were, reborn.

This, it seems to me, is significantly different from the diamond that lies at the heart of St Teresa's *Interior Castle*. Whereas she was content to contemplate the goal of the religious life, union with God, St John of the Cross finds that union is not an end but the beginning of a new life which he intends to nourish in order become the truth.

Writing in the Seventh Mansion of the *interior Castle*, St Teresa said this:

"The soul introduced into this mansion of spiritual marriage sees the Persons of the Blessed Trinity reveal themselves to it...all three communicate themselves to the soul and speak to it. They discover to it the meaning of the Gospel passage in which our Lord announces that he will come with the Father and the Holy Spirit to make his dwelling in the soul who loves and keeps his commandments."

Taking this still further, St John of the Cross declares with considerable daring:

"The soul can...love God as much as God loves it because it loves him with the same love with which He loves it and this is the Holy Spirit."[848]

"Granted that God in his goodness rises the soul to become deiform and unites it to the most blessed Trinity, making it divine by participation, how would it be hard to believe that it made its acts of intelligence, knowledge, and love in the Trinity, with the Trinity, like the Trinity, but by participation."[849]

In the end, this apparent difference might turn out to be no more than a difference of emphasis, but it is a difference which, I think, may be worth exploring on another occasion, or perhaps by scholars more skilled than I. For what is clear is that both Teresa and John poured many great spiritual riches into the deficit in the Carmelite treasury they inherited. Contemplative souls never cease to draw from their deposits. When the church made them "Doctors" of the

---

[847] *The Living Flame.* (Comment on the Last Stanza.)
[848] *Spiritual Canticle* Stanza 37.
[849] *Spiritual Canticle* Stanza 38.

church Christians were assured that they would find few more experienced guides through the twists and turns that our religious lives so frequently take.

Within the Carmelite order, there was a new "élan" given by St Teresa and St John of the Cross. Carmel entered into a period of prosperity and it began to add many people who were skilled both in theory and in practice such that many still regard the close of the sixteenth and the whole of the seventeenth century as a "golden age" for the Carmelite tradition. It was during this period, for example, that John of Jesus-Mary, Thomas of Jesus, Joseph of Jesus-Mary (Quiroga) Philip of the Trinity and Joseph of the Holy Ghost studied the whole question of the dynamics of the mystical life, especially the difficult problem of the relationship between "acquired and infused contemplation" which they found in the writings of St Teresa and St John of the Cross. Then the "Reform of Touraine", with the venerable John of Saint-Samson, strove to restore the primitive spirit of silence and solitude in all its purity.

Again, towards the end of the seventeenth century, a simple but somewhat quarrelsome brother, the cook of the convent of Rue de la Vaugirard—Brother Lawrence of the resurrection, brought back contemplative life to the practice of the presence of God. This he thought was exactly what the desert tradition was all about and thus, antecedently and according to the Carmelite legend, it was exactly what Elijah did too. Brother Lawrence said this:

"In the sight of God, thoughts count for very little. Love means everything. It is not necessary to have great things to do: I can turn my little omelette in the pan for the love of God; when that is done and if I have nothing more to do, I can prostrate myself on the ground and adore God who has given me the grace to do what I have done, then I rise happier than a king. When I can do nothing else, I can always pick up a straw from the ground for the love of God…"

"Men seek methods for learning how to love God. They want to reach their goal by; I do not know how many different practices. They go to a lot of trouble to stay in his presence in a great number of ways; is it not much shorter and far more direct to do all things for his love, to make use of all the duties of one's state to express our love for him, and to maintain his presence in us by our heart's commerce with him? We need not go about this in a subtle way. All we must do is simply to do what we do."[850]

---

[850] Brother Lawrence of the Resurrection (2013): *Spiritual Maxims*. Tunbridge Wells Kent. Start Publishing LLC.

For Brother Lawrence, it is faith and faith alone (*fides sola*) that makes it possible for the soul to remain in the presence of God. He goes on to extol the practice of the presence of God by faith in these words:

"O faith! O faith! O admirable virtue which enlightens men's minds and leads them to knowledge of their creator. It is faith that reveals to me the infinite perfections of God…that gives to me a perfect idea of his greatness that enables me to know him as he is. Faith teaches me in a short time more than I could learn in a long time in the schools…"[851]

Nevertheless, this faith has value in Lawrence's eyes only insofar and in the degree to which it is transformed into spiritual fire and kindles his love:

"All things are possible to one who believes, still more to one who hopes, still more and more to one who loves."[852]

We see a similar intensity and emphasis on faith in the female Carmelites who succeeded St Teresa. For example, Blessed Marie of the Incarnation was regarded as one of the foremost spiritual teachers in Paris at the time of Berulle and St Francis de la Sales. The same is true of Anne of Jesus and Anne of Saint Bartholomew who came to France from Spain in order to establish Carmelite houses and, having done so continued this mission in Belgium and at Beaune lived the humble Marguerite of the Blessed Sacrament. The widespread attraction of Carmel was felt by the repentant soul of Louis de la Valliere who became Louis of Mercy, and by Louise of France—the daughter of King Louis XV.

But the Carmelite influence spread further than Spain, France and the Low countries so that Florence was the home of St Mary Magdalene of Pazzi and, a century or so later, of St Teresa Margaret Redi too.

Yet beginning in the late eighteenth century there was a sudden and dramatic change in Carmelite life that lasted for more than a hundred years. This had nothing to do with the French revolution and the revolutionary fervour that haunted Europe, and everything to do with the fact that during this period Carmelite visionaries and mystics were completely silent. There was no new message to give or to live. It was as if the many riches of pervious centuries must suffice without adding to them further. In retrospect, however we see that this was but a dormant period preparing for the great flowering that was to be in St Theresa of the Child Jesus (of Lisieux).

---

[851] Ibid.

[852] Ibid.

It is a matter of great regret that those who concentrate on the life and work of St Theresa, who died at the age of twenty-four, have been so lost in wonder and admiration of her that their commentaries have too often lapsed into sheer sentiment and rather false piety. The task for much of the remainder of this chapter then, is to show how and why her teaching cannot be used in this way, for it is as original and profound as it is traditional. I will demonstrate that under the deceptive simplicity of her message about "the little way of childhood" is hidden a spiritual structure that is both strong in its own terms and finely balanced theologically.

There can be no doubt that the spiritual structure is authentically Carmelite encompassing many elements of her predecessors in the order. But Theresa has arranged them and divided them according to her own genius. Better still, a very sure theological instinct, enabled her to discern and sometimes rediscover the core of the Carmelite Spirit. Her life of love of the absolute and of absolute love shows a rare depth and fullness. It is this, in combination with certain tried and trusted spiritual principles which, in my view, constitute the true doctrine of "the little way of childhood" and nothing else. It is to this that we now turn.

I begin from the view that the doctrine of "the little way" is derived from a particular understanding of the Gospels which can be summarised thus: Since we are children of the same heavenly Father, inheritors together with Christ of the Kingdom of God, it is our duty and our joy to love our heavenly Father with a filial love full of confidence and abandonment. How that love is to be shown was first modelled by Christ who taught that we are God's children. In order to love our heavenly Father, we must be Christ-like.

The notion that we are God's children and heirs to the kingdom was, for Theresa, an *a priori* truth and that it was this which, unsurprisingly, led her teaching to have two complimentary aspects: a keen realisation of God's fatherhood towards us; and the need to develop a filial attitude of absolute confidence towards God our Father. If the confidence of St Theresa in the goodness of her father in heaven is absolute, this is because (somewhat circuitously) God is a Father and the Father is God. So it is that she rests her argument on this basic affirmation:

"We can never have enough confidence in God who is so good, so powerful and so merciful." From this, we can understand how on her lips the words "Papa the good God" are not childish, or a projection of parts of her relationship with her real earthly Father on to God. Rather they testify to the simplicity of her intimate life of prayer and to an absolute confidence derived from it such that she can say, "I know what it means to count on his mercy."[853]

It is easy to believe that such confidence was based on the surely somewhat odd assurance she had been given that she "had never committed any mortal sin". But she hastens to correct this idea:

"Make it clear, Mother, that if I had committed all possible crimes, I would still have the same confidence. I would feel that this multitude of offences would be like a drop of water cast into a blazing fire."[854] How could there be any limits to my confidence?[855]

Like St Teresa and St John of the Cross before her, St Theresa could not have reached this point had she not had a deeply personal, mystical, experience of God's love. Even though she always claimed that she had not known extraordinary graces, (and she never elaborates on those graces she *did* receive), it is clear that she had attained a high degree of union with God during a most painful dark night of the soul. But what might be quite illusory is that this mystical life was lived under the voluntarily obscure and detached sign of the little way of the spiritual childhood. After all, was she not eager not to do anything that "little souls" could not imitate? What, *exactly*, does this mean?

St Theresa had very great desires, yet she would never admit that she was a "great soul" or that she had the strength necessary to do great things, like the saints of old who had been proposed to her as spiritual role models. So she had to find a way in keeping with this littleness of which she was so deeply conscious. More than this, she sought a way that depended on this very weakness. Had not the Apostle Paul written, "When I am weak, then I am strong?" (2 Cor. 12:10) So that in searching the scriptures she found the words of Jesus, "Let the little children come to me and do not hinder them from coming to me, for of such is the kingdom of heaven." (Mtt.19:14) Such a statement accorded only too well to her knowledge, both of her own weakness and also of God's fatherly heart. It served too as a link between her spirit of childhood and her full confidence in the divine Fatherhood.

---

[853] St Theresa of the Child Jesus: *Maxims*. At Last Accessed March 2024.
[854] Novissima verba. P60.
[855] Letter of 14 September 1896. In The Letters of Saint Teresa of Jesus and the Andes. Trans Michael D Griffin OCD (1994) Washington DC. Institute of Carmelite Studies. Teresian Charism Press.

"I leave to great souls and lofty minds the beautiful books I cannot understand, much less put into practice and I rejoice that I am little because children alone and those who resemble them will be admitted to the heavenly banquet. I am glad that there are many mansions in the Kingdom of God, because if there were only those whose descriptions and whose road seems to me to be incomprehensible, I could never enter there."[856]

On this, Theresa was to advance unfalteringly and to draw all the necessary conclusions which follow from it with astonishing intellectual and spiritual courage. It is difficult to deny that weakness is a prime characteristic of newly born and infant children, but this weakness is the most sure of all guarantees to those who care for them and love them. In this context, Theresa remembered a text from the Prophet Isaiah that she copied in a notebook she used: "You shall be carried at the breasts. Upon their knees they shall caress you. As one whom a mother caresses, so I will comfort you." (Isa. 66:12)

Moreover, having learnt from experience about this "motherly" goodness of God, and knowing that the smaller the child the more it can count on the constant help and attention of its parents, Theresa resolved never to "grow up". This was not to be some Peter Pan-like idyll, but rather a way of practicing the presence of God through weakness. That is to say, she would no longer be concerned by her powerlessness but, on the contrary, rejoice in it.

"How happy I am to realise that I am little and weak, how happy I am to see myself so imperfect." She does not count on her works, but rather on her merits, she "keeps nothing in reserve" and she is not to be discouraged even by here faults:

"It is needful to remain little before God and to remain little is to recognise one's nothingness, expect all things from the good God, just as a little child expects all things from its Father. It is not to be troubled by anything, not to try to make a fortune. Even among poor people a child is given all it needs, as long as it is very little, but as soon as it grows up the father does not want to support it any longer and says: 'Work, now you are able to take care of yourself.' Because I never want to hear these words. I do not want to grow up…So I have stayed little and have no other occupation than of gathering flowers of love and sacrifice and of offering them to the good God to please him.'

---

[856] OP cir Letters. Letter of 15 May 1897 to Father Roulland.

To be little also means not to attribute to one's self the virtues that one practices, believing that one can do something, but to acknowledge that the good God has placed these treasures in the hands of his little child so that the child can make use of them as needed, but always as treasures of the good God.

Finally, it means not to be discouraged by one's faults because children often fall but they are too little to hurt themselves badly."[857]

This pleasant attitude and intuition gave Theresa many practical applications in the spiritual life. Above all it drew her along the path of confidence that was, for her, not only a virtue but the evidence of Christian hope in her life. Advancing with great boldness to the end of this hope and desiring no limits on God's mercy for those who love him with a complete filial love, she wrote to a sister:

"You are not sufficiently trusting; you fear God too much. I assure you that this grieves him. Do not be afraid of going to purgatory because of its pain, but rather long not to go there because this pleases God who imposes this expiation so regretfully. From the moment that you try to please him in all things, if you have the unshakeable confidence that he will purify you at every instant in his love and will leave in you no trace of sin, be very sure that you will not go to purgatory."[858]

And again:

"O how you hurt me! How greatly you injure the good God when you believe you are going to purgatory. For one who loves, there can be no purgatory. It seems to me that there will be no judgement for the victims of love, or rather, the good God will hasten to reward, with eternal delights, his own love which he will see burning in their hearts."[859]

St Theresa's confidence in God's infinite mercy leads her to this other certainty, as theologically balanced as the preceding, and one which she shares with Augustine of Hippo—that if God divides his graces unequally, he does so because of the same love.

"For some time, I have been asking myself why souls do not all receive the same amount of grace. Jesus deigned to instruct me about this mystery. Before my eyes he placed a book of nature and I understood that all the flowers created by him are beautiful…that if all the little flowers wanted to be roses, nature

---

[857] Novissima verba p 125 ff.
[858] Extract from a circular letter from Lisieux signed by R M Agnes 17 February 1924.
[859] Extract from a letter of Sister Marie de l'Eucharistie to M Guerin. 7 August 1897.

would lose her springtime garb. The same is true in the world of souls, the Lord's living garden."[860]

"God's love is revealed just as much in the simplest soul who does not resist as in the most sublime."[861]

Lastly this confidence in God leads Saint Theresa, by paths of poverty of spirit and self-forgetfulness, to a wonderful simplification of the religious life. In fact, how could she have failed to notice that the kingdom of heaven is offered not only to little children but also to the poor inspirit, and almost in the same words; "Blessed are the poor in spirit for theirs is the kingdom of heaven?" (Mtt.5:3) "Unless you turn and become like little children you will not enter the kingdom of heaven." (Mtt 18:3)

As Theresa made spiritual childhood her own, so she made her own poverty of spirit. She aspired to be nothing more than "a poor little child" who looks to her Father or everything and who obtains everything from him because of this same poverty. She cultivated this poverty and wanted to keep nothing for herself—not even her merits and good works: "There is only one way to force the good God not to judge at all, and that is to present oneself to him with empty hands…" When I think of this word: "I will soon come and I carry my reward with me to give each according to his works" I say to myself, "he will be very embarrassed for me because I have no works. Well, he will have to give to me according to his own works."

Theresa is forgetful of herself and counts on nothing. She is truly poor; "It is necessary to consent to remain poor and weak; this is hard. I have always longed to be unknown; I am resigned to being forgotten. It is necessary to count on nothing."

Thus, Theresa arrived at spiritual detachment, but in her own humble, hidden "little way". "I know well that it is not my great desires that please god in my little soul. What he likes is to see is the way I love my littleness and my poverty; it is my blind hope in his mercy, this is my only treasure…The weaker one is, without desires or virtues the more ready one is for the operations of this consuming and transforming love…God rejoices more in what he can do for a

---

[860] St Therese of Lisieux: Story of a Soul – The Autobiogra[phy of St Therese of Lisieux. Trans from Original Manuscripts by John Clark OCD Washington Dc ICS Publications. Third Edition (1996) Chapter 1. pp 11–30.
[861] Ibid.

soul humbly reigned to its poverty than in the creation of millions of suns and the vast stretch of the heavens."

She seems almost to bury herself with delight in this poverty; "I tell you that it is enough to recognise one's nothingness and to abandon oneself like a child in the arms of God."[862]

By abandoning herself into the arms of God, Theresa became marvellously free from herself and free for God. Her soul became wide open to the invasions of divine love. We, in fact, so often prevent God from coming to us and "flooding our souls with waves of his tenderness", because we do not open to him the place he yearns to occupy. Only when poverty is combined and united with confidence is God able to realise in us the desires of his love. It is very difficult for us to understand, much less describe, God's loving desire, but Theresa sensed that he wished, "…to love and make Love Loved". The deep reason for this begins to be evident in the following now famous paragraph:

"Merit is not to be found in doing much or in giving much, but rather in receiving and loving much. It is said that it is far sweeter to give than to receive, and this is true. But when Jesus wants for himself the sweetness of giving, it would not be gracious to refuse. Let him take and give whatever he wants."

To take and to receive, in these two cases Theresa will remain poor in order that she can receive the love that God has poured out on her: "I beg you to allow the waves of infinite tenderness hidden in you to overflow into my soul so that I may become a martyr in my soul." Then having received she will give it away to others: "As for me if I live to be eighty, I shall always be just as poor, I do not know how to economise. All that I have, I spend immediately in order to buy souls."[863]

Theresa was really flooded with divine love and that is why her life bore such fruit. This love transfigured two qualities that in her were always to remain united: love of God and love of others. She thought that the first was just as practical, but no less delicate, than the second. It was because of this that God could communicate with her and opened her to new dimensions of divine love. From the beginning of her religious life, Theresa was a true daughter of her order possessed of a deep, if somewhat extreme, understanding of her religious vocation. Yet it was only after she had offered herself to the divine outpouring

---

[862] Letter. 9 May 1897.
[863] Op cit Story of a Soul.

and surrendered herself to it that she discovered the vocation that God had prepared for her:

"I understand that love includes all vocations. I realise that all my desires are fulfilled. I have found my vocation. In the heart of the church, I will be love."

It was only then, too, that her vocation reached its full apostolic dimension and revealed the limits of its fruitfulness. In fact, she began to think and speak in quite universal and eschatological terms:

"I shall spend my heaven in doing good upon earth." "Yes, until the number of the elect shall be complete, I will take no rest."

- and Carmelite spirituality has maintained these dimensions ever since.

Chapter 23
St Francis De La Sales:
Inner Space as a Loving Heart

It is almost a truism of modern culture to say that symbols transmit a message even when their meaning escapes the conscious mind. This is because the symbols speak to the sub-conscious mind which absorbs the meaning of the symbols through our enculturation and socialisation.[864] To get a closer understanding of a symbol, (such as the loving heart), as it was used many centuries ago, it is necessary to acquire as much knowledge as possible of the dominant culture of era in question. Modern research in psychology has strongly suggested that our contemporary idea of the world and of human nature may be a serious impediment to a complete understanding of history because of the way we "see" the past, "coloured" as it is by our language, concepts and world view.

The paradigm of the time in which Francis de la Sales lived is the context of sixteenth century philosophy and theology as well as a baroque mentality which is characterised by a double movement: a call for introspective sincerity coupled with an intense desire for outward expression. In baroque art, this is seen in the choice of powerful effects which are intended to move the spectator to an experience of the greatness of God. The image of the heart is central to this since as a concept it is the manifestation of sincerity and devotion. Used as a religious image it has great force and power expressing as it does the heart's movement, always expanding and contracting and so corresponds to the baroque desire for introspection and outward expression.

---

[864] Mircea Eliade: "*Methodological Remarks on the Study of Religious Symbolism*" in Mircea Eliade and Joseph M Kitagwa (eds) (1959) *The History of Religions; Essays on Methodology.*" Cp the writings of Carl Jung and Joseph Campbell. University of Chicago Press Chicago. pp 86–107.

The medical profession at this time had a different understanding of the heart and, of course, it differs radically from our contemporary understanding of anatomy and physiology. They were educated according to the works of the second century physician Galen, and nothing of great significance had been added to his findings during the thirteen hundred years that followed![865] The part of medical science.[866] Hippocrates of Kos is considered the father of humoralism and his theory stated that health and temperament are determined by the equilibrium of the body's four constituent fluids. The fluids correspond to the four elements which compose all things; earth, air, fire and water and to four basic temperaments in the following way: *blood* corresponds to a sanguine temperament and to fire, *phlegm* corresponds to the phlegmatic temperament and to water, *bile* to the choleric temperament and to air, and finally *black bile* to melancholy and to earth.[867]

As blood was associated with fire it was the carrier of heat. That is why the heart is so often depicted at this time as a burning or smoking coal. The heat of the heart influenced a person's spirit as well as the body. The heart was, by its fire, thought to maintain body heat, the seat of consciousness, wisdom, courage, will and love. Thus, it was not only the most important organ in the body, but also the physical seat of the most important and central properties of the psyche.

At the time of Francis de La Sales, the ancient medical theory of "the humours" (humoralism—from the Greek for fluid or juice) had been penetrated by a renaissance understanding of Neo-Platonism.[868] According to the thoughts of this school of philosophy, especially as taught at Padua, every aspect of the world is a symbol that reveals an aspect of the creator. Like Ignatius then,

---

[865] For details of Galen and ancient ideas about the heart and its functions see John A Abruzzese (1985): *The Theology of Hearts in the Writings of Francis de la Sales.* Rome Pontifical University of St Thomas Aquinas.

[866] Vivian Nutton: *"Humoralism"* in W.F. Byum and Roy Porter (eds) (1993) *Companion Encyclopaedia of the History of Medicine,* **Vol 1**.

[867] For a consideration of the four temperaments in the context of Christian Spirituality see Jordan Aumann; *Spiritual Theology.*(2019) London. Bloomsbury Continuum. pp 140–145.

[868] Francis studied in Padua, an important seat of neo-platonic learning and according to Lajunne this influenced his own thinking in a number of different directions. See E.J Lajunne O.P. (1986/1987) *Saint Francis de la Sales, the man, the thinker, his influence,* pp93–97. **Vol 1 ii**, Bangalore. SFS Publications.

knowledge of the world gives knowledge of God. But this was now applied to the human body too since, as the Old Testament repeatedly makes clear it is made in the image and likeness of God himself. Moreover, before the final victory of the "objective" world view of modern science, the line of developing the physical reality, the symbol and its psychological content and its meaning was not as clear as it is today. The physical aspect on the one hand and the psychological or mystical aspect on the other hand were often, but by no means always, thought of as one and the same.

As we now approach Francis de la Sales more directly it is important to keep in mind that the texts of monastic and mystical theology, especially at this time, are normally meditative. Pure reason and rhetoric are not the issue of such texts. Monastic and mystical writers at this time are content to circle around a multiplicity of images to express a certain theological point. But this point is not primarily understood by examining the structure, logic and exposition of the text.

As in the case of St John of the Cross and Teresa of Avila theological points are to be understood by meditating on them slowly and carefully as a form of *lectio divina*. They are texts in which much of the meaning is to be found in tiny details that can be (and so often are) entirely missed and where a multiplicity of images is used because of the rich allusions they can give.

The dynamics of love are at the centre of Francis de la Sales use of the image of the heart. In his "*Treatise on the Love of God*" he quotes St Augustine of Hippo who famously said that the human heart is made for God and cannot find rest until it settles in the heart of God.[869] Francis wrote:

"True God, Theotimus, how amorous is the divine heart for our love! Would it not have been enough for him to give public permission whereby he would grant us leave to love him, just as Laban permitted Jacob to love his fair Rachel and win her by his services? No, he gives stronger expression of his passionate love for us. He commanded us to love him with all pour strength so that neither thought of his majesty and of our misery, which makes such an infinite disparity between him and us, nor any other pretext would turn us away from loving him."[870]

---

[869] St Francis de la Sales (1975) *Treatise on the Love of God (Treatise)* 3;6 **vol II** p179, Rockford Illinois. Tan Books and Publishers Inc, In what follows the number in brackets refers to the edition in the listed literature.
[870] ibid2:8 (vol 1 p 121).

On this view, the heart of a person longs for God and the heart of God longs for a person. This is the determinative idea of Salesian theology of the religious life. It is the dynamics of love, and the object of unity. It is intensely mystical in a way which Francis describes as the attempt "…to speak of God and to hear God speak in the depths of the heart."[871] So, for Francis, the heart is where our relationship with God is born, and he uses the heart as a symbol to introduce the theology of the dynamics of love.

In this mysticism of the heart we can, I think, see four distinct yet interrelated elements:

1) God's movement towards humankind in and through the heart of Christ.
2) The converse movement of the human heart towards God.
3) The union of the human heart with that of God.
4) The union of human hearts in holy friendship.

For Francis, these four elements provide the structure for the dynamics of love and so determine the way in which he uses the image of the heart. In what follows these dynamics will be illustrated by a focus on the heart of Christ.

In the first element, God takes the initiative. God moves towards his creatures, because his love is the source of all love. It is for this reason that the heart of Christ is the starting point of the dynamics of love.[872] Christ is God incarnate. This means that he is the embodiment of God, who is love. Since he is love incarnated, he is the standard by which all love is to be measured. Since love has its seat in the heart, Christ's heart is the symbol of that this love.

It is an important property of this love that it makes the lover shift his gaze from himself to the beloved. As a consequence "greater love has no man than this, that he lay down his life for his friends".[873] It follows from this that the love

---

[871] ibid 6:1 (vol 1 p 270–271).
[872] In *The Theology of Hearts in the Writings of Francis de la Sales* Abuzzese, *op cit*, treats the heart of God and the heart of Christ quite separately. I do not believe that Francis would have acknowledged such a division. To do so would have introduced a misleading and potentially false understanding of the Holy Trinity and of the love of which he wants to deal. In contrast to Abuzzese I will suggest that Francis uses the terms "heart of God" and "heart of Christ" to describe a single reality. I will also suggest that for all practical purposes, the two are exactly alike for their love is one.
[873] John 15:13.

of God is most profoundly revealed in Christ crucified, and to Francis de la Sales, he is the best teacher of the dynamics of love; "Mount Calvary is the best School of Love".[874]

In the second element, in which the human heart begins to move towards God, a central point in Salesian thinking is that *all* human people (*women* as well as men) are created with a longing for God.[875] This was a radical and, in some ways, dangerous departure from received wisdom which believed that such a longing was neither possible nor natural for women. The love of women, assuming that their souls were of equal characteristics and value of their male counterparts (and even this should be doubted!) was, it was believed, directed not to God but to earthly passions and especially to the physical enjoyment of sex and the procreation and care of children. Francis exposed the nonsense of received wisdom for what it was and countered it by saying that when women and men receive the love of God, it is natural to perceive it as an invitation. When women and men accept this invitation an upward movement towards God is accomplished in their hearts.

By means of the incarnation then, God challenges women as well as men to move towards him in love. The upward movement accomplished in the heart is the practical answer to this challenge. Once the motion has started, love is moved on by inner dynamics: the more a person loves, the more love God will place in his or her heart and in this way the upward movement accelerates.[876] But there is a hidden danger here. All is not as rosy as might at first appear to be the case, for sin cannot only slow this acceleration to a minimum movement it can drive out love completely. Only repentance can bring it back. Yet in this process God will not abandon the beloved but rather fill the lover with even more love and in this way human beings are brought closer together with God—for God *is* love as a matter of his identity not just by way of description.

In the third element in which the human heart becomes united with the heart of God, Francis argues that love alone is the answer to our human longing for God, for "love makes lovers equal".[877]

---

[874] Op cit *Treatise*. 12:13 (vol II p280).
[875] ibid. 1:15 and 1:16 (vol I pp90–95).
[876] ibid 3:2 and 3:3 (vol I pp 165–173).
[877] ibid 5;5 (vol I p 247) This is another radical concept. If it is misunderstood and taken to an extreme it may lead us to think that the epistemological distance between creatures and their creator is being overcome. It is not, for reasons that will be made clear below.

This element is very clearly seen to be at work in compassion. So, when Francis contemplates Christ's agony in the Garden of Gethsemane, his heart is filled with compassion to such an extent that he can begin to glimpse the nature of sorrow in the way that Christ did. It is for this reason that Francis believed that understanding and engaging in the corporal acts of mercy was a practical means by which the human heart could be more firmly united to the heart of God.[878] Love makes the lover share the life of the beloved in all its pain and hurt to the extent that it becomes his or her own and this, paradoxically, creates a great joy—for the strong identification of love accomplishes and creates closeness and unity with the beloved. And this is equally true of the love that God has for us.

For Francis, as for Bernard of Clairvaux before him[879] the lovers in the Song of Songs are among the most important images of this union, accomplished in love, of God with humankind. It is for this reason that the *Treatise* is full of quotations, little dialogues and scenes which seem to be inspired by this Biblical book:

"The devout soul says 'Ah you are beautiful, my beloved, you are beautiful! You are desirable, you are even desire itself! Such is my beloved, and he is the friend of my heart o you daughters of Jerusalem.'"[880]

The tradition of the allegorical interpretation of the Song of Songs is much older than Christianity and it may be for this reason that this highly erotic book was discounted as a sacred writing.[881] Certain parts of this poem may be older than Judaism, having their roots in Egyptian or Sumerian tales describing how the mother goddess gives blessings to the land through her love for her son the king.[882]

---

[878] Loc cit.

[879] Bernard of Clairvaux (2005) 'Sermons on the Song of Songs', *Bernard of Clairvaux—Selected Works*, Foreword by Vinita Hampton Wright. San Francisco. Harper Collins Spiritual Classics. pp 96–133.

[880] Op cit *Treatise* 5:1 (vol I pp 233–234) see also and compare *Song of Songs* 1:5 and 5;16.

[881] Martin H Pope (1985) 'The Song of Songs', *The Anchor Bible,* **vol 7c,** p 184 Garden City New York. Doubleday and Company Inc.

[882] Anne Baring and Jules Cashford (1993) *The Myth of the Goddess: Evolution of an image,* London. Arkana Penguin Books.

It is no wonder then that Jews and Christians alike have been convinced that this song, for all its eroticism, is in fact a song of divine love, the love between God and the soul. In the Christian tradition, this mystical marriage is not going to be consummated until after death but for Francis (in yet another radical break with history) this love is entirely possible in this life. When a person is united with Christ crucified through love compassion and acts of mercy, he or she already has a share of his resurrected life even in this life. It is this share in resurrection that makes mystical marriage this side of death a lived reality now.

Francis de la Sales claims that the human answer to the invitation of God's love cannot be confined to prayer and meditation. It has to result in concrete acts of love as well. The upward movement already described has to result in a movement towards our neighbour in which we try to incarnate little pieces of the love of God in human interaction. For Francis, this is absolutely necessary. The longing of humankind is towards the goal of unity with God, but this cannot be accomplished without acts of love. For God *is* love.

"Real living devotion…presupposes the love of God: it is in fact that very love, though it has many aspects. In so far as this love adorns the soul and makes us pleasing to God it is called grace; in so far as it enables us to do good it is called charity; when it is so perfect that it moves us, not merely to do good, but to do good carefully, frequently and readily it is called devotion."[883]

Everyone then has the opportunity to be devout wherever they are and in whatever they do. Devotion simply means doing the will of God and thus to renounce all self-centred action. According to Francis, this is the perfection of the human life, demonstrated to us by the last words of Christ on the Cross: "Father into thy hands I commend my Spirit."[884] However, rather like Benedict's notion of humility, this does not mean the extinction of self but rather its transformation:

"The soul that has flowed into God does not die. How could it die being plunged into Life? Yet it lives without living in itself. Without losing their light, the stars do not continue to shine in the sun's presence, but rather the sun shines in them and they are hidden in the sunlight. So too the soul, without losing its own life no longer lives when mingled with God, but rather God lives in it."[885]

---

[883] St Francis de la Sales. Allan Ross Ed. (2009) *Introduction to the Devout Life* (Introduction), New York. Dover Publications Inc1:1 p 7.
[884] Lk 23:46.
[885] Op cit *Treatise 6:12* (vol 1 p 302).

In choosing the good to the extent of always doing the will of God, lies apparent self-extinction, but this is only an apparent danger, and in reality, it is in the choice that the answer to all the longings of humankind are found.

The mystery of the Incarnation was essential for Francis de la Sales as well as for many of his contemporary theologians, such as Pierre de Berule and the so-called "French school". In fact, the incarnation was the source of their mysticism.[886] Since Christ was as human as any man or woman, his heart was thought to have all the qualities of a human heart,[887] which was believed to be the seat of the will, consciousness and emotions. Still, since Christ was not only human, but also God, his heart also had qualities that now human heart could have; the love and mercy of God himself. For Francis, Calvary was the place where god's love has its true significance. It was for him the meeting place of lovers[888] and the true school of love.[889] It is hard to overestimate the importance of the passion in his theology. In the pierced heart of the crucified Christ, the most extreme human suffering meets the fullness of the mercy of God.

The fact that Christ's heart was pierced and broken has a number of implications for Francis de la Sales: Firstly, the thrust of the spear represents the outer limits of the suffering of Christ, as his heart—his centre—was penetrated. Secondly, the wound reveals the fact that the heart of Christ had been wounded by love *before* the thrust of the spear. Thirdly, the wound affected the heart of Christ for all time is exposed and accessible for anyone who seeks it.

The deep devotion to the heart of Christ, in this sense, has its roots in the medieval devotion to the five wounds of Christ[890] Francis advises his spiritual disciple Jane to make a habit of meditation on the five wounds, and it is obvious that he thinks that meditation on the wounded heart lies at the core of this practice[891] and so raises the question of the significance that the *physica*l wound

---

[886] Howbeit that Francis de la Sales does not have much in common with the "French school".
[887] Cp. p1.
[888] Op cit *Treatise* 12:13 (vol II p 281).
[889] Loc cit.
[890] The devotion to the wounds and blood of Christ were characteristic of popular piety in the medieval period. It was tangentially connected to the stories of the quest for the Holy Grail. For a closer analysis of this connection and of the symbolism involved see Emma Jung and Marie Louise von Franz: *The Grail Legend*.
[891] Op cit Annecy Edition vol 12.p 358.

had for Francis. One important implication is that the heart, the innermost centre of the Word of God has suffered extreme human pain. The whole passion narrative shows how Christ is tormented and humiliated both physically and mentally and emotionally. The wound of the heart shows that he was spared nothing, and consequently that god cannot be said to be distant from any human suffering but rather is inextricably involved in it.

The wound also demonstrates that Christ was actually dead and did not merely appear to be so.[892] Many stepped in the medieval devotion to the wounds of Christ would find it natural to mention the water and blood that flowed from the wound, but Francis does not. To him, the central importance is in the wound itself, and in the fact that Christ endured even this for the sake of love. The violence continued even after death, for even when it was obvious that Christ was dead, the soldier was ordered to pierce him. The spear penetrated the heart that upheld Christ's life, the human incarnation of the Word of God.

Francis says that death without love of the saviour and love without the death of the saviour are both unhappy circumstances. Love and death are so interconnected in the passion that we cannot have the one in our hearts without the other.[893] If we let the love of God into our hearts, his death follows. When we are united to him in love, we cannot avoid experiencing that our own hearts are pierced by the spear of compassion and identification. As this compassionate identification grows, the spear kills everything in our hearts that is not love.

In the prayer that concludes the *Treatise*, Francis says:

"Ah! Come Holy Spirit, and inflame our hearts by your love! To love—or to die! To die—and to love! To die to all other love in order to live in Christ's love so that we may not die eternally."[894]

The insight here that it is necessary to die in order to live is one of the basic principles of the Christian faith, and this is especially important in monasticism from the moment of entering the community which is itself often regarded as a dying (to the world) in order to live (in the gathered community of Christ). This "acted" dying comes from the longing for God, the beloved. The effect of this longing is that one abandons the life that is based on selfish love and in this way

---

[892] Ibid Annecy Edition vol 9.p80. The gulf between appearance and reality at this point is, of course, one among many of the great barriers in contemporary Christian—Muslim dialogue.

[893] Op cit *Treatise*. 12:13, **vol II** p 281.

[894] Loc cit.

suffers death in order to live with Christ at the centre. It is important to mention here the close similarity between Francis and St Paul who believed that the aim and goal of all Christian devotion was to be able to say that "…it is no longer I who live, but Christ who lives in me."[895]

Like so many monastics, theologians and mystics Francis held that the heart of Christ was pierced and wounded by love long before the thrust of the spear. The physical wound has a mystical parallel. It is a "fact" for Francis that love wounds the hearts, and when the spear pierced Christ's side this was apparent.[896] Here, again it is clear how closely Francis connected love and death in the passion of Christ. It is also made clear in the following quotation from the *Treatise*:

"Theotimus, behold the divine redeemer stretched upon the cross as a pyre of honour! On it he dies of love for us, but with a love more dolorous than death itself…by a death more loving than love itself."[897]

By letting the concepts of love and death alternately throw light upon each other, Francis shows how intimately they are connected in his theology. For him, love will always be coupled with the death of Christ and with the death of our own selfish will. In the same way, death, even our own, is always marked by the love of Christ when we perceive it rightly.[898] For Francis, both death and love are given new and radical meanings as they are bound together in the death of Christ:

"Oh, how great was the flame of love that burned in the heart of our gentle saviour, since at the height of his suffering, at a time when the vehemence of his torments seemed to take him even from the power of praying for himself, he succeeded through the strength of his love in forgetting himself but not his creatures, and in a strong and intelligible voice said, 'Father forgive them.'"[899]

This quotation aptly illustrates the ancient belief that love has its seat in the heart and is one with the heat and fire of life residing there. It also shows how

---

[895] Galatians 2:20.
[896] Op cit *Treatise* 6:13 and 6:14, **vol I** pp302–309.0 See also Annecy edition vol 9 p80.
[897] Ibid 7:8 **vol II** p37.
[898] Though usually only in retrospect. Often our grief, at the time of death of someone we love, is too great for us to see and feel this. If we do so at all it is only very dimly.
[899] *The Sermons of Francis de Sales for Lent Given in 1622.* Ed. Fr Lewis S. Fiorelli. OSFS. Trans. Nuns of the Visitation. (1987) Rockford Illinois. Tan Books and Publishing Inc. p189.

the attention of Christ, even in his most intense suffering, was on his fellow human beings. His love for humankind was always stronger than his affliction, and this love has its source and seat in his heart.

Francis also tells how Peter's denial[900] and those who mocked him on the cross[901] pierced Christ's heart. When the heart is physically wounded it is a symbolic manifestation of unrequited love. During Francis' time, doctors were taught that the physical heart could literally burst from sorrow and, for Francis, it is obvious that this was exactly happened to Christ—the more so because Christ's love and sorrow were of a different proportion. Christ was Love itself, and his objective was to unite all things to himself through love. He knew what they dismissed when they rejected that love, and this knowledge causes the wound in his heart and his heart to finally burst through sorrow.

In the late medieval period, the heart of Christ was seen both as a refuge and a source of comfort and strength for the devout. Francis shared this conviction:

"See how he makes himself be seen through the wounds of his body and the opening of his side, as through windows, as through a lattice through which he himself looks out at us."[902]

"Yes truly…God's love is seated within the saviour's heart as on a royal throne. He beholds through his cleft side all the hearts of the children of men. His heart is the king of hearts,[903] and he keeps his eyes fixed on our hearts. Just as those who peer through a lattice see clearly while they themselves are only half seen, so too the divine love within the heart, or rather the heart of divine love, always sees clearly and looks on our hearts with his eyes of love, while we do not see him, but only half see him."[904]

It is significant that the first sentence includes a quotation from the *Song of Songs*. Christ is identified with the lover in the Song of Songs, and this draws the attention of the reader to the fact that the relationship between God and every human being is meant to be a relationship of love. This kind of allegorical interpretation of Scripture is important to Francis from the time he heard lectures on the subject in Paris in 1584. But this still leaves the question open as to how this text should be understood. Christ can no longer be seen, as he was when

---

[900] Ibid p191.
[901] Ibid p210.
[902] *Song of Songs* 2:8.9.
[903] Hence the title of this Chapter.
[904] Op cit *Treatise* 5:11 **vol 1** p263.

physically present, so we can no longer see the wound in his side or his heart through that open wound. When Christ died on the cross, he surrendered everything, both his outward dignity, and his inner integrity, peace and wholeness.

On the cross, he endured great sorrow and the greatest pain, and he did it out of love for us, and in obedience to the Father's will. This is the reason why his heart is the king of hearts, and because of this he can keep his eyes of love fixed on our hearts. He knows its conditions even in the most extreme of circumstances, since he himself has had the same experiences. Because of all this, the wound in his heart is an open window, a lattice for him to look through and see the hearts of everyone clearly and directly. Love wounded his heart in every conceivable way; so that he is acquainted with everything a human heart can harbour and endure. In this way, incarnation is completed in crucifixion.[905]

In the text, the wounds of Christ draw human beings to his side in love. According to St Francis, it is the wounds of Christ with which a person can most easily identify. For Francis, Christ is really alive and full of love even after having been wounded by the spear. For him, the red hot, glowing love is the hallmark of Christ, and it is evident from the text that he thinks made Thomas recognise the risen Lord.[906] In modern exegesis, this is certainly stretching the text to its limits, but for Francis this was a natural conclusion: Christ can be known by his heart which glows from love, and it is out of his heart that he knows us, as it is familiar with every human condition.

The scene where Thomas is allowed to place his hand in the wound of Christ is, for Francis, a description of the closeness that human beings and God long for, like lovers in their intimacy. The text shows us that the wound in the heart gives human beings access to the innermost regions God in Christ. To Francis, this is one of the most important qualities of the heart of Christ: that it is always open to those who seek unity with it through prayer, contemplation and meditation. This is a property of the heart of Christ which has been central to Christianity throughout the history of monasticism and of devotion. An excellent example of this is this prayer of the Cistercian William of St Thierry (1085–1148):

---

[905] See for example Treatise 10:17, **vol II**, p191) "*He poured himself completely into us and, so to speak, dissolved his grandeur so as to reduce it to the form of our littleness.*"
[906] Annecy Edition. Vl 10 pp 409–410.

"The treasures of your glory, Lord, were hidden in your heaven. But when your Son, our lord and redeemer was hanging on the Cross, the soldier opened his side with the spear and the sacraments of our salvation poured out as blood and water. Now we do not only place our finger or our hand in his side like Thomas did. We enter through the open gate, all the way in to the shrine of your soul where all the fullness of God dwells, and all our comfort and salvation. Lord, open the gates of this ark and let your chosen ones enter. Open the door of your body that all who desire the secrets of the Son can enter. And let them drink of your hidden wellsprings, and let them taste the price of redemption."[907]

Given its date and the character of its writing this prayer it is clear that this prayer is medieval. It is clear too in its use of images referring to Christ as a fellow human being in preference to his divinity. The legacy of this is evident throughout Francis de Sales' writings.

The theology of the heart of Christ found in the writings of Francis de Sales is not, however, focussed exclusively on the pierced heart of the crucified Lord. Another central aspect evolves from Mtt.11:29 "Take my yoke upon you, and learn of me: for I am gentle and lowly of heart". Gentleness and lowliness (humility) are among the virtues that Francis most cherished and this is one of his favourite Biblical quotations.[908] In the *Introduction to the Devout Life,* he wrote:

"The holy [oil of] chrism, traditionally used in the church for confirmations and consecration is composed of olive oil mingled with balm, symbolising…two virtues which shone out of our Lord and which he particularly loved and recommended, that by practising them ourselves we might better imitate him: Learn from me: I am gentle and humble of heart."

"Humility perfects our relationship with our neighbour. Balm…always sinks to the bottom of any liquid and so represents humility; olive oil always floats to the top and represents gentleness which rises above all things and is pre-eminent among the virtues, being the flower of charity which, St Bernard says, is made perfect when it is not only patient but also meek and gentle. Make sure

---

[907] As quoted in the Prayer Book of the Catholic Church in Norway, Compiled by Monsignor Michael Buckley p 283. For more on the Catholic Church in Norway see Last Accessed March 2–24.

[908] Francis de Sales to Jane de Chantal: *Letters of Spiritual Direction.* Ed. Wendy M Wright. (1988) Mahwah. Classics of Western Spirituality. Paulist Press p62.

however…that this is my special chrism, composed of gentleness and humility, is truly in your heart."[909]

This way of using examples is a common feature of the writings of Francis de Sales. It is an important aid when he popularises theology to make it as understandable to as many people as possible in his great circle of influence. It is also distinctive of baroque theological writings generally, and gives the text a characteristic exuberance.

Gentleness and lowliness are compared to the contents of the costly chrism. In this way, Francis shows how precious these virtues are and how, in his opinion, they ought to mark all the children of the church. For Francis, these are the foremost virtues of the heart of Christ. What is essential is that each person transforms his or her heart after the model of the heart of Christ by imitating these virtues. To achieve this, self-abandonment and asceticism are necessary, but first of all by inner self-chastisement, not primarily by long fasts and other physical torments. Even though he was not opposed to moderate asceticism, he thought it was a fundamental contradiction to seek humility by performing impressive acts of piety.

To achieve the virtues of the heart of Christ, he did not consider it necessary to wait for the right occasion to perform total self-abandonment. That could mean waiting for a very long time indeed! On the contrary, according to Francis we are Christians are to practice gentleness and lowliness in all the activities and encounters of daily life, as Christ did.

According to Francis, to be pleasant to an unpleasant person is preferable to the performance of daily mortification of the flesh.[910] He thought this because this kind of challenge is an ever-present reality and because this is true, we can so easily overlook it or think that it is a matter of common courtesy and good manners. It may be that, but it is also always far more than that. It is an occasion to practice the presence of God. In other words, it is of little use to be faithfully looking out for the chance to be a martyr if that makes us overlook the countless opportunities that help us forget ourselves for the transformation of our neighbour that come our way every day.

What kind of theology is illustrated by the imagery of the heart? It is a mystical theology with the love of God at its centre. It is the theology of the dynamics of love. This can be summed up in the following ways:

---

[909] Introduction III:8 (p111).
[910] Op cit.Francis de la Sales to Jane de Chantal. *Letters of Spiritual Direction*. p62.

- The heart of Christ is the core of the Incarnate Word of God. This means that it is both fully a person and fully God and is thus consistent with Orthodox Christian theology since Chalcedon. It harbours divine love and human emotions. It is where human suffering and divine mercy meet and converse.
- The fact that the heart of God is wounded also means that it is open and accessible to everyone as a place of refuge and as a source of strength and comfort.
- Since it is wounded, the heart of Christ is a symbol of mystical death. Love pierced it and penetrated the will that resides there so that only the will of the Father exists in it.
- The heart of Christ is an image of divine and human compassion. Christ loves all humanity and all human beings should do the same. Christ seeks the redemption of all and to assist in this task is the highest calling of every Christian. Christ's heart is wounded by the thought of all those who remain isolated and unredeemed because they turn their back on his love. The task of the Christian, like the Good Shepherd of Luke Chapter 15 is to seek the ones who are lost and bring them back to the sheepfold of the church.
- The heart of Christ is associated with the supreme virtues of lowliness and gentleness and from this it follows that the heart of Christ is a symbol for human self-abandonment into the constant love of God. To practice the virtues of lowliness and gentleness means, like Christ, to embrace <u>all</u> the circumstances that life brings; times of great joy and great sorrow and indeed those times which are neither joyful or sorrowful, but routine. Faithfulness to these little virtues of the heart of Christ is the main route to a Christ-like life in Salesian spirituality.
- The wounded heart of Christ implies that Christ knows all kinds of pain and sorrow and that means he is personally familiar with all the harsh circumstances of human life.

These are the principal elements of the Salesian theology of the heart of Christ. They are fully consistent with its general emphasis on the incarnation and the passion. The passion can be said to be the focal point of Salesian theology, and the Salesian theology of the heart is certainly centred there.

Part 8
Widening Spirituality and the Inner Space in the Modern World

Chapter 24
Parochial Monasticism: The Church of England and the Book of Common Prayer

The traditional view of much of the history of the Church of England is that having emerged from the dissolution of the monasteries and the largely Protestant Henrician, Edwardian and Elizabethan settlements it would and could have nothing whatever to do with monks, nuns and monasteries. But I wonder. After all, even though the semi-monastic community at Little Gidding[911] did not survive the death of its founder, Nicholas Ferrar, it was both tolerated and admired by many.[912]

---

[911] Nicholas Ferrar was born in 1592 and was the founder of a religious community at Little Gidding, Huntingdonshire after his ordination as Deacon. Ferrar seems never to have been ordained priest. His community was formed by him, his family and a few friends and it lasted from 1626 to 1646. They devoted themselves to prayer, fasting and almsgiving, taking control of the abandoned church building in which they held services, read the Book of Common Prayer and the entire Psalter every day. They took the injunction to "pray without ceasing" literally so that at no time, day or night, was the altar bereft of at least one member of the community praying before it. The community taught the local village children and were responsible for the medical and healthcare for many in the surrounding districts. They produced catechetical materials explaining the Christian faith and its practices. Every member of the community fasted with great rigour as a sign of their voluntary poverty and in order that they would have more goods to give to poor people who needed their material aid. It is interesting to speculate whether and to what extent Farrar's experiment at Little Gidding was a prototype of a new or secular monastic community.

[912] And is forever immortalised in TS Elliot's famous poem of the same name in his *Four Quartets*.

Writing only a hundred years or so after the dissolution of the monasteries one John Bramhall, sometime Bishop of Armagh, claimed that while the perceived covetousness of the monastic houses was a prime focus and motivation for reform throughout Europe, he saw no reason "…why monasteries might not agree well enough with reformed devotion."[913] Herbert Thorndike went even further: "It is certainly a blot on the reformation when we profess that we are without monastic life."[914] So, at the very least there would seem to be a longing for monasticism in Anglicanism if not its reality in wood and stone.

Perhaps then this longing was expressed not in buildings or in orders, but in liturgy so that monastic rhythms shaped and formed the spirituality of English women and men in much the same way as Cistercian practices moved from monastery to market place some half a millennium earlier. The focus of this chapter will be to try to determine to what extent that might be true and I begin with an exploration of the links, if any, between the Book of Common Prayer (BCP) and the spirituality that would have been most familiar to English people, namely that of the Benedictines on the one hand, and that the English mystical tradition of Rolle, Julian, Hilton and the author of *"The Cloud of Unknowing"* on the other.

One of the most interesting features of the BCP is that it insists that the regular celebration of the Eucharist and the daily cycles of morning and evening prayer should be said in the parish and available to all who wish to attend. These features are central to Anglican worship and make it distinctive and this insistence is still to be found in the more recent reforms of Anglican worship to be found in the current *"common worship."* While it might be argued that Catholicism of the Counter-reformation also developed patterns of devotion built around the Eucharist, this was increasing seen as the preserve of the clergy and the religious.

Since it was still celebrated in Latin it was not easily understood by common people whose devotion was now concentrated in the vernacular praying of novenas and the regular saying of decades of the rosary. Lutheranism at this time did celebrate the Eucharist in the vernacular but only intermittently throughout the year and in a truncated form. Their preference was for praise and prayer services in which the singing of psalms featured prominently.

---

[913] John Bramhall (1842) *Works*. Library of Anglo-Catholic Theology, Oxford, p118–120.

[914] Herbert Thorndike (1842) *Works* Library of Anglo-Catholic Theology, Oxford, p571.

The retention of morning and evening prayer created a direct link between the emergent Church of England, the desert tradition and the fathers of the early church. This is not as surprising as it might first appear because Cranmer, Hooker and other Anglican divines had a great interest in these periods of church history.[915] In this way, Anglican morning and evening prayer could be said to be an attempt to replicate the two main synaxes familiar to the Desert fathers and mothers and of the practice in the great cathedrals of the late Roman Empire in the fourth century. But Cranmer clearly knew the difference between the monastic practice of the desert dwellers and that of the cathedrals and in the BCP opts for the former over the later. It was his understanding and love of the Bible that led him to make this choice.

In the desert tradition, the emphasis on understanding the hours and scripture was on *listening* to and allowing oneself to be formed by the words of scripture. All other modes of worship were secondary to this. In the same way, and for the same reasons, Cranmer believed that the Bible was the living Word of God and that if "…his fellow countrymen could be induced to read the Word of God, or if illiterate to hear it read, it would in the course of time make its way into their hearts."[916]

So, Cranmer and his contemporaries clearly expected that ordinary women and men would be "monastic" in their liturgical outlook and for the most part seems to have been successful in this. Whereas Luther rejected "the hours" as a "work" opposed to the concept of *fides sola* (justification by faith alone), Cranmer's BCP retrieved the "monastic" quality of the hours.[917]

This does not mean that "cathedral" practices were absent either from the BCP or from lay and parochial devotion. On the contrary, it was (and is) predominant in Anglican cathedrals, minsters, schools and in some parish churches, but it was always balanced—perhaps even restrained by—the more common "monastic" practice and the centrality of morning and evening prayer

---

[915] It is an interest shared by the members of the Oxford Movement—Newman, Pusey, Keble etc—in their nineteenth century Anglo-Catholic reforms in the Church of England.
[916] Stephen Neil (1965) *Anglicanism Harmondsworth* Penguin. p54.
[917] It seems to me that Luther was quite wrong about this as in so much of his teaching and doctrine. There is no reason at all, as far as I can see, why the regular recitation of the office at key points through the day should not be an act of faith and confirm and increase the faith of the individual(s) saying them. Paul F Bradshaw has many interesting things to say about this in his *"Two Ways of Praying"* Abingdon. Nashville 1995 p39.

in the BCP prevented the church of England from becoming too clerical and any temptation to turn to the patterns being adopted in Counter-reformation Catholicism.

This was a peculiarly "English" balance and restraint reflecting our national preference for forming a complete or rounded view of any subject and this is no less true in religion than anywhere else. So, this balance between monasticism and the cathedral preferred listening to the whole Bible being read over a long period rather than repeated and selected portions of scripture[918] and this was expanded upon in writing and the preaching of sermons. It had a long history. Cranmer and his contemporaries, like the fourteenth century English mystics, sought a balance between the extremes of a potentially moribund theology and a sentimental popular piety that had nothing whatever to do with doctrine.

True piety, rooted and grounded in doctrine and linked with sound scholarship and learning was the ideal. In this way too, pastoral theology and practical pastoral care could be linked to the theological as well as popular understandings of the humanity of Christ—a tradition stretching back through Julian of Norwich and St Francis to St Bernard and beyond.[919] But in time, the balance shifted so that sound learning came to dominate. The results of this were by no means entirely negative and came about as a direct consequence of an interest in church history in the pre-Bernadine era.[920]

This balance may have been English but it was also intensely Benedictine. The Rule of St Benedict is all about balance, moderation and discretion, piety and learning and does so (like the BCP) in a liturgical context for the sake of cultivating a reflective spirit of prayer.

---

[918] It is, in my view, a matter of deep regret that the reading of scripture "straight through", as it were, over say three years is no longer possible in the current patterns of Anglican worship. In some churches, my own included, readings from the Old Testament are a rare treat, the Psalms are sung from the dozen or so at "the back of the hymn book" in a cleaned up and sanitised version. The Epistles are usually short periscopes from Pauline or pseudo-Pauline writings. The Pastoral and General Epistles are almost never heard at any length and even though the Synoptic Gospels each have their own Year, that for Mark, (year A), is always interrupted by John. So, what we have then is the same few readings repackaged and recycled year by year.

[919] This is a particular feature of the works of Donne, Herbert, Taylor, Ken and Andrews.

[920] Martin Thornton (1986) '*The Caroline Divines and the English Platonists*', *The Study of Spirituality,* C Jones, G Wainwright and E Yarnold SJ eds. Oxford OUP p 432.

By the late seventeenth and early eighteenth century, the balance shifted again away from the Desert fathers and the Bible towards good order and church discipline and this too was derived from the Benedictines. This meant not only a greater focus on the order and discipline brought about by the liturgical hours but also on other aspects of daily Christian living arising from the spirituality to be found in them. So, for example, prayers were composed that could be used for everyday occasions; waking, dressing, walking, saying grace before meals, embarking on a journey and so on.[921] This practice of prayers for the daily round and common tasks of life had a counterpart in certain periods of monastic history and endures in some communities to this day. Just as the Rule of St Benedict strives to cultivate a habitual sense of the presence of God in alternating patterns of work and prayer, so too does the BCP.

For those of us living in the twenty-first century, good order and discipline are often regarded as prosaic and somewhat boring, the playthings of "geeks" and "anoraks". But not so in the seventeenth and early eighteenth centuries when they were expressed in poetry. This was a good medium through which to communicate order and discipline because poetry is a means of expressing affections and sentiments in a sometimes mathematically precise way as in the writing of sonnets. It is therefore not without significance that, writing in the nineteenth century, John Henry Newman should characterise and distinguish St Benedict as a poet, from St Dominic the scientist and St Ignatius Loyola as a man of orderly and practical affairs.[922]

This leads directly to a consideration of another aspect of the spirituality made available to English women and men through the Book of Common Prayer: the beauty of language. For those who composed it, language and the spirituality it expressed were inseparable. This was again nothing new but a key aspect of the English mystical tradition, marked especially in Julian and *"The Cloud"*. It was certainly a concern of the Cistercians as we saw in the earlier consideration of their liturgical reforms. But, with one or two notable exceptions (The Shepherd of Hermas, Evagrius and Cassian spring immediately to mind) concern for the beauty of language was not a feature of early monasticism or for the desert dwellers. It may simply be a matter of literacy. Common to cultures in which an

---

[921] This has resonance with the Celtic tradition too. The Celts seemed to have a prayer for every possible event or action.

[922] John Henry Newman (1948) 'The Benedictine Schools', *Essays and Sketches* **vol iii** New York. Longmans Green & co, p 236.

oral, storytelling tradition, is dominant language is often attributed with magical powers and a talismanic potency because language, being spoken, is sounded and hence is full of power in a way which is not as true in cultures dependent on writing and books. Early monasticism and those who lived in the desert was just such a storytelling culture and so the compelling force and power of Scripture among them must have been due to simply hearing it spoken (whether from memory or hearing it read by others) during the synaxes. In primarily literate cultures such as that in which the BCP appeared, the same force and power needs to be experienced in a different way, so rendering it in a language which is rhythmical, poetic and compelling became the answer.

So it was that the BCP and the Authorised Version of the Bible appealed to the spiritual lives of English people in the seventeenth century. The Bible was read and the offices were prayed, both in a language that could be easily understood and made a lasting contribution to the encouragement of literacy throughout the land.[923]

The importance of Cranmer's use of language then was not only that it was in the vernacular and had a rhythm and power which can be appreciated to this day, but that it was one way of achieving his desire to involve all people of the church in its spiritual life, not as on=lookers but as active participants. So too the Rule of St Benedict is designed for a predominantly lay, that is non-clerical, community. Cranmer and Benedict alike expected more from their laity than a passive, largely uncomprehending, presence. They invested great confidence in the laity and expected a great deal from ordinary people.[924]

We know, however, that Cranmer's efforts to involve further lay participation in the Eucharist by insisting that it was not properly and rightly celebrated unless or until two or three people were present and able to receive Holy Communion met with a great deal of resistance.[925] But the evidence that survives about the numbers of people attending morning and evening prayer on a regular, sometimes daily, basis attests to the fact that his expectations were not always and everywhere disappointed.[926]

---

[923] Op cit Thornton pp434–435.
[924] Op cit Neil p54.
[925] John N Wall (1990) *Anglican Spirituality: A Historical Introduction* in *Spiritual Traditions for the Contemporary Church*. Robin Maas and Gabriel O'Donnel OP eds. Nashville. Abingdon Press p 278.
[926] Martin Thronton (1986) *English Spirituality*. Cowley Press. Oxford. p 241.

There are other common elements between the BCP and the Rule of Benedict. For example, Jeremy Taylor's injunction that "I would rather your prayer be often than long" echoes with Benedict's statement in the Rule (20:4) that "prayer should...be short and pure."[927] Both the spirituality of the BCP and the Rule of St Benedict inculcate a distinct strain of what Julian of Norwich called "homeliness"—a warm tolerant, individual devotion to God in Christ based on loving persuasion rather than threats of hell fire and brimstone or great oratory. Anglican spirituality is far more at home with the Benedictine imagery of supportive families than with, for example, the more militaristic imagery that was available to Cranmer and others when the BCP was written.[928]

The spirituality to be found in both the BCP and the Rule of St Benedict presuppose a stable and rational community and are seen very clearly in John Donne's emphasis on the Word of God being preached in a *"settled church"*.[929] The settled church was confident was characterised by a common office, empirical guidance within the family, rubrics relating to residential qualifications for marriage and burial. These characteristics and the whole notion of a *"settled church"* are elements evocative of Benedictine spirituality.

After the Council of Trent, Roman Catholicism began to separate moral from ascetic theology so that two distinct theological sciences (both intended to win souls for Christ and prepare them for heaven) developed. The first was occupied with questions of the legality or illegality of human actions, while the other was increasingly concerned with spiritual progress and holiness.[930] While such a distinction is still a feature of some parts of contemporary Catholicism, no such separation was ever made in Anglicanism and this again keeps pace with Benedictine history. Benedictine monasticism did not draw the distinction so sharply, if at all, preferring the notion that conventual life, with its daily

---

[927] Ibid p258.

[928] It is important that the image of family be kept in view at the present time. All families, however supportive they are fight from time to time—sometimes furiously. Our current situation in the Anglican Communion is one such time. The "trick", if there is one, is for the family to be so secure in its trust of all its members that it can find a way to respect each other's views and needs and to love each other just the same living together as under one roof.

[929] Op cit Thornton *English Spirituality*. P258.

[930] Ibid p241.

observances, is in and for itself a means of spiritual direction and moral instruction.[931]

Similarly, the BCP placed more emphasis on recollection in daily life than on particular techniques for formal prayer. Anglican spirituality, then and now, is far less concerned with formal "self-examination" before sacramental confession, than with the practical art of making moral decisions in daily life and training the conscience to be used in habitual recollection.[932]

The same is true of the BCP's approach to monastic vows. Quite obviously it could not ask members of a parish to take vows of obedience, stability or conversion of life, but it could suggest that these be adopted Christian virtues in everyday living.

But Cranmer, unlike Benedict, did not believe that every voice in the gathered community carried equal weight and he certainly was not a democrat! Whereas Benedict provides for the election of a superior from among the members of the monastic community, neither Cranmer nor the English parliament expected ordinary people to vote on who would be their rectors, vicars, bishops and so on.

This question of election brings up another major difference between traditional monasticism and Anglican practice. It is one which some might regard as a defect in Anglicanism and it is this: women and men become nuns and monks because they perceive in the monastic mode of life a spirituality to which they feel called. But not everyone is at home with monastic spirituality. Not everyone then should be expected to be at home with the monastic ethos of the BCP. Cranmer, however, wanted the entire English people to fit into a certain spiritual mould. While the spiritual ethos of the sixteenth century might have been sufficiently homogeneous and sufficiently "monastic" to sustain Anglican spirituality for a time, it clearly could not survive being made more explicit by Laudanism. Hence, in small part, the English Civil War.

It is also instructive to note that a book claiming to study Anglicanism as a religious and spiritual phenomenon makes no reference whatsoever to either the monastic influence in Anglicanism in general, or that of Benedict in particular.[933] It is as if, for the authors, there was no such influence. Or perhaps, if there was a

---

[931] Jean Leclerq (1990) *Spiritual Direction in the Benedictine Tradition* in *Traditions of Spiritual Guidance*, Lavinia Byrne Ed. Collegeville. Liturgical Press p28.
[932] Op cit Thornton *English Spirituality* p240–241.
[933] Stephen Sykes and John Booty. (1988) *The Study of Anglicanism*. London. SPCK.

monastic influence it must be denied or passed over in silence. For those of us intimately involved in contemporary Anglicanism, this must surely raise an important question: Has Anglicanism "outgrown" its monastic ethos, and if so, what is its ethos now? If we could begin to find an answer, we might, perhaps, begin to solve some of the internal quarrels that are everywhere present both at home and in the world-wide Anglican communion.

Chapter 25
Dietrich Bonheoffer: Life Together[934]

"Community" is a much-abused word. Politicians love it and claim to speak for it and to it. Philanthropists finance it. Anthropologists, historians and sociologists claim to be able to study it. Geographers, architects and town planners locate it. Story tellers, artists, playwrights and even musicians have mythologised it. Those who live in it are often oppressed by it. Christians want to create it and sometimes when things go horribly wrong what they create is a pale substitute, a bureaucratic institutional structure called Church. What all these people and ideas have in common is that they all want community to be composed of "good experiences." Community must always be a place where we experience the old revolutionary virtues of liberty, equality and fraternity, (or at least its modern equivalent—the much trumpeted "fairness").

When things go well, Christians understand that "community" is not about "good experiences" at all. On the contrary, they know that community happens only because it is first and foremost a divine gift. It is given not to answer the lack of some inherent human predisposition towards it, nor to promote it where it already exists, but only because community is the best (only?) vehicle we have for human communion with the divine.

Dietrich Bonheoffer knew this and insisted that Christian community concerns personal relationships "*abiding n Christ*". Christ is the one who *is* and who makes himself present in the life of the Body. Why and who Christ is—and

---

[934] The material for this chapter is a personal reflection arising from a reading of "*Life Together*" which was then given as a paper to a meeting of Anglican Lay Readers in the Diocese of Southwark. I have simply reproduced the paper here and it for this reason that what follows is rather informal in style and is not annotated or cross referenced to *Life Together* or to secondary sources.

what he has to do with a culture increasingly separated from Christian belief—remains central to Bonheoffer's insistence, for reasons that will become apparent.

"*Life Together*", Bonheoffer's book in which he describes his vision for a truly Christian community, is both profound and simple. Perhaps it is profound because it is simple. Or even the other way about! At any rate, it demands slowness and gentleness on our part. Much of it sounds somewhat predictably Lutheran and devotional and, at first, we may be tempted to dismiss it a merely a series of well-worn evangelical pieties from a particular time and place: well-intended (especially so in Nazi Germany) but bearing little weight for our post-modern, socially and religiously more complex and certainly more sceptical age. We would be entirely wrong to do so and for reasons that have nothing to do with Bonheoffer's personal integrity, his martyrdom, or his theological prowess. Rather, what we have in "*Life Together*" is exactly that—a means by which we might begin to live more faithfully in the world and even incorporate some of the insights and practices of the monastic tradition to our daily lives. For many, this book has laid the foundation of a "New or Secular Monasticism".

Its context is one which speaks of critical division and the need for authentic decision-making in the face of the Nazi dictatorship in Germany, not the comparatively easy pluralism of twenty-first century Britain. It is a text that arises from and speaks to the crisis of Christendom but is still able to presuppose much of its fabric—unlike Bonheoffer's prison writings, for example. Even so, there is a deep continuity between the different phases of Bonheoffer's writings and spiritual experience. It is necessary therefore to attend to him in that way, as well as noticing the evident differences.

What we might now call the "sub-text" of "*Life Together*" is startling, discomforting wisdom. So, it is important to persist with it, to dwell with it beyond any obvious point of bearing that we may feel. Its art and its prayerfulness do not consist in appealing to our many "feelings", it stretches them, or rather, it stretches us beyond them.

Bonheoffer's central message is that what we might call "true Christian community" (and what he more helpfully calls "Life Together") exists in Christ for the sake of the world, and that it only becomes possible when the dewy morning mist of hopes and dreams and visions have evaporated. Life Together is not to be confused with a romantic, or at least sentimental, "*sense of community*". Out too must go all our ideas of conventional Christian behaviour as the true way of Life. To exaggerate this for the purposes of illustration; is it permitted to smoke while meditating? Absolutely!

On this sort of small concern Bonheoffer's practice is less counter-cultural than it may seem, though no doubt "worthy" Lutherans were as suspicious of the daily pleasures of the flesh as we might expect them to have been. But Bonheoffer repeatedly insists that it is not our ideals or ideal behaviour that matters. It is the invisible that is killing us. What we do not see of common life is strangling us, and the invincible idealisations that lie behind our inaction are the source of our dying.

These days, for example, we speak easily of "fresh expressions" or "new forms of church" because many people have given up on the old, or because much of what we have inherited seems no longer to "work". So instead, we become advocates of the "café church" the "performance space church", the "fluid church", "family church" or "house church". We speak also of "churchless faith", of the "church beyond the congregation"—and even of a virtual church which exists only in so far as computer generated images on-line "exist".

Though some of this—deriving from ecumenical reflections of the missionary structures prevalent in the 1970s—was attributed to his influence, Bonheoffer would surely have been suspicious of "new ways of being church". Merely "changing church" is not enough. Where is the new (or old) form rooted? In whom or in what is it grounded? We can have variety and adaptability but we need also to concentrate on formation. The congregation is *not* dispensable. It is, as it were, "where the rubber hits the road" in terms of the Christian experience of God in relation to the world. That is by no means to dismiss experiments in missionary activities or the formation of base or intentional communities. It is certainly not to dismiss the formation of "secular" monastic communities, but it is to say that if these things are regarded as an alternative to or formed at the expense of the demanding simplicities of what Bonheoffer calls "life together," then we are gravely mistaken.

What we often want today is not to be church at all, but to discover ever-new "techniques" or skills that might "do" it for us. So, we create programmes, processes, guides, gurus and genii. Far from being the answer they can so often become the real problem. Nothing will "do" life together for us. We have to live together—in the company and presence of the world. If we do not really want this, or if we do so only on our own terms or in our own strength, we will be found out. If we do not in fact have life together then we also have no message beyond that of another group of individuals seeking individual happiness, meaning and extrication from problems ("salvation") in a "Jesusified" form. This is, of course, precisely what many people suspect is going on among us, and then we wonder why they stay away from our rhetoric and us.

Where concern for the world stands at the margins, or where it is nothing more than to create a world according to what we are concerned about, then church is not possible. All that is possible is a more or less formal gathering of people interested only in themselves—in their own rituals, their own beliefs and ideas (whether "right doctrine" or its "recreation") and their own ends. Only the real world can save the church from avoiding the challenges and demands of the saviour through the false but comforting illusions of religion.

How then can we move forward to the life together that Bonheoffer had in mind? Paradoxically, Bonhoeffer wrote about *"re-founding religious life"*. By this he meant, I think, not abstract, self-centred religious life, but a practical God-centred life for others, in the world. It is concept he developed as a result of his visits to a number of monastic and quasi-monastic communities in England while he was a pastor in London. He visited our Anglican Community of the Resurrection in Yorkshire, a grouping of the Society of Friends (Quakers) at Woodstock near Birmingham, Methodists in Richmond, Surrey, and the Roman Catholic Community of the Sacred Heart. So, it is a concept drawn from a wide spectrum of theological understandings and practices and Bonheoffer hoped that it might be applicable to all of them.

The *"re-founding of religious life"* is nothing less than a "secular monasticism"—a wholly new and radical concept for a Lutheran of his time and place—and its limits might have been even wider than we now envisage if his plans to spend with Ghandi had come to fulfilment. For Bonheoffer, Life Together, secular monasticism, is centred on Christ but not a Christ exclusive to or limited by the constraints of the church.

We see this in his own basic experiment in secular monasticism when he was Principal of a Lutheran Seminary. He took already intellectually able young men and opened and equipped them to the possibility of being radically reformed. Traditional German theological rigour could not have prepared them for that! Being forced to meditate on texts for longer than the mind could stand (*extended lectio divina?*), being subjected to a radically democratic common life in which decisions were taken as a result of consultation with every member, being required to bring their own personal reflections to the object of their study as well as those of accepted authority—all these broke the boundaries of theological education. The demands of this life together were regarded by many, including those who undertook them, as far from ideal especially since they also involved mutual confession. Bonheoffer included himself in this and clearly understood it as part of his accountability.

As a result, the notion of a corporate priesthood (similar perhaps to the older understandings of Canons Regular) was developed. This was wholly different from and posed a challenge to elevated sacerdotalism which somewhat ironically had become as much a feature of mid-twentieth century Lutheranism as anything to be found in Catholicism in the sixteenth. Bonheoffer believed that priest—hood is formed in all who exemplify priestly ministry and qualities but insisted that priesthood cannot be understood only in a limited sense.

Priesthood is, of course, defined by its sacramental ministry (even in Lutheranism) but Bonheoffer did not wish to make its understanding of the "priesthood of all believers" so vague and nebulous that it became meaningless and devoid of content. Central to corporate priesthood was the monthly celebration of the Eucharist. Bonheoffer's life together was seen as *Eucharistic* life together, not because the Eucharist was celebrated daily or as a matter of routine, but by virtue of its depth, quality and correspondence to authentic practices in the community and in the world. Bonheoffer. Eucharist is lived eschatology.

In all of this, the outward focus of life together is intrinsic to its meaning: service extends outside, it takes place not in the secure confines of the cloister but "in the presence of my enemies" (Ps. 23:5). Resisting Nazism while modelling something wholly different to its methods and ideas became central to the meaning of contemporary Christian discipleship for Dietrich Bonheoffer—insofar a Nazi ideology, structure and practice made alternative and deeply distorted death dealing claims about the nature of the world, human beings and God. It is at this point that Christ's command to love enemies became a distinguishing characteristic of Bonheoffer's community.

Community is a privilege realised by giving thanks for those who do not like it, and it opens up the possibility of transforming those who hate by bringing them (and us) into the presence of Christ. This is not the banal if well intentioned question "What would Jesus do…" but rather "Who is Christ and what does his Christ-ness demand of us and our mutual liberation?" This is, of course, the question for which Bonheoffer is well known, "Who really is Jesus Christ today?" and the possibilities of finding an answer are outlined in "*Life Together*".

Bonheoffer knew that the gift of community can so easily be trampled upon, lost or taken away on any day and at any point, *precisely because* it is a gift and not a possession, property or technique. *Non nobis, domine not* unto us but from the Giver. By the same token, precisely because it is a gift community can be experienced even in prison, as Bonheoffer discovered. Community is nothing but grace and grace completely changes what we regard as "realistic" in our Life Together. In the face of Nazi dictatorship, it was essential that Bonheoffer's community dispel the dream world in order to live fruitfully and faithfully in the real one—but at the heart of reality is the Giver who forbids our possession of the gift and so keeps us open to continual giving and receiving, like the manna in the desert.

But we might still ask; what is life together? Where is it to be found? How do we bring it about? Bonheoffer does not give a generalised or pre-planned answer. That is difficult and frustrating. Life together exists according to the specific and unique circumstance surrounding every particular secular monastic community. To a large extent it may only be recognised for what it is in hindsight or, to name it as the grace hindsight is, "*memory*".

It is easier in some ways to say what life together is not. It is not, as we have seen, an ideal. Those who love the dream of secular monasticism rather than its harsh reality destroy it. Disillusion overcomes them. What then? Do such people "get over it" by putting aside mere ideals, struggle on, or decide that the whole enterprise is not worth a candle? Bonheoffer reminds them, and us, that when we create community of any kind, we leave ourselves exposed to the deadly sin of pride, to judgement and hence to utter failure. Prayer is required.

Once again, the manner of prayer and inescapable mutual dependence that Bonheoffer has in mind cannot be manufactured through our own strength of will or intention. They come about only through Christ. "Through Christ" is a term which Bonheoffer uses repeatedly in "*Life Together*" and he attaches a specific set of meanings to it. First, Christ is our peace. He is the mediator not only between God and humankind, but between human beings and all that is. This means, secondly, that we know only through Christ and this in turn means, thirdly, that all our relationships are mediate, not immediate and it is they that matter most, not our individual selves. We exist in Christ and in Christ. It is a matter of obedience as it is for professed monastics and for exactly the same reasons. This is a difficult truth for most people to bear. Unfettered autonomy is so much part of the script of post-modernity that it feels like a burden rather than a release to be inescapably in mutual relationship. Living "through Christ" redefines those relationships in a liberating way, by freeing it to a call and blessing of service to others.

"But," we may ask, "what about those not in Christ?" This question entirely misunderstands what is going on here. Christ, according to the ancient Chalcedonian formula in mainstream Christian thought down the ages and so too in the writings of Bonheoffer, reveals all that is most fully human. In that sense, he is and will be all in all. Yet Christ only becomes a part by being apart—thus the identity and separation of the Christian community (including and especially monastic ones) that is finally for and not against the world. It seems to me that increasing numbers of Christians today take the opposite view and would far rather that we were against the world at every moment so it is necessary to tease out just what we mean, or rather what Bonheoffer might mean about being for the world.

The main reason for being for the world, even in the short term, is that it gives us a chance of discovering its potential in God, and in life together. This is what I call the "scandal of universality in particularity". The old conservative versus liberal or high church versus evangelical game, or even cloistered monastic versus secular monastic is about anxiously choosing and elevating one over the other—but it entirely misses the real point. The point is that the particularity by which we are offered God and the world as our liberation in Christ makes no sense outside the universal hope of a universal God, but also that we know nothing "universally"—we know only in and through the particular. Communication is about openness focussed in the specific, and a specificity that can point beyond itself. So, it is with Jesus Christ.

This sounds abstract and cerebral and yet the intention is practical, face-to-face and immediate. Christ is not a technique, a technology or a theory, but reveals all that is fully God (the other half of the Chalcedonian formula). As such he abolishes other mediations—such as materialism—that communicate anything less than the otherness of the Other and the others. Note, however, the danger of idealising this anti-idealism! This is what happens in much proselytising language about Christ which so often does violence to the integrity, meaning and purpose of Christ for the world. It is that "for-ness" that is lost in the abolition of the other. For Bonheoffer, however, it is central. That is why his message, though thoroughly Chalcedonian and Christocentric in character, is the opposite of many forms of proclamation that are so familiar to us at present which would confine the love of God only to a select (elect?) few.

So it is that, for Bonheoffer, we find that the so-called exclusivity of Christian devotion is nothing of the sort. Rather it confronts us with the anti-exclusivity of God's love. This love has, therefore, parallels and appearances elsewhere. We should celebrate these. Love of the other is immediately bound to the true nature and grounding of Christ. But Christian practice is not rooted in general values; it flows from the experience of community arising from a history going back to the eruption of Jesus into our assumptions about the world and God. It is sustained by the same presence and power that raised Christ from the dead. Bonheoffer did not express it in quite these terms, but this very broad and yet focussed vision is surely at the heart of his own spiritual and physical journey from *"Life Together"* to *"Letters and Papers from Prison"*.

Devotion, in the sense of loving attention to that which really matters is what shapes all of this. In *"Life Together"* intercessory prayers are the means by which we bring each other before God so that we can individually and as a community of faith, see each other as forgiven sinners, thus entirely changing our usual perspective and relationships. "Sin" is all that mars communication.

In prayer we are, according to Bonheoffer, "with Jesus" In prayer we come to know that in his body Jesus Christ bears our flesh and *vice versa*. We are the *Body* individually; we are spiritual-physical creatures. But we are most fully *"The Body"* when we freely participate in one another, take the consequences of doing so and offer *"The Body"* to the world as a sign of its hope. This is the basis of anything worthy in the name of the name of "secular monasticism". Everything else is secondary. What comes first is our accompaniment of one another in the presence of Christ, with devotion to God in Christ, through discipleship in the way of Christ, as partners of the Body of Christ in and for the world, and empowered by the same Spirit of God that is in Christ. That is what it means to live the Gospel in the every day. That is what it means to be truly evangelical, not in the sense of some ecclesiastical tribe, but in the sense of being orientated towards the "Good News". That too is what it means to be ecumenical, orientated towards not just other denominations but towards the whole inhabited creation. It is supremely what it is to be part of the *"One, Holy, Catholic and Apostolic Church"*—universal in our particularity.

For Bonheoffer then, and I hope for us too, through and with Christ is there the hope and actuality of life together. That is what we know. What we do with that knowledge is, painfully, up to us.

Chapter 26
Thomas Merton:
The Relevance of Irrelevancy

Over forty years have now passed since the tragic and early death of Thomas Merton. His death was replete with a number of ironies. He had fought to live in increasing monastic solitude for over a quarter of a century and yet died thousands of miles away from his hermitage. He was a convinced pacifist and yet his body was flown to the United States in a military aeroplane. The plane landed not at a civilian airport but a military one that was central to the war effort in Vietnam.

Now that such a time has gone by, we are in a good position to assess both Thomas Merton the monk and his many varied writings. That task is at once easy and extremely difficult. It is easy because he is one of the most familiar, prolific and accessible monastic writers of the twentieth century. His spiritual autobiography, *The Seven Storey Mountain* (1948) was regarded as a classic from the moment of its publication and was, and is, often favourably compared to the *Confessions* of St Augustine of Hippo.

Like Augustine, Merton had an ability to be ruthless in his self-criticism and yet ever so slightly smug, even triumphant at the same time! After that huge publishing success, Merton produced many learned tomes, articles and volumes of poetry. The sheer quantity of them, overlaid by his personal fame makes the task of assessment more difficult especially when we take into account the fact that that it was Merton who almost single-handedly introduced the American Roman Catholic community to the fruits of monasticism and the contemplative tradition.

Indeed, it was through Merton that the Catholic community in America (or at least it's more "liberal" branches) became gripped by all things monastic. It was not simply a matter of increased monastic vocations, though the Cistercian monasteries did experience phenomenal growth at this time, it was also seen in the more avant-garde journals of the day which were suddenly filled with articles about meditation, contemplative prayer, Gregorian chant and experiment in new or secular monasticism. Unfortunately, and through no direct fault of Merton himself, many viewed these things and monastic life in particular from a romantic, sentimental and therefore unrealistic standpoint. There is little evidence, I think, to suggest that Merton dissuaded people from taking this view or took steps to correct it. It was, after all, a view he shared, especially at the beginning of his exploration of his monastic vocation and his recurring desire to abandon the Cistercians in favour of the Carthusians.

With the advent of the Second Vatican Council, it may have been supposed that Merton would be eclipsed by the new writers for a new age such as Jacques Maritain and Dietrich Bonhoeffer (and even perhaps, Harvey Cox!). He suffered no such overshadowing, even though he increasingly seemed to be very much a child of the 1960s. Merton wrote no criticism of the new the new ecclesial order (though he had plenty of criticisms to make!) and nor did he become, like Hans Kung and other luminaries, a theological media guru. He seemed, in fact, to buck the trend. As the cry went up for relevance and greater engagement with the world, Merton pressed for what he wanted: further retreat from the world—the eremitical life.

From his hermitage, he continued to write books on spirituality, the need for east-west dialogue, volumes of poetry and resounding protests against racism and war. In the last years of his life, his influence was further underscored in that others began to write doctoral theses and other books about him and his theology. This was a trend which was to intensify after his death so that at present there is still a steady stream of writing, monographs and studies flowing year by year.

What explains and sustains this interest in a Cistercian monk? I think that question demands another and more basic one. It is this: What did Merton represent himself to be or, better, how has he been perceived by his many public admirers? He was not a professional theologian in the conventional sense of the word, although he did write some impressive works on ascetical theology,[935] but there were no books which provide us with systematic reflections on the datum of the faith. He was a poet and a literary critic, but I think that it does no

---

[935] For example, *New Seeds of Contemplation* (1962). London. Burns & Oates cardinal Books and *The Climate of Monastic Prayer* (2018). Foreword by Sarah Coakley. Collegeville. Liturgical press. to name but two.

disservice to his memory to say that his poetry was not quite of the first rank and that his criticism was eclectic, occasional and varying in quality to say the least. He was not a social critic either in any sustained fashion, although his social reflections could, and did, provoke strong and powerful responses. Even as a monastic commentator, Merton's output did not match the scholarship of, say, Fr. Jean LeClerq.[936]

Yet to attempt to "classify" Merton in any of these dualistic categories—as poet *or* theologian, as critic *or* monastic commentator—is rather to miss the point. Thomas Merton was primarily a Cistercian monk; that is the way he defined himself from the moment he entered the Gethesemanii Abbey, and that is the way he understood himself in the last months before his death. It is true that his notion of monasticism changed, developed and matured over the years. It is equally true that there were times when he seems to have hated his vocation or at least regarded it as a stifling burden. He had to shed all romantic notions of the monk as a pious figure shuffling about in a dusty cloister moving from cell to abbey church and from there to a library or a quiet study or gentle work in a garden or Grange. He had to do that in order to come to terms with the fact that a monk is a "marginal person who withdraws deliberately to the margins of society with a view to deepening fundamental human experience".[937]

For Merton then, the task and calling of a monk is to become more and more irrelevant, more and more invisible. It was that idea which, paradoxically, brought him to public notice and attention because it simply did not fit with the general mood of the 1960s. The quest for irrelevancy was not what that decade was about at all! Merton insisted that the monk needs to conduct his faith at the margins because he needs to live close to the edge of death. Only in that way can the monk understand the limits of life.

This concern with the particularities of the monastic vocation is especially prominent in Merton's book "*Contemplation in a World of Action*".[938] This brought together a number of Merton's essays and conference papers on the monastic life which had been written and delivered during the 1960s. In this

---

[936] His lectures to the novices at Gethsemanii on pre-Benedictine monastic rules are however, in my opinion, the exception to that general rule.
[937] Merton (1975) The *Asian Journal*, New York. New Directions Publishing. P 305.
[938] Merton: *Contemplation in a World of Action* (1998). Notre Dame. University of Notre Dame Press.

volume his idea of monastic irrelevancy is expressed in a somewhat different way:

"The monk is not defined by his task, his usefulness, because his task is not to do this or that but to be a man of God."[939]

It is from this perspective that the monk should be able to acquire a sense of the deepest meaning of life itself; he also "will be in some sense critical of the world, its routines, its confusions, and its sometimes-tragic failures to provide other men with lives that are fully sane and human."[940]

This sense of distance and marginality had to be lived in creative tension with the world and so it was important for Merton to delete the earlier idea of the Trappist that he had helped to create in *The Seven Storey Mountain*:

"The man who spurned New York, spat on Chicago, and tramped Louisville, heading for the woods with Thoreau in one pocket, John of the Cross in the other and holding the Bible open at the Apocalypse."[941]

In fact, Merton the solitary carried on a passionate, if critical, dialogue with the world. His writings and speeches attest to the post-Vatican II Catholic appetite for the problems and hopes of the modern world.

Indeed, I would argue that it is precisely through that peculiar angle of his life as a hermit that Merton proved his relevance to modern Catholic life. Many of the problems with which Merton struggled in the last decade of his life anticipated many of the topics that were to occupy the whole church in the 1970s, 1980s and beyond, but which seemed esoteric or even trivial at any earlier time.

First, Merton shared a marked interest in cultures and practices other than those born of the western enlightenment. He was a passionate student of the poetry and culture of Latin America and the Far East. One of Merton's novices at Gethsemanii, Ernesto Cardenal, became a famous poet in Nicaragua as well as one of his country's greatest social critics who influenced some of the thinking of the later liberation theologians in that land. Cardenal set up a small "basic community" at Soletiname which was organised on semi-monastic lines. It was destroyed by the police and Cardenal himself became a man on the run—the epitome of Merton's notion of monasticism at the margins.

Second, Merton had an abiding interest in Eastern thought, especially Zen and Tibetan Buddhism. Such an interest is now common among Christian priests,

---

[939] Loc citP27. My emphasis added.
[940] Loc cit P28.
[941] Op Cit. *Contemplation in a World of Action* p 159.

monks, nuns and lay folk alike. It has been of great and positive benefit to them in understanding the nature and depth of meditation and contemplative prayer and has helped us to appreciate not only the beauty of a tradition we do not share but also that of our own. For example, it has revived and broadened our appreciation of the Jesus Prayer and just what it might mean to try to pray unceasingly. But at the time all this was radical and many feared it. Some still do.

Merton was a pioneer in this important field. Merton's importance was that he consistently refused any and all facile and misleading appropriations of eastern spirituality. He exemplified to a significant degree that journey which the Notre Dame theologian John Dunne has described as "crossing over" without losing one's fidelity to the Christian tradition.[942]

Merton "crossed over" not as a teacher or missionary, but as student and pilgrim. He wanted to discover what the east had learnt about spirituality in general and monasticism in particular. His purpose, as fragments in his *Asian Journey* make clear, was to enhance the contemplative life of his own tradition. Merton was able to use Buddhist concepts to critique and clarify his own monastic life.

One example is sufficient. It is quite evident that his deep desire for greater solitude was tempered by the Buddhist concept of "compassion". He began to see how his monastic life had to oscillate between the anonymity of eremitical silence and openness to the needs of others on both an individual and social level. It was because of this clarification (that was apparently not available in his Cistercian studies) that Merton opted for a life which was to balance remote solitude with periods of availability.

Third, and most importantly, Merton was the foremost American spiritual writer of his (or perhaps any other) generation. He was a theologian in the ancient patristic sense of the word, by which I mean he could think and write and speak easily and existentially about his experience of God. He had a profound sense of the western spiritual tradition and was able to communicate in ways which made sense to a wide variety of modern audiences. In the 1960s, he was almost a *vox clamantis in deserto* (a voice crying in the desert) as he railed against a mindless activism cut off from the deep roots of prayer, contemplation and reflection.

---

[942] John Dunne (1978) *The Way of All the Earth -Experiments in Truth and Religion* Notre Dame. University of Notre Dame Press.

If Merton was indeed a lone voice then, he is a sane voice now, when interest in "spirituality" is manifest. Alas, even contemporary Christian circles are by no means immune to odd currents of pseudo-spirituality which are products of our fascination with the noise and nonsense of psychobabble. It is precisely in this area that Merton continues to provide a corrective and be a model for our day. He was able to be part of the ancient tradition of Christian monasticism while being alert to new ways through which that tradition can be enhanced, enlarged and made more available to ordinary (secular) lay women and men too.

The Church of the early twentieth century was in great need of people like Merton who could stand back from its turmoil and see it from a semi-detached point of view. We should seek them in our poets, musicians, composers and artists. We should seek them in our critics, drop outs, revolutionaries and nonconformists of all kinds. But we should never overlook the possibility of finding them where they have always been: in the monasteries. Thomas Merton was surely one of those rare souls who can turn the marginality of their own lives into a presence of importance for the whole church. St Thomas More was another. He is reputed to have said that what the world needed most were more houses for the poor and more real monks. I think he was right about that and ever so slowly we are getting the former. In rare, grace-filled moments, we also get the latter. For that small favour, we should thank Almighty God.

Chapter 27
John Main Meditating on the Mysterious Shape of God's Affection

"As long as our faith is seen as comprising a movement from man to God, we can only remain self-centred, earthbound. But in apprehending it as the movement from God to man we discover ourselves caught up in that movement, in its own depths, self-transcending and returning to the Father through the Son. Another name for this movement is Love."[943]

If we were to try and characterise the spiritual pilgrimage and teaching of John Main in the search for the development of inner space through a secular monasticism we could not, I think, do better than use that quotation.

The movement he describes there immersed him into the depths of divine providence; the mystery of the relationship of the Father and the Son in the love of the Holy Spirit. The silence of simplicity gave John Main the consciousness of being drawn into that reciprocated love of God through identification in his inner self with the risen Jesus.

This, in turn, seems to have been based on the prayer of Jesus for his disciples, "Father, I have made you known to them and will continue to make them known in order that the love you have for me may be in them and that I myself might be given to them." (John 17:26) To be in God as Christ is in God and to be in Christ as God is in Christ through the indwelling of the Holy Spirit is both the mystery of (Christian) human being and the grace of our calling. To experience that union is to be "caught up" in that returning movement.

John Main constantly spoke and wrote being caught up in the mystery which is wholly beyond us and yet contains us. Meditation must lead us to complete silence, to the necessary void of the desert experience precisely because the

---

[943] John Main (1980) *Word Into Silence*. London. Darton Longman and Todd. p37.

mystery, the paradox, ca never be finally fathomed; meditation is the silent consciousness of the mystery of God within us as made known in the sacraments and, especially, the Eucharist.

Thus, John Main embarked on his spiritual journey towards the mystery of God's affection, not by the futile effort of analysing and measuring what eternally eludes the grasp of human understanding, but by allowing himself to be totally immersed in the life of the Holy Trinity lived at the centre of his constantly expanding self. It is in this sense that John Main was a Trinitarian Christian. In other words, he was free of a created self that he had fully integrated and joyfully renounced to allow the Self of God, the loving relationship of the Holy Trinity, to rise at the centre of his consciousness. There he knew perfectly who he was. There he was totally attentive and present to himself because he was totally surrendered to God.

According to Main, we *must* find our true selves in a relationship of creature-creator. We are by nature dependent. In order to be a faithful disciple, the Christian must lose her finite self into the infinite Self of God. Meditation gives us that freedom. It is the freedom to accept our reality and to discover our liberated self. In meditation, says John Main:

"You just sit still and it is in that stillness that you gain the wisdom to see that you can only be yourself, you can only be yourself who is the person you are created to be, if you are willing to lose yourself. The truth that you can discover from your own experience is this—that any one of us can only find ourselves in the Other. No amount of self-analysis or self-examination will ever reveal to you who to you are. But if you can take the focus of your attention off yourself and project it forward then you will discover the Other and in discovering the Other, you will discover yourself. The Other is the ground of All Being, the Other we call God, Supreme Wisdom, Supreme Being, Supreme love. The name is not important. Indeed, in meditation and in the complete silence of it, we go beyond all words, to the Reality."[944]

Here we see, I think, a modern Benedictine reformulation of the Christian ontology found in the Augustinian tradition and an understanding of the human self, rooted in the mystical tradition which we noted in the Carmelite tradition in St Theresa of Avila and St John of the Cross. It is in this sense that John main

---

[944] John Main (1984) *Moment of Christ*. London. Darton Longman and Todd. p 86.

was, I think, able to pursue a unique and somewhat eclectic spiritual journey without censure from his superiors because it maintained this Orthodox course.

John Main was a teacher and leader in the tradition of St Benedict whom he characterised as a heroic leader. As we might expect, Benedict's inspiration was a determining influence in shaping his monastic profile:

"Now, St Benedict…is in the heroic mould because his vision of the Christian life which he is writing about in his Rule is a vision of life that is constantly expanding. The horizons are always opening and for him the reason for this is that the Christian life is…openness to the wonder and mystery of God. The wonder and mystery that is itself infinite."[945]

John Main's vision for developing the inner space through a secular monasticism did not depend on his assuming the responsibility of our pilgrimage for us. In this way, just like his predecessor and Holy Father St Benedict, John Main knew by spiritual instinct and experience that everyone has the unique and inescapable responsibility for walking alone in the power of God's Spirit, because every single individual has a unique place in a personal "I-Thou" relationship. This is, perhaps, why John Main never felt the urge to ally his theology with a particular school of thought or make it systematic. His is not a theology based on intellectual enquiry but the fruit of long experience brining the insights of monastic spirituality into the modern world.

One book, however, does, in my view, constitute a theological manifesto in the traditional sense and it has been of great importance in composing this chapter. It is *"Word into Silence"*, published in England in 1980. In it, we find his most profound teaching. Like the leitmotif of a great symphony, the theme recurs repeatedly in the orchestration of his many other books, pamphlets, articles and CDs. But once one has studied *"Word into Silence"* it's teaching is always identifiable. It is primarily from that source of information that much of the remaining material for this chapter is drawn the main focus of which will may rightly call his "spiritual theology", his understanding of what it means to meditate on the mysterious shape of God's affection for us in our daily, secular, lives.

As I noted above, John Main invites ordinary lay Christians to explore the nature of our human selves as a precondition to wholeness, serenity and harmony. Main is convinced that unless we have a healthy relationship with our

---

[945] John Main (1983) *Community of Love*. Montreal. The Benedictine Priory, p16.

own self, we cannot expect our religious pilgrimage to lead us anywhere than a dead end. To be relevant and effective, an authentic relationship with God must first be rooted and grounded in self-discovery, self-reconciliation and true self-love. The knowledge of our self, or better, the search for our true self, is already a sign of divine grace and is the right place to begin. As we move from the periphery to the centre, from complexity to simplicity, from word into silence, from action to agape solitude, from death to life, from immersion in the world to monastic solitude, we leave behind our egos which have been conditioned by the world of illusions and fed on ideological stimuli.

A medieval English mystic wrote of the *"Cloud of Unknowing"* but what Main is suggesting, I think, is that what we now need is a "Cloud of Forgetting" so that we can truly enter an inner space where our true self is the very Self of God, the ground of All Being, the source of All Love and the consummation of our human destiny. In other words, the attempt to create a secular monasticism and an inner space begins at this level of consciousness where conversion of life, *metanoia,* calls us away from illusion and into reality. In this way, the "Kingdom of God is at hand."[946]

For Main, it is through conversion of life, or integration of our self into the Self of God, that we discover reality and experience what he calls self-transcendence rather than self-fulfilment. The latter is a cultivation of the ego. The former is openness to the absolute of an unconditional love. The search for self and the need of love are one and the same pursuit.

The first step then, is to allow ourselves to be loved. It was to facilitate this that the Holy Spirit was sent into the world and into human hearts, to touch and awaken, to draw our minds into its redemptive light.[947]

More often than not our failure to engage or progress in the development of inner space, or our spiritual journeys generally, is symptomatic of our failure to find ourselves. Main saw the discipline of meditation as the primary and simple process by which we prepare ourselves to be at peace with our inner reality. Then and only then, can we appreciate and experience that deeper peace which the world cannot give which is the peace of God deep within the heart of God.[948] Finding the inner space in which heart can speak to heart, as the Blessed John

---

[946] John Main (1983) *The Hunger for Prayer*. Montreal. The Benedictine Priory. p16.
[947] Op cit *Word into Silence*. p37.
[948] And here we might note some similarities between what Main has to say and what St Francis de la Sales taught about the broken heart of Christ.

Henry Newman also believed, is the whole purpose and goal of the Christian journey. Such a goal can never be reached unless or until our daily secular walk in the world is informed and sustained by a clear understanding of who and what we are as human beings—as the most beloved children of God.

The first step then, is not just to allow ourselves to be loved but to *decide* that we want to be loved and at peace with ourselves. This occurs through the transformation of our consciousness as we gradually encounter the beauty of our being. This is, in fact, intensely Biblical. It is what the Letter to the Romans calls "the renewing of our mind" (Rom.12:2). The discipline of meditation allows us to do precisely that: to become aware of our self and to see that ultimately our life does not exist apart from the Reality of God. In meditation, we understand that it is God alone who gives existence, meaning and purpose to what we are meant to be and truly are in God's eternal now, not just abstractly but as a lived reality.

By the practice of meditation, we are challenged to pay attention to our self and to the mystery of the divine presence located at its centre. In the practice of meditation we concentrate on the self, attend to the self, not for the sake of the self but with the expectation that our consciousness and our whole lives will be made whole by merging with the whole life of God.

John Main says that such a moment of merger is not a one-off event but is potentially present every time we meditate, howbeit that we may be rarely aware that a moment of merger has occurred. He describes such moments as *"smashing the mirror"*, by which he means that when we are united with God *"as our supreme power source"*, we break through the screen of the *"hyper-self-consciousness of egos"*.

For him, original sin is nothing less than divided consciousness which comes about through the dualism of post-enlightenment thought. The divided consciousness of dualism puts, as it were, a mirror between us and God. This again looks very Pauline for, like St Paul's mirror (I Cor 13:12) it is tarnished, capable of reflecting only our image and not the image of God. The mirror which reverses the reflections of everything we see (including our self) must be smashed in order not to look backwards and meditation is the means of our restoration.[949] According to Main, Jesus insisted upon this smashing when he

---

[949] Op cit *Moment of Christ* p50.

said that no one could be a disciple unless they are prepared to leave the self behind.

Thus, John Main had much to say to those contemporary Christians who find theological debates arid and irrelevant and yet had difficulty in experiencing the power of the Gospel of Christ personally. He invited them to draw on the hidden, and often unknown and ignored forces at work in their inner self. Such people, he thought are looking for the perennial fruits of the Spirit: peace, liberty, joy the freedom and the power of Love. In short, they are looking for the strength and the courage to be. In this search they must come to terms with themselves at the most simple and most elemental level. This is neither new or innovative in the monastic tradition but rests on the comment of St Augustine of Hippo that "Man must first be restored to himself, make of himself a stepping stone and rise from self to God."[950]

As people embark on this process the basic discipline is to pay attention, to become alert, to awaken to the splendour of our relatedness to God. Created by God, we have a divine origin which is the source of our being, the energy of our doing, the restoration of our self and the object of our joy. But we cannot become aware of the beauty of our own creation or that of the world around us and within us, without sharing in the very glory of our creator. It is a glory we discover at the centre of our consciousness as we begin to live our lives as the outpouring of the power of our divine master.

This is the secret of all deep prayer, the prayer of silent union. The experience of prayer is the experience of coming into full union with the divine energy that created the universe. What Christianity has to proclaim to the world is that that energy is Love and it is the fountain head from which all creation flows. It is the fountain head that gives each one of us the creative power to be the person we are called to be—a person deeply rooted and established in Love.[951]

According to John Main, our spiritual experience should not be limited to our intellectual assent to a series of theological propositions. This is said so often from the pulpit and in all forms of Christian writing that it has become something of a cliché. As such its truth needs to be recovered. For Main spiritual reality does not come from theology, rather theology comes from spiritual reality.

That is to say, spiritual reality has an existential dimension which gives it authority: hence the importance of experiencing our own creation. In order to do

---

[950] Op cit *Hunger for Prayer* pp24–25.
[951] Op cit *Moment of Christ* p20.

so, we must try not to think of God as creator, but be with him and know him as the ground of our being. The experience is utterly simple. To be with God does not demand words, thoughts or discourses but the silent consciousness of God's presence. In saying this, John Main assumed the role of a prophet to his generation and to ours, reminding us that our spiritual journey has no future unless we are willing to accept the courage to become more and more silent.

Our inner space will not even begin to develop unless and until we are willing to accept the discipline of silence. Silence will teach us that we cannot apprehend God by thinking about him because God is a mystery infinitely beyond us and yet intimately within us. Silence frees us from the limitations of language. It frees us from the thought which would tend to reduce God to anthropomorphic categories. Silence allows us to communicate with God and be in communion with him as he is, not with a man-made intellectual image of the divine. Silence creates the inner space which opens us to the encompassing mystery of the divine instead of restricting us to the concrete materiality of an idol.

At this point, it is important to distinguish, as John Main does, between different sorts of silence. Main drew a contrast between the *"silence of oblivion"* and the "silence of full consciousness". The former is no more than an emptying, a void, whereas the latter is a filling of the mind with revelation. Silence of full consciousness reveals the Word of God free of all human intellectual speculation:

"What brings us out of the dead silence to the living conscious silence which leads us into the knowledge of our union with God is the Word…The personal experience of this power is the goal of the Christian pilgrimage of prayer. As we follow the pilgrimage we grow into an even deeper simplicity, an even sharper and more immediate encounter. We come less and less to see 'to experience the experience' but rather to allow the experience to be, to emerge, to expand and transform us."[952]

Whether we are aware of the mystical phenomenon or not, we are permeated by the light of the Holy Spirit. Writing on *Learning to be Silent* in the first chapter of *Word into Silence,* John Main remarked:

"In meditation our stillness [silence] is not a state of mere passivity but a state of full openness, full wakefulness to the wonder of our own being, full

---

[952] John Main (1983) *The Other-Centeredness of Mary*. Montreal. The Benedictine Priory. p9.

openness to the wonder of God, the author and sustainer of our being, and a full awareness that we are one with God."[953]

Meditation is a process of gradual revelation. Through it, we learn that we are called to that fullness of life for which Paul prayed on behalf of the Ephesians:

"And I pray that you being rooted and grounded in love may have power together with all the saints to grasp how wide and long and high and deep is the love of Christ, and to know this love that surpasses knowledge that you may be filled to the measure of all the fullness of God." (Eph3:19–20)

So according to John Main we enter into meditation precisely to seek that fullness of life already dwelling in each of us. This is the fullness of the risen Christ which the Holy Spirit, whose temples we are, presents as a sacrifice of praise and glory to the Father. John Main wrote of the human condition as seen from a faith perspective in this way:

"We have been allowed to enter the sphere of God's grace where we now stand. Jesus has blazed the trail for us and through his own experience has incorporated us into his present state which is glorious communion with the Father in his risen life, a life that now pervades the whole of creation. We stand in the sphere of God's grace because we are his and he is where we are. We are in him and his spirit is in us."[954]

Main does not therefore hesitate to say that we are infinitely holy, and indeed called to be truly united with God. This is a theme which is close to Eastern Orthodox mystical theology which we noted in an earlier chapter: *"...our vocation is to look upon and contemplate the Godhead and thus be ourselves divinised."*[955]

In meditation, we realise the depth of our intimate union with God our Father through Christ in the Holy Spirit. There at the very centre of ourselves we are purified in mind and heart, totally open to the transforming work of God's love for us. We quietly and peacefully reflect in all our relationships the light and heat and warmth of that love. To be perfectly at one with God in the tranquillity of one's heart is the fruit of the development of inner space offered by John Main.

Again, this is neither new nor innovative. The Benedictine tradition (of which Main was a part) called monks and lay people alike to experience prayer

---

[953] Op cit *Word into Silence*. p8.
[954] Op cit *Word into Silence*. p75.
[955] Ibid p20.

as silent communion within our own heart. Union brings us to communion, that is to a oneness with God and a oneness with all. It is a communion that is indescribably enriching because it takes us out of ourselves and into union with all, with the ALL, with God. Unity, union, communion is the threefold growth of Christian prayer.[956]

Main argues that when this growth blossoms we know that we have found our way back to our created centre where wholeness and harmony are achieved. Then we are fully conscious of our self and truly alive to others and to God. The continuing discipline of meditation helps us to remain within our self and thus in the presence of God our creator. There we no longer think about the past or the future but are totally immersed in the eternal now of the moment.

Freedom is the fruit and sign of our new grasp on reality. Living in the moment demands that we leave behind all false images of our self, all empty dreams of what we might have been and all illusions created by the stimuli of our peripheral egos. We are conscious of going through a new birth. First, we are unmade by experiencing the dying of Christ within our self. We become aware of being remade and then of being constantly created, and of springing from the creative love of the Father, returning to the eternal embrace.

This is a radical change; a conversion of life which John Main describes as follows:

"We are…made anew in the fact of entering into the ever-deeper centres of being, and of knowing ever more fully the harmony of all our qualities and energies in that ultimate centre of our being which is the centre and the source of all being, the centre of…Trinitarian Love."[957]

This needs a little sorting out. For Main, poverty is the inevitable corollary of turning the searchlight of consciousness away from ourselves and onto the Other - God dwelling within us. This is the essential insight that Mary exemplifies in the Gospel of Luke. There she is portrayed as living a poverty of spirit that is pure in heart because it is unsullied by the intrusion of the egotistical will seeking for an ever-new experience, desiring holiness, objectifying the Spirit or creating God in our own image. Mary reveals the basic simplicity of the Christian response in a poverty of spirit that consists in turning to God and away from the self.[958]

---

[956] Op cit *Moment of Christ* p20.
[957] Ibid p32–33.
[958] Op cit *The Other Centeredness of Mary* p15.

For Main, Mary's fiat is the way in which all Christians share in the risen life of Christ. In Mary, we see how a life becomes totally orientated towards Christ. It is already pre-figured for us in the sacrament of baptism in which we die with Jesus to the egocentric dimension of our existence and are reborn through the Spirit to the transcendent reality of Christ's risen life which is an eternal communion of love with the Father. These are a mystery, and because they are a mystery—so totally unfathomable to our human understanding that we cannot even desire to possess it—it has to be received as a gift in an attitude of complete poverty, in the experience of the void with complete single-mindedness the void demands complete self-denial with courage, commitment and openness.

Yet again, this is fully congruent with traditional Christian theology East and West which insists that the complete trust of faith is to experience in love what we cannot possibly understand with our intellect alone, nor embrace solely with the will. We need courage to renounce our anthropomorphic language, our discursive knowledge, our need to conceptualise and rationalise in order to take a leap of faith. At the time, we accept the discipline of contemplative prayer, or meditation, we realise that we cannot go on worshipping a god made in our own image, reflecting our own thoughts, ideas, aspirations and emotions, providing a spiritual security necessary to carry us on our own private pilgrimage. Rather we are called to naked faith.

Naked faith is the ability to accept the solitude and fear of the desert experience which lies at the very heart of all Christian belief. Naked faith enters the desert with no assurance that enlightenment thinking and the vitalisation we normally seek in life will unfold before us. Naked faith accepts that to enter the desert is to enter the void but it is in that acceptance and in that void that we find ourselves and find God. it is a painful and at times frightening process and it is precisely then that, however hard it is to do so, we need to pray and to meditate.

At the beginning at least, meditating with one word, without images, concepts and the curiosity of the analytical dualistic mind is a form of propose-consciousness of our intimate union with God our father, through Christ in the Spirit. But it is not a form of holy dozing! We dwell in ourselves as we dwell in God: we are truly found. The role of the mantra, then, is to open the door to the secret chamber of our hearts where we can live in the light, constantly listening to the Eternal Word, ever ready to follow his guidance and taste the fruit of his love. We should not stop saying the mantra when that brief breakthrough is made. By the constant repetition of our mantra, we keep our mind and our hearts firmly attentive to God, but the time may come when we stop saying the mantra and start listening to it linking the fullness of our being with the fullness of God. Then we enter the "cloud of unknowing" in which there is only silence and where we can no longer even hear the mantra. Jon Main put it in this way:

"Meditation is the essence of the art of concentration precisely because, the higher we toil up the mountainside, the fainter becomes the mantra sounding in the valley below us, and so the more attentively and seriously we have to listen to it. There then comes the day when we enter the 'cloud of unknowing' in which there is silence, absolute silence, and when we can no longer hear the mantra."[959]

The pace of meditation cannot be forced, nor should we be self-conscious about its quality. The essential attitude to be cultivated is the utter simplicity of the Blessed Virgin Mary as we say our mantra. We should not be concerned with anything else; certainly not expecting some sort of holy glow or moment of great enlightenment. Neither is true meditation, but holy dozing. For, in fact, most of the time we experience nothing at all—and that is precisely the point. All we need to do is to remain faithful to the mantra and so faithful to our need of God. But those take commitment and, at one level at least, knowledge of scripture. All the images used by John Main are taken from the Gospels and he speaks of purity of heart and of non-dualistic, undivided, consciousness as the concentration of our whole being on the Kingdom of God. Main does not hesitate to pint out the necessity of being single-minded towards the Kingdom in an ontological and not just a moral sense.

Such purity of purpose, however, demands openness to the other, to Jesus, whose presence we discover on the faces of all whom we meet, our spouses, our children, our friends and our neighbours. Our relationship to God deepens as we exercise greater sensitivity to all of his creatures. Indeed, contemplation and action are so interrelated that they spiritually feed each other and this is, of course entirely consistent with Main's own Benedictine tradition which emphasises the harmony, balance and moderation of the unity of prayer and labour:

"St Benedict then sees these two realties in our life-prayer and community— as essentially one. Concentration upon our neighbour in love and on God in prayer is, for St Benedict, the same sharing in the perpetual prayer of Christ which is his loving relationship to the Father. The monastery itself is based on and rooted in this loving relationship."[960]

---

[959] Op cit *Word Into Silence* pp54–55.
[960] John Main (1983) *The Monastic Adventure.* Montreal. The Benedictine Priory. p39.

The last phase of our loving relationship with the Father is, of course, death, because from birth to death we continually die to the egoism of our peripheral selves. From conversion to transfiguration, from *metanoia* to communion we are challenged to live in the now. In order to at least try to do that we must learn to die to the ego and the state of egoism that is constantly slipping out of the reality of the present by regretting the past or day-dreaming about the future.

As we fall away from our ego, we discover and experience the love of God whose Being is the very source of the person we are eternally becoming; we also discover that death is *the* essential phase of that process. It is the final and most demanding of the lessons that life teaches. It is the meaning of the absolute finality of the Cross that yet yields up into the infinite universe of the resurrection.[961]

The call to eternal life demands the radical conversion of death. Death is the readiness to lose oneself in the life of the Eternal other. It is the final generosity of love. Death, according to John Main, is an event *in* life (not separate from it, or its end point). For him, it is an act of love; and our physical death is but a passage to consecration and fulfilment. Death is a vision of Life:

"Within this vision, we see life as a preparation for death and we see death as a preparation for death. If we are to meet our own death with hope, it must be hope built not on theory or on belief but on experience. We must know from experience that death is an event in life, an essential part of any life which is perpetually expanding and self-transcending mystery. It seems to me that the only experience of the continuous death of the ego ca lead us into this hope, lead us into an ever-deepening contact with the power of life itself. Only our own death…can really persuade us of Death as the connecting link in the chain of perpetual expansion, the way to fullness of life."[962]

In conclusion, we can say that Main's contribution to the development of inner space lay in his invitation to everyone to see life as an adventure and in his specific invitation to Christians to look at their humanity and at themselves with great compassion. Part of that is to recognise that there are questions that must be asked but probably cannot be answered: questions about the nature of the self, of life, meaning, transcendence, reality and destiny.

According to Main, simply to ask those unanswerable questions confronts us with the divine mystery that Jesus, the Incarnate and eternal Word of God, fully

---

[961] Ibid p6.
[962] Ibid p7.

a person and fully God is indeed the way to be followed, the truth to be told and the life to be lived. In him, we contemplate the mystery in which we find our origin and end. That demands complete trust and a willingness to be guided through the Holy Spirit to live at the edge, on the limit of enquiry and beyond in a complete abandonment to the shape of God's love with a single-minded dedication which is nothing less than the monastic commitment down the ages.

Part 9

Chapter 28
Living in the Inner Space Today

Throughout this book we have seen that the monastic vocation is ultimately a call to unity. That unity can only be reached through a long and sometimes painful journey. It is a journey which implies a series of successive deep transformations, that is, through a long process of conversion.

Such a conversion is rooted and grounded in baptism. It is in baptism that we are introduced to that most radical of all conversions lived by a human being, the death and resurrection of Jesus Christ. No other conversion has any meaning unless or until it is related to that paschal mystery.

The paschal mystery stands at the very heart of human history. The two horizontal arms of Christ's cross span the whole of human history, from the dawn of creation with God breathing his breath of life into humankind, to the eschatological return of everything to God, in God in the Parousia. The Jesus will be at the centre, surrendering his Spirit to the Father and receiving it back to be the first fruits of the dead, partaking fully of the glory of the Father which is then extended to us too.

Our conversion, as a form of participation in the paschal mystery of Christ is an element in the global transformation of humankind and of the whole cosmos under the grace of the Holy Spirit of Christ himself. Although it is first of all a conversion of the heart, it takes its meaning from god's experience of human conversion in Christ, and the long journey of humankind that preceded it: and it will not be achieved without our active participation in creating the conditions under which the Kingdom of God might come on earth as it is in heaven.

The purpose of this chapter is simply to show how, why and in what ways all these aspects form a unified reality that receives its meaning from the paschal mystery into which *all* Christians, lay, ordained, clerical, monastic or religious—enter through baptism. It will do so in four ways: God's Experience of

Conversion in Jesus Christ, the Conversion of the Human heart as a journey towards the Self in God, the Conversion of Society into the Kingdom of God, and finally how all of this leads to what I will call a Final Integration.

1. God's Experience of Conversion in Jesus Christ

The first paradigm, or model, of conversion is certainly God's transformation to humanity as described in the Letter to the Philippians: "Though he was in the form of God, he…emptied himself and took the form of a slave, being born in the likeness of men…Because of this God highly exalted him and bestowed on him a name above every name." (Phil. 2:6–9).

If, in accordance with some contemporary evangelical preaching, we think of conversion simply as a passage from sin to virtue, then to speak of Jesus' conversion, or of God's experience of conversion in Jesus can make no sense at all. But it is, as it were, only by accident that conversion is for us a passage from sin to virtue—only because humankind has sinned. The reality of conversion is in itself something much deeper and larger. It starts with our conception and is a dimension of any passage from one stage of growth to another until we finally reach the perfection to which we are called. Jesus certainly went through such a process.

After the peaceful, largely uneventful and slow process of Jesus' growth in age, grace and wisdom, came the radical change at his baptism. As he went down into the water to be baptised by John, the Spirit came over him and he heard the voice of the Father saying: "You are my beloved Son." At that time, he experienced in his human psyche his identity as the Son of God. That gave him a new insight into his mission and ministry.[963] That sense of identity and that new insight were assumed through a long period of solitude in the desert, where he had to face terrible temptations as, indeed, we all do.

Jesus immediately began *not* to preach but to actualise the Kingdom of God, by healing the sick, forgiving sinners and announcing the Good News to the poor.

---

[963] In the Gospel of Mark, which represents the earliest tradition, the words of the Father are addressed to Jesus ("You are my beloved son.") and not, as in the Gospel of Matthew to the disciples and the crowd; ("This is my beloved Son."). To say that Jesus "experienced" his identity as the Son of God at that moment does not mean that it was his first revelation of it. On the contrary, most modern theologians will acknowledge a development in Jesus' awareness of his mission and ministry.

This was not done without encountering opposition and those confrontations through which new insights into his identity and his mission developed. The entire process came to completion in the radical transformation realised through Jesus' surrendering of his Spirit to the Father in crucifixion and being raised by him. The transforming experience lived by Jesus is the summit of our groping towards our end (*telos*) both as individuals and as a species: it gives meaning to the whole of human history.

When we are baptised, we enter into the long human experience of conversion that reached its culminating point in Jesus. By being immersed in Christ's paschal mystery, we are called to personal transformation that must bring us to full integration in God. Baptism does not so much establish us in a state, a so-called state of grace, as it sets us on a journey. That journey leads us beyond ourselves and beyond the limits of our own individual experience and the experience of the communities of faith of which we are part. As we reflect on that journey, we see not only where we have come from but where we might be headed. The road, however, is entirely ahead of us and where no map, compass nor "satnav" can guide us. This is the journey to which we are committed in baptism and to pursue unceasingly during every day of our Christian lives. It is nothing less than what traditional monastic literature describes as the "*conversation morum*", the conversion of life.

2. The Conversion of the Human Heart

The *conversatio morum* demanded by Jesus of his disciples was not simply a superficial modification of their moral behaviour. He demanded much more than replacing a personal ego by another which might be more respectable or more in conformity with the expectations and dictates of the society which surrounded them. Rather it required a radical and global transformation touching every dimension of what it is to be a human being at all—"spirit, soul and body"—to use the categories of Pauline anthropology.[964]

Quite clearly, such conversion must be, first of all, a conversion of the heart which, as we saw in the chapters on St Bernard of Clairvaux and St Francis de la Sales is (theologically) the source of everything that is either good or bad in human existence. In the Old Testament, the Prophet Ezekiel described in lyrical

---

[964] Cf. 1 Thess 5:23.

and poetical terms how the conversion of the heart would be characteristic of the new Kingdom of God: "I will give them a new heart and put a new spirit within them. I will remove the stony heart from their bodies, and replace it with a heart of flesh."[965] The journey to conversion is primarily an internal journey, the development of an inner space, a journey towards the discovery of the true self—that is the person we are called to be by God.

In the course of that creation of the inner space in the deepest part of ourselves, we may have to touch places that are unknown to us. We may cross unfamiliar and haunting lands in which we are strangers. This should not surprise us. It is the desert experience that lies at the heart of all true Christianity. Part of that is to be, like the Israelites of the Exodus journey, nomads in our own world. The first reality we encounter in the desert will be our own egos with all its pride and with all its limitations. When we venture to journey to our own inner space, we must expect to be confronted with fear, confusion and temptation—and even the feeling that we have entirely lost our faith.

The desert experience begins every great spiritual experience. After his baptism, Jesus began a new period of his life into solitude. It was the experience of the Prophet Elijah, growing through the awareness of his own spiritual poverty, his fears and his weakness, in the desert before the encounter with the glory of God on Mount Horeb. It was also the experience of St Paul, who spent a few mysterious years in the deserts of Arabia after his encounter with the risen Christ on the road to Damascus, and thousands of women and men, from the early days of monastic life in Egypt and Syria up to our times have deliberately gone into the physical desert for the very purpose of living such an experience.

That transforming journey may start with a very deep or even shattering experience, like that of Jesus at the time of his baptism, or that of Paul on the road to Damascus, or that of Elijah on Mount Horeb. But most of us will embark on that journey imperceptibly, not after any radical mystical experience, but simply, gradually, as we go on in life: passing from success to defeat, in our friendships, in our moral life and tasting the increasing frustration of unrealised hopes as we begin to count the number of our years by the marks they leave on our bodies. These may seem, at first, somewhat superficial things, but they touch us deeply, and if we accept them honestly and openly, they put us in touch with our deepest limitations, with our sinfulness and the idols we have been

---

[965] Ez. 11:19.

worshipping n wider society. This is the first step on the path to *conversatio morum*.

When the Desert Fathers described their struggles with yawning beasts and slimy snakes and grimacing devils (or even seductive women!) these were not just metaphors. They were describing the various aspects of their own inner space that the experience of the desert had forced them to discover. These are what Jung called the shadow side of our self, the unacceptable part of our personality with which, in the desert, we are brought face to face.

Such an experience of our sinfulness is not confined to the beginning of our spiritual journey. It can come at any time. It can be a sudden or lagging discovery after many years of prayer and faithful service to God. When it does come strong and persistent, doubts arise in our hearts about God and about our vocation. Intense passions flare. The meaning of truth grows stale. Questions abound and no answers appear. New kinds of spiritual darkness and sterility touch us deeply. These are not the charming little darkness's and dryness that convince us that we are making progress on the spiritual journey. On the contrary, they threaten to destroy the whole enterprise. The love of God that once sustained and motivated us is now elusive and illusionary.

When Jesus tried to describe the *conversatio morum* to the disciples, he used images that did not speak of smooth and gradual transformation, but images that reflected the two most traumatic events of human life: birth and death. He knew, more than anyone else, that the fullness of live cannot be reached without walking through the valley of the shadow of death.

To Nicodemus (Jn 3:5–6) he said: "I tell you solemnly, unless a man is born through water and the spirit, he cannot enter into the Kingdom of God: what is flesh is flesh: what is born of spirit is spirit." But later on, he described the conditions for such a life: "I tell you solemnly, unless a grain of wheat falls on the ground and dies, it remains only a single grain; but if it dies, it yields a rich harvest." (Jn 12–24–25). If, in the darkness of the desert, of our inner space, pleading to understand what is happening, we go to Jesus for advice and solace, we find that his response is as enigmatic as it was to poor Nicodemus.

Quite often in monastic history, entry into the postulancy has been considered as *the* conversion of life (or a second conversion if baptism is counted as the first). The rest of the monastic life is supposed (especially by those looking on form outside) to be a smooth, if not always easy, growth, development and faithful perseverance. The monastic vow of *conversation morum* has been understood as the commitment not to stop on a straight smooth journey to perfection. Though, of course, as this book has shown, it is nothing of the sort.

Similarly, some churches nowadays privilege "instant conversions" and sudden transforming mystical experiences. The danger of both this mistaken view of the monastic life and of "instant conversions" and the like is that they can be no more than changes of behaviour, the exchange of one ego for another. In any event, even the most extraordinary experience of God is usually only the first step on a long journey towards conversion, and it does not exempt a person from entering into the desert of his or her inner space and wandering about in it, sometimes for years, in exile. It is in that spirit that the first monks went into the desert to get in touch with their own inner space, with their own heart, and there do battle with the forces of evil and to defeat them after the example of Christ and, with his grace, to hasten the coming of the Parousia.

All the riches, hard won in pain, of such human experience of conversion can so easily be lost when undue emphasis is placed on extraordinary mystical experiences, on unrealistic charismatic enthusiasm, or when ascetical practices are substituted for the fullness of life to which we are called. Asceticism is necessary and indispensable, but it can also be an easy excuse to exempt ourselves from the painful process of learning to care, to listen, to live and to love. In this context, a word about spiritual formation both in the monastery and beyond is necessary. If spiritual formation is concerned only with transforming us into good edifying monks, or any other kind of Christian but does not encourage us to advance on that solitary journey through the desert of our sinfulness to the frightening encounter with the true and living God it is worthless.

All our activity will be no more and no less than an ego building exercise and certainly detract from creating the conditions of the Kingdom of God on earth. That so much spiritual formation has indeed been worthless may, in my view, account for the sorry state in which so many churches and whole denominations find themselves.

Paradoxically, to try to look outside ourselves and attempt to live up to external ideals and experiences can prevent the authentic conversion of life we are considering here. And I am afraid that very often much spiritual formation does just that. Instead of leading people to a painful conversion, we invite them to put on a new ego over their old one. When people attempt to find the ground of their identity solely in doing things and living up to society's goals or community's expectations, they unwittingly promote a false self. Ideals which are good in themselves can become obstacles to a deeper conversion. We are too often fearful to let go of our own creations and to allow God to touch us and give birth to our true selves.

If, however, we courageously continue our journey through the desert of our heart, we will eventually reach the ground of our being where it grows out of Being itself, where our own self is one with the Other who is the fullness of the Self, so that we can say with St Paul "*I do not live. He lives in me.*" Conversion of life, then, takes us to a renewed image of ourselves, of God and of other people. Or rather, it allows us to go beyond those images and to transcend them in a blessed simplicity, which is the ultimate end of all Christian life especially when it is explicitly monastic or adopts monastic insights into its practices. Conversion of the human heart keeps us away from ourselves and turns us towards God and our brothers and sisters.

3. Conversion of Society into the Kingdom of God.

Though conversion is first of all something extremely intimate and personal—the conversion of the heart—it cannot be so private as to be solitary. It must become a collective conversion through which the conversion of the church and society is realised.

Conversion can indeed happen to many people at the same time and they can form a community to sustain one another in their self-transformation, and to help one another in working out the implications and in fulfilling the promise of a new life. It is in that manner that cenobitic and secular monastic forms of community life were formed. During the optimistic days of the mid-nineteen sixties and shortly after the closure of Vatican II, it was believed that such conversion can pass from generation to generation and pass from one culture to another. Given the high degree of suspicion and distrust between age groups and between cultures some forty years on, the degree to which it might still do so must surely be a matter of doubt.

Jesus' own experience of conversion at his baptism was the discovery not only of his identity but also of his mission of preaching and actualising the Kingdom of God, at the beginning of its realisation. If our conversion is authentic, if, by becoming the person we are called to be, we become more our true self and therefore identified with the Other who is the prelude of the self, we will also receive the revelation of our personal unique mission in the building up of the kingdom.

That, certainly, was the experience of the apostles. It took them time to fully understand Jesus' message. Even at the moment of his death they were very far from, such an understanding. They were not only moral and physical cowards; they were intellectual and spiritual cowards too. Their scattering in fright at the time of Jesus' arrest and Peter's subsequent denial of ever having known Jesus is not just a physical event but a metaphor for their inability or unwillingness to face up to the full implications of a converted life orientated towards the Kingdom of God. Yet, in the forgiveness experienced in Jesus' passion, death and resurrection, they saw themselves in a new way and embraced Jesus as Saviour and Lord. They were bound to him in a new manner and thus they discovered their own role in the building up of the kingdom.

Our mission, rooted and grounded as it is in baptism, has to be discovered too. It is found in the deep experience of commonality and solidarity with all people affected by poverty, who live on the edge, who are weighed down by a sense of their own worthlessness and sin and who need healing. It is found wherever there are abandoned babies and mothers who can't cope, orphans and those leaving institutional care and who do not have the education and skills necessary for independent living, children and young people living with severe and complex needs because of their disability, and with vulnerable families—to name but four groups. Yet they are all those toward whom we easily experience prejudice and intolerance.

The Kingdom of God as preached by Jesus implies and entails a radical transformation of the whole fabric of society. Thus, individual conversion of the heart receives its meaning from being a small constitutive part of that great and profound transformation. That transformation of the Kingdom, of God, just like individual conversion requires, at some point, a radical break. The Kingdom does *not* evolve; it breaks in. it is not just a spiritual revolution but a social one undoing and replacing the structures of the old world. Hence it is presented as good news for the poor, sight for the blind, solace for the broken hearted, liberation for the oppressed, pardon for sinners, an enduring peace and new life for the dead. Such a Kingdom is not another world, but *this* world transformed and renewed.

This is the message of the Beatitudes. Too often preachers and theologian have spoken and written of them as though Christ promised blessedness only after death, achieved only in a far distant "Else-where-land".[966] If it is elsewhere is not right here right now—and may indeed be nowhere at all. Too often we have thought of the Beatitudes as saying "Blessed are the poor because after their miserable life on earth they will have the kingdom of heaven…blessed are those who suffer because they will have the joys in heaven…blessed are the hungry because after their present starvation, they will have heavenly food, and so on…" All this is a grave error.

It is not at all what Jesus taught. When Jesus declares the poor to be blessed, it is because he (and we) has come to deliver them from their poverty. When Jesus declares the sorrowful to be blessed, it is because he (and we) has come to replace sorrow with joy. When he declares the hungry to be blessed it is because he (and we) has come to feed them with real food and not nectar or ambrosia!

What Jesus began we are called to complete. The Kingdom of God must first be brought about here on earth. If it is realised here on earth, it will last forever because it is divine and because it is the realisation of the divine dimension of human being created in the image and likeness of God. Its completion will mark the end of time. Thus, the Beatitudes are not a spiritual narcotic meant to help us endure the hardships of this life in the expectation of a better "Elsewhere." Rather, they are a call to all of us to engage in the sort of mission and ministry that will transform the world.

This, of course, implies an eschatological expectation. The Kingdom of God is here but not in all its fullness. There is an urgency to achieve it. It also implies a constant struggle. The demonic powers that we find in ourselves and have to be confronted in the deserts of our inner space are present and active too in society. St Paul, employing the vocabulary of the Gnostics of his day, calls them the powers and principalities of this world. The purpose of developing our inner space and engaging in transformative mission and ministry is to hasten the final victory of the kingdom of light over the kingdom of darkness. The end of time,

---

[966] In this connection I am fond of quoting a piece of graffiti which could be seen in the late 1970s and early 1980s outside Paddington Station on the main railway line to Bristol and Bath. It read, *"The far away is near at hand in the images of elsewhere."* No doubt that somewhat opaque saying (some might say nonsense!) was no doubt written under the influence of drugs or drink. What we have so often had to say in terms of our Christian proclamation of the Kingdom of God has been no less narcotic—and one does not have to be a Marxist to think so!

therefore, is not the moment when the world will cease to exist, but the moment at which this world will be fully transformed into the Kingdom of God.

In the Gospels, Jesus makes it very plain that conversion of life is a choice between following two lords. Either we serve the principalities and powers of this world ("Mammon") or we serve the one true living and personal God ("Abba"). There are no grey areas. No in-between possibilities. There must be a personal choice.

That choice currently takes place at a time where one of the greatest manifestations of Mammon is the tremendous disparity between rich people and poor people, rich countries and poor countries and even between rich and poor regions in one country. The principal consequences of this disparity are hunger and war. So, the first step towards our conversion of life will be to understand the extent to which we contribute to those disparities.

Take a simple example: This morning I ate a good breakfast. I am wearing one of my best suits because later today I will attend a series of meetings. I will travel by bus and train. All these are things that countless millions of people cannot afford. The system that makes these things available to me is the same system that deliberately deprives others of them. The solutions are neither easy nor simple, but at least the fact that we do not have easy answers to hand should not blind us to the problem.

St Paul's conversion was a radical awareness of the identification of God with the marginalised and the oppressed: Saul, Saul, why do you persecute ME? By that simple question everything in him was shattered: his own identity, his understanding of other people and of God. Any real understanding of Matthew Chapter 25 (especially verses 40 and 45) and what political theologians call the "option for the poor" of this world, should affect in us the same conversion.

A second step in our conversion of life should be an analysis of the situation.

The awareness of both social mechanisms and the duty to act has nowhere been stronger than in our own day. It is remarkable to think, for example, that even twenty years ago things such as Fair-trade or Ethical Investment were regarded as odd, a little "hippyish" perhaps, but are now a mainstream part of our weekly shopping experience and of our savings. But, without burdening ourselves with doom laden notions of sin about all this (which I wrote about in a previous chapter) even this is not enough. We need to be more creative still in finding ways to disassociate ourselves—both individually and collectively—from any economic and social system in which poor people do not occupy the privileged place that has been assigned to them by the gratuitous and preferential love God has for them. It may well be that, in time, as the focus shifts from organisation and theology towards ethics secular monasticism will be a means of achieving this separation.

The Desert Fathers saw the evil in society of their time. They did not condemn society; they acknowledged the presence of the same evil in themselves and they fought it at that level. They expressed the struggle in their writings using a mythological form of language. The myths which they developed were very powerful in leading several successive generations to the experience of the conversion of life. For a few centuries now, although we find it charming at times to read those extravagant mythological stories of the Desert fathers, we have replaced their mythologies with our systematic theologies and spiritualities. But this replacement does not seem to be helping us very much. It may be that the new or secular monasticism will have to re-invent mythological language and a mythological expression of their experience which lies at the heart of the whole monastic way.

4. Final Integration.

At a time when the earliest gentile Christian communities were tempted to find psychological security and cohesion through anti-Semitism (because they thought that Jews were responsible for the death of Jesus, one of the most remarkable aspects of St Paul's conversion was that he resisted that sheer re-orientation of aggression found at the tome in other converts. Not only did he harmonise his own Jewish identity with his fidelity to Christ, but he dedicated three whole chapters in the Epistle to the Romans (chapters 9, 10 and 11) to a demonstration (howbeit sometimes rather laboured) of how, why and in what ways the Jews might be saved despite their rejection of Christ.

Through the centuries (and even now if we count the so-called war on Islamic terrorism) Christians have often given in to the temptation of tightening their ranks by waging crusades. Great monks have at times been drawn by Popes and Patriarchs into such movements. But nothing is more alien to the monastic concept of "*conversatio morum*".

By their ascent of the twelve steps of humility, Benedictines tend towards that purity of heart, or blessed simplicity that, in more modern jargon we could call "final integration". Those who have reached that final integration are not only converted in their own selves and therefore to the plenitude of the self, that is into Christ, but they are also one with every human being and the whole world. While belonging to a local community and living in a specific culture, they transcend all cultures, ideologies and systems. They can, in this way help society to be converted into the ultimate unity and to hasten the eschatological union with Christ. At a time when, in some political and church circles, the call seems again to engage in "holy wars", that aspect of the monastic tradition and monastic conversion seems to be worth remembering.

As we now bring this chapter to an end, let us sum up the process it has described. By virtue of their baptism Christians are called into a full participation in the paschal mystery of Christ. We do this through a long journey or conversion that leads us to find our personal identity in Christ. Insights from the monastic tradition suggest that this is first of all a conversion of the heart in which we receive the spirit of Christ who leads us into the desert of our inner space and in which we experience mercy and forgiveness. That experience develops in us another dimension of our inner space, a sense of compassion and solidarity that awakens us to our personal mission and ministry in the conversion of the world into god's kingdom. The ultimate aim and goal of that journey is not only our personal final integration, but the final integration of the whole cosmos—at last transformed into the visible Kingdom of God.

Chapter 29
Prayer, Reading and Hospitality

I begin with:

1. Centring Prayer

As I noted above, one of the key phrases in my spiritual journey so far, and certainly in my life of prayer has been that well known phrase from Psalm 46 "Be still and know that I am God." It sounds simple but actually it is turning into a lifetime project with all the struggles and dark nights of the soul that run along with it.

It is difficult to remember when I first stumbled across the phrase "centring prayer". It may have been when studying the Roots of Christian Mysticism with the World Community for Christian Meditation or when my then Vicar held one of his courses on Christian meditation. I was part of both at about the same time. Certainly, the practice of centring prayer has been part of me, on and off ever since and the quotation from Psalm 46 ends every session of meditation at the series of lectures and meditation held by "Silence in the City" at Westminster Cathedral.

When I first heard the phrase, "centring prayer" my first reaction was to ask, "But where is my centre?" I quickly learnt that it is not something I can find; it is far more intuitive than that. Often it is only something I "find" in retrospect, after meditation, after I have been acting in a centring way, when my behaviour has come out of that centre.

At other times, I can delude myself that I have been centred when I simply have not because the sound of internal chatter has covered over the silence of divine reality. As a result of my education, my understanding and practice of Christianity has been very "heads up", "ears open": very cerebral, too full of words. The problem is that words can so often give me a lot of knowledge about God and relatively little experience of God. I need both to make sense of both. In the words of an old man I met in the Sudan who had smoked raw tobacco most of his life and was offered a filtered cigarette by one of my colleagues: "No! No! That would be like kissing a girl through a glass window, I'd get the idea—but not the effect!" Centring prayer reminds me that ideas about and experience of are two completely different, and yet complimentary, worlds.

Finding my centre is done in God, for the sake of God. It is not just a project I do. I have to be quite frank here. I object to the view that it is simply a "project", a new initiative in the church to attract those who feel themselves excluded from traditional Christianity, directed at those who are spiritual but not religious. Some have even argued that centring prayer and silent meditation has nothing to do with God at all and everything to do, at best, with a narcissistic reflection or, at worse, some form of mind-bending. Others have even suggested that centring prayer is linked with the occult! All this is quite nonsensical and comes, I think, from a misinterpretation of the phrase from Psalm 46. "Be still and know that I am God" does not mean "If I am still I will know God" any more than it means "Be still and know that you are God" God is always unknowable. In centring prayer, I deepen that experience, but not conceptual knowledge and thus centring prayer is not some form of baptised transcendental meditation.

Centring Prayer is simply the deliberate act of putting myself in the presence of God in the same way and for the same reasons as the traditional monastic hours from which the practice of centring prayer is derived. As a matter of fact, as the monastic tradition of prayer repeatedly makes clear, it is always and everywhere quite impossible to be outside the presence of God.

I remember a rather overzealous evangelical academic colleague leading opening morning prayer in the college chapel with the words "Let us place ourselves in the presence of God and adore him" and my thinking "Where else do you think it is possible to be?" As the Book of Jonah points out, we can't ever run away from God, we can only run around God. We are already enfolded by God. It's like the song "*Hotel California*" by the group *Eagles,* to which my wife introduced me before we were married: "*You can check out any time you like, but you can never leave*"!

It is, curiously only a little distance from Eagles to John Cassian: but I return to John. He reportedly travelled to various desert monasteries talking to people about their spiritual practices, gaining bits of wisdom. When he returned to Gaul, what he taught was sometimes called "monologisitic prayer", from two words meaning "one word". This is the origin of saying a mantra during centring prayer, which frightens some people. They think that a mantra is something very exotic, a magical word—a "mind-bending" word. But on the contrary, it is simply a phrase, repeated, to help induce a sense of calm, a sense of silence, a means of concentrating on God without the distractions of inner chatter: in Zen Buddhism, "clear mind, clear mind, don't know," in Christianity, "O God come to my assistance, O Lord make haste to help me".

Centring prayer is, properly understood, like all other forms of prayer it reminds us that God cannot be grasped by concepts. Between us and God are two clouds: the cloud of unknowing and the cloud of forgetfulness. In centring prayer, we break through the clouds for until we do our hearts are restless until stayed on thee, as St Augustine of Hippo famously said. The only way to break through the clouds is through love, and love is expressed in the "prayer word" or mantra.

That, for me, is the whole basis of centring prayer and why I try to practice it. It is a means of giving and receiving love. Like all love, it can often be painful, challenging and tearful. At others it is warm, welcoming and secure leading to the understanding that although I am dust, and to dust I will return, I am nevertheless held securely in the hand of God who will never let his grasp slip, no matter what.

For those of us with an interest in adopting traditional monastic practices into our everyday lives, the practice of centring prayer is one way of keeping the silence. More than that centring prayer keeps alive part of the monastic tradition that has been lost and ignored by other parts of the church. The tradition of centring prayer has always been there, but it went underground. The fact is that centring prayer is part of our common Christian grammar and heritage. A contemplative dimension is part of everyone's life. When we stop long enough, when we stop grasping, wanting, objecting to the world, we can still discover something deep within us, another dimension of ourselves that wants to be still and rest in God, because God is the centre of centring prayer.

2. *Lectio divina*

Lectio divina and centring prayer are interrelated traditional monastic spiritual practices. I find that there is an ever-growing union between them such that *lectio* can melt into centring prayer and centring prayer can be a prime motive for l*ectio*.

Lectio divina is a Latin term which means divine reading. It describes a way of reading Scriptures through which we gradually let go of our own agendas, and especially an interpretation of the passage, to listen to what God has to say to us. Traditionally there are three, sometimes four stages through which the mind, or soul, passes in order to contemplate God. I no longer find these stages helpful. On the contrary, I find that they all get muddled up together so that it is sometimes impossible to say with any certainty, "Ah I am now at stage three" or "Oh my goodness, am I ever going to go beyond stage one?" *Lectio* is simply not like that and if it were it would no longer be the thing that it is—a way of *praying* the scriptures—but another cerebral, hermeneutical, academic exercise.

But for the sake of clarity and for the sake of tradition, let me mark out each of the four stages. At the first stage, I read the Word of God slowly and reflectively so that it sinks into me. Any passage of scripture can be used for this way of prayer but the passage needs to be very short. So, I have found that one of the sayings of the prophets or Jesus himself is to be preferred. In this way, some of the words or even one word can begin to form in us as a mantra. Micah 6:8 is an ideal passage containing as it does the concepts of Duty, Justice, Mercy, Humility and the Love of God all in a single sentence.

The second stage is about reflection. I think about the text I have chosen and ruminate upon it so that I take from it what God wants to give me. This thinking is both of the head and of the spirit. The more I ruminate, chew, the text the more the spirit will prevail over the rational mind and here again is a direct link to the practice of centring prayer.

Only in the third stage of *Lectio* am I in a position to begin respond to the text on which I have been ruminating. The response is not one of the mind but of prayer. Here I set all thinking aside and let my heart speak to God as he speaks to me. It is in the fullest sense of the phrase what the Blessed John Henry Newman meant by his motto, *cor ad cor, locquitor*, (Heart speaks to (or with) Heart).

At the fourth stage of *Lectio Divina* I find contemplation, rest, where I am able to let go of all ideas, all plans, and all meditations and of all holy thoughts and words too. This is the true heart of the practice of *lectio* and the point at which the boundaries between *lectio* and centring prayer (if there are any) break down and become one. Here there is only silence. Here I simply rest on the Word of God. I listen at the deepest level of my being to a God who speaks within me in a still small voice. As I listen and as my prayer mantra automatically kicks in, I am gradually transformed from within. Obviously, the hope is that this transformation will have a profound effect on the way I actually live, and the way I live is the test of the authenticity of my prayer. I must take what I read in the Word of God into the humdrum world of the everyday.

These stages of *lectio* are not fixed. There is nothing of a fixed rule about them. Rather they are, and have been from their origins in the earliest monastic communities, merely guidelines. From the first stage to the fourth, there is a natural movement towards ever greater simplicity. This is a hard lesson for me to learn because it involves less and less talking and more and more listening. Gradually the words of Scripture begin to dissolve and the Word of God is revealed before the eyes of my heart.

My experience of *lectio* has taught me many things about myself, other people and about God. If I were forced to sum them all up in a simple sentence, I would say this: "Know that the Word of God is alive and active and will transform each and every one of us if only we have the spiritual courage to open ourselves to receive what God wants to give us."

3. Hospitality

Hospitality holds the key to the future of traditional western monasticism and the new "secular" monastic movements. Religious orders, individual monks and those of us seeking to adopt and adapt monastic practices into our everyday lives need, I think, to be aware of this. Part of that awareness is to acknowledge that the practice of hospitality may require changes of life styles on the part of those who make their home in the monastery, those who visit them for retreat, study days and workshops, and those who seek to make their home a monastery.

A useful guide through what will undoubtedly become something of a maze if we are to find a balance is, once again, the Rule of St Benedict. While guests are spoken about in various places in the Rule[967] Benedict seems to have ambivalent feelings about them. While guests are to be welcomed "as Christ" he creates special rituals for them (such as prayers to avoid the devil!) and practical restrictions on them. He allows for a special kitchen in which their meals are to

---

[967] RB53 on the reception of guests and RB66 on the role of the porter are primary chapters here.

be prepared and limits the amount of conversation monks may have with their guests. All this is absolutely necessary if the rhythmic life of the monastery is to be maintained and if the community and the world are to intersect in a way that is balanced.

For Benedict, as we saw in earlier chapters, the monastery is in the world but not of the world. It is important to briefly revisit what he meant by that. "World", for Benedict, did not mean the whole of creation in a general sense because, as we have also seen, the whole of creation in Benedictine spirituality is sacred.[968] Rather "World" meant everything that is not centred on God. Benedict, like St Paul before him, believed in evil and its power and saw the ways of society as often being contrary to the life of Christian discipleship. Thus, Benedict wanted the monastery to be a place in creation in which God's creative love was continually felt, challenging and transforming all who came there.

In this context Benedict saw every person as unique, a created gift of God. The greatest gift was, of course, the person of Jesus now Christ the King of the world and every person, like Jesus, was a gift who resembled the greatest gift. Jesus is to be received as the gift in every guest to the monastery because as Jesus said himself: "I was a stranger, and you welcomed me." (Mtt.25:35 and RB53:1).

In one sense, everyone in a monastery is a guest, members of the community and visitors alike. Monks are guests in the sense that each one has somehow come into this house of God, this dwelling place of God. Some the original rituals of the monastic day, whether actually practised or not, reflect this concept of everyone being a guest (e.g. washing of the brother's feet. washing of the feet of guests, monks showing respect and even reverence when they greet each other, care of the sick).

When a monk loses this, overall sense of being a guest in the monastery, of seeing Christ in the monastic community and in those who visit it, his view of his vocation becomes distorted. The monastery is no longer a dwelling place of God but "my" place. Rules and timetables no longer exist "to amend faults and to safeguard love"[969] but to protect "my" personal comfortable way of life. The monk becomes the master not the disciple.[970]

In the same way then, those of us who are trying to adopt and adapt the insights of formal monastic spirituality into our everyday lives might also think

---

[968] See RB31:10.
[969] RB Prologue 47.
[970] RB6:6.

about our own homes in a different way. As a result of our great capital outlay and often financial sacrifice when we buy, lease or rent a property over many years we are accustomed to thinking of it as "my" place. And so, it is by virtue of our title to the property. But that is not all and it is certainly not all from a Christian perspective. Our homes too can be dwelling places of God. Members of our family and those who visit it can be respected, greeted and reverenced in love as signs and tokens of the presence of Christ in them and with us. That is one of the key principles underlying the Christian concept of marriage as a perpetual sacrament to those who are party to it.

All I am suggesting here is that this concept be broadened out so that that same sacramentality can be made available to all in the house for however long or short a time they are present with us. In that way too, as for the formal monastic community, rules and schedules can be for us a by which to "amend faults and safeguard love."

If we are to attempt to make that a practical possibility, we need to ask a number of searching questions and for the time being the word "monastery" will equally refer to our homes which are, in some sense at least, a "domestic monastery". The first question is this: Why do people come to the monastery? While guests come for a wide variety of reasons, those of us trying to create a domestic monastery must also hope that they come (as guests do in formal monastic houses) because they *also* see our homes as a dwelling place of God, a place where God can be felt and experienced in creation. Our guests can then expect our homes to be different, to be an oasis of peace away from the hassles of everyday life. If this is true, then our homes must be orientated in such a way as to make them conducive to listening, to providing silence as wells as social banter. They must feel a sense of prayer, not piety, a place in which they can hear and receive the Word of God. No small part of that is to have properly prepared meals of good, wholesome (organic?) ingredients, taken together and at a leisurely pace and in this way our common bread and common cup have the possibility of being Eucharistic.

The second question arises from this: What should the guest ministry of the contemporary monastery be? This, of course, depends on the particular monastery. Yet each monastic community should realise that the monastery is more than the sum of its parts, more than a work force, more than a place to live or a place to which one is attached. It is a definite place. It is place in which people attempt to live a balanced life and invite others to join them, no matter how long or short a time a person stays in the monastery, each is a guest in the house of God seeking to find again the creative gift of life that can so easily be lost in the modern world. Those who are professed as monks and those of us beyond the cloister need to believe this of ourselves and live it before we can even begin to think about sharing this with others.

Our monasteries need to look to the needs not of yesterday, but today and tomorrow. Monasticism cannot merely be the living of the past, like some religious theme park, it must also be living in the future by way of realised eschatology. A monastery, a family, lives in a past tradition which flows into the future, always the same but always changing, like a river.

A third question might be: does the concept of hospitality require monastics to go out of the monastery in order to serve? At times it may, but what monastics today need to realise is that the monastery, the dwelling place of God, has the power to transform people and thus transform the world.

In conclusion then, those of us seeking to build monastic type prayer, *lectio divina* and hospitality in to our lives and into our homes must understand that our greatest motivation, our greatest gift to the contemporary world is to offer a place of inner space where people live a balanced life, a place where peace is the quest and the aim.[971]

Above all, we offer a place not so interested in going out to save the world (important as that is in these days) but in letting the world experience the salvation already won in Jesus Christ, a place where *all* are guests in the household of God, respecting and cherishing each other, a place where hearts overflow "with the inexpressible delight of love".[972]

Richard Norton OBJN. CJN. MA. Stroud. Gloucestershire.

---

[971] RB Prologue 17.
[972] RB Prologue 49.